The Value of Conversation

Christoph Strosetzki
Editor

The Value of Conversation

Perspectives from Antiquity to Modernity

Editor
Christoph Strosetzki
Universität Münster
Münster, Germany

ISBN 978-3-662-67199-3   ISBN 978-3-662-67200-6 (eBook)
https://doi.org/10.1007/978-3-662-67200-6

© The Editor(s) (if applicable) and The Author(s), under exclusive license to Springer-Verlag GmbH, DE, part of Springer Nature 2023

This book is a translation of the original German edition "Der Wert der Konversation" by Strosetzki, Christoph, published by Springer-Verlag GmbH, DE in 2022. The translation was done with the help of an artificial intelligence machine translation tool. A subsequent human revision was done primarily in terms of content, so that the book will read stylistically differently from a conventional translation. Springer Nature works continuously to further the development of tools for the production of books and on the related technologies to support the authors.

This work is subject to copyright. All rights are solely and exclusively licensed by the Publisher, whether the whole or part of the material is concerned, specifically the rights of translation, reprinting, reuse of illustrations, recitation, broadcasting, reproduction on microfilms or in any other physical way, and transmission or information storage and retrieval, electronic adaptation, computer software, or by similar or dissimilar methodology now known or hereafter developed.

The use of general descriptive names, registered names, trademarks, service marks, etc. in this publication does not imply, even in the absence of a specific statement, that such names are exempt from the relevant protective laws and regulations and therefore free for general use.

The publisher, the authors, and the editors are safe to assume that the advice and information in this book are believed to be true and accurate at the date of publication. Neither the publisher nor the authors or the editors give a warranty, expressed or implied, with respect to the material contained herein or for any errors or omissions that may have been made. The publisher remains neutral with regard to jurisdictional claims in published maps and institutional affiliations.

Responsible Editor: Ferdinand Pöhlmann
This Palgrave Macmillan imprint is published by the registered company Springer-Verlag GmbH, DE, part of Springer Nature.
The registered company address is: Heidelberger Platz 3, 14197 Berlin, Germany

Preface

What is the value of conversation measured by? Are there more valuable and inferior types of conversation? What role do the contents, the people and the circumstances play? Do times and epochs shape their own conversations? These questions are explored in this volume using standards, as recommended in handbooks, and conversations reproduced in texts or reconstructed from texts, the latter also being called dialogues.

The contributions are categorised into three groups. While the first focuses on conceptual definitions and distinctions, the second is oriented towards contexts such as the salon and the meal, and the third on individual literary texts. The first and second groups proceed chronologically, the articles in the third are arranged according to reverse chronological order.

According to Wolfgang Pleger, the Platonic dialogue, unlike most conversations, is zetetic, i.e. searching and questioning. A distinction must be made between the eristic form, in which the interlocutor is to be refuted in an argument, the didactic form, in which the teacher knows the answer, which he wants to bring to light in the student through skilful questioning, and the agonal form, in which the interlocutor is not only to be refuted, but the argumentation is to arrive at a tenable statement. Finally, in the synergistic type of conversation, the interlocutor's opinion, which forms the starting point, is tested with an open mind through counter-assertions and pointed arguments in order to arrive at an insight into the matter itself after amazement, confusion, vacillation and aporia. In terms of reception, Pleger quotes Martin Buber, who sees in Socrates the "dialogical principle" that is the prerequisite of genuine conversation between I and Thou, and Habermas, whose dialogue free of domination is a fiction, "as if Socratic dialogue were generally and always possible".

Marcel Humar distinguishes an internal level in the Socratic conversations from an external level. While the interlocutors are unsettled and confused by Socrates, the external reader, at the latest by the second passage, can comprehend the course of the dialogue and see "the dialogues as training pieces in methodically guided conversation and correct argumentation". In the process, the Socratic *elenchos* becomes clear, i.e. his habit of refuting inadequately reasoned statements with the aim of freeing himself from apparent knowledge and moving closer to the truth.

Bernd Roeck blames the importance of conversation in the Italian Renaissance on a discourse revolution characterised by an increase in a variety of profane topics and the rehabilitation of a worldly *voluptasx*. The Quintilian *urbanitas*, which admits no discord, nothing coarse or peasantish, takes up Castiglione's *cortegiano*, whose *sprezzatura* contributes to the general merriment with jokes. When for Lorenzo Valla in *De vero bono* (1433) the small happiness on earth becomes the true good, Pontano praises the gentle speech of a *homo facetus* with his entertaining and witty humor. For Sperone Speroni, dialogue is something close to comedy in pleasure, to be distinguished from philosophical reasoning. If, according to Guazzo, knowledge begins with conversation and ends with it, in conversation the most powerful is only one of many, whereby authority is conquered by reason.

Christoph Strosetzki asks to what extent conversations are determined by historical world views or ideologies, or whether there are rather ahistorically valid constants for conversation elements and simply characteristics of different centuries. In 17th century France the *conversation enjouée* had a central place compared to the *conversation sérieuse*, and was characterised by pleasure, favour and the beauty of women, used trivial objects, was oriented towards the partners and used mockery and silence in a well-measured way. In the 18th century an *éloquence d'administration* emerged, substantive results mattered, half-knowledge was denounced, conversation became secondary and politeness was reinterpreted as charity or dissimulation. In the 19th century, the loss of the former light-heartedness of the salons and the model of women and the increase of material interests became clear. A comprehensive history of conversation could determine the boundary between these and the ahistorical rules that, in the sense of eutrapelia and *aptum*, avoid unpleasant interlocutors such as long-talkers, those who extol their own merits and grumblers such as momos. It could further show where the rhetorical appropriateness of conversation crosses over into the ethical and aesthetic.

Not to assertion, success and career at court, but to an "éthique chrétienne de la douceur", Christophe Losfeld traces the rules of conversation in the name of *honnêteté* at the end of the 17th century and in the 18th century in France. Thus Bordelon's appeal to be "omnibus suavis, nemini durus" can be traced back to the early medieval bishop Martin of Braga. The principle of pleasing became a demand for reciprocity and was derived from that *douceur* which the Apostle Paul sees in the *imitatio Christi*. It would be contrary to this to snub others, to contradict them or not to listen attentively. The one who mocks others lacks mercy and humility because he places himself above them. When the Abbé de Fourcroy in his *Catéchisme* presented virtuous interlocutors and edifying topics of conversation, as well as the mistakes of mockery and slander to be avoided, and Charles-Louis de Lantage advised conversation "with charity", to comfort, encourage and build others up without dropping "a word that harms anyone", then conversation could be seen to be derived from Christian ethics.

Adolph Freiherr Knigge's best-known book *Ueber den Umgang mit Menschen* (1788) is more of a moral philosophical or proto-sociological work than a mere primer on decency. According to Hans-Christian Riechers, Knigge, as a connoisseur and despiser of the court world, sympathised with republican ideas and shared with the young Goethe the aversion to the exclusion mechanisms of court society, in which others are whispered about behind their backs. From the duties towards others derived a bourgeois culture of conversation that took equal account of the freedom and dignity of the individual and differences of milieu and upbringing, and protected the weaker who is not to be ridiculed. From the duties against oneself arises the self-assertion of the moral subject in an adverse environment, whose adaptation, while preserving the inner value, may only be external.

Conversation shaped by the courtly environment can be reshaped in a bourgeois way, as Knigge does, or it can be contrasted with better alternatives. Simon Meier-Vieracker shows how the latter become critiques of conversation in 20th century German-language reflection on conversation. Nietzsche had already contrasted the dialogue as the perfect conversation with the sociable conversation in a larger circle, and Hirzel, in his work on literary history, had distinguished the dialogue, in which one sinks into the objects in discussion, from the conversation, in which jumping from one object to another was characteristic. In the 20th century, Martin Buber praised the immediacy of I and Thou as the persons connected in conversation and distinguished "genuine dialogue" from sham conversations, which were less concerned with communication and more with self-presentation—an approach shared by Siegfried Kracauer, Karl Jaspers, Helmuth Plessner and finally Martin Heidegger with his critique of "talk" in public. Ferdinand Tönnies links conversation, which is positively valued, with community and pleasantries with the more anonymous society characterised by etiquette. After the Second World War, it was the widespread Anglo-Saxon culture of discussion that was contrasted with conversation in national demarcation, which established the connection from person to person and opened up "the mutual essence".

There are contexts that are constitutive of conversation.

Petra Dollinger asks what became of the salons in the 19th century in Paris and Berlin and is able to present examples of a diverse and stimulating culture of conversation in the literary salons led by women. Already with the Huguenot refugees in the 17th century, people had become familiar with the French tradition. Later, Schleiermacher's "Theory of Sociable Behaviour" reflects his experiences in the salon of Henriette Herz (1764–1847). Rahel Levin-Varnhagen's (1771–1833) salon is philosophically influenced. Caroline Baroness de la Motte-Fouqué responded to Mme de Staël's criticism of German conversation culture with her essay "Ueber deutsche Geselligkeit in Antwort auf das Urtheil der Frau von Staël" (1814). Heinrich von Kleist and Clemens Brentano frequented the salon of Hedwig von Staegemann (1799–1891), which was influenced by Romanticism. A Parisian example of internationality is the salon of Mary Clarke-Mohl (1793–1883), a native Briton and wife of a German orientalist. Salon conversations could also turn to scientific topics or be frivolous, but they were meant to offer variety. Hedwig von Olfers, following Voltaire, says: "All genres are good, except the boring ones."—Martin Luther's table speeches appeared to be of such high value that his guests and listeners began to make conversational transcripts during his lifetime. Thomas Pittrof attempts to distinguish between quotation, addition, and editing in a text corpus of more than 7000 notes. Although Luther was aware of the monks' ban on silence at table, he offered consolation and joy as a remedy for melancholy. After all, the words are attributed to him: "One says, and it is true: ubi caput melancholicus, ibi Diabolus habet paratum balneum," against which help: "Company and conversation of godly and Christian people."– Rosmarie Zeller sees Georg Philipp Harsdörffer's *Gesprächspiele* (1641–1649) between knowledge transfer and pleasure, usefulness and entertainment. A group that is not too numerous and therefore enjoyable is supposed to deal with questions and answers. If still the Frenchman Charles Sorel in his *Maison des Jeux* compared the Platonic dialogues with such games, with Harsdörffer there are three male and three female persons of different age and status, who represent different opinions. A game master suggests the topics and questions, which can range from hunting to music, from painting to setting up a garden. If Italian academies were the model for these games, they seem to have found great interest at the court of Wolfenbüttel.—Wolfgang Adam sees the conversation at court in the Vies des Dames galantes by Pierre de Bourdeille, seigneur de Brantôme (1540–1614) characterized by violence and plaisir. Brantôme, who had contacts with the powerful of his time and insights into courtly life, shows in his work, which stands between memoir, historical account, and essay writing, how brutality and intrigue are hidden by politeness. Women are described in burlesque-obscene stories as fortresses to be stormed. As a member of the noblesse d'épée, Brantôme can look down on the essayist Montaigne, who belongs only to the noblesse de robe.—Forms of conversation can also be found in medieval texts. Corinne Denoyelle looks at the sequence of conversational themes in the 13th century prose novels about Lancelot and Tristan. She shows how a topic is introduced in courtly conversation, e.g., by the king, what possibilities there are to continue or refuse the proposed topic, or how a change of topic is possible with and without notice.

The individual contributions to this anthology offer insight into selected, significant aspects of conversation. If, for example, the "real" conversations of the 20th century took the Socratic Conversation as their model, it has been shown that in it correct argumentation is practised in a methodically guided manner and counter-assertions such as exaggerations are tested in an open-ended manner, so that truths, as in conversations, are only achieved after confusion, vacillation, amazement and aporia. In a complete history of communication consciousness (S. Meier), however, changes in the ideal conceptions of conversation and talk could be presented in such a way that even apparent opposites could dissolve or be differentiated in their opposites.

The core of the contributions, which go back to a conference that could not take place because of Covid, was expanded for the present anthology with additional essays. Thanks are due to Maike Dietz for the editorial standardisation of the manuscripts.

Christoph Strosetzki

Contents

Terms

**The Philosophical Dialogue. From Sophistic
Rhetoric to Socratic Dialectic** 3
Wolfgang Pleger

**Dimensions of Conversation and the Value of
Socratic Conversations in the Platonic Dialogues** 25
Marcel Humar

**The Renaissance of Conversation—A Short
History of Conversation in the Age of the Discourse
Revolution** 43
Bernd Roeck

Should One Talk? And If So, What About? Or What Not? 71
Christoph Strosetzki

**The Sweetness of Conversation According to Behavior Treatises
(Late 17th—Early 18th Centuries)** 95
Christophe Losfeld

Duties and Conventions of Conversation: Adolph Freiherr Knigge 123
Hans-Christian Riechers

**Back to Community. Criticism of Conversation in German-Language
Reflexion on Conversation in the 20th Century** 135
Simon Meier-Vieracker

Contexts

**Conversation in the Salon and Among Salonnières in
19th-Century Paris and Berlin** 157
Petra Dollinger

On Luther's Table Talks 189
Thomas Pittrof

Texts

**Conversation Between Knowledge Transmission and Enjoyment:
Georg Philipp Harsdörffer's Conversation Games** *Gesprächspiele* 209
Rosmarie Zeller

**"Here Are Some Fine Advisements and Conversations"—Forms of
Courtly Conversation in Brantôme's** *Les Dames galantes* 223
Wolfgang Adam

**"Et Lors Se Metent En Autres Paroles…" Changes of Subject in
Literary Conversation** 245
Corinne Denoyelle

Terms

The Philosophical Dialogue. From Sophistic Rhetoric to Socratic Dialectic

Wolfgang Pleger

Abstract

The second half of the 5th century BC is dominated in Athens by the Sophists. They represent the principle of enlightenment, new education and increased political involvement of citizens. Socrates (470–399) shares with them important topics, such as the criticism of myths, the rejection of natural philosophy, combined with an anthropological turn, the criticism of civic morality and finally, the rhetorical, pedagogical and political interest. However, in contrast to mere rhetoric influence technique, he develops a specifically philosophical question. His method is based on dialogical reason. His philosophy focuses on the problems of self-knowledge and the right way of life. He thus founded the philosophy of morality in European thought (Apel). The Platonic Socrates participates in different types of conversation. There is the eristic conversation, which aims at the defeat of the opponent, the agonistic conversation, in which truth is to be determined by argument and refutation in dispute, the synergistic conversation, in which in a friendly atmosphere in joint effort a result is sought and the didactic, which, conducted with young people, has the form of a teaching conversation.

Keywords

Ancient Greece · Sophistic Enlightenment · Anthropological Turn · Socrates · Dialogic Reason · Self-knowledge · Philosophy of Morality · Types of Conversation

W. Pleger (✉)
Universität Koblenz Landau, Koblenz, Germany
e-mail: pleger@uni-koblenz.de

The second half of the 5th century BC was dominated in Athens by the Sophists. They represented the principle of enlightenment, new education and increased citizen participation in political affairs. They questioned traditional city morality and were therefore regarded with suspicion by conservative circles, despite the great differences in their personal appearance.

For Aristophanes, the comedy poet, Socrates is also a Sophist, and the trial against him is the trial against a Sophist. In his eyes, Socrates is part of a line with the proceedings against Anaxagoras and Protagoras. It is also by no means denied that Socrates belongs to the intellectual current of Sophistic enlightenment. Therefore, it makes sense to clearly highlight the common themes. The question is: What is the meaning of the criticism of myths (1), the rejection of natural philosophy and the anthropological turn (2), the criticism of city morality (3), rhetoric (4), pedagogy (5) and finally political interest (6) for the Sophists, and in what way are these topics part of Socrates' thinking?

But even if one concedes that the agreement of the Socratic approach with Sophistic thought motives is greater than Plato, the declared opponent of the Sophists, allows in his dialogues, the unique and new, which is connected with Socrates, would be lost if one only emphasized the similarities. Occasionally, the relationship of Socrates to Sophism has been compared with Kant's to the Enlightenment[1]. Just as Kant belongs to the age of Enlightenment, but also overcomes and directs thinking into new channels, Socrates belongs to the age of Sophism, which he completes and transcends. There is no doubt that it is the merit of Plato to have characterized the moments in the figure of Socrates in a particularly clear way, which distinguish him from Sophism; and these moments are not inventions of Plato, because they are also confirmed by the other sources. They form a unity. The decisive difference of Socrates' thinking from that of the Sophists lies in the fact that, in contrast to the rhetoric developed by the Sophists, which aims at creating moods and influencing opinions, Socrates' thinking takes place in the dialogue, which serves self-knowledge and truth. The dialectic conceived by Socrates is to be understood as an art of conversation. It corresponds to a philosophy that is not only a form of thought, but also a way of life[2]. Historically reliable contents of Socrates' thinking can be found, in addition to Aristophanes, Xenophon and Aristotle, above all in Plato's early writings. But since Plato has also taken over Socrates' thought content in his middle and late dialogues, it is difficult to draw a clear line between the historical Socrates and the specifically Platonic one[3]. Therefore, the following will focus on the historical Socrates, but also the Platonic dialectic will be mentioned.

---

[1] Cf. Nestle 1975, p. 529.

[2] Cf. Pleger 2020, pp. 174–207.

[3] Cf. Pleger 2020, pp. 85–93.

1 Socrates and the Sophists—Similarities and Differences

The *first* moment of similarity between the Sophists and Socrates consists in their critical attitude towards the myth. The myth represents the world of the gods, which Homer and Hesiod represented in their epics and thus created at the same time. It was a poetic theology. The formula "fingunt simul creduntque", which was discussed much later by Vico with reference to Tacitus, can already be applied here[4]. The Homeric epics were an educational force whose importance can hardly be overestimated. They were not only the subject of grammar lessons, but also general education. Not a few educated people of this time knew both epics by heart. Nevertheless, they did not have the character of holy texts, as known from religions of revelation; it was not a dogmatic canonical text. The cults that formed around the gods mentioned by Homer, Hesiod, the lyricists and tragedians had their own roots and their own practice.

Criticism of the myth developed even before the Sophists. As one of the earliest witnesses, reference is made to some fragments of Xenophanes (ca. 580–ca. 485). With him, the accusation of anthropomorphism appears as the central motif of his criticism: "The Ethiopians represent their gods as black and flat-nosed, the Thracians on the other hand blue-eyed and red-haired". Also: "Everything Homer and Hesiod have imputed to the gods is only a scorn and a blame among men: stealing and adultery and cheating each other"[5]. But Xenophanes does not draw the consequence of the denial of God from this myth criticism. Rather, it is important to him to develop a theology that is free of any anthropomorphism. The "one God" he speaks of is free of all human passion. He is "completely eye, completely spirit, completely ear".

With regard to the Sophists, three positions should be remembered: the agnostic attitude of Protagoras, the rather myth-friendly attitude of Prodicus, who claims that the people of "primeval times" considered everything that is useful for life to be a god,—an attitude that already explains the myth without fighting it—and finally the "exposure" of the myth by Critias, who, according to his thesis, was "invented by a clever and thoughtful man"[6].

What position does Socrates take on this issue? The question is not easy to answer because the sources speak differently about it. For Aristophanes (ca. 445–ca. 385) Sokrates demythologizes Zeus by explaining his activities as natural, meteorological phenomena that are clouds[7]. For the writer and historian Xenophon (430—after 355), however, Socrates is a sign-believing, pious man of his time who was unjustly accused of impiety[8].

---

[4] Vico 1966, p. 68.
[5] D/K 21 B11.
[6] D/K 88, B25.
[7] Cf. Aristophanes 1990.
[8] Cf. Xenophon 1987.

Finally, with Plato, an ambivalent, difficult image arises. The dialogue *Euthyphron* and the *Apology* are two writings from Plato's early period. The *Euthyphron* is a conversation with a priest and soothsayer who is unable to justify his piety. He is embarrassed by Socrates twice. Firstly, because it is not possible to orient oneself to the will of the gods, because the gods are—as Homer describes in detail—themselves divided. However, the second problem is more serious. It leads to the question: Do the gods love what is just and pious, or is what is just and pious what the gods love? In the first case, the determination of the pious and just is a matter of human reason, in the second case the will of the gods is an own final criterion, and piety and justice are not rationally justifiable. The dialogue ends aporetically, and this means in this context that the situation of ignorance is to be stated with regard to the question of the gods. This is an agnosticism that already comes up in the *Apology* with regard to the question of the fate of the soul after death[9].

Nonetheless, Socrates differs from Protagoras's agnostic position. It should be noted that Socrates repeatedly and emphatically asserted obedience to "the" god, that is, to Apollo, the "Lord of Delphi", who has also been apostrophized as the god of truth. This obedience distinguishes him from the myth-critical attitude of the Sophists. According to Plato, Socrates dedicated his entire life and work to this god, and since there is no reason to doubt the historicity of the oracle consultation reported in the *Apology*, according to which no one would be "wiser" than him[10], the close relationship between Socrates and the god of Delphi must be accepted as a historical fact. Nonetheless, his worship of the 'god of truth' takes on its own, philosophical contour, which distinguishes it from all traditional piety. It takes the form of a search for truth on the way of a reasonable dialogue.

The *second* moment of agreement between the Sophists and Socrates lies in the anthropological turn taking place in their thinking. The anthropological turn, which can almost be interpreted as a paradigm shift in Greek thought, was introduced by Protagoras. His famous Homo-mensura-saying sets the new direction. Others have followed him. This also applies to Gorgias, who already specializes within anthropological thinking. The center of his efforts is rhetoric as the art of influencing people. This is only possible with the knowledge of psychological facts. Prodicus directs attention to the study of language, but also to ethical matters. In this context, one can speak of a paradigm shift in so far as the anthropological question takes the place of the physical explanation of the world. Anthropological turn therefore also means turning away from natural philosophy. But the Sophists, who use the word nature, like Hippias and Antiphon, do not ask about the nature of the universe, but about the nature of man.

What is the reason for this peculiar shift of interests? Perhaps a hint to be found in Xenophon is not out of the question. Xenophon states that natural philosophical thinking has not led to any generally accepted result. The natural philosophers

---

[9] Cf. 40 c/d.
[10] Cf. 21 a.

were rather hopelessly divided. There were conflicting views on the structure of the natural order. With regard to the number and exchange of basic substances, there were confusingly many ideas. For Xenophon, natural philosophy has come to a dead end.

Another reason to turn away from natural philosophy is that one has discovered a topic that is more urgent and closer at hand: namely, the "human things." Attributed to Socrates—the argument goes: What sense does it make to deal with the nature of the cosmos as long as we do not even know ourselves sufficiently accurately? For Socrates the turning away from natural philosophical questions is characteristic this is confirmed by Plato. This is most impressively described in the dialogue *Phaidros*. Socrates and Phaidros walk together outside the city along the river Ilissos and camp there under a plane tree to read a speech by the speaker Lysias, which Phaidros has brought with him. Socrates moves like a stranger in the immediate environment of Athens and admires the lovely landscape. When Phaidros asks him astonished whether he does not know the area, Socrates admits that he actually sees it for the first time and adds as justification: "Forgive me for this, best one. I am just curious and fields and trees do not want to teach me anything, but rather the people in the city"[11].

It is noteworthy how Socrates turned away from natural philosophy. Plato explains this in the dialogue *Phaidon*, a testimony which also has historical importance because it acknowledges Socrates' earlier involvement with natural philosophy. Socrates reports that he had learned the doctrine of Anaxagoras, according to which "reason is the ordering and cause of all things"[12]. This thought pleased him very much; for he associated with it the conjecture that Anaxagoras would explain the phenomena everywhere in terms of a generally successful order, and so he studied all of his books. But this hope was quickly disappointed, "as I progressed in reading and saw how the man does not get anywhere with reason"[13].

Socrates makes his disappointment about the failure of natural philosophy clear with an example. If everything that happens happens according to reason, then it should also be shown that he himself, Socrates, does what he does with reason. But if one asks why he is now sitting in prison and not fleeing, then the natural philosophers know of nothing else to say than "that I am now sitting here because my body consists of bones and sinews, and the bones are dense and separated from each other by joints, and the sinews are so arranged that they can be pulled and let go, and the bones are surrounded by flesh and skin, which hold them together. Since the bones float in their joints, the sinews, when I let them go and pull them, enable me to move my limbs now, and for this reason I am now sitting here with bent knees."[14] But that is—as Socrates says—not the true reason why he is now

---

[11] Plato: Phaidros 230d.
[12] Plato: Phaidon 97c.
[13] Ibid. 98b.
[14] Ibid. 98c/d.

sitting there; but it consists in the fact that the Athenians found it good to condemn him and imprison him, and he for himself found it good to accept the punishment and not to flee. The anthropological turn is connected with an ethical question for Socrates. "Sinews and bones" are undoubtedly natural preconditions for physical movement, but they do not contain reasons for action. These lie solely in the "reason"[15]. Socrates puts the "choice of the best" at the center of his action and that is only possible through the use of reason. Consideration, insight and decision are a matter of reason.

A *third* moment of agreement is found in the criticism of Polis-ethics. The criticism of traditional Polis-ethics initiated by the Sophists is characterized by the debate about the relationship of "Physis and Nomos"[16] which was discussed in the 5th century. The starting point for this topic were the insights into foreign societies gained through the lively Greek trade. Already in his work of history Herodotus points to the relativity of customs in different countries, e.g. to different burial rites[17]. But how can the custom, the "nomos" be justified? The answers of the Sophists are different. There is agreement on the following, often quoted words of Pindar: "The law (nomos) is king of everything, for mortals as well as for immortals"[18].

Now it is new in the age of the Sophists that the "nomos" is no longer interpreted as an expression of a divine commandment, as Sophocles tried with all emphasis in his "Antigone" performed in 442 BC. In this tragedy Kreon, king of Thebes, forbids to bury Polyneikes who fell in the fight against the city and orders to leave him to the prey of birds and dogs. Against the merely human law established by Kreon, Antigone invokes the "unwritten, unforgivable of the gods"[19].

The appeal to sacred law is not to be found anymore among the Sophists. They bring nature into effect as a new instance. However, the interpretation of nature is not uniform. While Thrasymachos and Kallikles, a Sophist mentioned by Plato, derive a right of the stronger from nature, Antiphon and Hippias emphasize the natural equality of all human beings. Protagoras takes a more differentiated position. For him, the "nomos" is a right that is naturally given to all human beings, but must be developed through education and practice. The law, understood as right, fulfills the task of guaranteeing the peaceful coexistence of human beings in the Polis.

What is Socrates' attitude towards traditional city-morality? Aristophanes and Xenophon present a contradictory picture. For Aristophanes, Socrates is a Sophist, for whom traditional custom has no meaning anymore. That a son owes obedience to his father, he—as the caricature of the Socratic doctrine in his comedy

---

[15] Ibid. 99a.
[16] Heinimann 1980, p. 110.
[17] Herodotus o. J., p. 220.
[18] Cf. Heinimann 1980, p. 67 (transl. W.P.).
[19] Sophocles 1961, v. 454 f.

The Clouds—considers to be an outdated custom that can be replaced at any time by another one. Xenophon, on the other hand, describes a conversation in which Socrates urges a young man to obey, to be grateful and to love his mother.

Plato's statement on this point is again ambivalent and difficult. On the one hand, he emphasizes the principle of legality as a characteristic feature of Socrates. Examples of this are his attitude in the Arginusae trial and in the arrest of Leon of Salamis, by which he resists illegal state orders[20]. This attitude is most clearly expressed in his acceptance of the death penalty, which he nevertheless considers to be a miscarriage of justice. The valid laws are to be respected—as the dialog *Crito* shows—as well as their application. Socrates obviously represents the principle of procedural justice, which forces him to accept a verdict that was formally correct. The principle of legality seems to guarantee him legal certainty alone. However, there are significant limits in this respect, which Plato highlights. Socrates is not willing to give up his previous philosophical way of life. A verdict that obliged him to do so, he would ignore[21].

It is also important to consider another aspect, which is extensively discussed in the dialog *Crito*. Crito appears in the dialog as a representative of traditional morality in the sense that he emphasizes the "opinion of the people" as a factor that cannot be neglected. If one considers how closely political, cultic, economic and military affairs were interwoven in a city, Crito's attitude is not incomprehensible, but rather appears as an expression of vital prudence. The norms of this traditional custom include certain maxims, which he also emphasizes towards Socrates and which culminate in the fact that he must flee.

But Socrates rejects the "opinion of the people" as something completely irrelevant. He says: "But good Crito, what should we care about the opinion of the people so much?"[22]. He emphasizes that he for himself only obeys the "logos", which "shows itself to be the best in the investigation"[23].

But Socrates does not put the venerable divine command in the place of custom—as Antigone—nor the law of nature—as the Sophists—but the examined logos to be determined in the exchange of arguments in conversation. The dialogical reason represents the instance that Socrates brings to the fore instead of the traditional custom.

In the relationship to the spoken word, a *fourth* characteristic of agreement and difference between the Sophists and Socrates becomes clear. Both are convinced of the power of the word. But here too, there are remarkable differences in the assessment. Within Sophism, the effort towards logos proceeds in two ways. On the one hand, there is Prodicus's interest in grammar in the broadest sense, on the other hand, Protagoras and Gorgias's rhetorical engagement. While one effort is

---

[20] Cf. Plato: Apology 32 b/c.
[21] Cf. 29d.
[22] Plato: Crito 44c.
[23] Ibid. 46b.

based on a language understanding in which nominal definitions play a major role, the other is part of an influence technique.

In Socrates the characteristic feature of logos is the emphasis on the contextuality of the word and speech. The word is not examined as a lexical size, but serves to represent the matter. The loosening of the relationship between word and matter carried out in Gorgian rhetoric is reversed by Socrates. This is clear from the already quoted Crito passage. Socrates always follows the "logos" that has shown itself to be the best. This means—as Schleiermacher translates—the sentence that best corresponds to the situation considered to be correct. Given that there are still authentic indications of Socratic thought in Plato's later writings, one should remember a passage in the *Phaedo*. There Socrates emphasizes that after his disappointment with natural philosophy, he has taken "refuge in the logos" and is looking for the truth in them[24]. Even more: The relationship of man to logos, to speech, must be seen as so close that "hostility to speech" is comparable to "hostility to man"[25].

As the *fifth* common theme between the Sophists and Socrates, one must point to the pedagogical interest. This is self-evident for many Sophists. Protagoras' declared goal is to prepare young men for their future political position, and for him—as indeed for Gorgias—this included the mediation of legal argumentation techniques. Other Sophists, such as Prodicus and Hippias, also seem to have striven to pass on literary and scientific education. Socrates' pedagogical Eros also seems to be characteristic. For Socrates, one could point to his conversation with the young Charmides, in which the topics of composure and self-control are discussed[26] and to the conversation with Lysis, in which the topic of friendship is discussed[27]. What is pedagogically significant is that, for him, the mediation of factual knowledge was not at the center of his activity, but the development of a dialogical relationship in which the young people are brought into a process of rethinking previously unquestioned opinions. The shaking of one's own opinions and convictions always means also the shaking of one's own self-understanding. The starting point of numerous conversations is a factual question, but the course of the conversation eventually leads to the question: How do I actually want to live? This is how a conversation partner summarizes the adventure of the Socratic dialogue in the *Laches*[28].

Finally, *sixth* the political interest. The relationship of Socrates to politics is paradoxical. While the Sophists were aiming to use the political opportunities available—at least for their students—Socrates is characterized by a distance from everyday political engagement. This is shown by Plato's *Apology* as well as

---

[24] Plato: *Phaedo* 99c.

[25] Ibid. 89d.

[26] Cf. Plato: Charmides.

[27] Cf. Plato: Lysis.

[28] Cf. 188a.

Xenophon's *Memorabilia*. The renunciation of the effort for political offices must not be interpreted as political disinterest. On the contrary: The question of politics forms almost a center of Socrates' work. In Plato's *Gorgias* he is attributed the statement: "I believe that I, with a few Athenians, so that I do not say, quite alone, devote myself to the true art of state and conduct state affairs quite alone today"[29]. And perhaps it is not coincidental that he was prosecuted in a way that, according to the understanding of politics at the time, could only be understood as political. The question that interested him was: What qualifications are necessary for a good politician, and how—if at all—can they be acquired? This is a philosophical question for him, and it differs significantly from the mere mediation of power techniques. It coincides with the question of what is specifically human (virtue). In the political context, as his confrontation shows with Thrasymachus in the first book of the *Politeia*, this is clearly the sense of justice[30].

Was Socrates a Sophist? Certainly, Socrates has central themes in common with the Sophists: the criticism of myths, the turn away from natural philosophy and the turn to anthropological questions, the emphasis on the power of logos and the pedagogical and political interest. But with him these themes receive a distinctive, own meaning.

2 Socrates and the Concept of Dialogical Reason

The dialogical method can be considered as the specific achievement of Socratic action. Aristotle has formed his own expression for the type of the 'Socratic dialogue'. He calls it "sokratikoi logoi"[31]. The question arises as to where Socrates got the motive to embark on this new way of philosophical research. Undoubtedly, the dramatic dialogue that impressed all Athenians was a model for the possibility of public debate about a 'human basic situation'. Vernant describes this situation accurately as follows:

> "In the debate opened by drama, the position of man himself becomes a problem, the mystery of human existence is put to the public, without the tragic search, which is taken up again and again and never completed, ever being able to provide a definitive answer and silence the question"[32].

This problem also characterizes the Socratic dialogue. It can be exemplarily illustrated by Sophocles' tragedy *King Oedipus* (first performed between 429 and 425), as the following sketch may show:

---

[29] 521d.
[30] Compare 335 e.
[31] Aristotle: *Poetics* 1447b.
[32] Vernant 1987, p. 198.

Oedipus is the rescuer and ruler of the city of Thebes. He freed it from the sacrifices that the Sphinx imposed on the city by solving her riddle. The riddle was: What goes in the morning on four legs, in the afternoon on two legs and in the evening on three legs? The answer is: man, who as a child crawls on all fours, as an adult walks on two legs and as an old man leans on a stick. This riddle is already symbolic in that it emphasizes the overwhelming helplessness of man. Giorgio Colli has pointed out in his book *The Birth of Philosophy* that the riddle contained in the myth is a preform of philosophy[33]. As harmless as the wording of the riddle may sound, so serious is its claim. It is part of the nature of the riddle that the Sphinx, after Oedipus *solved her* riddle, plunged into the abyss, while an unsolved riddle led to the death of the one who failed at it. Now the city has to be saved for a second time—this time from the plague. The condition is to "find the murderers" of Laius, the former king of the city. And with reference to his first rescue, Oedipus remarks: "Well then: I will clarify it from the bottom up again"[34].

This provides the key word for the action of the play. It is about solving a crime—it is about relentless pursuit of the truth. Oedipus is determined to do this. This search is carried out on behalf of the god Apollo. Schadewaldt observes: "Somehow it is as if Apollo were the immediate co-player, indeed the main player in the play. Apollo is the god of truth, who cannot tolerate that a crime remains undiscovered, who demands that things come to light and become apparent until they are expiated."[35] *King Oedipus* is a drama of truth-seeking and—mindful of the fact that the word truth in Greek also has the meaning of disclosure—a discovery and revelation drama. The tragic irony of the play is that Oedipus does not fail although he solves the case, but because he solves it. The murderer he is looking for is himself. The clarification of the hidden facts leads him to tragic self-knowledge.

The model of speech and counter-speech in court proceedings must be seen as just as decisive. The political discussion, which gained increasing importance in the time since the introduction of democracy, is also to be mentioned. They all contributed decisively to the fact that Socrates developed his model of the philosophical dialogue, which is to be understood as an open research process. The motives of truth-seeking and self-knowledge play decisive roles in it.

Points of contact for the method of the philosophical dialogue can be traced back to the *Apology*. The motive for its beginning is to be found in the Oracle story. Through the saying of the god of Delphi, he sees himself in the effort to understand it on the way of the "philosophy", "so that I would spend my life in search of wisdom and in examination of myself and others"[36]. This examination takes place in the dialogue and always includes three moments: examination of the other, self-examination and factual examination. Socrates brings this connection

---

[33] Colli 1981, pp. 45–54.
[34] Sophocles 1973, p. 15.
[35] Schadewaldt 1991, p. 278.
[36] 28e.

to the pithy formula in the *Protagoras*: "For I really only want to test the proposition, but it happens that in doing so, both I, the questioner, and the respondent are tested"[37]. The testing of which is spoken here and in the *Apology* has the character of a search, investigation, detection and research. The philosophical dialogue begun by Socrates is a zetetic i.e. investigative process. The refutation the elenchus, which is carried out inevitably in the background, is not the motive.

The Socratic dialogue pursues a zetetic intention and not an elenctic, refuting one. In accordance with its zetetic character, the Socratic dialogue is determined by question and answer; it is not a set of opinions, it strictly differs from mere conversation. But also the rhetorically embellished monologuing is excluded. The artfully constructed speech misses the goal of the examining investigation, which is thematized in the dialogical relation of the questioner, the respondent, and the investigated thing. Therefore, it is also not enough if the co-speaker offers to replace the long speech with the short one. Socrates insists on an "answer" to his question and does not accept a "speech" about it. The goal of the speech is the assent of the listeners, that of the conversation the joint insight into a matter. Assent and insight are not the same.

In the Socratic conversation, the question has priority. The question contains two moments: It is an expression of the non-knowledge of the questioner and an appeal to the person questioned to answer or to admit his own non-knowledge. The answer provokes the next question, and in this way the dialogical investigation gets going.

If we are allowed to believe Plato, Socrates developed a method of questioning. According to it, there is a certain order. There are questions that must be answered before the next one can be asked. The method of questioning proceeds from the general to the particular. Before, for example, the question was not answered, what rhetoric is, it makes no sense to ask about its value. The ability to question presupposes a knowledge that not all conversation partners bring with them. Socrates obviously has this knowledge. It is an implicit knowledge that guides the course of the conversation. It is explained when the conversation stalls or disagreement arises about the conversation.

In Xenophon as well as in the early, "Socratic", dialogues of Plato a second moment of Socratic conversation leadership is expressed. The starting point of the conversation is the "opinion" of the conversation partner. The opinion has its "seat in life" of the respective person and in the concrete situation in which it is located. This can be explained by a number of examples. In the dialogue *Euthyphron* the starting point for the conversation is the intended lawsuit by Euthyphron against his father because of the suspicion of murder. Although his relatives are horrified that he is suing his own father, "But badly, o Socrates, they do not know how the divine behaves, what is pious and what is impious"[38]. With that the topic of

---

[37] 333c.

[38] 4e.

the conversation is found. It is closely linked to the person and the situation of Euthyphron. With whom could one better talk about the topic of piety than with a priest and soothsayer who is furthermore about to act according to his conception of piety? Just as self-evident it is when Socrates in the dialogue *Ion* talks with a rhapsode about poetry and oratory. With the boy Lysis he talks about the just awakened friendship to another boy[39]. And in the dialogue *Kriton* Socrates talks in prison with his friend Kriton about the question of the right to flee. There is a concrete, life-world determined starting point for the Socratic dialogue. The participants in the conversation have an opinion about their situation, which they express to Socrates. This opinion is examined in the conversation. The Socratic dialogue is to be understood as a method of opinion testing. But the opinion is only the starting point. The goal is to come to a "logos", that is, to a statement about the thing itself that is free of contradiction. In order to achieve this goal, a methodologically disciplined conversation leadership is necessary.

The starting point of the conversation is thus historically situated, in a certain sense contingent; the goal, on the other hand, is to be understood as an insight into the invariant structure of the thing itself and has general significance. The course of the conversation therefore represents an abbreviation of the way to philosophy. If in the *Euthyphron* the question "Is it pious to sue one's father?" served as the starting point, then in the course of the conversation the question takes the form: What is piety at all? In this sense, Aristotle is right when he attributes the character of induction or, more precisely, of "epagoge" to the Socratic conversation. It is not just a method of generalizing individual cases, but a reversal of the direction of questioning of the conversation partners. The sense of this reversal is to come first from the situation determined by everyday life to the insight into the structure of the thing itself and from there to an answer to the initial question. In his middle phase, Plato sought to clarify this double reversal with the help of the cave allegory in Book VII of the *Politeia*. This double reversal is extremely laborious and ends in many early dialogues of Plato in an aporia. At the end of the dialogue *Euthyphron* neither knows what piety is, nor whether it is pious to sue his father. What remains are only the situation of the disturbance and the insight into the untenability of the previous opinion.

The Socratic dialogue is anything but the uninterrupted course, discourse, from opinion to knowledge; rather, it is very often characterized by confusion, hesitation, astonishment, aporia, interruption of the conversation. For example, Euthyphron is repeatedly admonished by Socrates to bring the necessary discipline to the conversation and to answer the questions asked, and even in the dialogue *Laches* the conversation partners agree that a form of courage of their own is necessary to be able to cope with the new difficulties of the conversation. But it is not only Socrates who plunges his conversation partners into bewilderment,

---

[39] Cf. Plato: *Lysis*.

occasionally he himself gets into confusion and interrupts the conversation. In the *Hippias major* he says: "Just hold still, dear friend, for I am again afraid of what we are going to bring up." And the rhetoric-conscious Hippias replies incomprehensibly: "Why are you again afraid, Socrates, since your speech is now going splendidly forward?"[40]. But it is not the unrestrained flow of speech that is the goal of the Socratic dialogue, but its questioning. The questions always have the character of back-questions, and this means that the self-evident direction of movement, which is characteristic of the expression of opinion, is interrupted again and again. The conversation offers the possibility of such interruptions. In contrast to the flow of speech, the Socratic conversation is characterized not only by the back and forth between the conversation partners, but also by a forward and backward in the course of argumentation.

In the dialogue *Protagoras* the paradoxical situation arises that at the end of the conversation the starting positions of the conversation partners have almost reversed. While Protagoras initially claims the teachability of virtue, at the end he is no longer convinced of it, and while Socrates initially doubts the teachability of virtue, at the end he at least considers it to be a knowledge that is teachable as such. Often these uncertainties in the conversation lead to expressions of anger. The ones who are unsure in the conversation laugh or scold, threaten or remain silent. These expressions are a clear indication that more is at stake than the correctness of a thesis. The existence of the conversation partner himself is called into question. Just because the starting point of the conversation is often interwoven with the personal situation of the conversation partner, the questioning of the matter also questions the person. Only a few show the greatness like Gorgias, who also takes part in the further conversation after his refutation by Socrates, in the situation of the shaking of their self-understanding. But in addition to victory and defeat in the conversation there is the possibility of gaining new insights and the resulting change of one's own person. It has the consequence of a changed practice.

The dialogue *Charmides* indicates such a process, and something similar applies to the dialogue *Laches*. In addition, there is the situation that the development of an insight is slower than the course of the argumentation. As a result, the unwilling conversation partner has to admit that he has nothing more to oppose to the Socratic proof, nevertheless insists that he is not convinced and does not believe Socrates.

From here it is also possible to try an answer to the question of the teachability of virtue, which Socrates asks again and again. Virtue is not *teachable* in the sense of a propositional knowledge[41], but it is *learnable* on the arduous way of the conversation, that is, through the acquisition of practical insights. This includes self-change.

---

[40] Plato: Hippias I, 396 a/b.
[41] Cf. Wieland 1982, pp. 224–235.

A total of four different types of dialogue occur in Plato's work. These are the eristic type, the didactic, the agonistic and the synergistic.[42]

The eristic is a dispute with the aim of refuting the conversation partner without asserting one's own thesis. An example is the dialogue *Euthydemos,* from Plato's middle period. Socrates emphasizes that he has no interest in this type of conversation.

The didactic conversation is a teaching conversation in which the teacher already knows the answer that he wants to bring to light through clever questions with the student. An example is the teaching conversation about the question of doubling the square with the young slave Menon in the dialogue of the same name. The concept of this didactic conversation is based on the anamnesis doctrine, which has its origin in the Pythagorean doctrine of the reincarnation of the soul, which Plato only picks up. For this reason, it can be attributed to the Platonic, but not to the historical Socrates.

The agonal conversation, like the eristic, is a dispute, but in contrast to this, the goal is not the mere refutation of the opponent, but the attempt to come to a tenable statement through argument and counter-argument, through assertion and refutation. This type of conversation can be found in *Protagoras,* in *Gorgias* and in *Thrasymachus.* While the eristic conversation has an exclusively elenctic character, the agonal conversation is elenctic and zetetic at the same time. The conversation partner is to be refuted, and through the elimination of the arguments proven to be false, the sought-after tenable statement is to be filtered out quasi. The search for truth takes place 'via negationis'. The statement that contains no contradiction and thus asserts itself is true.

In general, the Socratic dialogue proceeds strictly logically. The subject of the conversations are not factual assertions or experience sentences. There are neither examples in the "Socratic" nor in later dialogues of Plato that a factual assertion would be disputed. Not even the thesis put forward by Socrates that the leading politicians have failed in the education of their sons is denied by the later accuser Anytos.

Topics of the conversation are opinions about the understanding of central ethical issues. The question of virtue discussed in *Protagoras* is exemplary. What is virtue? Is it one, or does it break down into parts? And—if it breaks down into parts—how are the parts related to the whole of virtue and how are they related to each other? This results in a wealth of questions to which very different answers can be given. The characteristic of the Socratic dialogue is that an opinion stated in this way is not rejected as false, and it is not confronted with a counter-claim. Rather, the opinion presented is accepted and now its logical compatibility is checked with further, derived or complementary claims. This leads to a remarkable sharpening of the concept of truth. According to the rules of the agonistic dialogue, the statement must be true if it can be asserted without contradiction.

---

[42] Cf. Pleger 2009, pp. 207 ff.

In modern terms, it can be said that the agonistic conversation is not based on a correspondence theory of truth, but on a coherence theory. While the correspondence theory defines truth as the correspondence of sentence and state of affairs, the coherence theory is content with the consistency of statements. However, it is not exactly clear whether this was only understood by Socrates as a negative criterion of truth.

The synergistic conversation type has a different character. It represents the highest form of philosophical dialogue. It is characterized by the fact that the conversation partners do not defend a thesis against their conversation partner, but that they admit their ignorance with regard to the problem under discussion. Here too opinions form the starting point; but now it is a matter of arriving at the truth to be discovered together by bringing together the opinions and the cooperation of the conversation partners. It is obvious that this type of conversation requires a friendly conversation atmosphere and that the "heavy weapons" that characterize the agonistic conversation are not needed. Examples of synergistic conversations are to be found in Plato's early dialogues *Lysis*, *Euthyphron* and *Ion*, to a certain extent also *Hippias major* and *Hippias minor*. Only in a synergistic conversation it is possible to admit one's own mistakes without having been convicted of a contradiction and to support the other in his argumentation. In the dialogue *Menon* Socrates characterizes the synergistic conversation as one that is "dialectical" than a dispute; for in it a claim is not simply made, but the agreement of the conversation partner is sought[43].

In describing and characterizing the dialogical method, the early Platonic dialogues deserve special attention; but of course it must be borne in mind that these are already literarily shaped dialogues. However, some of the features mentioned here can also be found in Xenophon. The conversation types he encounters can be divided into a pedagogical-persuasive and in an agonistic. The pedagogical-persuasive, for example, refers to the admonishing conversation between Socrates and Chairekrates[44], while agonistic are, for example, his conversations with the Sophist Antiphon[45].

In summary, it can be said that Socrates, following the forms of the dramatic dialogue in tragedy and comedy, the court speech and the political discussion, and in distinction from eristic and elenctic conversation forms, introduced the philosophical dialogue, which, according to the zetetic method, seeks the "best logos" and follows the principle of dialogical reason. In place of the rhetoric developed by the Sophists, which serves to refute or persuade, enters the dialectic, i.e. an art of conversation, which is committed to the search for truth. The goals of the dialogical method developed and practiced by him are the self-knowledge of the participants and a life in accordance with this insight. With the dialogical reason

---

[43] Cf. Plato: Menon 75d.
[44] Cf. Xenophon 1987, p. 107.
[45] Ibid. p. 67.

developed and practiced by Socrates, a turning point in the history of European thought has been reached. It is therefore no exaggeration to say that "the foundation of moral philosophy by Socrates" took place[46].

3   On the History of Reception and Impact

Only examples can be given of the immediate impact of Socrates[47]. To the immediate impact of Socrates belongs the Socratics and the Socratic schools. Euclides of Megara, Antisthenes of Athens, Aristippus of Cyrene, Aeschines of Athens and Phaedo would have to be mentioned. Of all, Plato is the most important, to whom we owe not only the so-called Socratic dialogues, which are probably based on Socrates himself, but also important testimonies about him. By adopting the dialogue as a philosophical method from Socrates, Plato himself is the undoubtedly most important Socratic. Aristotle is not a Socratic in the strict sense of the word, but he develops his problem-solving method with the methodological examination of argument and counter-argument in the wake of Socrates' concept.

In the Middle Ages, dialectics becomes the preferred method of intellectual engagement. This is shown by the writings of Augustine, Anselm of Canterbury[48] and Nicholas of Cusa[49] that are written in the form of dialogues. An exemplary dialogue of Augustine shall be explained. In his book *Soliloquies (soliloquia)*, which was written in 386, Augustine does not want to achieve the knowledge that is decisive for his life through a prayer, but on the way to certain knowledge. Inspired by his close contact with ancient philosophy, he conceives the book in the form of a Socratic dialogue. The conversation partners are him, 'Augustine', and 'Reason'. 'Reason' takes on the role of the questioner quite exactly, as Socrates does in the Socratic dialogues. Also the topic is similar to Socratic thinking. It is about self-knowledge and, moreover, about knowledge of God. Like many Socratic dialogues, it ends with an aporia regarding the initial question. Because of the central importance that this conversation has for Augustine's self-understanding, the beginning shall be quoted:

> "Augustine: So I have prayed to God. Reason: So what do you want to know?
> A.: Everything that I have said in the prayer. R.: Summarize it shortly.
> A.: I want to know God and the soul. R.: Nothing else?
> A.: Nothing. R.: So start asking. But before that, explain to me at which point of the representation of God you will be able to say: it is enough.
> A.: I do not know to which point it must be represented to me, so that I can say: it is enough. For I believe I do not know anything as I want to know God"[50].

---

[46] Apel 1988, p. 432.

[47] Cf. Pleger 2020, pp. 218–276.

[48] Anselm of Canterbury 1994, pp. 101 ff.

[49] Nicholas of Cusa 1982, Vol. III, p. 481.

[50] Augustine 1986, p. 19.

It is a philosophical dialogue with which Augustine deals with the topic of faith. It shows the ambivalent position that Augustine still occupies at this time between philosophy and theology. But even in the same year, i.e. 386, his experience of conversion takes place, which leads him to completely turn away from philosophy and to criticize it in the sense of the Bible, as the only authority that is now recognized by him.

For the 18th and 19th centuries, see Hamann, Kant and Nietzsche. In his work *Socratic Memoirs* from 1759, the untimely philosopher and theologian Johann Georg Hamann places the Socratic sentence *"I know nothing!"*[51] at the center of his considerations. For him, this statement is not a trick, but meant seriously. As a theologian, he is convinced that the solution to the problem of imperfect human knowledge is only possible after the appearance of Christ[52]. The figure of Socrates offers him the opportunity to surpass philosophy itself with the philosophy of this paradoxical thinker and to complete it with theology. At the same time, Socrates is thus given a place in Christian salvation history.

Kant evaluates Socrates quite differently. In the introduction to his lecture on logic, he gives a brief overview of the history of philosophy and, after a reference to Pythagoras and his school, remarks: "The most important epoch of Greek philosophy finally begins with *Socrates*. For it was he who gave philosophy and all speculative minds a completely new *practical* direction"[53]. The Socratic dialogue, oriented towards reason, plays a central role here. Kant first divides the "erotematic", i.e. questioning, method into the *"dialogical" or "Socratic"* and the "catechetical". The one is directed to reason, the other to memory. He remarks: "Erotematically one can only teach by means of the *Socratic dialogue,* in which both have to question and answer each other in turn; so that it seems as if the pupil himself were the teacher. The Socratic dialogue teaches by means of questions, by teaching the pupil his own principles of reason and sharpening his attention to them"[54]. Kant thus places his own thinking in the tradition of Socratic philosophy.

Nietzsche also has a very intense relationship with Socrates. For him, Socrates is an exceptional figure. He sees in "Socrates the one turning point and vortex of the so-called world history"[55]. However, unlike Kant, he does not see him as a role model, but as a historical misfortune. In his first work *The Birth of Tragedy from the Spirit of Music* from 1872, he explains how tragedy, with its emphasis on musical and Dionysian-intoxicating elements, which formed the center of the "tragic age of the Greeks", lost importance through the increasingly strong emphasis of the rational moments of dialogue absorbed into it. While tragedy is pessimistic in its anthropological basic attitude in its realistic assessment of the

---

[51] Hamann 1959 II, p. 133.
[52] Ibid. p. 147.
[53] Kant 1998, III, p. 453.
[54] Ibid. p. 582.
[55] Nietzsche 1980, Vol. I., P. 100.

situation of man, the dialectic, the art of dialogue, developed by Socrates, "the mystagogue of science", is optimistic. The result is: "The optimistic dialectic drives the music out of tragedy with the scourge of its syllogisms: that is, it destroys the essence of tragedy, which can only be interpreted as a manifestation and connection of Dionysian states, as a visible symbolization of music, as the dream world of a Dionysian intoxication"[56]. Nietzsche does not believe that the further progress of science is the future of humanity, but that the lost Dionysian world view of the Greeks must be regained.

Mentioned in the 20th century are Freud, Buber, Arendt, and Habermas. Freud's conversation psychotherapy is in several respects in the tradition of Socrates. The statement that Socrates made in the *Apology* about his research into himself, which he conducted through dialogue, served the concern for the "soul, that it might fare well,"[57] is taken over by Freud without him expressly referring to Socrates. He formulated his approach as follows: "Our way of strengthening the weakened ego proceeds from the expansion of its self-knowledge"[58]. The methodological approach offers the conversation in a therapeutic session. "Such a session therefore proceeds like a conversation between two equally awake people, one of whom saves himself from every muscular effort and every distracting sense impression which could interfere with the concentration of his attention on his own psychic activity"[59]. Another moment of Socratic conversation practice is added. It is the maieutic method. The therapist does not confront the patient with his diagnosis, but is merely a kind of midwife in the attempt of the patient to bring himself to speech and thus to achieve self-knowledge and ultimately healing.

A direct reference to Socrates can be found in Martin Buber, who directly builds on Socrates with the "dialogical principle" he represents. Buber understands dialogue in a comprehensive sense. It is the interpersonal relationship between I and You, in which each conversation partner can develop into a person. "The main prerequisite for the emergence of a real conversation is that each one means his partner as this one, as this one person. I become aware of him, become aware of the fact that he is different, essentially different from me, and I accept the person I have perceived, so that I can address my word to him, precisely as him, in all seriousness."[60] But dialogue is also the response of the human being to the changing situations of the world in which he finds himself. By responding to a situation, he is responsible for it. In this way, dialogue is connected with an ethics of responsibility. Buber finds Socrates as the decisive forerunner of the dialogical principle. He says: "But how beautifully and rightfully the Socrates' I sounds! It is the I of the endless conversation, and the air of the conversation surrounds it on all

---

[56] Ibid. P. 95.
[57] 29e.
[58] Freud 1994, p. 72.
[59] Freud 1975, p. 102.
[60] Buber 1984, p. 283.

its ways, even before the judges and even in the last prison hour. This I lived in the relationship to the human being, which is embodied in the conversation."[61].

Hannah Arendt not only dealt with the totalitarian trends of the 20th century in her political philosophy, but also researched the roots of political thinking in ancient Greece. In this context, she also addresses Socrates in his historical context. She asks why Socrates failed in court. Her answer is: He failed because he did not adhere to the usual rules of defense in court. He did not use the tricks of rhetoric with which an accused can create a favorable mood for himself. He treated the judges like his conversation partners and tried to find a common, binding truth in dialogue with them. "Socrates insisted on dealing with his judges in the same way as he dealt with all possible topics with individual Athenian citizens or with his students, and he believed that he could arrive at a truth and convince the others of this truth,"[62]. But not only that! Socrates—according to Arendt—believed that the common life in the 'polis' could be formed "in a truly dialogic" way on the basis of friendship. The statesman as ruler would thus become superfluous. "Should such an understanding—with the resulting practice—arise without the help of a statesman, then the prerequisite for this would be that every citizen can articulate himself in order to show his opinion in its truthfulness and therefore also to understand his fellow citizens,"[63]. The dialogue forms the basis of political sovereignty.

For Habermas too, the "authority-free dialogue", whose model is the Socratic dialogues, becomes the guiding thought of his social-critical considerations. Building on Max Weber's concept of the "interest in knowledge"[64] he develops the concept of the "knowledge-guiding interests". He distinguishes three: The empirical sciences pursue the "interest in knowledge in the technical disposal of objectified processes"[65]. The hermeneutic sciences research with the practical interest "the preservation and expansion of the intersubjectivity of possible action-oriented communication"[66]. This communication is already dependent on dialogue in a special way. The "emancipatory interest in knowledge" finally has an "interest in maturity". It forms the goal of his considerations. "Of course, in an emancipated society that had realized the maturity of its members, communication would have unfolded into the authority-free dialogue of all with all, from which we would always borrow the pattern of a mutually formed identity of the ego as well as the idea of true agreement. In this respect, the truth of statements is based on the anticipation of a successful life"[67]. In the current situation of society, however, it

---

[61] Ibid. pp. 68 f.
[62] Arendt 2016, p. 46.
[63] Ibid. pp. 53 ff.
[64] Weber 1988, p. 161.
[65] Habermas 1969, p. 157.
[66] Ibid. p. 158.
[67] Ibid. p. 164.

is—according to Habermas—a "fiction that the Socratic dialogue is generally and at any time possible"[68]. Nevertheless, he adheres to it as an ideal. In his discourse ethics, which he conceived together with Apel, Habermas has more precisely explained the conditions of a "authority-free dialogue"[69].

References

Quellen: Textausgaben und Übersetzungen

Aristophanes: Die Wolken. Stuttgart: Reclam 1990.
Aristoteles: Poetik. München: Deutscher Taschenbuch Verlag 1983.
Diels, Hermann und Walther Kranz: Die Fragmente der Vorsokratiker. Griechisch/deutsch. Dublin/Zürich: Weidmann 1974 (zitiert als D/K).
Herodot: Neun Bücher über die Geschichte. Essen: Phaidon. o. J.
Platon: Werke in acht Bänden. Griechisch/deutsch. Darmstadt: WBG 1977.
Sophokles: Antigone. Griechisch/deutsch. Göttingen: Vandenhoeck & Ruprecht 1961.
Sophokles: König Ödipus. Frankfurt a. M.: Insel Verlag 1973.
Xenophon: Erinnerungen an Sokrates. Griechisch/deutsch. München/Zürich: Artemis Verlag. 1987.

Sonstige Literatur

Anselm von Canterbury: Freiheitsschriften. Lateinisch/Deutsch. Freiburg: Herder 1994.
Apel, Karl-Otto: Diskurs und Verantwortung. Das Problem des Übergangs zur postkonventionellen Moral. Frankfurt a. M.: Suhrkamp 1988.
Arendt, Hannah: Sokrates. Apologie der Pluralität. Berlin: Matthes & Seitz 2016.
Augustinus: Selbstgespräche. Lateinisch/Deutsch. München/Zürich: Artemis Verlag 1986.
Buber, Martin: Das dialogische Prinzip. Heidelberg: Verlag Lambert Schneider 1984.
Colli, Giorgio: Die Geburt der Philosophie. Frankfurt a. M.: Europäische Verlagsanstalt 1981.
Freud, Sigmund: Abriss der Psychoanalyse. Frankfurt a. M.: Fischer Verlag 1994.
Freud, Sigmund: Studienausgabe. Schriften zur Behandlungstechnik. Ergänzungsband. Frankfurt a. M.: Fischer-Verlag. 1975.
Habermas, Jürgen: Technik und Wissenschaft als ‚Ideologie'. Frankfurt a. M.: Suhrkamp 1969.
Habermas, Jürgen: Vorstudien und Ergänzungen zur Theorie des kommunikativen Handelns. Frankfurt a. M.: Suhrkamp 1984.
Hamann, Johann Georg: Sokratische Denkwürdigkeiten. Hauptschriften erklärt. Bd. 2 Gütersloh: Verlagshaus Gerd Mohn 1959.
Hegel, Georg Wilhelm Friedrich: Vorlesungen über die Geschichte der Philosophie I. Werke in zwanzig Bänden. Bd. 18. Frankfurt a. M.: Suhrkamp 1971.
Heinimann, Felix: Nomos und Physis. Herkunft und Bedeutung einer Antithese im griechischen Denken des 5. Jahrhunderts. Darmstadt: WBG 1980.
Kant, Immanuel: Werke in sechs Bänden. Hg. von W. Weischedel. Darmstadt: WBG 1998.

---

[68] Ibid.
[69] Cf. Habermas 1984.

Kierkegaard, Sören: Über den Begriff der Ironie mit ständiger Rücksicht auf Sokrates. Gesammelte Werke in 31 Bänden. Bd. 24. Gütersloh: Verlagshaus Gerd Mohn 1989.

Nestle, Wilhelm: Vom Mythos zum Logos. Die Selbstentfaltung des griechischen Denkens. Stuttgart: Alfred Kröner Verlag 1975.

Nietzsche, Friedrich: Sämtliche Werke. Kritische Studienausgabe. Hg. von G. Colli und M. Montinari. München/Berlin/New York 1980.

Nikolaus von Kues: Philosophisch-Theologische Schriften. Drei Bände. lat./dt. Wien: Herder Verlag 1982.

Pleger, Wolfgang: Platon. Darmstadt: WBG 2009.

Pleger, Wolfgang: Sokrates. Zur dialogischen Vernunft. Darmstadt: WBG 2020.

Schadewaldt, Wolfgang: Die griechische Tragödie. Tübinger Vorlesungen Bd. 4. Frankfurt a. M.: Suhrkamp 1991.

Vernant, Jean-Pierre: Mythos und Gesellschaft im alten Griechenland. Frankfurt a. M.: Suhrkamp 1987.

Vico, Giambattista: Die neue Wissenschaft über die gemeinschaftliche Natur der Völker. Reinbek bei Hamburg: Rowohlt 1966.

Weber, Max: Gesammelte Aufsätze zur Wissenschaftslehre. Tübingen: Mohr/Siebeck 1988.

Wieland, Wolfgang: Platon und die Formen des Wissens. Göttingen: Vandenhoeck & Ruprecht 1982.

Dimensions of Conversation and the Value of Socratic Conversations in the Platonic Dialogues

Marcel Humar

Abstract

Plato's dialogues are masterpieces of conversation: both on the level of the text, which presents Socrates in conversation with different types of interlocutors to the reader, and on the text-external level, where Plato implicitly adresses his reader. The early dialogues are characterized in particular by a special conversation practice of Socrates aimed at bewilderment and—as a result—the *aporia* of the interlocutors. Conversations stagnate, produce confusing results and the course of argumentation sometimes seems to be incoherent. This essay presents, after preliminary remarks on the dimensions of the Platonic dialogue, selected passages from the *Meno,* which show how Plato marks errors or inaccuracies in the argumentation of his figures, which ultimately lead to the *aporia* or to unsatisfactory results. Plato makes those (not inevitable) mistakes visible and comprehensible to the reader, so that the reader can understand the progression of the dialogue and overcome the (sometimes erroneous) conclusion.

Keywords

Socrates · Dialogue · Rhetoric · Character · Reader guidance · Aporia · Meno · Dimension of conversation · Plato

M. Humar (✉)
Freie Universität / Humboldt-Universität zu Berlin, Berlin, Germany
e-mail: m.humar@fu-berlin.de

1 Introduction

No figure of antiquity is more closely linked to the process of conversation than Socrates. In Plato's dialogues, our main source for the (historical) Socrates[1], a multifaceted image of different conversation modes is unfolded to the reader, especially in the earlier dialogues,[2], ranging from eristic dispute[3] up to empathetic instruction[4].

The Platonic dialogue features three fundamental dimensions of conversation within its structure. One is the personal dimension: Plato presents his Socrates encountering various 'characters'[5] in the dialogue. The figures appearing in the Platonic dialogues have a highly differentiated characterisation[6]; they are by no means just 'interlocutors' who serve as a vehicle for conversational contributions[7]. Rather, the thoroughly elaborate character of each interlocutor can be deciphered on a single pass through a dialogue. Further, the figures significantly influence the dynamics and progression of the dialogue[8]. Most of the figures in the early dialogues are sophists, but members of specific occupational groups who claim to be experts in a certain area are also often present. In the later dialogues, other figure types are presented, which overall appear less 'naive' and more professional than the figures in the earlier dialogues.[9]

In addition, the interactive dimension is to be mentioned: Conversation means interaction. This can also be observed on the level of the text. Socrates and his interlocutors show a complex conversational behavior and interact with each other in different ways[10]. Socrates is often depicted as adapting the conversation

---

[1] On this, see Vlastos 1971, p. 1. Benson 1990, p. 128 n. 2, assumes that Plato's early dialogues provide a relatively accurate picture of the historical Socrates.

[2] For the grouping of Plato's dialogues, see Söder 2017, pp. 23–27.

[3] For example, large parts of the *Gorgias* or the *Hippias minor*.

[4] The "geometry lesson" with the slave in the *Meno* could be cited as an example. But also large parts of the *Charmides* or *Laches* fall into this category.

[5] For the characters in Plato, see Blondell 2002 and Charalabopoulos 2012.

[6] Concerning the different types of interlocutors, as far as I know, there is no comprehensive work. Their importance is already emphasised by Teloh 1986.

[7] If it were only about the dialogue form in which a philosophical problem is to be discussed, neither the detailed characterisation of the individual figures in the dialogue nor the high variance with regard to the different types of Socrates' interlocutors and their special properties would be necessary. Cf. Rowe 2007, pp. 10–11.

[8] See Humar 2017a, especially p. 26. For the *Gorgias* in particular, see the brief research overview in Kaiser 2017, pp. 232–233.

[9] Cf. Humar 2017a, pp. 36–39. A brief overview of the different types of interlocutors can be found in Beversluis 2000, pp. 28–30.

[10] For the interaction of the interlocutors, see, for example, Conventry 1990, Arieti 1991, Beversluis 2000, Blondell 2002, Charalabopoulos 2012 and Humar 2017b.

in accordance with the individual progress of his interlocutors[11]. With regard to this interactive dimension of the dialogues, a change of the interaction of the figures from the early to the late dialogues is especially discernable[12]; also the figure of Socrates alters from the early to the late dialogues and is portrayed less as a doubtful questioner and bewildering, rhetorically versed interlocutor in the later texts[13]. The first dimension and the second dimension seem to be in a reciprocal relationship: Depending on which 'type' Socrates is confronted with, his behavior changes.

Finally, a thematic dimension can be found in the dialogues: Many dialogues tackle the question about the nature of a 'thing'[14] as their starting point; some dialogues develop more complex questions and offer numerous excursions[15]. Others again have sections that are only (at least from the perspective of one of the figures) experienced as superficial 'chatter' and do not seem to claim to address important issues[16]. The relevance of the topic for the individual interlocutors also plays a role in how they interact with Socrates and how they react to him[17]. All three dimensions play a role in the design of the Platonic dialogues and must be taken into account if one wants to ask about the 'value of conversation' as will be outlined briefly below.

2 The Value of the Socratic Conversation

The question of the 'value' of the Socratic conversation in Plato can be addressed from two sides at first, which consider the two communication systems inherent in the dialogue: On the *text-internal* level, as we may call it,[18] Plato lets his different figures enter into conversations with each other about specific topics in a

---

[11] Cf. Kahn 1983, pp. 75–121 and Blondell 2002.

[12] This was already noticed by the ancient Plato commentator Proclus in relation to the typical Socratic irony, which this dialogue only uses towards the sophists. In the later dialogues this is not present anymore; cf. Proclus *In tim*. 1, 62, 26–28.

[13] For this development, see Nehamas 1990, pp. 12–14.

[14] All early dialogues start from a question of the scheme "What is X?"; see Puster 1983 and Fröhlich 2007.

[15] This is most prominently the case in the *Politeia*.

[16] This is best seen in the figure of Cephalus in the *Politeia*: The conversation between Cephalus and Socrates has (at least for Cephalus) a rather casual character. But as the conversation gets deeper, Cephalus withdraws from the conversation with the excuse that he now has to sacrifice; he hands the conversation over to his son. Rosen 2005, pp. 30–31 comments: "Cephalus bequeaths the argument to his son, since he himself must now attend to the sacrifices. The symbolism is obvious; at this point, the conversation leaves the dimension of social conventions and turns to argument."

[17] Cf. Humar 2017a, pp. 228 ff. For Callicles' reaction in the *Gorgias* to Socrates as reflexes to Socrates' painful interventions, see Kaiser 2017, p. 235.

[18] Kaiser also speaks of an internal dialogue level ("interne Dialogebene") in 2017, p. 233.

very specific way, as explained above by the three dimensions. Thus, this level concerns the conversation in which the interlocutors address each other. In the early dialogues, a constant image emerges: A supposed expert in one area claims to have knowledge about a certain subject or at least makes the assertion that he can clearly define and explain the object of his field of study[19]. In the progression of the conversation Socrates always manages to first call this supposed knowledge into question and finally lead the conversation partner into a state of *aporia* (bewilderment, insecurity). He often uses rhetorical devices as well. The previous claim to knowledge by the supposed expert is thus (usually) destroyed step by step. This moment of aporetic bewilderment can then, under certain circumstances, serve as a starting point for a re-evaluation of the definitions or the own standpoint and ultimately contribute to the (intellectual) development of the interlocutor[20]; here the maieutic art of Socrates begins and, after the aporetic insecurity and the destruction of false assumptions, they try to generate new knowledge step by step together. However, the willingness to engage in these processes depends heavily on the character of the interlocutor: Many choose to exit the conversation or prefer a change of subject due to the initial experienced injury, which makes a successful or at least satisfactory outcome of the dialogue impossible[21].

Accordingly, the conversation with Socrates could provide the characters on the *text-internal* level of the dialogue some value in itself, which consists in being stimulated to reflect, to check one's own positions or claims to knowledge and—after overcoming the *aporia*—to make a step forward in their own intellecutal development. In this way, Plato demonstrates through his characters in the dialogue the performance of the Socratic dialogue and the positive effect of Socrates on his interlocutors. It becomes (not always) clear: The Socratic *elenchus* serves reflection, not destruction[22], even though painful experiences during this procedure cannot be avoided. This effect of Socrates and the intention behind it are described by Plato with a popular image: In the *Symposium* Plato lets the drunk Alkibiades appear who comes to the house of Agathon and begins to praise Socrates in front of the audience:

---

[19] Many interlocutorsin the early dialogues introduce the definitions with the remark that it would not be difficult (οὐ χαλεπόν) to say what this or that thing is; cf. *Alc.* I 106b7–8, *Lach.* 190e4, *Lys.* 206c8 and *Men.* 71e1.

[20] See, for example, Dejardins 1990, pp. 4–6, who sees the *aporia* as the prerequisite for the further willingness of the interlocutors to make new considerations. Only then can they gain better insight. See also the comprehensive analysis by Politis 2006.

[21] See below nn. 25 and 26.

[22] In this respect, the Socratic conversation practice differs from the display of rhetorical skills by the sophists. See, for example, Nehamas 1990 and Humar 2017a, pp. 28–32 with further references regarding this distinction.

> For though this is a point I did not mention at the beginning of my speech, it is also Socrates' discourses that are very like those images of Silenus[23] which open up. If you let yourself listen to them they all seem utterly ridiculous at first hearing, because he wraps everything up in words and phrases which are indeed like the hide of some rude satyr. His talk is all about pack-animals and blacksmiths and cobblers and tanners, and he always seems to be saying the same things in the same words, so that any simple-minded bystander unused to this kind of thing might simply laugh at what he was saying. But if ever you see his discourses opening up and you get inside it, first you will find that his is the only discourse which has a meaning in it, and then that it is also most divine and contains the greatest number of images of virtue. Moreover, it has the widest application, or, rather, it applies to everything that one should consider if one intends to become fine and good. (*symp.* 221d–222a; Translation by M. C. Howatson 2008)

This passage is also a short description of the dimensions of conversation presented in my introduction above: On the thematic level, Socrates often takes detours and leaves topics by introducing digressions, (for the interlocutors) seemingly strange examples or analogies. This often provokes a specific reaction: His interlocutors begin to laugh and sometimes mock Socrates and do not take him seriously; in extreme cases they react angrily[24]. However, this has to do with their individual character – they do not recognize the potential of this kind of conversation, because they are too inexperienced and also ignorant (summarized in *symp.* 221e–222a: ἄπειρος καὶ ἀνόητος ἄνθρωπος πᾶς ἂν τῶν λόγων καταγελάσειεν). But, and this is where the value of the conversation lies, the Socratic conversation always has a "meaning in it" (222a: νοῦν ἔχοντας ἔνδον μόνους). However, only for those who can look behind the, occasionally ridiculous, facade of the conversation and have the distant goal of the dialogue in mind: personal development and factual knowledge. Then—that is the quintessence of the playful praise of Alcibiades—every interlocutor can profit from a conversation with Socrates. However, this value is not recognized by all participants during the conversation, which can also be explained by the three dimensions described above: Either the conversation partners do not allow themselves to be open to a re-examination due to their psychological disposition, but leave the conversation narcissistically offended[25] or simply try to avoid it[26]. Or it turns out that they never really had an interest in the subject (thematic dimension) and consequently are

---

[23] Sileni were originally nature demons in animal form and were later assigned to the entourage of Dionysus. Finally, the equation of Silen and Satyr took place (see the further excerpt from the *Symposium* above; cf. Martens 2004, pp. 24–25. The passage here probably refers to figures that could be bought. For the topic of Satyr and Silenus in the *Symposium* and for parallels in other texts, see Usher 2002.

[24] Compare, for instance, the extensive list of accusations against Socrates in the *Gorgias*. There Callicles is indignant that Socrates deliberately intends to misinterpret (490c9–d1 and 491a1–3), talks nonsense (490e4), deliberately uses sophistical tricks (497a7), asks meaningless questions (497b7–8), is aggressive (505d4) and even quarrelsome (515b5). See also *Hipp. min.* 373b4–5, *Charm.* 169c, *Euthyphr.* 11b.

[25] This is how Euthyphro behaves, for example, in the dialogue of the same name (*Euthyphr.* 15e).

[26] Cf. *Hipp. min.* 369b8–c8.

also not willing to continue the examination or to take on the necessary commitment. Finally, if one wants to grasp the value of the Socratic conversation, it must be noted that this always depends on the individual's psychological disposition and the relevance of the topic for every individual interlocutor: There is value in the conversations, but not for everyone.

The value of the Socratic dialogue, as presented by Plato, is also evident in another respect. This value lies in the intellectual training of the reader[27] through a careful reading of the dialogues. This value can therefore be described as being situated on a *text-external* level. The reader becomes a witness to a conversation and, through careful (and perhaps repeated[28]) reading, understands the progression of the dialogue and the argumentation presented in it. The reader can follow the development of the conversation and its (aporetic) outcome[29]. If the reader did not understand the course of the argument (and the result) the first time due to the rhetoric of Socrates and, like the characters in the dialogue, became uncertain[30], a second reading can lead to reflection on the course of the dialogue and, eventually, a deeper understanding of it. This shapes the dialogues as exercises in methodologically guided conversation and correct argumentation[31]. The reader can also follow the role of Socrates and understand the function of his peculiar rhetoric. This has been thoroughly fleshed out in Michael Erler's monograph on the purpose and meaning of *aporia* in Plato's dialogues.[32] Erler, in his book, is concerned with the question of whether and to what extent the reader is involved in the dialogues.[33] He concludes that there are things left unsaid in the dialogues and the reader has to fill this gap[34].

---

[27] For the sake of readability, this article uses the generic form "reader", which of course always refers to people of all gender identities.

[28] This is assumed by some interpreters; see, for example, Usener 1994 or Kersting 1999. Blößner (1997, 2011) emphasized that Plato expected and even intended that the dialogues are read several times. For interesting observations on this, see Blößner 1997, pp. 284–288. On the importance of reading for understanding a work, see Quintilian *inst. orat.* 10,1,19: *lectio libera est nec actionis impetu transcurrit; sed repetere saepius licet, sive dubites sive memoriae penitus adfigere velis. repetamus autem et retractemus, et ut cibos mansos ac prope liquefactos demittimus, quo facilius digerantur, ita lectio non cruda, sed multa iteratione mollita et velut confecta, memoriae imitationique tradatur.*

[29] See, for example, Gooch 1987, p. 200 in relation to the *Meno*: "While the printed word cannot answer his questions in new speech, the stability of written argument does allow him to retrace the path to the conclusion. When he walks the argument's course again, he may see that its end is not inevitable." Similarly, Kersting 1999, p. 42 in relation to the *Politeia*.

[30] See Erler 2015, p. 110. On the transfer of the *aporia* to the reader, see Vöhler 2013, p. 77.

[31] Similarly, in relation to the *Meno*, Blößner 2011.

[32] Erler 1987.

[33] This has previously been remarked by Szlezák 1985, pp. 138–139. For the learning progress that the Platonic dialogue can initiate in its reader, see Cotton 2014, esp. pp. 265–266. For the involvement of the reader in the dialogues, see also Hoerber 1960, p. 94, Westermann 2002, pp. 48–49, Blößner 2011, Kaiser 2017.

[34] For this, see Erler 1987, p. 8.

Subsequently, attempts were also made to find clues in the text that are intended as hints for the reader but are not noticed by or are not relevant to the figures in the texts. The function of those hidden remarks has been seen to enable the reader to understand the progression of the dialogue (these clues can be complex ironic statements or just single terms[35]). This means that clues and hints towards an alternative reading can be extracted from the dialogue, which are intended for the reader on a *text-external* level. By reading the dialogues carefully and being attentive to hints, the reader is led to a deeper understanding with regard to the progression of the dialogue, while the characters in the dialogue fail to do so. In this way, the *aporia* inherent in the dialogue can be overcome by the reader or at least traced back to its origin through intensive reading; this also enables the reader to analyse the argumentative paths carried out in the dialogue. The conversations end in bewilderment but they point to possible solutions, as Erler emphasises: "Die Gespräche enden zwar in Ratlosigkeit (Aporie), deuten aber Lösungsmöglichkeiten an. Platon bietet dem Leser also einen Wettkampf um Sinn und Zweck kommunikativer Methoden und damit gleichsam einen Eigenkommentar zu den in seinen Schriften illustrierten philosophischen Auseinandersetzungen an."[36]

The following passages from the *Meno* shall prove the remarks concerning the double value of the Platonic dialogues made in the introduction. The passages under discussion have been less considered in research so far with regard to the reader[37].

3 The Dialogue *Meno*

The (assumed) middle dialogue[38] begins with the question of Meno, a student of Gorgias, to Socrates, whether *aretē* (ἀρετή[39]) is teachable, or the human being acquires it by training, or whether it comes to the human being by nature or in some other way (70a1–4: Ἔχεις μοι εἰπεῖν, ὦ Σώκρατες, ἆρα διδακτὸν ἡ ἀρετή; ἢ οὐ διδακτὸν ἀλλ' ἀσκητόν; ἢ οὔτε ἀσκητὸν οὔτε μαθητόν, ἀλλὰ φύσει παραγίγνεται τοῖς ἀνθρώποις ἢ ἄλλῳ τινὶ τρόπῳ; Can you tell me Sokrates, whether *aretē* is teachable? Or is it not teachable, but trainable? Or neither trainable nor learnable, instead it comes to humans by nature or in some other way?). Socrates assumes as a premise that one can only answer the question if one first

---

[35] For comments by the figures in the Platonic dialogues as clues for the reader, see Humar 2017a, pp. 244–273 with further literature references and some examples from other dialogues.

[36] Erler 2017, p. 92.

[37] I am thus methodologically following my own work (Humar 2017a and 2017b).

[38] Cf. Thomas 1980, pp. 10 ff. For the dating of the conversation, see Bluck 1961, pp. 108–120; the dating is shortly discussed by Hoerber 1960, pp. 79–80.

[39] In the following, the term *aretē* is left untranslated (as in Blößner 2011 and Hallich 2013). In general, the term includes any form of excellence of a person (virtue) or thing (quality) and can sometimes be difficult to reproduce in English.

clarifies what *aretē* is at all (search for a definition). That one must first know what an x is in order to then make statements about whether something is an x, is a basic principle in the Socratic dialogues[40]. Meno believes to know exactly what *aretē* is (71e1: Ἀλλ' οὐ χαλεπόν, ὦ Σώκρατες, εἰπεῖν[41]), which is why he does not question this methodological requirement by Socrates. He seemsto be sure to be able to give the answer quickly. After the introduction, Meno presents three definitions of *aretē* in the first part; all of them are rejected or refuted by Socrates. The second part focuses on the processes of learning and teaching (exemplified by the "geometry lesson" with a slave), while the third part of the dialogue again addresses the question of the acquisition of *aretē*. Anytos, one of the three accusers of Socrates, is also included in the dialogue as an interlocutor In the following, I will pick out two significant scenes as examples of the statements made at the beginning with regard to reader guidance and understanding the dynamics of the dialogue.

3.1 First Example: The Refutation of the Definitions in the First Part

In the first part of the dialogue[42], Socrates attempts with Meno to define *aretē*. The first definition fails because Meno does not grasp the nature (72b1: οὐσία) of *aretē* but lists many different *aretai* that come to different objects like the *aretē* of a man, a woman, a slave, etc. (thus, *aretē* would be a relative concept[43], which has different forms depending on the reference). The *aretē* of a man, for example, would be to administer the state (the *polis*), that of a woman the house. Socrates focuses on the multitude of examples that Meno had offered him and points out that there must nevertheless be a common form (72c7: εἶδος) of *aretē* underlying all of them[44]. The first definition is thus quickly refuted[45], despite Meno's hesitation to make concrete concessions (73a).

Interestingly, Socrates expands Meno's definition at this point in the dialogue with a small detail: "How was that? Didn't you say that the *aretē* of a man consists in administering the *polis* well [εὖ], but [that of] a woman the house [well]."[46] Plato

---

[40] Cf. Geach 1966 and Santas 1972.

[41] The Greek text follows here and in the following the edition by J. Burnet (Platonis Opera, rec. Ioannes Burnet, Vol. 1–5, Oxford 1900–1907, and more often). The translations from the *Meno* are by the author.

[42] For a complete outline of the dialogue, see Holzhausen 1994, p. 149 and Hoerber 1960, pp. 85–87. A brief overview can be found in Söder 2017, pp. 44–45.

[43] On relativism in the first definition, see Hallich 2013, pp. 36–39.

[44] Examples in definitions are often rejected by Socrates; see, for example, *Euthyphr*. 6d–e and *Lach*. 190e–192b. These passages are also named in Hallich 2013, p. 39 n. 9.

[45] However, this definition is not as deficient as it might seem from Socrates' statement; see Bluck 1961, p. 218 and Thomas 1980, p. 83.

[46] *Men.* 73a6–7: τί δέ; οὐκ ἀνδρὸς μὲν ἀρετὴν ἔλεγες πόλιν εὖ διοικεῖν, γυναικὸς δὲ οἰκίαν;

has Meno agree here, although he never said that: There was never any word about a qualitative evaluation of this administration (good)[47]. And now Socrates can build on this addition and bring in other concepts: In the following passage he addresses the aspects of composure and justice and (always with Meno's agreement) concludes that excellent (ἀγαθοί)[48] men and women can only be excellent if they do so in a reasonable and just manner (73a9: σωφρόνως καὶ δικαίως). Now a very simple argument can be quickly created: All those who administer well (εὖ) are then excellent (ἀγαθοί) men or women if they are just and reasonable; and thus they always have *aretē*. Hence, according to Socrates, there can't be different *aretai*.

The second definition[49] (73c9) is quickly refuted: Meno offers to define *aretē* as the ability to rule over other people. Socrates reacts with a simple question:

> SOK. But is this also the *aretē* of a child, Meno, or the one of a slave, to be able to rule over the master? And, in your opinion, is the one who rules still a slave?[50] (73d2–4)

Meno vehemently denies this (73d5: Οὐ πάνυ μοι δοκεῖ, ὦ Σώκρατες) and Socrates confirms this denial. At this point, Meno (at least implicitly) is clearly refuted and the definition has failed; this time Meno also makes clear concessions. But Socrates immediately provides (for the argumentation or the refutation at this point not necessary) an addition, which is also clearly highlighted as such: ἔτι γὰρ καὶ τόδε σκόπει (73d6). And Plato lets Meno react in a very special way:

> SOK. Being able to rule [that is your definition]. Shouldn't we just add to it: in a just way, not in an unjust way?
> MEN. I think so. For justice is *aretē*, Socrates.
> SOK. Is it *aretē*, Meno, or some *aretē*?[51] (73d7–e1)

---

[47] For the inserted εὖ, see Weiss 2001, p. 25.

[48] From *Men*. 87d8–e1 it becomes clear that excellent (*agathoi*) people are excellent if they have *aretē*.

[49] This is presented explicitly as derived from Gorgias (Socrates had asked for a definition of Gorgias). Aristotle mentions that Gorgias' educational program consisted in learning his teachings by heart, cf. Arist. *Soph. El*. 183b35–184a2: For even those who taught eristic verbal contests, the educational program was similar to that of Gorgias. For some gave out rhetorical texts to learn by heart, others eristic texts, and each of them promised to apply their speeches to the often [sc. held] speeches for and against a matter. Therefore, the instruction for the pupils was quick, but unprofessional [i.e. without scientific basis]. καὶ γὰρ τῶν περὶ τοὺς ἐριστικοὺς λόγους μισθαρνούντων ὁμοία τις ἦν ἡ παίδευσις τῇ Γοργίου πραγματείᾳ· λόγους γὰρ οἱ μὲν ῥητορικοὺς οἱ δὲ ἐρωτητικοὺς ἐδίδοσαν ἐκμανθάνειν, εἰς οὓς πλειστάκις ἐμπίπτειν ᾠήθησαν ἑκάτεροι τοὺς ἀλλήλων λόγους. διόπερ ταχεῖα μὲν ἄτεχνος δ' ἦν ἡ διδασκαλία τοῖς μανθάνουσι παρ' αὐτῶν·—My translation. Hence, it is not surprising that Meno can offer a (maybe heard) definition but cannot explain it. Anderson (1971, p. 225) comments: "Trained by Gorgias, Meno is a man with an excellent memory, but very little understanding;"

[50] ΣΩ. [...] ἀλλ' ἆρα καὶ παιδὸς ἡ αὐτὴ ἀρετή, ὦ Μένων, καὶ δούλου, ἄρχειν οἵω τε εἶναι τοῦ δεσπότου, καὶ δοκεῖ σοι ἔτι ἂν δοῦλος εἶναι ὁ ἄρχων;

[51] ΣΩ. [...] ἄρχειν φῂς οἷόν τ' εἶναι. οὐ προσθήσομεν αὐτόσε τὸ δικαίως, ἀδίκως δὲ μή; MEN. Οἶμαι ἔγωγε· ἡ γὰρ δικαιοσύνη, ὦ Σώκρατες, ἀρετή ἐστιν. ΣΩ. Πότερον ἀρετή, ὦ Μένων, ἢ ἀρετή τις;

This distinction (*aretē* vs. some *aretē*) is again established as the starting point of the following section: Based on the justice that was brought into play, and the finding that it is one *aretē* of many, as well as the addition that also courage, prudence, wisdom and generosity each is one *aretē*[52], Socrates can conclude:

> SOC. Meno, the same thing happened to us again. We have found many *aretai* again, while we were looking for one, in a different way than before. But the one that exists in all of these, we cannot find.[53] (74a7–10)

Through this digression, the conversation of the two interlocutors turns in a circle: Meno was refuted, he had indirectly admitted this through his vehement rejection of the consequences of his definition. The digression, however, is—on the *text-internal* level—completely unnecessary: Meno is refuted again by an addition of terms that Socrates introduces and does not justify[54], even though it was already clear that the definition does not hold. At this point, the reader wonders why Plato here lets Socrates make further statements that do not bring the dialogue foward. This digression only receives its full function in the third definition, as I will explain in the following. After a parenthesis on colors and shapes[55], Socrates asks Meno again for the definition of *aretē* (75b4); this time with the necessary addition that Meno should not break it down into many again (thus, a mistake like in the first definition is prevented). Based on an ambiguous quotation from a poet, Meno then comes to the definition that *aretē* is "to desire the beautiful and to be able to procure it" (77b3). In a short interlude, the definition is shortened and reduced to the statement: *aretē* is then present if one can procure the beautiful (τὰ ἀγαθά). When asked what is meant by the "beautiful", Meno only narrows down his definition to property or prestige objects such as gold, silver, or duties (78c6)[56]. How these are acquired does not seem to be important for Meno; but he confirms on Socrates' request that they must be acquired with justice, prudence or decency (ὁσιότης):

> SOC. Or do you want to add to this acquisition, Meno, that it is just and honorable, or does it make no difference to you, but if someone unjustly acquires them, you would still call it *aretē* in the same way?
> MEN. Certainly not, Socrates.
> SOC. But you would call it wickedness?
> MEN. Clearly.

---

[52] These conversation steps are carried out in 74a1–6.

[53] ΣΩ. Πάλιν, ὦ Μένων, ταὐτὸν πεπόνθαμεν· πολλὰς αὖ ηὑρήκαμεν ἀρετὰς μίαν ζητοῦντες, ἄλλον τρόπον ἢ νυνδή· τὴν δὲ μίαν, ἣ διὰ πάντων τούτων ἐστίν, οὐ δυνάμεθα ἀνευρεῖν.

[54] Cf. Hallich 2013, p. 51.

[55] For this digression and its function in the dialogue, see Klein 1965, pp. 55–70 and Hallich 2013, pp. 52–59.

[56] Socrates assures himself of this again in 78c7.

SOC. Hence, as it seems, justice or prudence or decency, or some other part of *aretē* have to go along with this acquisition.[...]
SOC. Did we not just now say that each of these qualities is a part of *aretē*, justice and prudence and all such [qualities]?
MEN. Yes.
SOC. Yes, then, Meno, are you making fun of me?[57] (78d3–79a7, with omissions)

Meno is refuted in two ways: First, it becomes clear from the argumentation that *aretē* does not aim at the possession of goods or positions, but at the evaluation of the action that leads to these (just, prudent, etc.). And he lets himself be led into a methodological error by Socrates again, which generates the deficient definition from the beginning (there would be several *aretai* again). Meno reacts to Socrates' request to start again from the beginning (79e5: ἐξ ἀρχῆς) with the famous comparison of the sting-ray[58]: his aporetic uncertainty reaches its peak. He no longer wants to participate in the conversation, but tries to push the topic aside with the provoking image of Socrates.

It is interesting how Plato makes this development transparent[59] for the reader: First of all, Plato lets Socrates use all the techniques on the dialogical level that also occur in other dialogues (substitution of concepts, additional extensions, etc.). Jens Holzhausen remarks[60] about the passage: "Bei der Widerlegung des zweiten Teil der dritten Definition [...] passiert etwas Erstaunliches, was ebenfalls Menons Charakterisierung dient. Denn Sokrates widerlegt ihn mit genau demselben 'Trick', mit dem er schon die zweite Definition zurückwies."[61] This is correct because the two terms reappear; but actually the second definition is not rejected by this "trick" (as Holzhausen calls it), but by the previous argument (73d: the *aretē* of a slave or a child cannot consist in ruling). The insertion is basically irrelevant or not without alternative for the course and the refutation of the second

---

[57][ΣΩ.] πότερον προστιθεὶς τούτῳ τῷ πόρῳ, ὦ Μένων, τὸ δικαίως καὶ ὁσίως, ἢ οὐδέν σοι διαφέρει, ἀλλὰ κἂν ἀδίκως τις αὐτὰ πορίζηται, ὁμοίως σὺ αὐτὰ ἀρετὴν καλεῖς; MEN. Οὐ δήπου, ὦ Σώκρατες. ΣΩ. ἀλλὰ κακίαν. MEN.πάντως δήπου. ΣΩ. δεῖ ἄρα, ὡς ἔοικε, τούτῳ τῷ πόρῳ δικαιοσύνην ἢ σωφροσύνην ἢ ὁσιότητα προσεῖναι, ἢ ἄλλο τι μόριον ἀρετῆς· [...] ΣΩ. Οὐκοῦν τούτων ἕκαστον ὀλίγον πρότερον μόριον ἀρετῆς ἔφαμεν εἶναι, τὴν δικαιοσύνην καὶ σωφροσύνην καὶ πάντα τὰ τοιαῦτα; MEN. Ναί. ΣΩ. εἶτα, ὦ Μένων, παίζεις πρός με;

[58] *Men.* 80 a1–b7.

[59] This of course presupposes that Plato is always aware of the error in the dialogues himself; there are significant indications for this. For the general transparency of logical conclusions for the reader see Geiger 2006, especially p. 20. Blößner also assumes this transparency and shows that in *Politeia* Book 1 Plato lets his figures interact in a specific way in order to make the reader aware that a premise has not yet been proved; so this one could find out at which point in the argumentation the error is to be found and in addition of what kind the error is and what one would have to do to avoid it; see Blößner 1991, pp. 69–70. For another example, see Blößner 1997, p. 286. Seeck 1997 also rejects errors in thinking at Plato.

[60] Holzhausen 1994, p. 134.

[61] See also Klein 1965, p. 81.

definition. Holzhausen[62] asks the following question after his observations: "Ist Sokrates Menon gegenüber so einfallslos, daß er dessen Definition zweimal auf dieselbe Weise und noch dazu mit denselben Worten widerlegen muss?" That could be. But whoever has studied the Platonic Socrates in the other dialogues has to admit that it is difficult to assume that Plato wants Socrates to use the same trick twice without any thought behind it; there are certainly many alternatives possible[63]. It is therefore advisable to think about at least one more function of this addition of terms, which leads to a refutation again[64].

The double repetition of the same procedure is intended for the reader whom Plato wants to show how and why the definitions fail. By repeating the added pair of terms (in a *just* and *pious* way, δικαίως καὶ ὁσίως) the attention is automatically concentrated on this pair which is often used throughout the part. If the reader had overlooked the terms the first time, Plato gives a second chance to the reader, now to discover[65] how easily Socrates refutes Meno here and thus shows that the addition plays a crucial role in the refutation of the definition. Of course, Meno does not notice anything and falls into the trap twice. But the reader can, with Plato's help, overcome the partial, text-internal *aporia* of Meno and understand why the definitions fail and what role the concept pair repeatedly added by Socrates plays. In addition, as already noted, the central problem in the refutation, the parts of *aretē* (78e1: μόριον ἀρετῆς), is repeated several times in the sections before this refutation[66]; this also increases the reader's attention. It seems as if Plato wants the reader to discover the development of the dialogue here. That such techniques of reader guidance are not an isolated case in the *Meno* should be illustrated by a second example.

3.2 Second Example: The Question of the Teachers of *Aretē*

The question of the teachability of *aretē* raised at the beginning of the dialogue is answered at 96c10: If there are no teachers and no students of *aretē*, then it is not teachable. But how do both interlocutors come to this insight? The foundation for this conclusion starts at 89d4 and is linguistically striking. At Meno's request, Socrates confirms the previously discussed assumption that *aretē* must be

---

[62] *Ibid.*

[63] That Socrates has a whole arsenal of rhetorical devices is manifest in the other dialogues; see Humar 2017a in detail.

[64] Klein 1965, pp. 79–80: "[…] Meno's acceptance of Socrates 'addition' means that Meno repudiates his own statement."

[65] Hallich 2013, p. 75 also notes: "Die Parallelität zwischen der (modifizierten) dritten undder zweiten Bestimmung der Tugend ist so augenfällig, dass erstaunlich ist, dass Menon sie nichtbemerkt." What function this part has with regard to the reader and his understanding is not discussed by Hallich.

[66] For example, 79a3, b2, b5 and 6, b9 etc. Cf. Klein 1965, p. 80.

teachable if it is a form of knowledge (*epistēmē*)[67]. He does not want to take this back either; but he wonders whether *aretē* is actually knowledge:

> SOK. [...] Tell me, if anything can be taught (*didakton*), not only *aretē*, isn't it necessarily true that there must be teachers and students of it?
> MEN. It seems so to me.
> SOK. Wouldn't we also rightly suspect, if we suspected that that for which there are neither teachers nor students is not teachable (*didakton*)?[68] (89d6–e3)

What is decisive here is the Greek word *didakton* (διδακτόν), which can be translated both as teachable and as 'taught'. The word thus has a decisive ambiguity inherent in it, which Socrates does not make clear. This has already been pointed out by Paul Gooch: "However, *didakton* masks an ambiguity which needs to be exposed. The phrase *hê aretê ouk esti didakton* may mean either "virtue is not taught" or "virtue is not teachable", and the difference is important."[69] Because it makes a difference whether one assumes that something is not taught because (at the moment, for certain reasons) there are no teachers and students, or whether one (incorrectly) infers from this assumption that the object is not teachable in general. And that Socrates does not necessarily assert this last interpretation becomes clear from the construction: Plato has Socrates formulate his question cautiously in the optative: Wouldn't we be right?[70]

Meno asks if there are not after all teachers of *aretē*. From this question a further discourse about the sophists ensues, which Socrates conducts with Anytos and which tackles the question of who the potential teachers of *aretē* could be (89e6: τινες εἶεν διδάσκαλοι). All candidates (sophists, excellent men) are gradually excluded. Therefore, Socrates can conclude that, if neither sophists nor excellent (ἀγαθοί) men are teachers in this matter, then there are apparently no other teachers (96b7–8). Now Socrates recurs to the statements made at 89d6–8: If there are no teachers, then are there also no students? (96c1) Meno agrees. Socrates then refers directly to the premises set in 89e1–2: "But we agreed that a thing for which there are neither teachers nor students is also not teachable (*didakton*), right?" (96c3–4). Meno immediately confirms this (96c5). Socrates can then transfer this general statement to *aretē*: "But now there are no teachers of *aretē* to be seen anywhere, are there?" (96c6) Meno agrees to this again. Socrates asks in exactly the same words again:

---

[67] This is also dealt with in the *Protagoras*; see *Prot.* 361a–b. See also *Politeia* VI, 492e3–5.

[68] [ΣΩ.] τόδε γάρ μοι εἰπέ· εἰ ἔστιν διδακτὸν ὁτιοῦν πρᾶγμα, μὴ μόνον ἀρετή, οὐκ ἀναγκαῖον αὐτοῦ καὶ διδασκάλους καὶ μαθητὰς εἶναι; ΜΕΝ. Ἔμοιγε δοκεῖ. ΣΩ. Οὐκοῦν τοὐναντίον αὖ, οὗ μήτε διδάσκαλοι μήτε μαθηταὶ εἶεν, καλῶς ἂν αὐτὸ εἰκάζοντες εἰκάζοιμεν μὴ διδακτὸν εἶναι;

[69] Gooch 1987, p. 200. On this ambiguity, see also Ionescu 2007, p. 122.

[70] See Ebert 2018, p. 132. Similar also Ionescu 2007, p. 122.

SOC. If there are no teachers, then are there also no students?
MEN. It seems so.
SOC. So *aretē* would not be teachable? (96c8–10)[71]

Even here Socrates does not formulate clearly, but remains in the optative. Why? The course of the dialogue, the premises set, and the investigations carried out make no other conclusion possible. The error lies in the misinterpretation of *didakton* as "not teachable" and not as "not taught"; Socrates narrows down the understanding of the term decisively and Meno does not notice this. The conclusion is not inevitable: If one takes the latter meaning, one would conclude that the absence of teachers and students indicates that a certain thing (at the moment for certain reasons) is not taught. There are no subjects and objects of teaching at that time. However, this does not prove the principle of unteachability of this thing, as Socrates suggests[72]. At least one could have specified the term. Paul Gooch asks, however, whether Plato wants to enable his reader to discover this issue and find a solution: "Did Plato intend his reader to make the move Meno fails to make?"[73] In my opinion the answer is: yes. The decisive hint is given to the reader by Meno himself; in response to Socrates' question of whether *aretē* would then be teachable, he says: "It does not seem to be the case if we undertake the investigation in the right way (εἴπερ ὀρθῶς ἡμεῖς ἐσκέμμεθα)." And this comment by Meno is also directed at the reader: Unlike the figures on the level of the dialogue, the reader can go back and realize that the investigation was *not* carried out in the right way and has to correct the error. It also does not seem to be a coincidence that Plato has Meno use the term *aretē*, which is decisive for the outcome of the dialogue, in the very first sentence of the dialogue (see above). But not only that: Meno uses the word *didakton* once, but also the word *mathēton* (μαθητόν), which can be translated as learnable[74]. For the question it is irrelevant whether one asks whether *aretē* is teachable (*didakton*) or learnable (*mathēton*) (and in addition trainable or learnable). But for the reader there is a hint here that Meno wants to understand the word *didakton* in exactly this sense. Socrates will later turn it around. The reader may notice when rereading the dialogue right from the beginning: A clear distinction of the terms right from the start and a terminological focus on *didakton* and *mathēton* during the investigation might have given the dialogue a different course.

The unsatisfactory conclusion that follows from the dialogue—namely, that *aretē* comes to people by divine providence and can by no means be taught—is clearly grounded in a faulty investigation as well as in the inaccuracies introduced

---

[71] ΣΩ. Εἰ δέ γε μὴ διδάσκαλοι, οὐδὲ μαθηταί; ΜΕΝ. Φαίνεται οὕτως. ΣΩ. Ἀρετὴ ἄρα οὐκ ἂν εἴη διδακτόν;

[72] This is also noted, inter alia, by Ionescu 2007, p. 122.

[73] Gooch 1987, p. 201.

[74] For the distinction between the two terms, see Hoerber 1960, pp. 91–92.

deliberately by Socrates and accepted by a careless Meno[75]. The reader has the chance to figure that out. Even more: He can see that the deliberately used ambiguity of the term *didakton* lies in the fact that Plato here uses it in a restricted sense and Meno understands it in a specific (misleading) way. In this way, the conversation makes a contribution to the understanding of (in)correct argumentation[76].

4   The Socratic Tactic and the Value of Conversation for Plato's Readers

The fact that Meno fails his attempts at a definition in the first part and in the investigations in the second part has two causes: First, it may be due to the fact that Meno, as can be distilled from the entire course of the conversation, does not seem to have particularly well-developed cognitive abilities; he makes many mistakes in his definitions and lets himself be quickly led astray by Socrates. In line with this observation, several interpreters do not attribute outstanding skills to him[77]. But why did Plato create his Meno in this way? As James Arieti has noted, the composition of the dialogues plays an important role for Plato[78]. For the planned failure of the conversation, exactly such a figure as Meno is needed.

That Plato wants his Meno to fail is obvious; hence, figure and result must therefore be consistent. At the same time, however, Plato provides hints for the reader at the two decisive points, which enables him to overcome the *aporia*, to understand the internal structure of the conversation and to see the methodological errors. He can, in contrast to Meno and Anytus[79], the other interlocutor in the dialogue, undergo a development. Hence, the dialogue serves as an exercise in philosophical conversation. This, however, only works if Plato lets his figures act accordingly naively and carelessly and in return leaves clues that make mistakes in the argumentation recognisable. The reader is thus indirectly included in the dialogue and can understand the conversation in its finest structure if he is able to interpret the hints correctly. This may not have been possible for every reader in antiquity. Thus, the 'value' of the Platonic conversation on the *text-external* level corresponds to the principle already mentioned above for the *text-internal* level: There is a value in the conversations, but not for everyone.

---

[75] Cf. Ionescu 2007, p. 137.

[76] Similarly, according to the interpretation of Hoerber 1960, Plato seems to want to show at another place in the dialogue that it is important in a conversation to either define terms precisely or at least to avoid vague terms. Thus, his Socrates uses the key words *epistēmē* and *phronēsis* synonymously several times in the discussion of knowledge and its distinction from true opinion, leading to false assumptions; cf. Hoerber 1960, p. 90.

[77] Hoerber 1960, p. 100, Klein 1965, pp. 54–55, Thomas 1980, pp. 92–93, Holzhausen 1995.

[78] Arieti 1991, p. 201: "[…] the cast of characters in frequently a clue to Plato's intent."

[79] See Hoerber 1960, p. 99: "The characterization of Meno and Anytus in the *Meno* makes it clear that any insight into cause or any knowledge based on the Ideas is beyond their ken, and that Meno and Anytus must continue to live in the world of opinion […]."

References

Arieti, James A.: Interpreting Plato: The Dialogues as Drama. Lanham: Rowman & Littlefield Publishers 1991.
Anderson, Daniel E.: The Theory of Recollection in Plato's Meno, in: Southern Journal of Philosophy 9,3, 1971, pp. 225–235.
Benson, Hugh H.: Meno, the Slave-boy and the Elenchos, in: Phronesis 35, 1990, pp. 128–158.
Beversluis, John: Cross-examining Socrates. A Defense of the Interlocutors in Plato's Early Dialogues. Cambridge: Cambridge Univ. Press 2000.
Blondell, Ruby: The Play of Character in Plato's Dialogues. Cambridge: Cambridge Univ. Press 2002.
Blößner, Norbert: Zu Platon, ‚Politeia' 352d–357d, in: Hermes 119,1, 1991, pp. 61–73.
Blößner, Norbert: Dialogform und Argument: Studien zu Platons Politeia. Stuttgart, Mainz: Franz Steiner Verlag 1997.
Blößner, Norbert: The Unity of The Meno, in: Philologus 155, 2011, pp. 39–68.
Bluck, Richard S.: Plato's Meno, edited with Introduction and Commentary, Cambridge: Cambridge Univ. Press 1961.
Charalabopoulos, Nikos: Platonic Drama and its Ancient Reception. Cambridge: Cambridge Univ. Press 2012.
Conventry, Lucida: The Role of the Interlocutor in Plato's Dialogues: Theory and Practice, in: Cristopher Pelling (ed.), Characterization and Individuality in Greek Literature. Oxford: Clarendon Press 1990, pp. 174–196.
Cotton, Anne K.: Platonic Dialogue and the Education of the Reader. Oxford: Oxford Univ. Press 2014.
Dejardins, Rosemary: The Rational Enterprise: Logos in Plato's Theaetetus. Albany: State Univ. of New York Press 1990.
Ebert, Theodor: Menon. Übersetzung und Kommentar. Berlin, Boston: Walter de Gruyter 2018.
Erler, Michael: Der Sinn der Aporien in den Dialogen Platons. Übungsstücke zur Anleitung im philosophischen Denken. Berlin, New York: Walter de Gruyter 1987.
Erler, Michael: Vom admirativen zum irritierten Staunen. Philosophie, Rhetorik und Verunsicherung in Platons Dialogen, in: Ramona Früh, Therese Fuhrer, Marcel Humar, Martin Vöhler (eds.): Irritationen. Rhetorische und poetische Verfahren der Verunsicherung. Berlin, New York: Walter de Gruyter 2015, pp. 109–123.
Erler, Michael: Kontexte der Philosophie Platons, in: Christoph Horn, Jörn Müller, Joachim Söder (eds.): Platon-Handbuch. Leben – Werk – Wirkung. Stuttgart: J. B. Metzler 2017, 2. Aufl., pp. 64–104.
Fröhlich, Bettina: Die sokratische Frage: Platons Laches. Berlin, Münster: LIT Verlag 2007.
Geiger, Rolf: Dialektische Tugenden: Untersuchungen zur Gesprächsform in den Platonischen Dialogen. Paderborn: Mentis 2006.
Geach, Peter: Plato's Euthyphro: An Analysis and Commentary, in: The Monist 50,3, 1966, pp. 369–382.
Gooch, Paul W.: Irony and Insight in Plato's Meno, in: Laval théologique et philosophique 43,2, 1987, pp. 189–204.
Hallich, Oliver: Platons Menon. Darmstadt: Wissenschaftliche Buchgesellschaft 2013.
Hoerber, Robert G.: Plato's Meno, in: Phronesis 5,2, 1960, pp. 78–102.
Holzhausen, Jens: Menon in Platons ‚Menon', in: Würzburger Jahrbücher für die Altertumswissenschaft N.F. 20, 1994, pp. 129–149.
Humar, Marcel: Rhetorik der Verunsicherung – Affekt-Strategien in den platonischen Frühdialogen. Berlin, Boston: Walter de Gruyter 2017(a).
Humar, Marcel: (De)legitimierungsversuche in Platons Laches – zur Personenkonstellation der sokratischen Gesprächspartner, in: Gymnasium 124,3, 2017(b), pp. 203–223.
Ionescu, Cristina: Plato's Meno. An Interpretation. Lanham: Lexington Books 2007.

Kahn, Charles H.: Drama and Dialectic in Plato's Gorgias, in: Oxford Studies in Ancient hilosophy 1, 1983, pp. 75–121.
Kaiser, Bernhard: Argumentativ überwunden, aber nicht überzeugt? Zur Wirksamkeit der sokratischen Elenktik in Platons Gorgias, in: Graeco-Latina Brunensia 22,2, 2017, pp. 229–240.
Kersting, Wolfgang: Platons Staat, Darmstadt: Wissenschaftliche Buchgesellschaft 1999.
Klein, Jacob: A commentary on Plato's Meno. Chapel Hill: Univ. of North Carolina Press 1965.
Martens, Ekkehard: Sokrates: Eine Einführung. Stuttgart: Reclam Verlag 2004.
Nehamas, Alexander: Eristic, Antilogic, Sophistic, Dialectic: Plato's Demarcation of Philosophy from Sophistry, in: History of Philosophy Quarterly 7,1, 1990, pp. 3–16.
Politis, Vasilis: Aporia and Searching in the Early Plato, in: Lindsay Judson, Vassilis Karasmanis (eds.): Remembering Socrates: Philosophical Essays. Oxford: Oxford Univ. Press 2006, pp. 88–109.
Puster, Rolf W.: Zur Argumentationsstruktur platonischer Dialoge: die „Was ist X?" Frage in Laches, Charmides, der größere Hippias und Euthyphron. Freiburg im Breisgau, München: Alber Verlag 1983.
Rosen, Stanley: Plato's Republic: a Study. New Haven, London: Yale Univ. Press 2005.
Rowe, Christopher: Plato and the Art of Philosophical Writing. Cambridge: Cambridge Univ. Press 2007.
Santas, Gerasimos X.: The Socratic Fallacy, in: Journal of the History of Philosophy 10, 1972, pp. 127–141.
Seeck, Gustav A.: Nicht-Denkfehler und natürliche Sprache bei Platon: Gerechtigkeit und Frömmigkeit in Platons Protagoras. München: C. H. Beck 1997.
Söder, Joachim: Zu Platons Werken, in: Christoph Horn, Jörn Müller, Joachim Söder (eds.): Platon-Handbuch. Leben – Werk – Wirkung. Stuttgart: J. B. Metzler 2017, 2. Aufl., pp. 20–61.
Szlezák, Thomas A.: Platon und die Schriftlichkeit der Philosophie. Bd. 1: Interpretationen zu den frühen und mittleren Dialogen. Berlin, New York: Walter de Gruyter 1985.
Teloh, Henry: The Importance of Interlocutors Characters in Plato's Early Dialogues, in: Boston Area Colloquium in Ancient Philosophy 2, 1986, pp. 25–28.
Thomas, John E.: Musings on the Meno, Den Haag, Boston, London: Springer Netherlands 1980.
Usener, Sylvia: Isokrates, Platon und ihr Publikum: Hörer und Leser von Literatur im 4. Jahrhundert v. Chr. Tübingen: Narr Verlag 1994.
Usher, M. D.: Satyr Play in Plato's Symposium, in: The American Journal of Philology 123,2, 2002, pp. 205–228.
Vlastos, Gregory: Introduction: The Paradox of Socrates, in: Gregory Vlastos (ed.): The Philosophy of Socrates: a Collection of Critical Essays. New York: Anchor Books 1971, pp. 1–21.
Völer, Martin: Rhetorik der Verunsicherung. Platons Konzeption der Sokratischen Methode in der Apologie, in: Martin Baisch, Andreas Degen u. Jana Lüdtke (eds.), Wie Gebannt – Ästhetische Verfahren der affektiven Bindung von Aufmerksamkeit. Freiburg: Rombach Verlag KG, pp. 73–92.
Weiss, Roslyn: Virtue in the Cave. Moral inquiry in Plato's Meno, Oxford: Clarendon Press 2001.
Westermann, Hartmut: Die Intentionen des Dichters und die Zwecke der Interpreten: Zu Theorie und Praxis der Dichterauslegung in den platonischen Dialogen. Berlin, New York: Walter de Gruyter 2002.

The Renaissance of Conversation—A Short History of Conversation in the Age of the Discourse Revolution

Bernd Roeck

Abstract

The article provides an overview from a historical perspective of aspects of the—essentially Italian—prehistory of "classical" conversation, as it developed in France in the 17th century. It starts from the "discourse revolution", a central phenomenon of the Renaissance: it is characterized by the differentiation and expansion of the objects of literature, science and fine art, and thus by the increase in profane topics. In addition to political and social conditions, the wide reception of ancient patterns was decisive for this. In this context, the revival of the literary genre of the dialogue and the parallel increase in reflections on manners and thus also on norms that a successful conversation should correspond to took place. The rehabilitation of *voluptas* is reminded of as a prerequisite for the positive evaluation of conversation in the narrower sense. The world-historical importance of the Renaissance dialogue—the delimitation of the genre from conversation is only possible to a limited extent—lies in the fact that it indicates the principle of exchanging ideas and critically discussing them. In other cultures this practice was far less common.

Keywords

Dialog dialogue · Konversation conversation · Renaissance · Diskursrevolution discourse revolution · Voluptas · Säkularisierung secularization · Erste Aufklärung First Enlightenment

---

B. Roeck (✉)
Universität Zürich, Zürich, Switzerland
e-mail: roeck@hist.uzh.ch

© The Author(s), under exclusive license to Springer-Verlag GmbH, DE, part of Springer Nature 2023
C. Strosetzki (ed.), *The Value of Conversation*,
https://doi.org/10.1007/978-3-662-67200-6_3

1 Terms

Giovanni della Casa's widely read "Galateo" instructs, as the subtitle states, through the person "of an old, uneducated man who is teaching one of his young men", on the manners, "which one must observe or avoid in general conversation".[1] For example, rules for appropriate clothing are also discussed. The general idea of social interaction remained associated with the term well into the 17th century.[2] Restrictions to the speech or chatter necessarily associated with social contacts, finally the "informal conversation in a small group", which obeys certain rules, apparently took place first in French.[3] Distinctions from "dialogue"—whether as oral conversation or as a literary genre—are difficult, if one does not want to make the purpose-free character of the conversation, which would thus be assigned a lower rank, the criterion.[4]

Of course, long before the "age of conversation", conversations took place that were not only dedicated to the pursuit of knowledge with holy seriousness, but also served as entertainment. The one is hardly separable from the other purpose. Even the more or less fictional conversations that Greek and Roman wisdom teachers of all directions staged were by no means exclusively committed to the investigation of ultimate truths. Significantly, the boom of the genre "dialogue" in the Renaissance and the theoretical reflection on the dialogue and the "art of conversation" went hand in hand with the rehabilitation of *voluptas*, which is why it will be given some attention below.

2 Ancient Patterns: Good Conversations, Sweet Dessert

Most of the standards that the "good conversation" should orient itself to already show blueprint of the "classical" conversation. They were laid out in ancient texts on rhetoric, moral philosophy or politics.[5] They also resulted implicitly from the epochal dialogues of antiquity. According to Cicero, the passions were always to be moderated, propriety and appropriateness, the *aptum*, to be maintained; the term meant approximately the same as later *bienséance*.[6] In the conversation, even reproaches were to be brought mildly, but yet, if there was no other medicine, with

---

[1] This is the title of the Milan edition of 1559: "Treatise by Mr. Giovanni della Casa in which, under the guise of an old idiot teaching his young man, the ways are discussed that one must either keep or shun in common conversation".

[2] Emmelius 2010, pp. 8 ff.; Plotke 2008.

[3] Strosetzki 2013, pp. 51–55; Montandon 1995, p. 125.

[4] Häsner, Bruni, pp. 120 ff.; Strosetzki 2013, pp. 16 ff.

[5] Aschenberg 2005, p. 279 ff.

[6] Cic. off. I, 96; orat. 70; Ansgar Kemmann, 'prepon', in Horn and Rapp 2008, p. 368 ff.; *bienséance*: Strosetzki 2013, p. 246–261.

vigor, if necessary with simulated anger.[7] To actually be angry was not becoming. The angry person showed himself to be a slave of his emotions.

Cicero distinguishes the peaceful, friendly *sermo* in a small circle—the prefiguration of the "true" conversation—from the competitive debate, as it takes place in court, in the senate or in the public assembly.[8] While rhetoric provides rules for the speech, he writes in *"De officiis,"* there are none for such conversations. The *sermo communis* should be unagitated, of fine humor and by no means stiff and stubborn, *minimique pertinax*. Important questions were to be discussed seriously, cheerful with wit. It was to stay on the topic, however, taking into account that not all people were equally interested in the same thing. One should neither mock nor slander those who are absent; those present were to be met with appreciation.

The exemplary participant in an ancient conversation circle has characteristics that also distinguish the good citizen, statesman or wise philosopher. He is just, calm and honest; in everything he observes $\mu\varepsilon\sigma\acute{o}\tau\eta\varsigma$, the middle.[9] So he does not talk too much, but does not remain silent either. Neither does he boast, nor does he flirt by self-deprecation. He always tells the truth. He not only has virtues, but also *urbanitas*.

In the Augustan period, the rhetoric teacher Domitius Marsus, author of a work *"De urbanitate"*, gave a definition of this concept that was to have a far-reaching effect. "A urbane person will be the one from whom there are many good sayings and answers, and who in conversations, in society, at banquets and in assemblies, in short, everywhere speaks wittily and aptly."[10] Quintilian adds: "In my opinion, 'urbanitas' is that which does not allow anything discordant, anything rude, anything rustic, anything confused, anything foreign to be found either in meaning or in words, language or gestures, and not so much in individual statements as in the whole color of speech."[11] If one changes the original stage for the appearance of the "Urban", the city, and gives him the court as an environment, he shows himself as the forerunner of the *cortegiano*, as Castiglione will characterize him.

Conversation, in particular pleasant conversations as a pastime, has certainly always existed. Dion Chrysostomus, Plutarch and others formulate rules for this, which essentially correspond to Quintilian's and Cicero's recommendations.[12]

---

[7] Cic. off. I,3; II, 48; Kennerly 2010, p. 133, 136.

[8] What follows: Cic. off. I, 132–136.

[9] Patrick Unruh, 'mesôtes', in Horn and Rapp 2008, p. 32; Friedemann Buddensiek, ibid., p. 275; Richard Bosley, et al. (eds.), 1995; Fortenbaugh 1975; Morel 1969.

[10] *"Urbanus homo erit, cuius multa bene dicta responsaque erunt, et qui in sermonibus, circulis, conviviis, item in contionibus, omni denique loco ridicule commodeque dicet"*: Inst. VI, 3, 105; Leidl; Pons.

[11] Inst. VI, 3, 107: "…*Nam meo quidem iudicio illa est urbanitas, in qua nihil absonum, nihil agreste, nihil inconditum, nihil peregrinum neque sensu neque verbis neque ore gestuve possit deprendi, ut non tam sit in singulis dictis quam in toto colore dicendi.*"

[12] Dion. Chrys. orations 27; Plutarch VI, 502b–515a; VIII, 8; Anna Ginestí Rosell, 2013; this. 2021.

What distinguishes the view of some philosophers of antiquity most clearly from the assessments of almost all Christian authors of the Middle Ages is that they approve of sociability as an end in itself and give hints on how to make symposia pleasant.[13] Marcus Terentius Varro suggests that one should chat about topics from everyday life, about which one has no time to talk in court or in business. Even the dessert served as dessert, *bellaria,* is mentioned.[14] Varro loves puns: Sweets are sweetest when they are not sweet—otherwise they would be bad for digestion. What is talked about at the edge of the meal that Varro and his mediator Aulus Gellius describe comes quite close to a modern concept of "conversation". The conversation is background noise of a good meal. Not too serious and not too light, it is not about truths and certainly not about ultimate truths. It is enough if it gives pleasure, *voluptas,*—precisely what emerges in 17th century France as the central goal of all conversation, namely *plaisir* and *divertissement*.[15]

3 The Dialogues Fall Silent

No medieval theologian would have come up with the idea of discussing the quality of desserts in connection with thinking about the rules of social behaviour. The pagan sage had passed on his position as a role model to the pious Christian, who knows that true happiness will only be granted in heaven. earthly happiness, pleasure or even lust are regarded as insignificant in this respect, possibly dangerous for the salvation of the soul. Monks and hermits appeared as the most perfect embodiment of the Christian man, who did everything but maintain the middle. A social history of silence finds very talkative sources in monastic rules.[16]

The first post-ancient discussion of the norms to which a good conversation should suffice was written by the jurist Albertanus of Brescia (1195—after 1251).[17] The treatise *Ars loquendi et tacendi* intended for his son Stefano deals with the topic according to the leading questions of communication theory: "Who, what and to whom you say something" is to be asked, and thus also "why, how and when". In addition to Christian scriptures, Albertanus draws on a rich fund of ancient authors, among which Seneca and Cicero occur most frequently. Thus, in his discourse one finds the usual positions of the Stoa, such as not to speak in anger or with envy. Always one must stay with the truth and ask oneself whether what one wants to say is useful and serious, *grave,* or empty and false. Also one should beware of gossip. It was the object of mockery and contempt from time

---

[13] Schnell 2006.
[14] Gell. noctes Atticae XIII, 11; Dion. Chrys. Orationes 77, 3 f.
[15] Strosetzki 2013, pp. 238–245, 296–306.
[16] Müller 1984.
[17] Powell 1992; Friedlein 2002, p. 62 ff. (lit.).

immemorial. Horace's satire "The Boor" takes it to task, as do Dion Chrysostomus and the author or authors of the *"Novellino"*.[18]

The Middle Ages otherwise did not produce more extensive theoretical reflections on the topic.[19] There is one or the other remark on courtly manners. In the *"Roman de la rose"* Love admonishes the lover not to use vulgar, coarse words.[20] In ancient tradition, *urbanitas* or also "measure", *mesura,* are valued as positive qualities.[21] An example is Hermann Damen, a North German Sangspruch poet of the late 13th century: "Whoever wants to speak without thinking / is of stupid mind ... to speak moderately, whoever can / and also to moderate silence / moderate clothes in honor wait; / we think he is a [wise] man, / who does not rise above moderation / and moderate holds up all the time."[22]

The book "On Love", written by the cleric Andreas "Capellanus" between 1174 and 1186, is an exception.[23] It presents pattern dialogues between passionate suitors and reserved women of different social classes. In doing so, it differentiates between the social positions of the speakers, for example, by giving hints on how the *plebeius* should speak to the higher-ranking lady or the aristocrat to the aristocrat. In addition to beauty, wealth, a good character and other things, it is finally the *copiosa sermonis facundia* that should be of use in acquiring love: "The eloquence in conversation often drives the hearts of those who do not love to love. The adorned speech of the lovers is used to set the arrows of love in motion and leads to the assumption of the inner value of the speakers."[24]

Andreas' writing seems to have found many readers; at least Bishop Étienne Tempier of Paris felt compelled in 1277 to condemn the treatise in a cover letter to his decree, which was directed against 219 theses of Averroism and Aristotelism.[25] In doing so, Andreas had anticipated in the third book of his work: It advises against giving in to the types of love that he had just described, because eternal rewards can be obtained through chastity. The moral volte, which is rather cursory in comparison to the rest, was obviously intended to legitimize the libertinage that Andreas had allowed himself in the two preceding books. What he actually undertakes is an attempt to analyze language, communication and the various functions of discourse—he is not only, but primarily, a discourse about discourses.[26]

---

[18] Hor. ser. I, 9; Dion. Chrys. orationes 27; Novellino: Kocher 2005, p. 128 ff.

[19] Cf. Schnell 2008.

[20] Roussel 1995, p. 185.

[21] Godo 2003, pp. 53–86.

[22] von der Hagen 1838, pp. 165–166.

[23] Andersen-Wyman 2007, p. 9.

[24] Knapp 2006, pp. 22–28.

[25] Andersen-Wyman 2007, pp. 12–18.

[26] Andersen-Wyman 2007, p. 24; Classen 2002, p. 342.

4 Discourse Revolution

His treatise, among many other sources, documents a process that could be described with the term "discourse revolution". He means the increasing variety of objects that were dealt with in treatises and books, so that the first gradual, then intensifying advance of profane topics.[27] *Varietà* becomes the signature of the Renaissance.[28] The reception of ancient texts had a major impact. Its prerequisites were found in the specific social and political conditions of Latin Europe. The spaces of the discourse revolution appear to be relatively permeable societies with more or less strong middle classes, which in some cases exercised political influence. The cities and states competing with each other on the cultural field had almost immeasurable patronage potentials. Whoever had made himself unpopular had good chances of finding a feeding trough elsewhere. Of enormous importance was the containment of the "pastoral power". Certainly Latin Europe remained a Christian, God-fearing country. But the influence of the religious functionaries on secular affairs, and thus also on philosophy, literature and art, declined in importance.

The progress of the discourse revolution can be illustrated by the increasingly unprejudiced assessment of worldly pleasures. Only the gradual rehabilitation of this-worldly *voluptas* will make it possible to establish the conversation for pleasure as a positively connoted social practice. Thomas Aquinas took the first step in this direction when he saw "friendly words and gestures" as factors that promote socialization; with Aristotle he saw man, the *"πολιτικόν ζῷον"*[29], destined for a life in community. So he allows conversation as a game that provides relaxation. If wit and clever turns caused cheerfulness, they curbed exuberance and thus found the virtue of moderation.

How much the spaces of the world expanded soon, illustrated Boccaccio's *"Decameron"*. The poet allows the protagonists to have cheerful conversations under the most pleasant circumstances (but claims that the customs were more relaxed in the "old days"[30]). If you take the stories they tell, they leave nothing to be desired in terms of openness.[31] And even the "pastoral power"—when it appears in the form of lustful monks—is ridiculed with biting mockery. In addition to the serious occasion of fleeing the plague, the purpose of the conversations in the *"Decameron"* is above all entertainment. The essence of this outstanding document of the discourse revolution is documented in the title of the first English translation, which appeared in London between 1620 and 1625: *"The Modell of*

---

[27] Roeck 2009; Roeck 2007, pp. 257–268; Roeck 2020, p. 17.

[28] Brinkmann 2001, pp. 12 ff.

[29] Aristot. Pol. 1.1253a; the following: Strosetzki 2013, pp. 334–338; Schrott and Strosetzki, 2021.—Practices: Schatzki 2002, pp. 70–73.

[30] Klinkert 2016, p. 41.

[31] Salwa 2019, pp. 61–78; Cox 1992, pp. 15 ff.

Wit, Mirth, Eloquence, and Conversation. Framed in ten days, of an hundred curious pieces, by seven honourable ladies, and three noble gentlemen".[32]

5 The Rehabilitation of *Voluptas* and the Renaissance of Dialogue

But the simultaneity of the non-simultaneous is to be registered. What the Florentine Boccaccio allows to happen with self-evidence, namely to provide this-worldly pleasure, *diletto,* through conversation, still appears problematic under the pen of his contemporary Petrarch. Certainly, Petrarch's *"Vita solitaria"* also knows the conversation with select friends; but seclusion is not the mode of existence in solitude.[33] How suspect mere this-worldly pleasures still are to the author is illustrated by two sections of his *"De remediis utriusque fortunae"* (1354–1366). In it, reason leads a dialogue with joy, *gaudium,* about painting and sculpture. More precisely, it is rather a monologue, since *gaudium* only stereotypically (albeit with increasingly defiant emphasis) declares its joy in "painted panels" and statues, while *ratio* dismisses them as empty, "vain" pleasures in wordy fashion. That reason is right is clear from the beginning. Pleasure and wonder, she says, distracted from the higher. "But you, if you are still pleased by this, which is falsely painted in worthless colors, shadowy, raise your eyes to him who painted the human skeleton with senses, the soul with reason, the heaven with stars and the earth with flowers—and you will despise those whom you admired as artists."[34] Only religious sculptures could be useful to devout people because they reminded them of heavenly things and moved their souls. "But the profane, even if they sometimes hold the soft with the memory of the noble to virtue, should not be loved and dealt with too much, so that they do not become witnesses of stupidity, servants of greed and rebels against the true religion and that very famous commandment: 'Beware of idols!'"[35]

Leon Battista Alberti saw things quite differently in his treatise on painting (1436). He has no problem praising the enjoyment and pleasure *(volutta, diletto)* that viewing paintings brings.[36] He even likes it when painters show how wind blowing makes the fabric covering the body flutter and reveal a lot of nudity.[37] Shortly before *"Della pittura"* was completed, Lorenzo Valla had taken up the rehabilitation of worldly pleasure. His treatise *"De vero bono"* (1433), a revised version of *"De voluptate,"* attracted the attention of scholars, not least because

---

[32] Castiglione 1625–1620; Castiglione 1935.

[33] Rüegg; Lee 2012, S. 260 f.; Lee 2017, S. 4 f.

[34] The text passages in Baxandall 1971, S. 141, 143; Maurach and Echinger-Maurach 2014, L 5.

[35] Ibid., LI, 13.

[36] Alberti 2007, pp. 37–39; references: Ibid., p. 100 f.; p. 106–109; p. 110 f.

[37] Alberti 2007, p. 45, p. 138 f.

its author extensively discussed the "rhetoric of debate."[38] The dialogue poses the question of what the true, highest good is—Valla considers it by far the most important of all philosophy—and discusses it in an unprecedented way. The lawyer Catone Sacco is allowed to represent the Stoic view that it is equivalent to *honestas*, "honesty." Maffeo Vegio explains with Epicurus *voluptas* as the highest good. The Franciscan theologian and rhetorician Antonio da Rho finally provides a synthesis of pagan and Christian positions.[39] He argues that the "true good" is indeed *voluptas*, but in the final escalation that pleasure which will be enjoyed in heaven. But it will also be experienced physically. What would be the point of the resurrection of the body otherwise?[40]

Valla's protagonists not only represent different positions on the right of *voluptas*, they also argue in different ways. Sacco argues with the weapons of dialectics. Vegio emphasizes the priority of rhetoric and thus the freedom from the binding to the teachings of a philosophical "sect", in this case the Stoics.[41] The third discussant, da Rho, brings poetry into play. Like moderate *copia dicendi*, the wealth of rhetorical means, it is suitable to overwhelm by evoking emotions.[42] In addition, the treatise itself should provide *voluptas*. In *"De voluptate"* one first meets in a colonnade, then in a garden together. That this refers to the Stoics and the Kepos of Epicurus—the two philosophical directions whose dealings with the troublesome play the main roles in Valla's treatise—is obvious.[43] The reader is offered a subtle intellectual game, the deciphering of which not least provides pleasure.

Valla's deliberations process patterns of the Ciceronian dialogue.[44] From him and other ancient authors one could learn that even the small happiness on earth has its rights and that it is worth making thoughts about what it consists of.[45] This view distinguishes Valla's deliberations on the "true good" from church teachings; among the heresies condemned by Bishop Tempier was also the sentence: "That happiness is to be possessed in this life and not in the other."[46]

Valla was a friend of the witty conversationalist who, in addition to eroticism, also appreciated good food and drink, and in general was inclined towards

---

[38] Westermann 2006, p. 31; Vilar 2014; Saviello 2019; on the (possibly four) different versions with different titles: de Panizza Lorch 1970, p. XI; this. 1985, p. 5.

[39] In the first version, the dialogue figures were Leonardo Bruni, Antonio Beccadelli and Niccolò Niccoli: Müller 2002, p. 165f.

[40] Valla 2004, III, 24f., p. 348–350; Leinkauf 2017, p. 173f., 185, 352 f., 357 f.; Roeck 2020, p. 502 f. (Lit.).

[41] Nauta, 2009; Müller 2002—with a view to the first version—S. 191.

[42] Müller 2002, S. 177 f.; Panizza Lorch 1985, S. 116.

[43] Müller 2002, S. 168 f., 179 f., 188–193.

[44] Vilar 2014, S. 351–356; Unkenntnis Lukrez': S. 350; Panizza Lorch 1985, S. 29.

[45] Thomä, 2011, S. 144–147.

[46] Piché and Lafleur 1999; Art. 176: *"Quod felicitas habetur in ista vita, et non in alia"*; Bubert 2019, S. 144, Anm. 303.

a refined lifestyle.[47] But he by no means spoke of pure hedonism. However, he did offer modifications of the previously condemned "epicurean" concept in a Christian sense.[48] Conversely, passages from his treatise could actually be read as Epicurean-tinged criticism of the Christian devaluation of *voluptas* (pleasure).[49] The pursuit of pleasure appears at least in Valla as what it is: as an elementary force in life—not simply sin and therefore an obstacle on the way to eternal bliss. And he meets stoic *rigiditas* (rigidity) with laughter.[50] The real Leonardo Bruni, whose *alter ego* in the first version had to defend the stoic-Aristotelian system of virtues, was, as his reaction to Valla's dialogue shows, anything but satisfied with this result.[51]

Not only Valla tried approaches to Epicurean positions.[52] At the same time, the fanning out of profane topics escalated. The spectrum was expanded to include art theory and urbanism, new perspectives in the natural sciences were opened up by the rediscovery of Lucretius' *"De rerum natura"*[53]*;* Antonio Beccadelli's *"Hermaphroditus"* shocked the prudish with pornography. There had been nothing like this since Ovid's *"Ars amatoria"*. And Platina, in his work *"De honesta voluptate et valetudine"* printed in 1474, worked out a differentiated dietetics as a prerequisite for physical well-being. He also provides an epochal cookbook: a manifesto against monastic asceticism and sour stoics who, as Platina mocks, passed judgment with raised eyebrows—not on human experience, but only on the sound of words.[54]

The examples could be multiplied indefinitely and supplemented with art-historical findings. One could refer to the enormous increase in portraits and self-portraits in a naturalistic style in the 15th and 16th centuries, or to the appearance of new genres such as still-lifes, genre paintings or cityscapes.[55] The earliest autonomous landscape is Albrecht Altdorfer's "Danube landscape with Schloss Wörth" (c. 1520/1525), a small-scale painting which is today in the Alte Pinakothek in Munich. In this way, secular spaces gradually increased in the arts as well.[56] The type of painting known as the *"Sacra Conversazione"*, which dates from the

---

[47] Panizza Lorch 1985, pp. 39 ff.

[48] Ibid., p. 59.

[49] Müller 2002, pp. 175 ff.

[50] Panizza Lorch 1985, p. 45.

[51] Müller 2002, pp. 200 ff.; in *"De vero bono"* (On the True Good), Catone Sacco takes over Bruni's part.

[52] Saviello 2019, p. 129; Allen 1944; Fois 1969, pp. 122–128.

[53] Greenblatt 2011.

[54] Milham 1998, p. 101.

[55] Roeck 2020, p. 679.

[56] Roeck 2004, pp. 122f.; Roeck 2015. A quantitative evaluation of dated paintings showed that the proportion of paintings with secular themes increased from 5% to 22% between 1408 and 1539: Burke 1972, pp. 152, 279.

Renaissance, does not contradict this. The term is not contemporary.[57] The saints gathered around the Madonna in most of the paintings of this type do indeed communicate with each other through gestures, but they do not speak to each other. They bear witness to veneration, some of them seek eye contact with the audience—but not with the Virgin Mary, who remains in her higher sphere.[58]

The causes of this partial "disenchantment of the world" are complex.[59] Among other things, they had to do with the increasing spread of ancient models.[60] Italy became the centre of the new humanist leading culture also because the writings of the ancients were more easily accessible here than elsewhere. In addition, the wealth of "manners books" reflects the self-dynamics of the expanding book market. If you wanted to be successful, you had to offer something new. If more and more treatises were written discussing the norms of conversation, their authors also wanted to exploit niche markets.

The comparatively few dialogues of the Middle Ages were almost exclusively concerned with religious questions.[61] Early examples of the rebirth of the genre in the Renaissance—they have been called a "dialogic culture epoch"[62]—offer Petrarch's "Secretum" and Bruni's "Dialogi ad Petrum Paulum Histrum".[63] Lukian, who influenced Alberti's "Momus" and his "Intercenales", also spiced up Antonio Galateo's "Hermita", a satirical church criticism that circulated only in secret.[64]

6   The art of speaking

Coluccio Salutati, one of the participants in Bruni's *Dialogi*, notes that conversations refresh the mind tired from book study, sharpen presence of mind, and allow one to test one's own eloquence. In this way, they could increase one's own fame; if one were to lose, this would arouse the ambition to do better next time.[65] He thereby highlights quite banal, profane benefits of conversations. Certainly there is talk of "truth"; the conviction that it could be won through conversation is shared by most early dialogues.[66] But ambition also appears as a positive affect, just as

---

[57] Peters 1981, p. 8.
[58] Fehl 1992, p. 37.
[59] Roeck 2020, pp. 223, 238, 287, 427, 1079 and passim.
[60] Häsner 2006; Roeck 2006; Fubini 2003; Marsh 1980.
[61] Cardelle de Hartmann 2007; Häsner 2002, pp. 118 ff.
[62] Guthmüller and Müller 2004, p. 7 (introduction).
[63] Quillen 2010, pp. 363–385.
[64] Häsner and Lozar 2006; Marsh 1980 p. 7.
[65] Häsner 2002, p. 121; Baker 2015, p. 94.
[66] Cox 1992, p. 62; Westermann 2006, pp. 38–39.

the acquisition of fame is an desirable goal. So not even some Stoics would have argued, and certainly no theologian. But Bruni's attitude towards scholastic *ars disputandi* is critical. Unlike Niccolò Niccoli, he pleads for the renewal of the dialogical principle in the sense of Cicero's rhetoric.[67]

The fifteenth century discussed the question of what makes a good conversation more intensely than the centuries before; one "talks about talking."[68] In the intellectual hothouse climate of humanistic Florence, for half of Europe was experiencing a "renaissance of eloquence," of which Bruni was considered the restorer.[69] Rhetorical rules could be found in etiquette books and even in theories of art, as in Alberti's treatise on painting.[70] Albertanus's treatise was occasionally referenced; some thirty prints of it are known from the fifteenth century. It also attracted attention beyond the Alps. The "Mirror of True Rhetoric" by the Freiburg writer and printer Friedrich Riederer, the first German-language rhetoric theory, shows Albertanus's influence.[71] The book published for the first time in 1493 was based on the then still attributed to Cicero "Rhetorica ad Herennium".[72] The most invoked ideal of *mesotes* is illustrated by a woodcut: It shows the fall of Icarus. The image is supposed to remind not to fly too high or too low, thus "in the middle … to act".[73] In addition to rules for oral communication, the book provides patterns for speeches in court and the drafting of letters and contracts. Riederer deals with his topic according to the questions formulated by Albertanus. Gentle speech promotes love and unity; thus the author turns against scolding, cursing, mockery and all speech that sows discord and endangers "Burgersche Vereynung". He admonishes the appropriateness of words and gestures and turns against the "foolishly rough people", who, instead of listening to the word of God in church, rather liked to "indulge in conversation with each other" at that time, "to spend it uselessly".[74] In pious pre-Reformation Germany—and in the bourgeois environment in which the author moved—it was beyond Riederer's horizon to approve of casual chatter.

Something closer to the topic of what makes for good conversation in the modern, narrower sense of the term is "Dello optimo cortesano" (On the Ideal Courtier) the author Diomede Carafa (1406-1487) was a statesman and military leader closely associated with the Neapolitan court.[75] Like Albertanus's treatise, his was originally intended as instruction for his own son. The text, printed in an

---

[67] Bruni was not an extreme classicist: Mori 2020, pp. 328, 337–338.

[68] Marsh 1980, pp. 27–28.

[69] Baker 2015, p. 51 and passim (Chap. 1); Plett 1993; Helmrath 2006.

[70] Bätschmann 2017; Kuhn 1984; Baxandall 1971; Spencer 1957; Horace: Gilbert 1943/45.

[71] Riederer 1493.

[72] Knape 2002; Riederer 2008, XII; Riederer 1493, aIII.

[73] Riederer 1493, LXI v.

[74] Riederer 1493, aIV.

[75] Carafa 1489; new edition: Carafa/Paparelli 1971. On Carafa: Petrucci 1976; Hinz 1992, p. 139 (lit.).

edition of 300 copies in the 1480s, then bears a dedication to Beatrice of Aragon. Carafa's little book provides guidance on how to please the prince through service and behavior. For him, the best *"cortesano"* is a passive executor of the prince's will. The final arbiter of what he should or should not advise the prince is his conscience and, with it, God—and not, as later for Castiglione's *"Cortegiano,"* its usefulness.[76] He has *"urbanitas,"* but should listen more than talk. After all, God has equipped humans with two ears and only one mouth. Once something has been said, it has been said and cannot be taken back: "The words are now your masters." Certainly empty talk about *"cose uane"* is not allowed.[77] Making jokes is the province of *"boffoni"* and not of wise, cautious people, *"homini descreti."* Carafa does allow his readers to occasionally say something pleasant, *"qualche cosa piacevole,"* but always little and, if so, honorable.

Like Carafa, Valla and Beccadelli, Giovanni Pontano (1429–1502) earned his money at the court of Alfonso of Naples. In his treatise *"De sermone"*, written down in the first years of the 16th century, he distinguishes with Cicero *sermo, "speech"* or *"discussion"*, from *sermocinatio, "conversation"*.[78] His *homo facetus* is a forerunner of the *Cortegiano*.[79] He has wit and pleasant manners, which Pontano describes as *facetudo*—one of many of his neologisms. Furthermore, the advantages of the *homo facetus* correspond to Aristotelian standards.[80] As Beccadelli's successor, Pontano led the academy named after him in Naples, the first modern institution of this kind. In it, the *homo facetus* could unfold his charm. However, opposites should not be obscured by compliments or hidden under silence. Pontano knows that a conversation operating with clever words and spiced with jokes entertains and relaxes—Cicero speaks of *relaxatio animi*: "We philosophize, but we enjoy ourselves at the same time."[81] Pontano wrote his own cheerful, sometimes playing burlesque comedies in the style of Lucian.[82]

Since time immemorial and to this day, conversations, including their civilized variant "conversation", have been means against melancholy.[83] They make the hardships of everyday life forget. Roger Ascham addresses this function at the beginning of his *"Schoolmaster": "The Lord Secretary [Sir William Cecil] had*

---

[76] Cox 1992, pp. 52–53.

[77] Carafa 1489, fol. a3r; c4r/v, c5r/v.

[78] So Nauta's translation (Nauta 2011, p. 485). However, *sermocinatio* could also mean the rhetorical figure. In Stieler 1691, p. 2103, there is an example of application that anticipates the meaning of the later established loanword *"conversation":"conversatio"* appears here, inter alia, as a *"very pleasant, familiar conversation"*, a *"sermocinatio suavissima, familiaris"*. Similar French definitions: Strosetzki 2013, pp. 51–55; *"entretien familier"*: Ibid., pp. 60–63.

[79] Pigman III 2001; For the following Bistagne 2008 (introduction); Dicke 2008.

[80] For example, he is always honest and also observes the middle in conversation: *"Et in sermone servandam esse mediocritatem."* Pontano 1509, lib. I, aIII.

[81] Bistagne 2008, p. 277.

[82] Marsh 1980 p. 100 ff.

[83] So Stefano Guazzo: Montandon 1995 p. 128.

the habit, although his head had been full of the most important affairs of the kingdom, that he nevertheless seemed to lay them aside at dinnertime and always found the appropriate opportunity to talk pleasantly about other things. "[84] One of the most famous scenes of the Renaissance illustrates the same function. It shows Machiavelli in intimate conversation with absentees, with statesmen and philosophers of antiquity.[85] "They answer me affably. For four hours I don't feel bored, forget all my troubles, don't fear poverty, and death doesn't scare me: I completely identify with them." Reading and imaginary dialogues here appear as practices of leisure, of *loisir*, which Montaigne will determine as a period of reflection, imagination and their taming by writing.[86] The dialogues with oneself or with great spirits of antiquity, of which Machiavelli and later Montaigne write, appear as secularizations of the soul conversations that seek God as a dialogue partner.[87]

7 The *"Cortegiano"* and the license to smile

The flood of treatises in dialog form had grown into the unmanageable with the escalation of the discourse revolution in the Cinquecento. It is estimated to include several thousand titles. The description of an ideal conversation offers Thomas More in the second book of *his "Utopia": "prohibited."* Both dinner and supper are begun with some lecture of morality that is read to them; but it is so short that it is not tedious nor uneasy to them to hear it. From hence the old men take occasion to entertain those about them with some useful and pleasant enlargements; but they do not engross the whole discourse so to themselves during their meals that the younger may not put in for a share; on the contrary, they engage them to talk, that so they may, in that free way of conversation, find out the force of every one's spirit and observe his temper… They never sup without music, and there is always fruit served up after meat; while they are at table some burn perfumes and sprinkle about fragrant ointments and sweet waters—in short, they want nothing that may cheer up their spirits; they give themselves a large allowance that way, and indulge themselves in all such pleasures as are attended with no inconvenience." The *convivium* of the Utopians resembles, down to the *"bellaria"*, which are served after the main course, the model banquet, which is described by Aulus Gellius (and his source Varro).[88]

Morus had read Plato's "State" as well as the "Attic Nights" exactly. The relaxed Laughter, at least smiling, gradually became acceptable. Valla had pointed

---

[84] "*M. Secretarie hath this accustomed maner, though his head be neuer so full of most weightie affaires of the Realme, yet, at diner time he doth seeme to lay them alwaies aside: and findeth euer fitte occasion to taulke pleasantlie of other matters …*": Roger Ascham, The Scholemaster (…), Ascham 1570, Preface.

[85] Roeck 2020, pp. 647–648.

[86] Klinkert 2016, pp. 73–78.

[87] Wild 2014, pp. 19–36.

[88] To More's knowledge of Aulus Gellius: Schoeck 1960, S. 127–129; Baumann 1983.

out that it counted among the gifts that God had given to man alone—but still noted that *risus* was less valuable than speech and *vinum*.[89] Smiling people are rarely encountered in Renaissance artworks. The anonymous one on a portrait of Antonello da Messina in the Museo Mandralisca in Cefalù is popular mainly because he smirks. And the "Mona Lisa" became the most famous portrait in art history not least because of her smile.

Castiglione's ideal "Cortegiano" has a sense of humor and gives witty responses. He speaks about this and that, always circumspect and reserved, with "good and appropriate arguments"; he knows how to "with a certain affability refresh the spirit of the listeners, and with pleasing expressions and jokes to make them sensitive to cheerfulness and laughter, and that without becoming annoying or causing boredom, he is constantly pleased."[90] He will not condescend to clowning, "descendere alla buffoneria", just as Pontano's vir facetus and later the honnête homme.[91] Like his ancient and medieval counterparts, he controls passion, avoids self-praise. In everything he observes Cicero's decorum and maintains the middle.[92] As Boccaccio did before him, the "Cortegiano" grants women equal positions. Castiglione describes the conversation style of the perfect "Cortegiano" and his entire behavior with the neologism sprezzatura.[93] The term, of course, refers to a mixture of noble nonchalance, ease and friendliness that should also determine everyday conversation, conversare cottidiano. As well as one can, one should avoid affectation "like a rough and dangerous reef."[94] So a man of sprezzatura dissimulates and represents in one.[95]

None of the earlier writings devotes as much attention to the rules of conversation as Castiglione does. He constitutes them as an *art*. A good conversation appears to him as a structure whose beauty can be measured according to the same criteria as a good speech or a painting by Titian. Agostino Nifo will bring this view to a head a few decades later when he characterizes the "graceful courtier" as someone who, in conversations, gestures and business dealings, *beauty*.[96] Much later, in 1677, such a comparison also seemed obvious to a French author,

---

[89] Panizza Lorch 1985, S. 89–93; 58 f.

[90] Cortegiano, Libro I, XLI.

[91] Cortegiano, Libro II, L; Strosetzki 2013, S. 82–89.

[92] The same applies to the ideal speaker, as Vives conceives him: Havu 2015, S. 294–297.

[93] Cortegiano, Libro I, cap. XXVI. Quondam, Introduzione, in: Castiglione/Quondam 1981, S. XI; for the genealogy of the term: Waters 2019.

[94] Similarly, the French theory of the late 17th century: Strosetzki 2013, S. 100; Gabriel Harvey found the formulation "ars casus videatur" for one aspect of sprezzatura (Burke 1995, S. 89).

[95] Quondam 1981, p. XIII; Paulicelli 2014, p. 65; for further development: van Delft and Lotterie 1993. Castiglione also draws on Cicero's "De oratore": Hinz 1996, p. 1488; Häsner 2002, p. 137 (lit.); Marsh 1980, chap. 1.

[96] Nifo 1645, p. 302: "*Hinc patet quis gratiosus aulicus sit: est enim qui in sermonibus et gestibus et rebus pulchritudine utitur.*"

Chevalier de Méré.[97] In turn, terms that could characterize the ideal courtier, such as *grazia* and later the *je ne sais quoi,* were used to assess works of art.[98]

Rabelais emphasizes in the prologue to *"Gargantua et Pantagruel"* that fun and seriousness need not exclude each other. As an example, he takes the Platonic dialogue, obviously with the intention of justifying his own "pantagruelic" opus. Drawing on Erasmus' *"Adagia,"* the learned doctor compares the "Silen" Socrates (as Alkibiades is said to have called him) to a painted box, a *silène,* as found in the *bouticques des apotecaires.* Like these boxes painted with cheerful motifs, the cheerful, ugly, poor philosopher has kept a "priceless, heavenly drug": outstanding intelligence, wonderful mental strength, sobriety, composure and freedom from everything that drives people.[99]

Friedrich Dedekind, Rabelais' distant German relative, uses burlesque humor as a didactic tool. The heroes of his "Grobianus"—which owes many suggestions to Brant's "Ship of Fools"—do not smile, they "split their bellies" with laughter; they crack jokes, make crude jokes, drink, scream "like the burglars" and talk nonsense in their drunkenness with "mumble / murmur / and snore."[100] The recommendations reverse the rules of table manners literature. "You should not be ashamed of any crude jest: For where people now come together / With wine / to people / and in taverns / You don't hear anything serious being said / But whoever is serious and crude / And does a lot of it / deserves great praise."[101]

8 The Conversation as Comedy

"Grobianus" parodies the common virtue teachings. In the preface, Plato, Cicero, Erasmus—Dedekind has in mind his "De civilitate morum puerilium"—and the "Disticha Catonis" are mentioned. Dedekind praises monstrous behavior to entertain and educate his audience. The motto of the title page makes this clear: "Read this little book often and much / And always do the opposite." This mocks the style cultivated in Castiglione's circle of conversation and also suggested by Brant's "Ship of Fools".[102] If someone wants to talk to "Grobianus", he should interrupt him with "Scream" and thus destroy the speech.[103] The "Grobianers" also lie that the beams bend: "Just lie so that your mouth doesn't stand / And always go like a windmill. Either talk and snore too / And don't delay eating."[104]

---

[97] Strosetzki 2013, p. 50.

[98] Toutain- Quittelier and Rauseo 2021, Vigliarolo 2021, pp. 86–87; Scholar 2005.

[99] Raible 1966; Deupmann 2002, pp. 105–106.

[100] Dedekind 1551, fol. 54, 73.

[101] Dedekind 1551, fol. 55 (emphasis B.R.); Arinobu 2021, pp. 132–138.

[102] Brant 1495, fol. 110a: "On table manners".

[103] Dedekind 1551, fol. 127.

[104] Dedekind 1551, fol. 100.

This corresponds to the recommendation for the "Grobiana"—the female edition of "Grobianus", which Dedekind supplemented with his work in 1567—to talk for hours "about loose things".[105]

In a very different way, Stefano Guazzo, a lawyer and statesman in the service of Gonzaga, teaches "La civil conversazione" in good speech and proper behavior.[106] Guazzo sets the usual rules. He advises *accommodazione,* which probably means adaptation to customs and engagement with the respective other.[107] He also turns against the "tyranny" of those who only wanted to talk and not listen; that is, as if one monopolized wine at a meal. His plea for the middle includes gestures: They move between the immobility of statues and the gesticulation of monkeys, *instabilità dell simie.*[108]

In the center is also for Guazzo the importance of "civil conversation" (in the old, broad sense of the term) as a factor of socialization. In addition, he emphasizes the community-forming and emotional functions of language with Aristotle.[109] The fourth book tells of conversations in the circle around Vespasiano Gonzaga, which have all the ingredients of a successful conversation: jokes, witty proverbs, irony.

Not only the conversational style, which Guazzo, Dedekind and their colleagues advocated, should be entertaining, but also the dialogues and treatises on everything and everyone that they put on paper. Sperone Speroni (1500–1588) confronted strict philosophical reasoning with the game of pros and cons of staged conversations in his *"Apologia dei dialoghi".* The latter should be given the preference: "In short, the dialogue is a pleasant garden, and the topics and people introduced into it are its healing herbs—not all of them are beautiful in the same way, nor all good, nor healthy; and to see them all gathered in this place, if they are rare, is an entertaining wonder; if they are known to the people in general, the fact that they are arranged with gentle art—in addition to the fact that this is already a beautiful praise—makes the observer hope that the one who arranged them in this way can also distinguish, according to his judgment, the high, greater things and nobler intentions with the same order."[110] The dialogue that Speroni describes so poetically is not a classical

---

[105] Dedekind 1586, fol. 4v.

[106] Guazzo 1574/Brescia 1574; Quondam 1993.

[107] Patrizi 2003; Miller 2001; Cox 1992, p. 41.

[108] Burke 1992, p. 77; Roodenburg 2004, p. 27; Strosetzki 2013, pp. 137–142.

[109] The same applies to other authors, such as Pontano (Nauta, 2011, pp. 486–490) or Vives (Havu 2015, pp. 1–3).

[110] dal Bello 2018, S. S. 178: *"Brevemente il dialogo è un giardino dilettevole e le materie con le persone che sono in esso introdotte sono i suoi simplici, non tutti belli ad un modo né tutti buoni né salutiferi; e tutti questi se rari sono, vedergli accolti in quel luogo è dilettevole maraviglia e, noti essendo communemente alle genti, il ben disporli con gentile arte, oltre che in fatto è una bella laude, fa ancor sperar chi ciò mira che chi così li ordinò collo istesso ordine possa distinguere a suo arbitrio le cose alte e maggiori e di più nobili intendimenti".* The garden metaphor can already be found in Plato: Plat. Phaidr. 276b, 276d.

work of art. There is something entertaining about it—each dialogue has not a little of a comedy, he once wrote[111]—and also ugly things. In the end it offers no victorious opinion, but a panorama of points of view.[112] Doubt is given room. The "path of the dialogue" leads to a pleasant labyrinth, according to Speroni. It allows participation in the search for truth, does not strive for it with rigidity. The dialogue is more elegant and enjoyable, *più civile e più dilettevole,* than arguing with syllogisms.

The rehabilitation of *voluptas,* which Thomas Aquinas had initiated and Valla, Alberti, and others had carried out, now made it possible to justify conversation as a pleasure. Compared to the joy of conversation among "noble minds," Nifo observed, the pleasures of festivals, tournaments, comedies, and the like were nothing.[113] He stated bluntly: *"Conversari cum similibus, voluptatis est causa."*[114] In connection with his presentation of the *vir aulicus,* a successor to the *"Cortegiano,"* he provided a sort of theory of laughter that distinguished, for example, natural from simulated *risus.*[115] What was called "Verhöflichung des Lachens", "laughter becoming courtly"[116] could be demonstrated as early as the seventeenth century in the paintings of Jan Steen, whose tavern scenes would serve as illustrations for the "Grobianus." The master of coarse revelry is shown in his "Self-Portrait with Lute," painted around 1663/1664, with a broad, cheerful laugh; a few years later he presents himself—now a quite fashionable gentleman—with a light smile.[117]

9 Market conditions, "real" conversations, and the limits of freedom of opinion

"Every day one writes many books / great volumes, and countless large and small treatises", so "the making of books has no end", Aegidius Albertinus noted in 1600 in the dedication of his "Court School", the translation of two works by Fray Antonio Guevara, to Duke Ferdinand of Bavaria.[118] This is done, among other things, out of a desire for fame and "for the sake of acquiring human favor and temporal enjoyments". With this he speaks very earthly conditions of Renaissance literary production—in particular of those writings that conveyed norms of behavior "at court". Its usefulness was obvious: A lifestyle appropriate to the courtly

---

[111] Häsner 2002, S. 115.

[112] dal Bello, S. 192.

[113] Cox 1992, p. 22.

[114] Nifo 1645, p. 258.

[115] Nifo 1645, pp. 289–298.

[116] Schörle 2007.

[117] Roodenburg 2004, pp. 139–140 (figs. 48, 49).

[118] de Guevara and Albertinus 1600 (*Menosprecio de corte y alabança de aldea/Aviso de privados y doctrina de cortesanos,* Valladolid 1539), Preface.

world was symbolic capital that could be converted into real capital.[119] Carafa quotes the proverb *"Cortesia vale assai e costa poco"*.[120]

A famous example is Leonardo da Vinci. He was by no means perceived by his contemporaries as an introverted eccentric, but rather as an elegant courtier with *sprezzatura*.[121] His facetiae, rebuses and essays show him as a witty entertainer at the courts of Milan and Amboise. His exquisite wardrobe and his perfumes—rose water, lavender—suggest that he sometimes appeared like a dandy. Unlike in the case of the French nobility of the later 17th century, the theory of conversation in Renaissance Italy probably reminds us less of the need to camouflage power loss.[122] Rather, Italy's elites were eager to acquire accessories of a lifestyle that would make their rank—and their real power—visible and suitable for outbidding status rivals. The same purposes were served by castles, works of art and festivals.

The mass of authors and, since about 1600, increasingly also women among them[123], must have desperately sought new topics in order to survive in the book market. The discourse revolution unfolded its own dynamics. One copied from each other, compiled from a some books an new one.[124] Some topics were discussed with tiresome tenacity, for example the *paragone* of the arts, the *questione della lingua* and also works that were instructed in good manners and the rules of conversation. The fortunes of the *"Cortegiano"* illustrate these connections. Ruth Kelso counted over 2000 writings that take up its theme and variantly discuss it.[125] The Hofmann found his way into the cities, and patterns of behavior that he demonstrated influenced the bourgeois habitus—a classic case of vertical culture transfer.[126] Guazzo's *"Civil conversazione"* was also a European success. Up to the middle of the 17th century, 43 Italian editions followed the two first editions printed in Venice and Brescia in 1574, as well as translations into German, Latin, English and French.[127] Guazzo's most famous reader was Montaigne.

It is naturally difficult to answer how the flood of Renaissance dialogues, etiquette books and theoretical discussions of the art of conversation relate to real speech.[128] Hardly any light is cast on conversation situations. Poggio Bracciolini does give us such an insight in the afterword to his *"Facezie"* (1438/51).[129] Most of the stories were told in the *bugiale*, "a kind of lying workshop" set up by the

---

[119] Cox 1992, pp. 34 ff.; On the terminology: Bourdieu 1983.

[120] Hinz 1992, p. 141.

[121] Roeck 2019, pp. 148 ff.

[122] Cox 1992, pp. 24 ff.

[123] Hacke 2001, p. 17; Werner.

[124] Doubt 2022 (announced); on Villalón's editing of the "Cortegiano": Cox 1992, p. 130, n. 9.

[125] Burke 1995, p. 82.

[126] Roeck 2007, pp. 26–28; Strosetzki 2013, pp. 42, 311; Tarde 1890/2009.

[127] Hübner 2012, pp. 192–199.

[128] Cox 1992, pp. 13–17; Häsner 2002, pp. 125 f., 148 f.

[129] Maglio 1998, pp. 43–46.

secretaries of the Curia "for laughter." He nostalgically recalls the "good custom of jokes and conversation," *"il buon uso dello scherzo e del conversare"* of past times. It is also reported of the circle around Marsilio Ficino in his *academiola* in Careggi that Fazetien were told and lively sociability was cultivated.[130]

The usually fictional Renaissance conversations are mostly artfully stylized and have an *locus amoenus* as a stage.[131] Did the dying Lorenzo de' Medici really still have the strength to hold *sermones urbanos* from his bed?[132] Almost nothing is handed down about conversations on the market square or in the tavern. Sometimes court records act as witnesses. They report, for example, on the interrogation of two weavers who had been summoned to the city hall in Augsburg in July 1589.[133] A conversation about confessional questions and the entrustment of power to the Augsburg guilds by Charles V after the Schmalkaldic War had degenerated into a quarrel and brawl. It had started as a peaceful conversation: "We have talked about all sorts of things," one of the offenders testified. It would be nice to know what about...

The case reminds us that no authority tolerated being made fun of, if a dialogue—whether it had actually taken place or was literary fiction—touched upon religion, power, or both. Conversely, the genre could become a weapon in political disputes. An early example is Alamanno Rinuccini's dialogue *"De libertate"*[134] which was directed against the Medici. The Reformation was also accompanied from the beginning by dialogues. They were among the catalysts of the "generalized convictions" that made Luther's revolt a mass movement.[135]

In the confessional age, there were no shortage of attempts to control the unleashed speech and writing brought about by the Discourse Revolution. Even some of the writings quoted in this article were banned. In 1559, the Inquisition banned *"The Decameron,"* Valla's *"De voluptate,"* more of his writings, and all of Erasmus' and Lucian's works. Castiglione's *"Cortegiano"* was not spared from censorship; a "purified" version appeared in 1584. Christóbal de Villalón's *"El scholástico,"* a Spanish adaptation, could not be published during the author's lifetime due to Erasmian positions and sympathies for pagan thinkers such as Plato and Seneca.[136] Even the defense of equality for women aroused suspicion.[137] In many dialogues of

---

[130] Poncet 2013; Batkin 1979, pp. 193 f.

[131] Andersen and Toftgaard 2012.

[132] Batkin 1979, p. 187.

[133] Roeck 1989, pp. 129, 177.

[134] Müller 2004.

[135] Becker 2013; Kampe 1997; Baumann et al. 2015, here Introduction, p. 7 ff.—"Generalized convictions": Smelser 1963.

[136] Burke 1995, pp. 102–106, 85; Platonic and Lucianic models appeared less "honorable" than Cicero's dialogic style: Cox 1992, p. 32. See also Speroni: Hempfer in Hempfer 2002, p. 28.

[137] Cox 1992, p. 81.

the later Cinquecento, rhetoric lost importance to dialectic.[138] Order, not *vaghezza*, and truth, not pleasure should be provided. In Guarini's *"Segretario,"* there was not even anything decent to eat during the conversations.[139]

But the great conversation was only interrupted. The experience of religious strife and religious wars was probably the prerequisite for the second, "great" Enlightenment that followed the first Enlightenment. It picked up patterns of thought from the Renaissance and perfected the art of conversation. For Montesquieu, Kant and others, conversation appeared as a specifically French enterprise.[140] They owed much to the Italians and, with them, to the ancient forerunners.[141] Here the word was freer than in the Counter-Reformation south. And there was no court in Europe where it would have been more lucrative to master the rules of courtesy than at Versailles—and thus no city whose fascinating court performance encouraged its citizens to imitate it, as in Paris.

10 The value of conversation

Whether Gutenberg's invention would have found markets without the discourse revolution is open to question. No other world culture experienced a comparable revolution of speaking, writing and communicating before modern times, in which not only a few intellectuals took part. Guazzo notes that the works went through the hands of a hundred thousand readers and made their authors famous and immortal in the world.[142] Even in China and Korea, where printing with movable types (albeit not the screw press) was available much earlier than in Europe, the media revolution did not take place.[143] In addition to capital-strong middle classes—whose older members had glasses and could therefore read for longer—and thus markets for books, there was a lack of political freedoms here. In Islamic states, the dictate of religion already set tight limits on all communication.

The great conversation of the Renaissance had a world-historical impact due to the principle learned from antiquity of gaining knowledge through questions, further questions, and consideration of pros and cons—Cicero's *"disputare in utramque partem"*.[144] In the discussion, as Cicero had argued and thus given the dialog of the humanists a guiding principle, "we must not seek the weight of

---

[138] Cox 1992, p. 89, the following p. 101; Valla's opposite position: Marsh 1980, p. 75.

[139] Cox 1992, p. 111 (Guarini 1594, p. 52).

[140] Strosetzki 2013, p. 47; Montandon 1995, p. 145.

[141] Fumaroli 1996; Montandon 1995. One example is the ideal of *médiocrité*, the French version of Aristotle's μεσότης or the Stoic *mediocritas*, which was recommended by Riederer as well as by Castiglione and Guazzo. See morel 1969; Strosetzki 2013, pp. 265–270.

[142] Cox 1992, p. 40.

[143] Cf. Roeck 2020, 1069 f., 1119 f.

[144] Plat. Phaidr. 276e–277a.; Ax 1995.

authority so much as that of reason."[145] Without a discourse revolution, printing press and, as a result, the dissemination of the principles of dialog according to ancient patterns, the scientific and technological upheavals of the modern era would most likely not have taken place. The example of all examples is Galileo's "Dialogue Concerning the Two Chief World Systems", which probably contributed more to the acceptance of the Copernican world model than any other text.[146] Not respect for the old, but criticism of it and the overcoming of established paradigms, founded the Western version of modernity. Guazzo was right when he stated: "It seems to me quite obvious that knowledge begins with conversation and ends with conversation."[147] Only through conversation can the scholar put his knowledge to the test, just as the blacksmith tests the strength of the armor by firing a musket or thrusting a spear.

The dialogues of the Renaissance are an expression of a globally unique intellectual culture that favored the open exchange of ideas and arguments. A message that went out from the discourses in the academies, villas and gardens of Italy was once formulated by Cicero: Some, no matter how powerful, could appear in conversation like "one of many".[148] Conversation circles of the "first Enlightenment" constituted protected spaces in which conscience could be articulated and, in principle, freedom prevailed to talk about anything—$\pi\alpha\rho\rho\eta\sigma\acute{\iota}\alpha$ in the positive sense of the term. They therefore belong to the prehistory of the bourgeois world: its pathogenesis, but also its achievements.[149]

References

Alberti, Leon Battista: Della Pittura- Über die Malkunst. Oskar Bätschmann und Sandra Gianfredda (Hg.). Darmstadt: Wissenschaftliche Buchgesellschaft 2007, 2. Aufl.
Allen, Don Cameron: The Rehabilitation of Epicurus and His Theory of Pleasure in the Early Renaissance, in: Studies in Philology 41,1, 1944, S. 1–15.
Andersen, Michael Høxbro und Toftgaard, Anders: Dialogo & conversazione. I luoghi di una socialità ideale dal Rinascimento all'Illuminismo. Florenz: Olschki 2012.
Andersen- Wyman, Kathleen: Andreas Capellanus on Love? Desire, Seduction, and Subversion in a Twelfth- Century Latin Text. New York: Palgrave Macmillan 2007.
Arinobu, Mamina: Ordnung des Tisches bei Hofe. Die Rolle und die Funktion der Tischzuchtliteratur und die Gast- und Festmähler in der Hofgesellschaft im Hoch und Spätmittelalter. Baden- Baden: Tectum 2021.
Ascham, Roger: The Scholemaster (…). London: John Daye1570.

---

[145] Cic. nat. I,10; Marsh 1980, S. 33 ff.

[146] Kalverkämper 1996, S. 683–745.

[147] Guazzo 1574, I, 30: "…*mi pare assai manifesto che'l sapere comincia dal conversare e finisce nel conversare*"; Montandon 1995 S. 128.

[148] Cic. off. I, 109.

[149] Koselleck 2010; Roeck 2020, pp. 1172 ff.; Parrhesia: Foucault 2011.

Aschenberg, Heidi: Sprachdialoge der Renaissance – pragmatisch gesehen, in: Angela Schrott und Harald Völker (Hg.): Historische Pragmatik und historische Varietätenlinguistik in den romanischen Sprachen. Göttingen: Universitätsverlag Göttinge 2005, S. 279–289.

Ax, Wolfram: Disputare in utramque partem: Zum literarischen Plan und zur dialektischen Methode Varros in de lingua Latina 8–10, in: Rheinisches Museum für Philologie 138,2, 1995, S. 146–177.

Baker, Patrick: Italian Renaissance Humanism in the Mirror. Cambridge u. a.: Cambridge UP 2015.

Batkin: Leonid M., Die italienische Renaissance. Versuch einer Charakterisierung eines Kulturtyps. Übers. Irene Faix. Basel, Frankfurt a. M.: Stroemfeld/Roter Stern 1979.

Bätschmann, Oskar: Leon Battista Alberti (1404–1472): De pictura, in: Wolfgang Brassat (Hg.): Handbuch Rhetorik der Bildenden Künste. Berlin, Boston: De Gruyter 2017, S. 253–268.

Baumann, Uwe: Herodotus, Aulus Gellius and Thomas More's Utopia, in: Moreana 20, 1983, Heft 77, S. 5–10.

Baumann, Uwe u. a. (Hg.): Polemik im Dialog des Renaissance-Humanismus. Formen, Entwicklungen und Funktionen. Göttingen: V & R Unipress 2015.

Baxandall, Michael: Giotto and the Orators. Humanist Observers of Painting in Italy and the Discovery of Pictorial Composition 1350 – 1450. Oxford: Oxford UP 1971.

Becker, Ulrich: Ulrich von Huttens polemische Dialoge im Spannungsfeld von Humanismus und Politik. Göttingen: V & R Unipress 2013.

Bistagne, Florence (Hg.): Giovanni Gioviano Pontano, *De Sermone. De la Conversation*. Paris: Champion 2008.

Boccaccio, Giovanni: The Modell of Wit, Mirth, Eloquence, and Conversation. London: Isaac Jaggard for Mathew Lownes 1625–1620; ND Basil Blackwell: Oxford 1935.

Bosley, Richard u. a. (Hg.): Aristotle, Virtue and the Mean. Edmonton: Academic Print. & Pub. 1995.

Bourdieu, Pierre: Ökonomisches Kapital, kulturelles Kapital, soziales Kapital, in: Reinhard Kreckel (Hg.): Soziale Ungleichheiten. Göttingen: Schwartz 1983, S. 183–198.

Brant, Sebastian: Das Narrenschiff. Basel: Bergmann von Olpe 1495, 2. Aufl.

Brinkmann, Brigitte: Varietas und Veritas: Normen und Normativität in der Zeit der Renaissance. Castigliones ‚Libro del Cortegiano'. München: Fink 2001.

Bubert, Marcel: Kreative Gegensätze: Der Streit um den Nutzen der Philosophie an der mittelalterlichen Universität. Leiden, Boston: Brill 2019.

Burke, Peter: Culture and Society in Renaissance Italy, 1420–1540. London: Batsford 1972.

Burke, Peter: The Fortunes of the Courtier. European Reception of Castigliones ‚Cortegiano'. Cambridge: Polity Press 1995.

Burke, Peter: The Language of Gesture in Early Modern Italy, in: Jan Bremmer und Herman Roodenburg (Hg.): A Cultural History of Gesture. Ithaca: Cornell UP 1992, S. 71–83.

Carafa, Diomede: Dello optimo cortesano, Gioacchino Paparelli (Hg.). Salerno: Beta 1971.

Cardelle de Hartmann, Carmen: Lateinische Dialoge 1200–1400. Literarhistorische Studie und Repertorium. Leiden, Boston: Brill 2007.

Castiglione, Baldassar: Il Libro del Cortegiano, Amedeo Quondam (Hg.). Milano: Garzanti 1981.

Classen, Albrecht: Epistemology at the Courts: The Discussion of Love by Andreas Capellanus and Juan Ruiz, in: Neuphilologische Mitteilungen 103,3, 2002, S. 341–362.

Cox, Virginia: The Renaissance Dialogue. Literary Dialogue in its Social and Political Context, Castiglione to Galileo. Cambridge u.a.: Cambridge UP 1992.

dal Bello, Alessandra: ‚A guisa di Aceste commetto i colpi alle nuvole': I dialoghi di Sperone Speroni. Diss. Padova 2018.

de Guevara, Antonio: Institutiones vitae aulicae, Oder Hof- Schul, übers. v. Aegidius Albertinus. München: Nikolaus Heinrich 1600.

de Panizza Lorch, Maristella: A Defense of Life. Lorenzo Valla's Theory of Pleasure. München: Fink 1985.

de Panizza Lorch, Maristella (Hg.): Lorenzo Valla, De vero falsoque bono. Bari: Adriatica éditrice 1970.
Dedekind, Friedrich: Grobianus und Grobiana. Mühlberg: Wendelin Hellbach 1586.
Dedekind, Friedrich: Grobianus/von groben Sitten/und unhöflichen geberden (...), übers. v. Caspar Scheidt. Worms: Hermann Gülfferich 1551.
della Casa, Giovanni: Trattato ... nel quale sotto la persona d'un vecchio idiota ammaestrante un suo giovinetto, si ragiona dei modi che si debbono o tenere o schifare nella comune conversazione, cognominato Galatheo. Milano: Giovanni Antonio de' Antoni 1559.
Deupmann, Christoph: ‚Furor satricus'. Verhandlungen über literarische Aggression im 17. und 18. Jahrhundert. Tübingen: Niemeyer 2002.
Dicke, Gerd: Homo facetus. Vom Mittelalter eines humanistischen Ideals, in: Nicola McLelland u. a. (Hg.): Humanismus in der deutschen Literatur des Mittelalters und der Frühen Neuzeit. XVIII. Anglo- German Colloquium Hofgeismar 2003. Tübingen: Niemeyer 2008, S. 299–332.
Emmelius, Caroline: Gesellige Ordnung. Grundlegende Konzeptionen von geselliger Kommunikation in Mittelalter und Früher Neuzeit. Berlin, New York: De Gruyter 2010
Fehl, Philip: Saints, Donors, and Columns in Titian's ‚Pesaro Madonna', in: Philip Fehl: Decorum and Wit. The Poetry of Venetian Painting. Wien: IRSA 1992, S. 30–43 (zuerst in: Renaissance Papers, Chapel Hill 1974, S. 75–85).
Fois, Mario S. J.: Il pensiero cristiano di Lorenzo Valla nel quadro storicoculturale del suo ambiente. Rom: Libreria editrice dell'Università Gregoriana 1969.
Fortenbaugh, W. W.: Die Charaktere Theophrasts: Verhaltensregelmäßigkeiten und aristotelische Laster, in: Rheinisches Museum für Philologie NF 118, 1/2, 1975, S. 62–82.
Foucault, Michel: The Courage of Truth: Lectures at the Collége de France II, 1983–1984. Hg. v. Frédéric Gros, übers. v. Graham Burchell. Palgrave: Basingstoke 2011.
Franca Petrucci: ‚Carafa, Diomede', in: DBI 19, 1976, S. 524–530.
Friedlein, Roger: Geleit auf dem Weg zur Wahrheit. Dialoge im Duecento, in: Hempfer, Klaus W. (Hg.): Möglichkeiten des Dialogs: Struktur und Funktion einer literarischen Gattung zwischen Mittelalter und Renaissance in Italien. Stuttgart: Steiner 2002, S. 39–73.
Fubini, Riccardo: Humanism and Secularization. From Petrarch to Valla, London. Durham: Duke UP 2003.
Fumaroli, Marc: ‚La conversation', in: Pierre Nora (Hg.): Les Lieux de mémoire, Bd. 3,2. Paris: Gallimard 1996, S. 679–743.
Gilbert, Creighton E.: Antique Frameworks for Renaissance Art Theory: Alberti and Pino, in: Marsyas 3, 1943/45, 87–106.
Godo, Emmanuel: Une histoire de la conversation. Paris: Classiques Garnier 2003.
Greenblatt, Stephen: The Sverve. How the Renaissance Began. London: Bodley Head 2011.
Guarini, Giambattista: Il Segretario. Venedig: Roberto Meietti 1594.
Guazzo, Stefano: La civil conversazione. Venedig: Andrea de Alarise 1574.
Guthmüller, Bodo und Müller, Wolfgang G.: Dialog und Gesprächskultur in der Renaissance. Wiesbaden: Harrassowitz 2004.
Hacke, Daniela (Hg. u. Übers.); Moderata Fonte. Das Verdienst der Frauen. Warum Frauen würdiger und vollkommener sind als Männer. München: C.H. Beck 2001.
Häsner, Bernd und Lozar, Angelika: Providenz oder Kontingenz? Antonio Galateos Eremita und die ‚Lukianisierung' des religiösen Diskurses, in: Hempfer, Klaus W. (Hg.): Grenzen und Entgrenzungen des Renaissancedialogs. Stuttgart: Steiner 2006, S. 13–58.
Häsner, Bernd: Dialog und Essay. Zwei ‚Weisen der Welterzeugung' an der Schwelle der Neuzeit, in: Hempfer 2006, S. 141–203.
Häsner, Bernd: Leonardo Brunis Dialogus ad Petrum Paulum Histrum: Darstellung und Selbstkonstruktion einer humanistischen Kommunikationskultur, in: Hempfer, Klaus W. (Hg.): Möglichkeiten des Dialogs: Struktur und Funktion einer literarischen Gattung zwischen Mittelalter und Renaissance in Italien. Stuttgart: Steiner 2002, S. 115–161.

Havu, Kaarlo Johannes: Between Concord and Discord. Juan Luis Vives (1492/1493–1540) on Language, Rhetoric, and Politics. Diss. Florenz 2015.
Helmrath, Johannes: Der europäische Humanismus und die Funktionen der Rhetorik, in: Thomas Maissen und Gerrit Walther (Hg.): Funktionen des Humanismus. Studien zum Nutzen des Neuen in der humanistischen Kultur. Göttingen: Wallstein 2006, S. 18–48.
Hempfer, Klaus W. (Hg.): Grenzen und Entgrenzungen des Renaissancedialogs. Stuttgart: Steiner 2006.
Hempfer, Klaus W. (Hg.): Möglichkeiten des Dialogs: Struktur und Funktion einer literarischen Gattung zwischen Mittelalter und Renaissance in Italien. Stuttgart: Steiner 2002.
Hempfer, Klaus W.: Lektüren von Dialogen, in: Hempfer, Klaus W. (Hg.): Möglichkeiten des Dialogs: Struktur und Funktion einer literarischen Gattung zwischen Mittelalter und Renaissance in Italien. Stuttgart: Steiner 2002, S. 1–38.
Hinz, Manfred: Rhetorische Strategien des Hofmannes. Studien zu den italienischen Hofmannstraktaten des 16. und 17. Jahrhunderts. Stuttgart: J.B. Metzler 1992.
Horn, Christoph und Rapp, Christof (Hg.): Wörterbuch der antiken Philosophie. München: C.H. Beck 2008.
Hübner, Helga: Stefano Guazzo La civil conversazione in der französischen Kultur des 16. und 17. Jahrhunderts. Frankfurt a. M. u. a.: Lang 2012.
Kalverkämper, Hartwig: Die Kultur des literarischen wissenschaftlichen Dialogs – aufgezeigt an einem Beispiel aus der italienischen Renaissance (Galilei) und der französischen Aufklärung (Fontenelle), in: Hartwig Kalverkämper und Klaus- Dieter Baumann (Hg.): Fachliche Textsorten. Komponenten – Relationen – Strategien. Tübingen: Narr 1996, S. 683–745.
Kampe, Jürgen: Problem „Reformationsdialog". Untersuchungen zu einer Gattung im reformatorischen Medienwettstreit. Beiträge zur Dialogforschung. Tübingen: Niemeyer 1997.
Kennerly, Michele: Sermo and Stoic Sociality in Cicero's De officiis, in: Rhetorica 28,2, 2010, S. 119–137.
Klinkert, Thomas: Muße und Erzählen: ein poetologischer Zusammenhang. Vom ‚Roman de la Rose' bis zu Jorge Semprún. Tübingen: Mohr Siebeck 2016.
Knape, Joachim: Albertanus Brixiensis: Die Räte von der Rede, in: Joachim Knape und Bernhard Roll (Hg.): Rhetorica deutsch. Rhetorikschriften des 15. Jahrhunderts. Wiesbaden: Harrassowitz 2002, S. 235–244.
Knapp, Fritz Peter (Hg.): Andreas aulae regiae capellanus/Andreas königlicher Hofkapellan: De amore/Von der Liebe – libri tres/Drei Bücher. Berlin, New York: De Gruyter 2006.
Kocher, Ursula: Boccaccio und die deutsche Novellistik. Formen der Transposition italienischer ‚novelle' im 15. und 16. Jahrhundert. Amsterdam, New York: Rodopi 2005.
Koselleck, Reinhart: Kritik und Krise. Eine Studie zur Pathogenese der bürgerlichen Welt. Frankfurt a. M.: Suhrkamp 2010, 11. Aufl.
Kuhn, Rudolf: Albertis Lehre über die Komposition als die Kunst in der Malerei, in: Archiv für Begriffsgeschichte 28, 1984, S. 123–178.
Lee, Alexander: Petrarch and St. Augustine: Classical Scholarship, Christian Theology and the Origins of the Renaissance in Italy. Leiden, Boston: Brill 2012.
Lee, Alexander: The look(s) of Love: Petrarch, Simone Martini and the Ambiguities of Fourteenth- Century Portraiture, in: Journal of Art Historiography 17, 2017, S. 1–12.
Leidl, Christoph G.: ‚Urbanitas', in: Gert Ueding (Hg.): Historisches Wörterbuch der Rhetorik, Bd. 10. Berlin: De Gruyter 2012, Sp. 1344–1364.
Leinkauf, Thomas: Grundriss Philosophie des Humanismus und der Renaissance (1350–1600), 2 Bde. Hamburg: Meiner 2017.
Maglio, Gabriella: Poggio Bracciolini e il ‚Bugiale' come osservatorio del suo tempo, in: Esperienze Letterarie, 23, 2, 1998, S. 43–61.
Marsh, David: Dialogue and Discussion in the Renaissance, in: Glyn B. Norton (Hg.): The Cambridge History of Literary Criticism, Bd. 3. Cambridge u. a.: Cambridge UP 2006, S. 265–270.

Marsh, David: The Quattrocento Dialogue. Classical Tradition and Humanist Innovation. Cambridge MA: Harvard UP 1980.
Maurach, Gregor und Echinger- Maurach, Claudia (Hg.): Francesco Petrarca on Panel Painting and Sculpture. De tabulis pictis; de statuis, aus: Francesco Petrarca, De remediis utriusque fortunae (1354–1366). Dialogus XL. Dialogus XLI (Fontes. Quellen und Dokumente zur Kunst. 1350–1750, 78), 2014 (http:/archiv.ub.uni-heidelberg.de/artdok/volltexte/2014/2209 URN: urn:nbn:de:bsz:16- artdok- 22098: 9. 11. 2021).
Milham, Mary Ella (Hg.): Platina, on Right Pleasure and Good Health: A Critical Edition and Translation of *De honesta voluptate et valetudine*. Tempe Ariz: Medieval & Renaissance Texts & Studies 1998.
Miller, Peter N.: Friendship and Conversation in 17th- Century Venice, in: The Journal of Modern History 73, 2001, S. 1–31.
Montandon, Alain: „Conversation", in: Montandon, Alain (Hg.): Dictionnaire raisonné de la politesse et du savoir- vivre du moyen âge à nos jours. Paris: Seuil 1995, S. 125–153.
Morel, Jacques, Médiocrité et perfection dans la France du XVIIe siècle. Paris: Arman Colin 1969.
Mori, Giuliano: Competing Humanisms: Debating Culture Identity in Leonardo Bruni's *Dialogi ad Petrum Paulum Histrum*, in: Journal of Medieval and Early Modern Studies 50,2, 2020, S. 323–347.
Müller, Gernot Michael: ‚Nam quid ego priscam illam dicendi licentiam cum hodierna taciturnitate conferam?' Alamanno Rinuccinis ‚Dialogus de libertate' und die Auflösung einer humanistischen Diskussionskultur in Florenz unter Lorenzo, in: Guthmüller, Bodo und Müller, Wolfgang G.: Dialog und Gesprächskultur in der Renaissance. Wiesbaden: Harrassowitz 2004, S. 125–152.
Müller, Gernot Michael: Diskrepante Annäherungen an die ‚voluptas'. Zur Funktion der Figureninteraktion in Lorenzo Vallas Dialog ‚De voluptate', in: Hempfer, Klaus W. (Hg.): Möglichkeiten des Dialogs: Struktur und Funktion einer literarischen Gattung' zwischen Mittelalter und Renaissance in Italien. Stuttgart: Steiner 2002, S. 163–213.
Müller, Ivo: St. Galler Klosterplan und monastisches Schweigen, in: Zeitschrift für schweizerische Kirchengeschichte 78, 1984, S. 3–9.
Nauta, Lodi: In Defense of Common Sense. Lorenzo Valla's Humanist Critique of Scholastic Philosophy. Cambridge MA: Harvard UP 2009.
Nauta, Lodi: Philology as Philosophy. Giovanni Pontano on Language, Meaning, and Grammar, in: Journal of the History of Ideas 72,4, 2011, S. 481–502.
Nifo, Agostino: De re aulica, in: Opuscula moralia et politica (…). Paris: Gabriel Naudaeus 1645.
Patrizi, Giorgio: ‚Guazzo, Stefano', in: DBI 60, 2003, S. 544–538.
Paulicelli, Eugenia: Writing Fashion in Early Modern Italy: From Sprezzatura to Satire. Farnham: Ashgate 2014.
Peters, Hans Albert: Giovanni Bellini oder Antonello da Messina, Zur Entstehung der sogenannten Sacra Conversazione. Diss. Phil. Bonn 1981.
Piché, David und Lafleur, Claude: La condamnation parisienne de 1277. Paris: J. Vrin 1999.
Pigman III, George W. (Hg.): Giovanni Gioviano Pontano, The Virtues and Vices of Speech. Cambridge MA: Harvard UP 2001.
Plett, Heinrich F.: Rhetorik der Renaissance – Renaissance der Rhetorik, in: Heinrich F. Plett (Hg.): Renaissance- Rhetorik (…). Berlin: De Gruyter 1993, S. 1–20.
Plotke, Seraina: Conversatio/Konversation: Eine Wort- und Begriffsgeschichte, in: Schnell, Rüdiger: Konversationskultur in der Vormoderne. Geschlechter im geselligen Gespräch. Köln: Böhlau 2008, S. 31–120.
Poncet, Christophe: Ficino's Little Academy at Careggi, in: Bruniana & Campanelliana 19, 1, 2013, S. 67–76.
Pons, Alain: Civilité- Urbanité, in: Montandon 1995, S. 91–109.
Pontano, Giovanni: De bello neapolitano et de sermon. Neapel: Sigismundus Mayr 1509.

Powell, James M.: Albertanus of Brescia. The Pursuit of Happiness in the Early Thirteenth Century. Philadelphia: University of Pennsylvania Press 1992.

Quillen, Caril: The Uses of the Past in Quattrocento Florence: A Reading of Leonardo Bruni's Dialogues, in: Journal of the History of Ideas 71, 2010, S. 363–385.

Quondam, Amedeo (Hg.): Guazzo, Stefano, La civil conversazione, 2 Bde. Modena: Panini 1993.

Raible, Wolfgang: Der Prolog zu 'Gargantua' und der Pantagruelismus, in: Romanische Forschungen 78, 2/3, 1966, S. 253–279.

Riederer, Friedrich: Spiegel der waren Rhetoric vß M. Tvlio. C. vnd andern getütscht. Freiburg: Friedrich Riederer 1493.

Riederer, Friedrich: Spiegel der wahren Rhetorik (1493), Joachim Knape und Stefanie Luppold (Hg.). Wiesbaden: Harrassowitz 2008.

Roeck, Bernd: „...die ersten Gemälde der Welt". Über die Entzauberung des Raumes in der europäischen Renaissance, in: Dirk Syndram u. a. (Hg.): Luther und die Fürsten. Selbstdarstellung und Selbstverständnis des Herrschers im Zeitalter der Reformation. Dresden: Sandstein 2015, S. 47–63.

Roeck, Bernd: Das historische Auge. Kunstwerke als Zeugen ihrer Zeit. Von der Renaissance zur Revolution. Vandenhoeck & Ruprecht: Göttingen 2004.

Roeck, Bernd: Der Morgen der Welt. Geschichte der Renaissance. München: C.H. Beck 2020, 6. Aufl.

Roeck, Bernd: Eine Stadt in Krieg und Frieden. Studien zur Geschichte der Reichsstadt Augsburg zwischen Kalenderstreit und Parität. Göttingen: Vandenhoeck & Ruprecht 1989.

Roeck, Bernd: Gedruckte Worte, geschnittene Bilder und die verzauberte Welt. Zur Geschichte der Phantasie im Zeitalter der frühneuzeitlichen Massenkommunikation, in: Francia 34,2, 2007, S. 257–268.

Roeck, Bernd: Introduction, in: Herman Roodenburg (Hg.): Forging European Identities, 1400–1700 (Cultural Exchange in Early Modern Europe, Bd. 4). Cambridge: Cambridge UP 2007, S. 1–29.

Roeck, Bernd: Leonardo. Der Mann, der alles wissen wollte. Biographie. München: C.H. Beck 2019, 3. Aufl.

Roeck, Bernd: Religious Crisis 1400–1700. Some Considerations, in: Troels Dahlerup und Per Ingesman (Hg.): New Approaches to the History of Late Medieval and Early Modern Europe. Selected Proceedings of Two International Conferences at The Royal Danish Academy of Sciences and Letters in Copenhagen in 1997 and 1999. Kopenhagen: Det Kongelige Danske Videnskabernes Selskab 2009, S. 445–462.

Roodenburg, Herman: The Eloquence of the Body. Perspectives on Gesture in the Dutch Republic. Zwolle: Waanders 2004.

Rosell, Anna Ginestí: Der Umgang mit negativen Figuren in den Dialogen Plutarchs, in: Gernot Michael Müller (Hg.): Figurengestaltung und Gesprächsinteraktion im antiken Dialog. Stuttgart: Franz Steiner 2021, S. 189–204.

Rosell, Anna Ginestí: The Sophist and his Beard. Working Papers in Nervan, Trajanic and Hadrianic Literature 1.7, 14/4/13. (https://arts.st-andrews.ac.uk/literaryinteractions/wp-content/uploads/2013/04/The-Sophist-and-his-Beard.pdf, 21. 10. 2021).

Roussel, Claude: „Courtoisie", in: Montandon 1995, S. 175–196.

Rüegg, Walter: Die humanistische Lebensform des Gesprächs bei Petrarca, in: Walter Rüegg: Anstöße. Aufsätze und Vorträge zur dialogischen Lebensform. Frankfurt a. M.: Metzner 1973, S. 9–28.

Salwa, Piotr: ,Cacciato e isfolgorato dalla fortuna': Variazioni sul tema dell'esilio, e gli inizi della novella italiana, in: Gabriel Siemoneit u. a. (Hg.): Exil und Heimatferne in der humanistischen Literatur von Petrarca bis zum Anfang des 16. Jahrhunderts. Tübingen: Narr Francke Attempto 2019, S. 61–78.

Saviello, Alberto: Lorenzo Valla, in: Romana Sammern und Julia Saviello (Hg.): Schönheit – Der Körper als Kunstprodukt. Kommentierte Quellentexte von Cicero bis Goya. Berlin: Reimer 2019, S. 125–131.

Schatzki, Theodore R.: The Site of the Social. A Philosophical Account of the Constitution of Social Life and Change. University Park PA: Penn State UP 2002.

Schnell, Rüdiger: Gastmahl und Gespräch. Entwürfe idealer Konversation, von Plutarch zu Castiglione, in: Alois Hahn (Hg.): Norm und Krise von Kommunikation. Inszenierungen literarischer und sozialer Interaktion im Mittelalter. Für Peter von Moos. Berlin u. a.: Lit Verlag 2006, S. 73–90.

Schnell, Rüdiger: Konversation im Mittelalter. Bausteine zu einer Geschichte der Konversationskultur, in: Schnell, Rüdiger: Konversationskultur in der Vormoderne. Geschlechter im geselligen Gespräch. Köln: Böhlau 2008, S. 121–218.

Schnell, Rüdiger: Konversationskultur in der Vormoderne. Geschlechter im geselligen Gespräch. Köln: Böhlau 2008.

Schoeck, Richard J.: More's Attic Nights: Sir Thomas More's Use of Aulus Gellius' 'Noctes Atticae', in: Renaissance News 13, 2, 1960, S. 127–129

Scholar, Richard: *The Je- Ne- Sais- Quoi in Early Modern Europe. Encounters with a Certain Something.* Oxford: Oxford UP 2005.

Schörle, Eckart: Die Verhöflichung des Lachens. Lachgeschichte im 18. Jahrhundert. Bielefeld: Aisthesis 2007.

Schrott, Angela und Strosetzki, Christoph (Hg.): Gelungene Gespräche als Praxis der Gemeinschaftsbildung. Literatur – Sprache – Gesellschaft. Berlin: De Gruyter 2021.

Smelser, Neil: Theory of Collective Behaviour. New York: The Free Press of Glencoe 1963.

Spencer, John: Ut rhetorica pictura, in: Journal of the Warburg and Courtauld Institutes 20, 1957, S. 26–44.

Stieler, Kaspar von (Spaten): Der Deutschen Sprache Stammbaum und Fortwachs (…). Nürnberg: Johann Hofmann 1691.

Strosetzki, Christoph: Konversation als Sprachkultur. Elemente einer historischen Kommunikationspragmatik. Berlin: Frank & Timme 2013.

Tarde, Gabriel: Die Gesetze der Nachahmung. Übers. v. Jadja Wolf (1890). Frankfurt a. M.: Suhrkamp 2009.

Thomä, Dieter: Glück in der Philosophie der Renaissance und der Frühen Neuzeit, in: Dieter Thomä u. a.: Glück. Ein interdisziplinäres Handbuch. Stuttgart, Weimar: J.B. Metzler 2011, S. 143–149.

Toutain- Quittelier, Valentine und Rauseo, Chris (Hg.): Watteau au confluent des arts. Esthétiques de la grâce. Rennes: Presses universitaires de Rennes 2014.

Valla, Lorenzo: Von der Lust oder Vom wahren Guten/*De voluptate sive De vero bono*. Lateinisch- deutsche Ausgabe, hg. u. übers. v. Peter Michael Schenkel, eingel. v. Eckhard Keßler. München: Fink 2004.

van Delft, Louis und Lotterie, Florence: Torquato Accetto et la notion de ‚dissimulation honnête' dans la culture classique, in: Alain Montandon (Hg.): L'honnête homme et le dandy. Tübingen: Narr 1993, S. 35–57.

Vigliarolo, Luca: Die Geste der Kunst: Paradigmen einer Ästhetik. Bielefeld: transcript 2021.

Vilar, Mariano: La construcción dialógica del placer en el *De vero bono* de Lorenzo Valla, in: Studia Aurea 8, 2014, S. 347–368.

von der Hagen, Friedrich Heinrich (Hg.): Minnesinger aus den Jenauer, Heidelberger und Weingarter Sammlungen und den übrigen Handschriften und frühen Drucken (Minnesinger III,1). Leipzig: Johann Ambrosius Barth 1838.

Waters, Roderick- Pascal: La ‚sprezzatura': enjeux et concepts. Diss. Paris 2019.

Werner, Edeltraud: Das Dialogmuster im italienischen Geschlechterdiskurs bis 1600. Am Beispiel von Baldassare Castigliones Cortegiano und Moderata Fontes il merito delle donne, in: Baumann, Uwe u. a. (Hg.): Polemik im Dialog des Renaissance-Humanismus. Formen, Entwicklungen und Funktionen. Göttingen: V & R Unipress 2015, S. 253–289.

Westermann, Hartmut: Wie disputiert man über das Gute? Lorenzo Vallas *De vero bono* als Debatte über die richtige Debatte, in: Jahrbuch Rhetorik 25, 2006, S. 30–54.

Wild, Cornelia: Aus zweiter Hand. Dialog und Providenz, in: Matthias Hausmann und Marita Liebermann (Hg.): Inszenierte Gespräche: zum Dialog als Gattung und Argumentationsmodus in der Romania vom Mittelalter bis zur Aufklärung. Berlin: Weidler 2014, S. 19–36.

Zweifel, Simone: Aus Büchern Bücher machen. Zur Produktion und Multiplikation von Wissen in frühneuzeitlichen Kompilationen. Berlin: De Gruyter Oldenburg 2021.

Should One Talk? And If So, What About? Or What Not?

Christoph Strosetzki

Abstract

If Aristotle had named the ability to converse with the virtue of Eutrapelia, in the early Middle Ages, jokes and chatter were rejected in view of the hereafter, until Thomas Aquinas rehabilitated conversation in the sense of Aristotle in the High Middle Ages. In 17th century France, conversation was characterized by pleasure, favor, orientation to the partner, dominance of women and trivial objects. In the 18th century, morality, substantive results and efficiency dominate, so that politeness appears as superfluous fraud. In the 19th century, technology and the dominance of material interests have displaced the old carelessness. The question arises as to where conversation is determined by ahistorical rules, or where, in the sense of Foucault's discourse, which determines what should be said and what should not be said, historical determinations dominate.

Keywords

Eutrapelia · Favor · Women · Pleasure · Politeness · Discourse · Rules · *Aptum* · *Bienséance* · Ethics · Aesthetics

Aristotle says that one should talk. After all, the ability to converse is a virtue for him. He calls it *Eutrapelia* and places it next to the other virtues of social interaction such as composure and justice. As a moral virtue, it consists in adhering to the

C. Strosetzki (✉)
Universität Münster, Münster, Germany
e-mail: stroset@uni-muenster.de

right middle and forbids any excess, e.g. of praise or criticism.[1] There are examples from Antiquity of what and how one should not talk. The Greek gods silenced Momus by throwing him out of Olympus. As a contrarian, grumbler and notorious killjoy, he exaggerated and got on everyone's nerves.[2] Plato would have liked to throw the Sophists out of Athens and assigns them the second worst place in the soul migration, followed only by the tyrant.[3] For him, Sophists are not oriented towards truth, but only towards opinion. They are hunters, whose prey caught by persuasion are paying customers, and teachers of a debating art, also called eristics, which proves and disproves at will without regard for truth and with its fallacies and apparent contradictions quickly and concisely presents different things as identical and nonexistent things as existent.[4] So what Momus and the Sophists had to say was unwanted.

When it comes to the hereafter, one should not talk about this world. This was at least the opinion of the church fathers in early medieval times, which is why Ambrose wanted to avoid jokes in conversations, as they could rob more serious topics of their dignity.[5] For Chrysostom, the world is not a theatre for laughter.[6] Benedict had specified for the monks of his order that they were to remain silent and not speak unless they were asked. For while the chatterbox lacked orientation, the wise man was known by the few words he spoke.[7] Gregory the Great transferred this approach to all clerics when he saw the much-talked about—like an open city without fortifications—exposed to attacks, as it was easy to move from useless conversation about the affairs of others to slander, disputes and hatred. He quotes several Bible passages to the clerics: "Gossip does not go without sin;"[8] "The service of justice is silence;"[9] And finally: "People will have to give an account on the day of judgement for every useless word they speak."[10] He comments on the latter quote: "Useless is a word that lacks a justifiable or good, useful purpose. So if an account is already required for every useless word, let us

---

[1] Aristotle 1995, pp. 96–98.

[2] For example, he criticized the creatures of Zeus, Athena and Prometheus, that the bull should have its horns below the eyes, a house should have wheels to escape from disliked neighbours, and in humans the heart should be attached outside and visible, so that one could more easily recognize its badness. Cf. Aesop 2005, pp. 100–103.

[3] Plato 1964, p. 66–67.

[4] Plato 1967.

[5] Ambrose of Milan 1917, p. 872 f.

[6] John Chrysostom 1862, p. 70 (VI, 6).

[7] Benedict of Nursia 2007, p. 131 (VII, 56–61).

[8] Proverbs 10, p. 19.

[9] Is. 32, p. 17.

[10] Matth 12, p. 36.

consider what punishment awaits gossip, in which one also sins through harmful words."[11]

In the High Middle Ages, it is Thomas Aquinas who turns against Ambrose and Chrysostom, sees conversation as necessary recreation from work and wants to know that it is again guided by the Aristotelian virtue of eutrapelia.[12] It would contradict the desirable happiness to be unpleasant and to suppress what is funny or cheerful. If Thomas combines conversation with friendship, truth and justice, he sees it directed towards others, insofar as one reveals to the other what concerns him. Here, the Aristotelian mean serves as a guideline: "But there is an excess in the one who talks about his affairs at the wrong time, and a deficiency in the one who conceals when he should reveal."[13]

In Antiquity, therefore, the right measure is recommended, which prohibits exaggerations of praise and criticism, and prefers factuality on opinion-based polemics. In the Middle Ages, silence is opposed to the chatterbox and the much-talker. Cheerfulness and wit are considered to be useless on the one hand against the background of the afterlife, on the other hand guided by virtues as conducive to human happiness. With this, criteria have been set by which the assessment of the conversation can also take place in modern times, which vary depending on the historical context. The question now is whether there are historical conditions that make further specifications. Is there a different ideology, a different view of the world in the 17th century than in the 18th or 19th century? Based on expository texts that can be assigned to moralistics, i.e. the description and discussion of customs, ways of thinking shall be pointed out, which determine certain ways of speaking and types of conversation.

Foucault's definition of discourse as what is sayable, what is to be said, what cannot be said, and by whom, when, and in what way it can be said, can be transferred from the scientific level to everyday conversation here. One could also think of his concept of epistemes, which, as a strategic dispositif, prescribes which statements are acceptable.[14] One could also apply Dilthey's philosophy of world views, which attributes different priorities to the seat in life and historical consciousness.[15] For Max Scheler, the respective world view would be an expression "for the organic and historical way in which large groups of people, world, soul and life are actually viewed and valued."[16] In the following, the view of conversation in the 17th century, historically conditioned, will be discussed first. In the course of the text, authors will only be mentioned occasionally, as many of them are little

---

[11] Gregory, Liber regulae postoralis, 173: https://bkv.unifr.ch/de/works/152/versions/171 (13.01.2022).

[12] Thomas Aquinas 1993, Vol. 22, p. 338–339 (II–II, q. 168, a. 2).

[13] Thomas Aquinas, 1943, Vol. 20, p. 124 (II–II, q.109, a.1, ad 3).

[14] Foucault 1981, p. 74; Foucault 1978, p. 124.

[15] Dilthey 1991, pp. 3–7.

[16] Scheler 1963, p. 7.

known, they usually complement each other and the moralistic genre basis is relatively uniform.[17]

Historically, the first is the importance attributed to conversation. In 17th century France it has a central importance. If man is traditionally defined as a social being, it is above all the conversation that makes him so.[18] For the property of having a good conversation, there are adjectives like "conversable" and "affable" and descriptions like "d'une conversation agréable" or "d'une aimable conversation" or "homme rare et d'une exquise conversation".[19] In conversation, it is about winning sympathies: "Rien n'est plus important pour le commerce de la vie, que de plaire dans la Conversation."[20] The king's favor is what everyone at court is striving to win.[21] One should take care to avoid any kind of ridiculousness, as this could be off-putting and would only diminish the pleasure of the gathering.[22] It is not easy to please, as one should always be able to say something nice and take care that everything one talks about is entertaining.[23] Pleasure is what it is all about in conversation.[24] Conversation is therefore the opposite of work. It is even recommended as a guideline for people of status to occasionally interrupt their pleasures with a little work.[25] Conversation is a particularly beautiful pastime: "La conversation est ce semble, ce qui fait passer le temps agreablement." [26]

The goal is the *conversation enjouée,* which is possible with different people on different topics and may be interspersed with gallant, mocking, witty remarks, references and spontaneous replies, in order to serve the pleasure and entertainment[27]. These are well-expressed trifles that make the conversation enjoyable and "cette manière de badiner"[28] appear extremely entertaining. As an ideal conversation

---

[17] For relevant research literature see: Strosetzki, Christoph: Conversation as language culture. Elements of a historical communication pragmatics. Berlin: Frank and Timme 2017, pp. 11–37; Schrott, Angela and Christoph Strosetzki (eds.): Successful conversations as practice of community building. Berlin: de Gruyter 2020, pp. 7–8.

[18] Chalesme 1671, p. 178.

[19] La Bruyère 1694 (1951), p. 19.

[20] Ortigue de Vaumorière 1701^4, p. 4.

[21] "But to come to that, the common goal to which all Courtiers aim, is to win the favor of the Prince. In this point lies all their science, and all their work is employed." Eust. Du Refuge 1618, p. 182.

[22] Morvan de Bellegarde 1723, vol. 1, p. 1.

[23] "One must study so many things to please; […] one must always have some pretty thing to say, and that all the subjects one proposes are diverting." (Morvan de Bellegarde 1688, p. 296 ff.)

[24] "to divert oneself, as in fact, is the main goal of conversation." (Chevalier de Méré 1930, vol. 2, p. 102 ff.)

[25] "I want you to [honest diversions] taste more by interspersing them with a little work." (A. de Courtin 1673, p. 179 ff.)

[26] Clément 1664, p. 2.

[27] "au plaisir et au divertissement" (Claude Irson 1656, p. 255)

[28] La Rochefoucauld 1658 (1964, pp. 4–5)

partner, as a *honnête homme,* one should not know everything about something, but something about everything. This is then necessary if one does not want to be silent too often in a conversation. What is required is a vague knowledge of the most pleasant questions that are discussed in good society.[29] If one has to talk about everything, that does not mean that one should bring up as many topics as possible in a short time.[30] It is also to the liking if one does not insist on one's own opinion, but is flexible. It is advisable to be more flexible towards important conversation partners, although the line to flattery should not be crossed.[31] One is successful with others when one pretends to have the same opinions and inclinations as they.[32] One takes another step towards the others when one does not want to be witty oneself, but gives the conversation partner the opportunity to be witty himself.[33] Here, the one who knows too much and is constantly trying to instruct others with his knowledge and to insist dogmatically on his opinion is unpopular.[34]

Conversation serieuse et sçavante is a conversation about theology, philosophy, jurisprudence, medicine, history, politics, mathematics, geography, or fine literature that also deserves the name *conférence,* because it clings so persistently to speculation that one gets the impression that the sciences bring forth uncivilized barbarians. If a "Pédant importun, ou son Ecolier ridicule"[35] gets excited, then the zeal to get rid of his knowledge suggests the pressure that science seems to exert on him. Someone who knows a lot is in danger of considering himself a "phénix des beaux esprits", who claims attention and admiration from others.[36]

Nor can it be called conversation if it is talked for business reasons, for example when a party to a lawsuit talks to the judges, a merchant negotiates with another, a general gives orders, or a king discusses political issues in his cabinet. All of this is possible without that conversational talent that beautifies life and is rarer than one might think.[37] The actual conversation, the *conversation enjouée,* is thus opposed to the serious conversation, which in turn is to be distinguished from the factual business type. It is "ou de Doctrine (Chrétienne – Prophane) ou d'Affaires (Publiques ou Politiques-Particulieres)".[38] In the actual conversation, it is therefore not about the content, but about the well-being of the conversation partners. "Il faudroit que les Sciences obscures et les grandes Affaires eussent

---

[29] "une médiocre teinture des plus agréables questions qui s'agitent quelquefois dans les bonnes compagnies" (N. Faret 1630 (1932), p. 60)

[30] Mlle de Scudéry 1680, vol. 1, pp. 32–33

[31] Morvan de Bellegarde 1723 (new edition), vol. 2, pp. 529–530 and p. 552.

[32] Morvan de Bellegarde 1693, p. 251.

[33] Ortigue de Vaumorière 1701 (4th ed.), p. 13.

[34] Abbé Goussault 1692, pp. 270–271; cf. also: ibid. p. 277.

[35] Cl. Irson 1656, p. 52; see also pp. 250 ff.

[36] Morvan de Bellegarde 1723 (new edition), vol. 1, p. 31.

[37] Mlle de Scudéry 1680, vol. 1, pp. 2 ff.

[38] Claude Irson 1656, p. 250.

moins de part dans leurs discours, que la bienséance et le divertissement."[39] Especially with scholars one has the impression that their knowledge is hidden in mysterious folds, which is why it takes so much effort to bring it to light slowly and cumbersomely. The opposite is a cosmopolitan and cultivated personality who is used to moving in conversations and can express himself effortlessly on all possible topics.[40]

He attributes the inability of those who have had a long school education to carry on an easy conversation to the fact that they have been taught in school how to assert themselves in arguments, but not how to give in to others where appropriate. The special ability of women to carry on a conversation, on the other hand, is due to the fact that they bring the opposite qualifications to the table. Because they are not burdened by thorough knowledge, they easily express what their senses perceive, what delights or grieves them, what intrigues they are hatching or what disputes occupy them: "pourvû qu'on ne parle que de bagatelles, elles ont toujours de quoi fournir à la conversation."[41] When they touch on a variety of conversation topics superficially, the women's approach seems to have been modeled on that of the *honnête homme*: "Nous devons aux Dames cét art de varier, parce qu'elles ont ordinairement plus de delicatesse, que de sçavoir, de sorte qu'elles ne prennent que la fleur des choses, sans vouloir trop les penetrer."[42]

Their way of speaking is supported by their natural beauty.[43] It is more pleasant to talk to women because they have a certain gracefulness, express themselves more clearly and entertainingly than men.[44] Women owe the sovereignty of their manners not least to the fact that they are exempt from hard work.[45] In Courtin's "Traité de la presse, ou l'art de bien employer le temps en forme d'entretiens" (1673), such women, who are relieved of all manual work, are the subject of satire: "quand je voy l'immobilité et la molesse de nos Maistresses, qui sont toute une matinée dans une chaise, sans aucune action, comme si elles estoient des idoles."[46] Politeness can be learned better from women than from reading books.[47]

---

[39] Ortigue de Vaumorière 1701 (4th ed.), p. 5.

[40] Morvan de Bellegarde 1697, pp. 292 ff.

[41] Morvan de Bellegarde 1723 (Neuausgabe), Bd. 1, S. 118; vgl. auch S. 31.

[42] Chalesme 1671, S. 207 f.

[43] Grenaille 1639–40, 3. Bd., S. 209.

[44] „Quand elles ont l'esprit bien fait, j'aime mieux leur conversation que celle des hommes; on y trouve une certain douceur qui ne se rencontre point parmi nous, et il me semble, outre cela, qu'elles s'expliquent avec plus de netteté et qu'elles donnent un tour plus agréable à ce qu'elles disent." (La Rochefoucauld 1658 (1964), S. 6)

[45] Ortique de Vaumorière 1688, S. 44.

[46] A. de Courtin 1673, S. 118.

[47] „ce n'est qu'en frequentant les Dames, que nous acquerons cét air du monde, et cette politesse que nul conseil, ny aucune lecture ne peuvent donner." (Chalesme 1671, S. 197)

A topic of conversation must not directly concern the conversation partners, which is why irrelevant objects are to be preferred.[48] They also have the advantage of not revealing any weaknesses even if, as is usual, everyone at court is spying on each other.[49] Such irrelevant topics are, for example, fashion, love affairs and excursions.[50] In this way, the art of talking about the most insignificant things becomes the ability to create something out of nothing.[51] The fact that the satisfaction of the conversation partner has priority over the choice of conversation topic results in the demand that one should not say what one considers worth mentioning oneself, but what might please the conversation partners.[52] So when choosing a conversation topic, one should orient oneself towards the partners.[53] This means in concrete terms that one should converse differently with older people than with young people; with noblemen one should talk about matters concerning honor, with rich people one should admire their wealth, and with officials one should express respect. One should agree unconditionally with those of higher rank, as far as possible with those of equal rank, while subordinates may be patiently convinced of one's own opinion. If one has to do with kings, one must pay attention to whether they are warlike, peaceful or educated. Depending on this, one can talk to them about war, about dangerous plans, about the order and discipline in the armies, or in the second case about justice, about the order within the country, about finances and trade. In the third case, choose the branch of culture that interests the king most.[54] In front of young people who have opera and comedy in their heads, one should not behave like a thoughtful philosopher and not look glum in front of the ladies who are thinking about dancing. So it is primarily to be judged for whom which conversation topic is appropriate. However, this can be difficult if one is facing unknown persons. Since they have to be treated with different politeness according to their rank, one has to deduce their status from their posture and their behavior.[55] In general, it is said that speaking little of oneself and letting

---

[48] „Pour les matieres du discours toutes me sont bonnes pourueu qu'elles soient indifferentes;" (F. de Grenaille 1642, S. 268)

[49] La Conversation: „Elle doit mesme autant qu'il se peut rouler sur des matieres indiférentes, sur tout entre des Personnes de la Cour, qui sont d'ordinaire les Espions les uns des autres." (La Chétardie 1683, Bd. 1, S. 54 f.)

[50] "l'on is not concerned at the Court about modes, about love affairs, about gambling, about parties, and what grieves honest people most is that one ordinarily dares not talk about anything else there." (R. Bary 1673, p. 38)

[51] La Bruyère 1694 (1951), p. 168.

[52] "In order to make our conversation agreeable, we should not always want to say what seems good and curious to us, but entertain those with whom we are talking about what is to their taste and what they like." (Goussault 1692, p. 117)

[53] La Rochefoucauld 1731 (1964), p. 510.

[54] N. Faret 1630 (1932), pp. 169 ff. and p. 103 f.

[55] Ortigue de Vaumorièie 1688, S. 10–11, 28.

others speak much of themselves makes it possible to please in society. The most popular friend is the one who has the talent to make us speak about ourselves.[56]

Not only in terms of topics, but also in terms of conversation level, one must adapt to the partner in order not to bore. "Le plus grand secret de la conversation est de se proportionner au caractere des personnes que l'on frequente;"[57] For if the conversation partners believe themselves to be on the same level, they are delighted with each other and with themselves and see themselves confirmed in their self-love. Equality with others is advantageous, which means that the middle between too little and too much must be observed. Too much good also carries the danger of habituation or envy. Rather, agreement with others is pleasing: "C'est la conformité qui fait qu'on se plaist ensemble."[58] Whoever appears excellent in everything and constantly elicits admiration will be unbearable. If the goal is "me rendre agréable dans la Conversation,"[59] then one must not please too much in order to please really. In any case, one pleases others most when one gives them the opportunity to please in turn. If the other believes himself to be appreciated by his conversation partner, then he is also convinced of his merits.[60]

In general, the different behaviors in conversation can be related to different character traits that can be inferred from these behaviors. Whoever talks too much is unreasonable. Whoever speaks too loudly shows pride. Whoever speaks too eagerly is shy. Whoever says nonsense is a joker. Whoever often mocks is a fool. Whoever insults has a quick temper. Whoever lies is a villain. And if someone tells bad things about others, he is envious or malicious.[61] Whoever talks uninterruptedly, is likely to be suspected that he does so out of fear that his stupidity might otherwise be discovered. People who talk a lot tell stories from the most remote centuries and places. What they say, they also express at inappropriate times.[62] Whoever talks a lot runs the risk of repeating himself often, because he no longer knows what he has already said and what not.[63]

The list of unpleasant conversation partners is long. These include those who talk constantly and for a long time, who only tell trivialities, who cannot say anything without extensive introductions and preliminary remarks, who easily get

---

[56] Laurent Bordelon 1694 (2. Aufl.), S. 253 f.

[57] Morvan de Bellegarde 1723 (Neuauflage), Bd. 3, avertissement; vgl. auch S. 17.

[58] Méré 1930, Bd. 2, S. 106, vgl. auch 108, 120–121.

[59] Ortigue de Vaumorière 1701 (4. Aufl.), S. 2 f.

[60] "Cela fait qu'ils n'ont point de peine à convenir de vostre mérite, parce qu'ils croyent vous avoir persuadé du leur, qu'ils disent mille biens de vous, et qu'ils vous élevent au dela de ce que vous auriez pû le prétendre." Trotti de La Chétardie 1683, Bd. 2, S. 12 f.

[61] Bordelon 1694 (2nd ed.), P. 250 f.

[62] La Bruyère 1694 (1951), P. 379.

[63] "But why resist the boredom of hearing the same thing said a hundred times? […] Is it that the pleasure they have in talking takes away their reflection and memory, since they no longer remember that they said, a moment ago, what they repeat with so much emphasis, and what they recite as if it were something new." (Morvan de Bellegarde 1696 A, P. 181 f.)

excited and become angry without reason, the obstinate, who only let their opinion count, and finally those who speak so loudly that their listeners get headaches from it.[64] No less unpleasant are the bad joke makers, those who spread bad rumors, those who are unable to contribute to a conversation, the superficial ones and those who, for the sheer joy of opposition, always contradict.[65] A separate group are the obstinate, who insist on their opinion under all circumstances.[66] Suspicious conversation partners easily become tyrants who embarrass others because they always misunderstand something, interpret every laugh as malicious, think that one only speaks of them and only tells negative things about them. No better are those who irritate by always rejecting what others say, while they remain untouched by good remarks and applaud stupidity.[67] As is well known, conversation with women is the most pleasant. But it is also the most complicated[68] because they are so sensitive that they can easily interpret casual remarks to their disadvantage and become disturbed by them, which is why explanations and justifications of what one has said are often necessary with them.[69]

It is hard to endure the prying "espions publics" who have nothing better to do than go from house to house, gossiping about others and spreading the latest news.[70] It seems as if such a "nouvelliste"[71] is born to hear the news of others, to pass it on, to know all the rumors and stories of the city, and to be able to give information about them. News is always popular when one is the first to tell of an important marriage, the birth of a prince, a victory or a conquest, or of a measure to optimize the external security of peoples, the beautification of cities, a long-planned festival at court, or a new fashion at court.[72] In addition to those of the residential district, there are the big news, such as battles, city sieges and other world-shaking events. Some only express themselves when they can report such news, so that one might think that the gods only change the face of the universe so that those in conversation do not run out of topics.[73] Whether geographical,

---

[64] A. de Courtin 1672 (2nd ed.), P. 67 ff.; Courtin, Ant. de: Nouveau traité de la civilité qui se pratique en France parmi les honnestes gens. Paris 1672² (Paris 1671).

[65] Morvan de Bellegarde 1723 (reprint), Vol. 1, P. 11.

[66] Mme de Sablé 1678 (1971), P. 235.

[67] Morvan de Bellegarde 1688, P. 312–313, 29.

[68] N. Faret 1636 (1932), P. 175.

[69] "the slightest word said to their disadvantage, and which they always interpret in a bad light, gives them strange worries; […] most of their conversations take place in explanations and apologies, to give a good sense to what has been said," Morvan de Bellegarde 1723 (reprint), Vol. 1, P. 321.

[70] Mlle de Scudéry 1680, Vol. 1, p. 31.

[71] La Bruyère 1694 (1951), p. 123.

[72] Ortigue de Vaumorière 1688, Ibid., p. 9 ff.

[73] Mlle de Scudéry 1680, Vol. 1, p. 29 ff.

political or genealogical questions arise in conversation: "Un Nouvelliste répond à tout."[74]

In addition to the character flaws of unpleasant conversation partners, there are also behavioral problems. It is not well received if one helps the person who is looking for a word too quickly and without being asked with the matching word. The same applies if one dares to answer first in the presence of higher-ranking persons. This even applies to questions about the time or the date. "We must let the people who are most qualified in front of us answer, unless we are directly informed about it."[75] A casual family style is appropriate among equals who know each other well, but it is an impertinence towards a superior, and towards a person of lower rank it can even be interpreted as a sign of goodwill.[76]

Conversations are not only based on rank, but also on the number of people involved. They are tiring in a large circle, because only very general things are talked about there: Most of those who prefer large companies only testify to their inability to have a conversation one-on-one.[77] On the other hand, it is a mistake to focus on one particular person in a large circle and to ignore the others. Groups that meet regularly develop their own laws, customs, their own language and their own jokes, which remain incomprehensible to an outsider.[78] However, if you come across a group of people who are talking, it is inappropriate to join the conversation without further ado, especially if the people concerned have withdrawn to exchange secrets. Nor is it appropriate to ask about the subject of the conversation when you join a group. It could be something confidential, which would then require a secretive answer. Instead, the group should inform the newcomer in turn or change the subject.[79] Care must also be taken when ending a conversation and assessing whether one is desired or tolerated: "a skilled man knows if it is appropriate or if he bores; he knows how to disappear just before the moment when he would be too much somewhere."[80]

What should one not talk about in conversation? What topics are inappropriate? It is certainly unpleasant, if an unknown person, who by chance takes the seat next to you in a carriage, at a party or at a play, has nothing more important to divulge than his name, his residence, his financial situation, his offices, those of his father, those of his mother's family, his relatives and his coat of arms, from which one can deduce that he is noble, has a castle, beautiful furniture, servants

---

[74] Ortigue de Vaumorière 1688., p. 421 ff.

[75] A. de Courtin 1672², p. 38.

[76] Antoine de Courtin 1672², pp. 16 ff.

[77] "Large assemblies tire; one can't talk about anything but general things there, which almost always bore, and which nobody is interested in. Nevertheless, the majority like the crowd; it is a sure sign of their bad taste, or that they distrust themselves, and that they do not believe they can support themselves in a tête-à-tête." (Morvan de Bellegarde 1723 (reprint), vol. 2, p. 392 f.)

[78] La Bruyère 1694 (1951), p. 621, 223.

[79] René Bary 1673, p. 282, 285.

[80] La Bruyère 1694 (1951), p. 168; see also p. 175.

and a carriage. This results in the demand not to talk long about oneself or to give oneself as an example.[81] But how does one find the topics and the knowledge that one needs for a conversation? One possibility is to read again and again in books or excerpts and to memorize everything that can occur in a conversation.[82] One can also collect and organize what one has read in a notebook, so that on one side the tragic and sad events are standing and on the other side the successful and happy events. One can then fall back on the respective repertoire, depending on the mood of the conversation partner.[83] If now someone talks constantly about tragic events or unpleasant matters, this is generally considered unpleasant. Conversations of this kind resemble long, lamentable and sad news.[84] To support such eternal complainers with advice is not very meaningful, as it only confirms them in their way.[85]

If you have guests from the provinces, the experience and knowledge from which they chat is so uninteresting and unenlightening that it would be better if they were silent than to talk about their farmers, their dogs, their horses, their hunting or their coursing, and the number of pheasants they killed, specifying how many gray and red ones there were, so that they could almost name them.[86] Country life is tedious for the city-dweller or courtier. For it is generally true that whoever only talks about the same thing wants to make himself the master of the conversation.[87] The remedy is variety, which leads to agreeableness.[88] The most diverse things should be discussed on different levels: "If you will believe me, we should go everywhere that genius leads us, without any other division or distinction than those of common sense."[89]

There are some special components of a conversation for which there are special rules. These include mockery. So one should not mock about congenital defects, about the appearance rather than the psyche of a person, about ascribed rather than real merits, about actions that are meaningless for a status rather than

---

[81] "Il faut éviter de parler longtemps de soi-même, et de se donner souvent pour exemple." (La Rochefoucauld 1731 (1964), p. 509).

[82] "afin d'éprouver si l'on s'en pourra servir dans la conversation ordinaire, ou dans les occasions les plus importantes." (Ch. Sorel 1672, p. 300).

[83] Ortigue de Vaumorière 1688, pp. 332 ff.

[84] Mlle de Scudéry 1680, vol. 1, pp. 10, 12, 25 ff.

[85] Morvan de Bellegarde 1696 A, avertissement.

[86] Morvan de Bellegarde 1723 (new edition), vol. 1, p. 10 ff.

[87] "It is dangerous to always want to be the master of the conversation, and to talk about the same thing too often; one must enter indifferently into all the agreeable subjects that present themselves, and never show that one wants to lead the conversation to what one has a mind to say." (La Rochefoucauld 1731 (1964), p. 510).

[88] "It is variety that gives pleasure;" (Ortigue de Vaumorière 1688, p. 8 ff.)

[89] Méré 1668/69 (1930), vol. 1, p. 67.

those that are connected with the status honor.[90] When mocking, one should consider how the conversation partner will receive the mockery. Women are particularly sensitive and can take harmless jokes as mockery and react violently against it.[91] Another component of conversation is silence. It is considered a virtue as long as it retains a function within the conversation, as long as it is eloquent silence or as long as one prefers it for the sake of consideration of the speech. If a conversation partner is limited to uninterrupted silence, then he should do without the company of others, because he only burdens them: "People who are so taciturn should renounce society. They are a burden to everyone, and their conversation is nothing but tedious."[92] On the other hand, eight functions of silence in conversation can be distinguished: a cautious one that is appropriate according to time and place, an artificial one that is supposed to surprise others, a conciliatory one that renounces contradiction and signals agreement, a mocking one that allows one to secretly enjoy the other's ridiculousness, an attentive one that shows interest, a stupid one in which tongue and mind have become motionless, an affirmative one that is limited to non-verbal signals, and a rejecting silence that proudly and coldly refuses a reply.[93]

It can be concluded that conversation was the subject of numerous writings in the 17th century, that the *conversation enjouée* was striven for, in which, relieved from work, one could give priority to the conversation partner over the topic, make him appear witty through tolerance, mockery and silence were subordinate to entertainment and equality made a pleasant family-like intercourse possible where there were no hierarchies.

For the 18th century, a decline in treatises on *honnêteté* and an increase in moral and religious publications can be observed at first.[94] Conversation is now content-related and understood as "communication des idées"[95] Where now compliance is desired, it should serve the success of the business man acting circumspect and modest.[96] Normally, it is less about the well-being of the conversation partners, but about content-related results "pour retirer du fruit de la conversation".[97] From the discussions and the meeting of different opinions, unexpected results arise as in chemical processes.[98] Reason and usefulness are the new terms that dominate. Rhetorical subtleties can therefore be dispensed with. Because

---

[90] A. de Courtin 1672 (2nd ed.), 243 ff.; also La Bruyère (1694 (1951) p. 186) recommends mocking only about insignificant faults.

[91] Abbé Goussault 1694, p. 8 f.

[92] Morvan de Bellegarde 1688, p. 195.

[93] Morvan de Bellegarde 1696 B, pp. 12 ff.

[94] Reichardt/Höfer 1986.

[95] Calvel 1722, p. 1.

[96] Mallet 1753, p. 131.

[97] Préaux 1750, p. 299.

[98] Chapelle 1763, p. 193.

an amusement is not expected, but a service.[99] A new administrative rhetoric, an *éloquence d'administration,* deals with state revenues, resources, agriculture and trade. Reason-oriented, as it is, it is only rewarded when it proves to be useful.[100] Conversation is therefore no longer the pleasure, where it primarily matters to please the other, no matter what is being talked about. It becomes a efficiency-oriented means, which is then justified when it succeeds in bringing projects to success.[101]

The *honnêteté,* which in the 17th century referred to a perfectly formed external behavior, regains its original moral dimension in the 18th century. This is shown in sentences like: "L'honnêteté qui est une imitation de la charité, est aussi une des vertus de la société."[102] Not compliance and submission are required, but the completion of tasks.[103] The pedant as an antithesis to the *honnête homme* is adapted to the changed conditions. He is no longer the one who can only talk about one subject in conversation because he knows no more, but he becomes the semi-knowing one who arrogates himself an opinion about things he does not understand. This makes the pedant harmful and obstructive to any further development of the sciences and the mind. The undigested knowledge of the pedant is praised by his peers as erudition. In reality, however, they are nothing but a chaos from which the true scientists and scholars have to beware.[104] In any case, these are only relevant to a part of society, since it is generally more important to produce morally good citizens for society.[105]

If, therefore, the pedant is now accused of superficiality, this is precisely the quality that was lacking in him in the 17th century and the presence of which adorned the *honnête homme.* Is a similar revaluation of values taking place with the woman, who stood paradigmatic for the principle of pleasure, that is, for the priority of orientation towards the conversation partner over content-related and subject-related orientation? It is not worth it, it is said, to please women by paying attention to finesse and tact in expression and thereby risking the loss of time in which new knowledge could have been discovered.[106] Immediately after the French Revolution, political speech in public was clearly in the foreground compared to conversation in private. On the public tribunes of the legislative

---

[99] "ce n'est pas un amusement qu'on leur demande, mais un service." (Batteux 1774, p. 68).

[100] "ouverte par la raison pour l'humanité, où le talent n'obtenait de couronne, que lorsqu'il se rendait utile." (Dampmartin 1794, p. 75).

[101] Préaux 1750, p. 271.

[102] Lambert 1748, p. 183.

[103] "ce sont vos services qui doivent parler pour vous." (Marquise de Lambert 1729, p. 33).

[104] Boyer 1755, pp. 143, 151–154.

[105] "Former des citoyens, des hommes bons et vertueux est le premier devoir de la société." (F. J. P. Aubert 1792, p. 104).

[106] "Thus, the scholars who, out of a desire to please women, write with more eloquence and clarity, lose by leveling the path they have traveled, in precious time that they could have used to make new progress." (Ferlet 1772, p. 49).

assemblies, excellent speakers[107] have developed a new rhetoric with which the rights of man are proclaimed, traitors are exposed, the oppressed are taken into account and tyranny is broken.

Even scientists and scholars appear as silent spectators in comparison to these heroes fighting for freedom.[108] If the latter are distracted from their actual concern in the quieter post-revolutionary times when they try to accommodate the women in their presentation, then the women who served as a model for the *honnête homme* in the 17th century become a model for the pedant characterized by superficiality. This is particularly the case when they jump from one subject to another and come from frivolities, news or fashion to politics and science, where their knowledge is limited to a few words and everything is tolerated except reason.[109] If it is then said of the woman that she is not born for political discussion, but for the domestic happiness[110] and should take care of children and husband, then the Enlightenment turns out to be a setback for the emancipation of women.

In the educational writings of the 18th century, in which a canon of knowledge is established, the still central *science du monde* is missing. If at all, only conversational behavior is mentioned in passing. An example is the Jesuit Duchesne, who in *La Science de la jeune noblesse* in 1729, considers heraldry, geography, history, versification, arithmetic, fortification and the genealogy of old French families to be worth knowing, but not conversational behavior.[111] Also the Jesuit Buffier comes in his *Cours des sciences sur les principes nouveaux et simples* (1732) only after 1100 pages to conversation, to which he devotes about twenty pages, in order to warn in a general way against the unpleasant conversation and the arrogant, piquant, strange, vexatious, absent-minded, precious and pedantic manners and behaviors.[112] And where it comes to the principle of pleasure in conversation, it is no longer polite behavior that forms the basis, but rather virtues that are based in religion, "la source de toutes les vertus sociables"[113]. Now who contributes to the happiness of others pleases. External politeness and pleasure are seen from a moral point of view as lessons of meanness and as inappropriate submissiveness.[114] Politeness is taken out of social life as goodwill[115] to love of neighbor and charity. The politeness that forbade contradicting a superior could only be observed in a tribe of savages who patiently listen to the truths of the

---

[107] "distinguished speakers" (Fourcroy 1793, pp. 14–16).

[108] Biot 1803, p. 34.

[109] "where one suffers everything except good sense." (Ferlet 1772, p. 60).

[110] "made for the inner happiness of society and not for the movement of camps or the discussion of councils," (Rousseau 1790, p. 32 ff.)

[111] Duchesne 1729.

[112] Buffier 1732, S. 1102–1127.

[113] Moncrif 1738, S. 187.

[114] Lambert 1729, S. 33.

[115] "fond de bienveillance" Chapelle 1763, S. 223.

gospel as well as the explanations of the missionaries who want to convert them to Christianity. "Vous les croyez convaincus, point du tout, c'est pure politesse."[116] Not because they were convinced of the teachings, but out of politeness they remain silent.

There are also moralistic texts in the 19th century that describe and discuss customs. The following refers to the genre of physiology, which was particularly widespread in the middle of the century. The generic term *physiology* is taken over from medicine, where it stands for the doctrine of the life processes in the organisms of all living beings. In the literary *physiologies* the life and behavior of different social groups and representatives are demonstrated. If these texts look back wistfully to the 17th century, it is regretted that the salons and with them the rule of women belong to the past.[117] After all, they used to have influence on politics and even on the selection of ministers. While the lady of the house dominated, the lord of the house was inconspicuous or absent. In nostalgic retrospect, the effort to receive guests and attend witty conversations again and again seems less hard than the present compulsion to attend balls or theater performances. For the citizen of the 19th century, an invitation is a challenge. He lacks the composure and skill of the nobleman in the 17th century. Therefore, he has to choose guests, menu, day and time long before the actual event. Because he is naturally clumsy, precise preparation is a duty for him. Whether at parties, weddings or baptisms: "Exactitude in fulfilling one's duty is one of the dominant qualities among the bourgeoisie."[118]

If in the 17th century the court and the salons were the central places of conversation, in the 19th century it seems to be the Parisian *Café*. Four factors have changed the situation: the technology, the dominance of material interests, also the loss of carefreeness and the model of the woman. The noise of the big locomotives and the huge steam engines have drowned out philosophy and literature. Only the industry has remained as the only form of nobility.[119] The attention is focused on wealth, increase in assets and social ascent. A zeitgeist is diagnosed that is oriented towards material interests. One's head is no longer free in the face of constant material demands that fill the imagination. Everyone is so busy with themselves that conversation has been lost. Anyone who wants to dedicate themselves to conversation needs leisure. And the women who used to talk about literary topics now play "Landsknecht" *(lansquenet)* or "Whist", the former a game in which several parties compete against a banker, the latter a card game similar

---

[116] Aubert 1792, S. 91.

[117] "The empire of the salons has passed with that of women." (Gay 1837, p. 1).

[118] Monnier 1841, p. 119.

[119] "L'industrie devient la souveraine des temps modernes et la seule noblesse possible." (Mériclet/Guitton 1848, p. 3–4).

to bridge. Compared to this, the salons of the 17th century stood for an epoch in which women could enjoy sovereign power.[120]

In the bourgeois 19th century, however, numerous rules of court culture from the 17th century are also adopted. Even today it is still considered the worst of all evils to expose oneself to ridicule.[121] If a woman makes herself ridiculous, she can be sure of the attention of others. After all, everyone wants to see from up close what others are gossiping about. But if you don't want to be made fun of, you have to follow the rules and join the required general uniformity.[122] Social hierarchies have not disappeared either. They are just illustrated in other contexts. An example is the porter's wife who treats the tenants of a house differently depending on the floor they live on. Towards those of the first floor she is overzealous, those of the second floor she honors with a bow, while for the third floor she has the necessary politeness and for the other floors an immovable face and no words left.[123]

The phenomenon of the man who talks all the time is also addressed in the 19th century. One manifestation is the *blagueur*, who offers up meaningless, half-true, or false statements in a tone of conviction. "Toujours prompt à parler, il souffre de la nécessité de se taire."[124] He can be found in a variety of professions, such as politics, diplomacy, business, law, or banking. He is also illustrated by the example of the representative who talks a lot, says nothing, and never wants to stop: "Ils ne veulent pas descendre de la tribune: il faudra qu'ils en tombent."[125] He is like a squirrel, which does nothing but run on the wheel it is on. Therefore, by not contributing anything to the matter and not making any political proposal, the representative is violating the *aptum*, that is, what others expect as appropriate behavior. The same applies to another illustrative example. Imagine that a family doctor has consulted with four specialists, who, instead of discussing the patient's illness, first discuss who should make the first diagnosis, to which the others would then probably be happy to agree. But this does not happen because they debate the value of a painting, a box seat at the opera, exchange rates, politics, the English queen, and Antoine Gibus's hats.[126] On their way out, they briefly confirm the diagnosis of the family doctor, prescribe the patient sixty leeches and a strict diet, before they themselves have a hearty dinner. So here all the expectations are satirically thwarted that one would bring to a conversation with specialists. A final example takes us into the stagecoach. What topics can be expected

---

[120] "l'époque de la véritable puissance des femmes, où elles regnèrent en souveraines." (Mériclet/Guitton 1848, p. 160); see also p. 3–4, 34, 88.

[121] Gay 1846, p. 1.

[122] "Conventions have taken over everything, and, except for a few manners, a few expressions that the distinguished world still reserves for itself, uniformity would be complete." (Gay 1846, p. 21).

[123] Rousseau 1841, p. 14.

[124] Société en commandite 1841, S. 27.

[125] Bernard 1841, S. 24–25.

[126] Huart 1841, S. 37.

during the journey? While the coachman offers an inexhaustible treasure trove of scandalous stories from his city, the conversation of the travelers depends on the time of day. While they are grumpy and sleepy in the morning, they are happy to talk in the evening about philosophical, political, and culinary topics.[127] Such a routine is plausible, but rather natural, since the circumstances of a stagecoach ride determine the conversation more than the expectations of others.

It should now be asked how to deal with the conversation rules. Are these absolutely or only conditionally binding? Do the rules provide for exceptions or freedoms? How clearly visible may the rule compliance be? These questions were of particular interest in the 17th century. The demands for appropriateness appeared to be all-encompassing: "Les bienséances sont d'une étendue infinie."[128] It is enough to observe them in order not to displease anyone and not to expose oneself to ridicule. They therefore belong to the *science du monde*.[129] The rule to pay attention to persons, time and place sets a formal framework within which there is the freedom that fashion determines and temporarily changes. François de Grenaille recognizes the unlimited power of fashion in his book *La mode, ou caractère de la religion, de la vie, de la conversation, de la solitude, des compliments, des habits et du style du temps* (1642), which is able to make the lowest things appear valuable and vice versa.[130] He wants to represent the fashionable appearances of behavior and sciences. He shows the fashionable life, the compliments and the conversations that appear modern, modern clothing and modern apartments that offer more diversity in one century than in many past centuries. This corresponds to fashions in theology, philosophy, jurisprudence, rhetoric and poetry in the sciences. One can ask at this point to what extent the dictate of fashion is comparable to that of discourse.

If fashion also occupies free spaces in the rules of conversation in its own way, then following the rules, regardless of the level, must not be visible. On the contrary, a semblance of unawareness of the rules should be created by signs of naturalness and casualness, making them invisible to us. Affectation and artifice are therefore to be avoided. Instead, everything should look as if it were unintentional and involuntary.[131] Only in this way are the "Loix de la Conversation"[132] or the "regles pour la conversation"[133] applied correctly as laws and rules. But

---

[127] Gourdon 1842, S. 88.

[128] Morvan de Bellegarde 1723 (Neuauflage), Bd. 1, S. 332.

[129] de Callières 1664, S. 285.

[130] "On peut dire encor que la Mode apporte cela dans le môde comme vne de ses proprietez, qu'elle y rend precieuses les choses les plus viles du monde, et rend viles celles qui estoient precieuses." (de Grenaille 1642, S. 132); see also S. 115.

[131] "Affectation, which tarnishes and soils the most beautiful things, and the use everywhere of a certain negligence which hides the artifice, and testifies that one does nothing but as if without thinking about it, and without any kind of pain." (Faret 1630 (1932), p. 51).

[132] Irson 1662 (1973), p. 203.

[133] Mlle de Scudéry 1680, vol. 1, p. 38.

the comparison with the greater freedom that is customary among the provincial population in conversation and manners, but leads to nothing, shows that they are meaningful, justified and valuable: "But what advantage do you get from a freedom that leads to nothing? Is it worth the constraint that contributes to our fortune?"[134]

The rulebook, whether historically conditioned or ahistorical, goes back, as shown at the beginning, to ancient designs in rhetoric, poetics and ethics, which is quite conscious in the 17th century when the totality of social behavior rules is summarized in the concept of *bienséance*, of appropriateness. If you do not think of the totality, but of the individual rules, then the word *bienséance* appears in the plural. Courtin refers in his definition to the first book of Cicero's *De officiis*. He defines *bienséance* as the doctrine of putting everything one does or says in its proper place. You have to orient yourself according to your own age and status, the status of the partner, as well as time and place: It is enough to violate one of these rules to make everything appear rude.[135] René Rapin does not refer to Cicero in his version of *bienséance*, but to Aristotle and Horace: "Il faut enfin que les moeurs soient proportionnées à l'âge, au sexe, à la qualité, aux emplois et à la fortune des personnes: et c'est particulièrement dans le second livre de la *Rhétorique* d'Aristote et dans la *Poétique* d'Horace qu'on peut apprendre ce secret."[136] A brief look should be cast on the texts of the ancient authors to see what their specifications are.

In his Rhetoric, Aristotle defines appropriateness, which corresponds to the French word *bienséance* and the Latin *aptum*, as an appropriate use of passionate expression and ethical awareness, that is, of pathos and ethos, so that one does not speak solemnly about trivialities and casually about important matters.[137] For Aristotle's Poetics, appropriateness means that the characters are to be designed in accordance with expectations, and, for example, a woman is to be brave in a different way than a man.[138] To illustrate the lack of appropriateness, Horace paints the picture of a lovely female head, followed by the neck of a horse, colorful feathers, and a fish tail, to visualize a book where head and foot do not belong to the same shape. In the same way, the language is to match the speaker, and Achilles is not to speak like Medea, a god like a diligent nurse, or a merchant, and a hero adorned with royal gold must not engage in banal conversations in dark taverns.[139] Aristotle also sees appropriateness in ethics, namely as an unchangeable natural law where, for example, in Sophocles' play Antigone buries her brother in

---

[134] Ortigue de Vaumorière 1688, p. 342.

[135] A. de Courtin 1672 (2nd ed.), P. 4 ff.

[136] R. Rapin 1675 (1970), p. 44.

[137] Aristotle 2007, p. 165.

[138] Aristotle 1994, p. 47.

[139] Horace 1984, pp. 5, 11–12, and 19.

defiance of the decreed law of Creon.[140] Starting from appropriateness in poetry, which is manifested, for example, in the fact that a character is to act and speak in accordance with his role, the Roman Cicero arrives at appropriateness in ethics and aesthetics. Decency in action manifests itself in moderation and restraint. Just as the beauty of a body is addressed to the eye through the appropriate arrangement of the limbs, "so this appropriateness, which manifests itself in behavior, evokes the approval of those with whom one lives, through the order, constancy, and observance of measure in all expressions and actions."[141]

If the place of appropriateness, of *bienséance* and of *aptum,* that is to say, not only in conversation and in poetry, but also in ethics and aesthetics, is to be found, then it suggests that conversations are also to be evaluated with ethical and aesthetic criteria. We already encountered the ethical dimension at the beginning, when Aristotle placed the virtue of *Eutrapelia* as the ability to converse next to other virtues and Gregor saw garrulousness and gossip as sins in the *Ilias.*[142] The ideal of a natural connection between the beautiful and the good, that is, between the aesthetic and the ethical, in man was introduced by Homer in the *Ilias.*[143] In our context, the connection with aesthetics is already shown in the principle of appropriateness, which in conversation as in poetry helps to avoid the ugly. It is further shown in the conversation principle of pleasure and in the paradigm of the woman, whose speech is supported by her natural beauty.

Fashion takes a special place, regardless of whether it changes the historically determined conversation rules or the freedom it leaves. It shows paradigmatically the change that is also taking place in customs and morality, for example, the medieval understanding of garrulousness as a sin has neither been preserved in the 17th nor in the 19th century. Finally, a summary of the historically shaped conversation forms should be given before more constant elements are mentioned.

Dilthey's world view or Schelers's world view served as well as the Foucauldian discourse to mark the historical imprints, such as the great importance that was attributed to conversation in the 17th century, where pleasure and enjoyment were basic principles. The latter was achieved through a superficial knowledge of all possible topics, through flexibility and by avoiding pedantry. It was entertaining to give the other the opportunity to be witty, to consider guests from the provinces as uncouth and to use mockery deliberately. If in the 17th century it was about pleasing others in conversation, which was considered a pleasure, more emphasis was placed on the contents of a conversation in the 18th century, which should instruct and benefit. Nowadays, the orientation of the conversation to benefit and efficiency, the definition of the pedant as a semi-educated person, the primacy of the citizen over the scholar, the loss of the dominance of the woman

---

[140] Aristotle 2007, p. 68.
[141] Cicero 1999, p. 87.
[142] Homer, Iliad, XXIV, p. 52.
[143] Plato, Gorgias, 470e 9 ff.

and the criticism of politeness as dishonesty are characteristic. In France, finally, in the 19th century, the popular place of conversation was no longer the salon, but the coffee house and the focus was on material interests and duty fulfillment. Hosting became a civic duty, the old carelessness was replaced by industry and material problems, conversation was replaced by card games.

In addition to such historical imprints, there are more general norms that seem to be valid timelessly. So the much-talked-about man of the 17th century can be found again in the *blagueur* of the 19th century, who is just as unpopular as those who only talk about themselves or make jokes at the wrong time. Also the circumstances of a carriage ride probably gave rise to the 17th century to speak little in the morning and more in the evening. This shows that in addition to the discursively determined, historically changing conversation elements, there are also conversation forms that could be described as ahistorically constant. The always recurring warnings not to talk about oneself, to pay attention to social hierarchies, to take into account the character traits of the conversation partners, to avoid unpleasant conversation partners, to take into account the situation when telling tragic and happy events or news, show constancy. Much-talked-about men were as unpopular in the 17th century as one or two centuries later. But where is the exact boundary between constant conversation elements and those that are determined by fashions or discourses? A "histoire de la Conversation", as Guez de Balzac 1665 wishes, where one can read how Scipio and Lailius or Atticus and Cicero conversed, could provide more insight.[144]

References

Ambrosius von Mailand: De officiis ministrorum, J. E. Niederhuber (Hg.). Kempten: Kösel 1917.
Aristoteles: Poetik, Manfred Fuhrmann (Hg.). Stuttgart: Reclam 1994.
Aristoteles: Nikomachische Ethik, Günther Bien (Hg.). Hamburg: Meiner 1995.
Aristoteles, Rhetorik, Gernot Krapinger (hg.), Stuttgart, Reclam, 2007
Aesop, Fabeln, Thomas Voskuhl (hg. und übers.), Stuttgart, Reclam 2005
Aubert, F. J. P. : Études sur l'éducation. Paris : 1792.
Bary, René : Actions publiques sur la rhétorique françoise. Paris : 1658.
Bary, René : La fine philosophie, accommodée à l'intelligence des dames. Paris : 1660.
Bary, René : L'esprit de la cour ou les conversations galantes. Paris : 1662.
Bary, René : Journal de conversation, où les plus belles matières sont agitées de part et d'autre. Paris : 1673.
Batteux, Charles : Principes de la littérature, Bd. I. Paris : 1774^5.
Benedikt von Nursia: Die Benediktsregel, G. Holzherr (Hg.). Freiburg: Paulusverlag 2007.
Bernard, Pierre : Physiologie du député. Paris : 1841.
Biot, Jean-Baptiste : Essai sur l'histoire générale des sciences pendant la Révolution Française. Paris : 1803.
Bordelon, Laurent : La belle éducation. Lyon/Paris : 1694^2.
Boyer, Jean Baptiste de, Marquis d'Argens : Critique du siècle ou lettres sur divers sujets par l'auteur des 'Lettres Juives', Neue Aufl. Bd. 1. La Haye : 1755.

---

[144] Guez de Balzac 1971, p. 435.

Buffier, Claude : Cours des sciences sur les principes nouveaux et simples pour former le langage, l'esprit et le coeur, dans l'usage ordinaire de la vie. Paris : 1732.
Callières, Jacques de : La fortune des gens de qualité. Paris : 1664.
Calvel, Étienne : Encyclopédie littéraire, t. 1. Paris : 1772.
Chalesme, L'homme de qualité, ou les moyens de vivre en homme de bien et en homme du monde. Amsterdam : 1671.
Chrysostomus, Johannes: Homiliae in Matthaeum, in: J.-P. Migne (ed.): Patrologiae cursus, t. 57. Paris: Migne 1862.
Cicero: De officiis. Vom pflichtgemäßen Handeln, Heinz Gunermann (ed.). Stutgart: Reclam 1999.
Clement, Elis.-Marie : Dialogue de la princesse sçavante et de la dame de famille, contenant l'art d'élever les jeunes dames dans une belle et noble éducation. Paris : 1664.
Courtin, Ant. de : Nouveau traité de la civilité qui se pratique en France parmi les honnestes gens. Paris : 1672[2] (Paris 1671).
Courtin, Ant. de : Traité de la paresse, ou l'Art de bien employer le temps en forme d'entretiens. Paris : 1673.
Dampmartin, Anne-Henri Cabet de : Essai de littérature, à l'usage des dames, t. 1. Amsterdam : 1794.
Dilthey, Wilhelm: Das geschichtliche Bewußtsein und die Weltanschauungen, in: Ges. Schr. 8. Göttingen : Vandenhoeck 1991.
Du Preaux, Abbé: Le chrétien parfait honnête homme, ou l'art d'allier la piété avec la politesse, et les autres devoirs de la vie civile, 2 t. Paris: 1750.
Du Refuge, Eustache : Traité de la Cour, ou Instruction des Courtisans. Paris : 1618.
Duchesne, Jean Baptiste : La science de la jeune noblesse, 2 t. Paris : 1729.
Faret, Nicolas : L'art de plaire à la court (1630), M. Magendie (ed.). Madrid/Paris/Buenos-Aires : 1932 (Paris 1636).
Ferlet : Discours sur le bien et le mal que le commerce des femmes a fait à la littérature. Nancy : 1772.
Foucault, Michel: Dispositive der Macht. Über Sexualität, Wissen und Wahrheit. Berlin: Merve 1978.
Foucault, Michel: Archäologie des Wissens. Frankfurt a.M.: 1981.
Fourcroy, Antoine François de : Discours sur l'état actuel des sciences et des arts dans la République Française. Lycée des arts 7.4.1793.
Gay, Sophie : Salons célèbres. Bruxelles : Meline 1837.
Gay, Sophie : Physiologie du ridicule. Paris : 1864 (1833[1]).
Gourdon, Edouard : Physiologie des diligences et des grandes routes. Paris : 1842.
Goussault, Abbé : Le portrait d'un honneste homme. Paris : 1692.
Goussault, Abbé : Le portrait d'une femme honneste, raisonnable et véritablement chrétienne. Paris : 1694.
Gregor, Liber regulae postoralis: https://bkv.unifr.ch/de/works/152/versions/171
Grenaille, Fr. de : L'honneste fille, 3 Bde. Paris 1639–40.
Grenaille, Fr. de : La mode, ou caractère de la religion, de la vie, de la conversation, de la solitude, des compliments, des habits et du style du temps. Paris : 1642.
Grenaille, Fr. de : L'honneste Garçon ou l'Art de bien élever la noblesse à la vertu, aux sciences et à tous les exercices convenables à sa condition. Paris : 1642 A.
Guez de Balzac, J.-L. : Œuvres, Val. Conrart (ed.), 2 t. Genf : 1971 (Paris 1665).
Guitton, Antoine (Pseudonyme: A. G. Mériclet) : Physiologie de l'esprit. Paris 1848.
Horaz : Ars Poetica, Eckhart Schäfer (ed.). Stuttgart : Reclam 1984.
Huart, Louis : Physiologie du médecin. Paris : 1841.
Irson, Claude : Nouvelle Méthode pour apprendre facilement les principes et la pureté de la langue françoise. Paris : 1656.
Irson, Claude : Nouvelle Méthode pour apprendre facilement les principes et la pureté de la langue françoise. Genf : 1973 (Paris 1662).

La Bruyère : Œuvres complètes, Julien Benda (ed.). Paris : 1951 (Paris 1694[8]).
La Chapelle, Jean Baptiste de : L'art de communiquer ses idées, enrichi de notes historiques et philosophiques. London/Paris : 1763[3].
La Chetardie, Trotti de : Instruction pour un jeune seigneur, ou l'idée d'un galant-homme. Paris : 1700, Privilège : 1684.
La Rochefoucauld : Œuvres complètes, L. Martin-Chauffier (ed.). Paris : 1964.
Lambert, Anne-Thérèse de Marguenat de Courcelles de : Lettres sur la véritable éducation. Amsterdam : 1729.
Lambert, Anne-Thérèse de Marguenat de Courcelles de : Avis d'une mère à son fils et à sa fille, in: Œuvres, t. 2. Paris : 1748.
Mallet, Edme : Essai sur les bienséances oratoires, 2 t. Amsterdam/Leipzig : 1753.
Méré, chevalier de : De la vraie honnesteté (S. 1–95), De l'éloquence et de l'entretien (S. 96–146), De la délicatesse dans les choses et dans l'expression (S. 147–193), Dissertation sur la Tragédie (S. 337–356), in: Œuvres posthumes. Paris : 1700.
Méré, chevalier de : t. 1: Les conversations (1668/69). Discours de la justesse (1671), t. 2: Les Discours. Des Agrémens (1676). De l'Esprit (1677). De la Conversation (1677), t. 3: Les Aventures de Renaud et d'Armide (1678). Œuvres posthumes (1700), in: Charles-H. Boudhors (ed.) : Œuvres complètes. Paris : F. Roches 1930.
Moncrif, Françoise Augustin de : Essais sur la nécessité et sur les moyens de plaire. Paris : 1738.
Monnier, Bourgois : Physiologie du bourgeois. Paris : 1841.
Morvan de Bellegarde : Refléxion sur ce qui peut plaire ou déplaire dans le commerce du monde. Paris : 1688.
Morvan de Bellegarde : Les règles de la vie civile avec des traits d'histoire pour former l'esprit d'un jeune prince. Paris : 1693.
Morvan de Bellegarde : Conduite pour se taire et pour parler, principalement en matière de religion. Paris : 1696 B.
Morvan de Bellegarde : Modèles de conversation pour les personnes polies. Paris : 1697.
Morvan de Bellegarde : Réflexions sur le ridicule et sur les moyens de l'éviter, où sont représentez les mœurs et les différens caractères des personnes de ce siècle. Paris : 1696 A.
Morvan de Bellegarde; Œuvres diverses: t. 1: Les Réflexions sur le ridicule, et sur les moyens de l'éviter (1696), t. 2: Les Réflexions sur la politesse des mœurs (1698), t. 3: Les modèles de conversation pour les personnes polies (1697), t. 4: Les règles de la vie civile, avec les traits d'histoire pour former l'esprit d'un jeune prince (1693). Paris : 1723 (Neuauflagen).
Ortigue de Vaumorière, P. de : L'art de plaire dans la conversation. Paris : 1688.
Ortigue de Vaumorière, P. de : L'art de plaire dans la conversation. Paris : 1701[4].
Platon: Phaidros, Wolfgang Buchwald (ed.). München: Tusculum 1964.
Platon: Der Sophist, Reiner Wiehl (ed.). Hamburg: Meiner 1967.
Preaux, Abbé Du : Le chrétien parfait honnête homme, ou l'art d'allier la piété avec la politesse, et les autres devoirs de la vie civile, 2 t. Paris: 1750.
Rapin, René : Les réflexions sur la poétique de ce temps et sur les ouvrages des poètes anciens et modernes (1675), E. T. Dubois (ed.). Genf : 1970.
Reichardt, Rolf und Annette Höfer: Honnête homme, Honnêteté, Honnêtes gens, in: R. Reichardt und E. Schmitt: Handbuch politisch sozialer Grundbegriffe in Frankreich 1680–1820, VII. München: 1986.
Rousseau, Charles-Louis : Essai sur l'éducation et l'existence civile et politique des femmes. Paris : 1790.
Rousseau, James : Physiologie de la portière. Paris : 1841
Sablé, Mme de : Les maximes, G. Toso Rodinis (ed.). Padua : 1971 (1678).
Scheler, Max: Schriften zur Soziologie und Weltanschauungslehre. Gesamtvorrede (1922), in: Gesammelte Werke 6. Bern: Francke 1963.
Scudéry, Mlle de : Conversations sur de divers sujets, 2 t. Paris : 1680.
Société en commandite : Physiologie du blagueur. Paris : 1841.

Thomas von Aquin: Summa theologica, t. 20: Tugenden des Gemeinschaftslebens, übers. und komm. von Dominikanern und Benediktinern Deutschlands und Österreichs. München/Heidelberg: Kerle 1943.

Thomas von Aquin: Summa theologica, t. 22: Maßhaltung 2. Teil, transl. and comm. by the dominicans and benedictines of Germany and Austria. Graz/Wien/Köln: Styria 1993.

The Sweetness of Conversation According to Behavior Treatises (Late 17th—Early 18th Centuries)

Christophe Losfeld

Abstract

Maints auteurs des XVIIème et XVIIIème siècles, à l'horizon de l'effort qu'ils prodiguent pour améliorer les mœurs, formulent dans les traités de comportement des règles minutieuses et complexes destinées à régir la conversation. Ces règles, dont on peut faire découler les limites de ce qu'il est licite d'exprimer, sont notoirement indissociables de l'honnêteté. Qu'elles aient pu faire l'unanimité tient aussi à ce qu'elles émanent d'une éthique chrétienne de la douceur, une notion constituant comme le point d'articulation des différentes qualités d'une bonne conversation.

Keywords

Civilisation des mœurs · éthique chrétienne

1 Introduction

Starting in the sixteenth century, the awareness that it was necessary to rethink human relationships in order to improve life on earth led to a vast movement of reflection on the meaning and conditions of life in society and the means of improving it by perfecting behavior and substituting gentleness for the brutality that characterized it previously.

C. Losfeld (✉)
Martin-Luther-Universität Halle-Wittenberg, Halle, Germany
e-mail: christophe.losfeld@romanistik.uni-halle.de

The innumerable French treatises published at that time were, of course, based on a certain number of founding texts written during both classical antiquity and patristic times as well as during the Italian and Spanish Renaissance.[1] Drawing inspiration from this triple tradition, they formulated a system of rules governing conversation and determining the limits of what one is allowed to say, a rigorous and particularly stable system that would last at least until the French Revolution—which does not foreshadow debates on the meaning of this system. These rules have been well known since the groundbreaking work of Christoph Strosetzki and Alain Montandon[2], who have clearly shown the links they had with honesty and absolutist society, so that any remark about the codes of good conversation formulated during what is known as "the age of conversation" can only be an afterthought.

The latter expression obviously refers to the masterful picture painted by B. Craveri[3] of the trade of elites from the reign of Louis XIII to the Revolution, a picture that makes it possible to perceive, through anecdotes or misadventures[4] such as Voiture's in the blue room, what was permitted or not permitted to be said. In fact, the apparent freedom of conversation characteristic, for example, of salons does not mean that everything could be said there. And perhaps this conversation was also governed by this code with very distant origins, of which the treatises on behavior published between the end of the seventeenth and eighteenth centuries are an echo.

2 The Theological Horizon of Gentleness

Martin de Braga, in his *Formula vitae honestae*[5] demanded thus as early as the 6th century: "Be kind to all, bland to no one, familiar to few, equal to all", a formula which eleven centuries later Bordelon takes up again, in *La Bonne éducation*, in the following variant: "Be familiar with few in conversation, sweet to all, and harsh to no one. Be familiar with few, sweet to all, harsh to no one."[6]

Even two centuries before Martin de Braga, one finds a similar precept in Saint Ambrose of Milan who invites us to be "mild, gentle, moderate" (mitis, mansuetus, modestus). And to add:

> If someone watches over all this, he becomes mild, gentle, moderate. For by watching over his mouth and restraining his tongue, and by not speaking before he questions, weighs and examines his own words to see if he should say this, if he should say it against

---

[1] See, for example, D'Amico 2001 and Hübner 2012.
[2] Strosetzki 1984, pp. 186–210 and 2013, pp. 246–286 and Montandon 1995, 2004 (these references are by no means exhaustive).
[3] Craveri 2002.
[4] Ibid., pp. 102–205.
[5] Braca 1950, p. 172.
[6] Bordelon 1693, p. 240.

that one, if now is the time for this speech, this man assuredly practices moderation, calm and patience, so that he does not break out into speech in indignation and anger, that he does not reveal in his words any indication of passion, that he does not reveal in his speech the flames of ardent desire and the presence in his discourse of the goads of anger; he finally avoids that the speech which should make inner riches manifest, should reveal and display some fault in character[7]

It goes without saying, and this has been shown sufficiently, that Ambrose is largely inspired by Cicero's 37th chapter of the first book of *De Officiis*. But while Cicero makes a distinction here between "sustained discourse" and "conversation", noting that for the latter there is no rule[8]—it is precisely this that he undertakes to remedy —, Ambrose subsumes this difference:

the question of discourse is divided into two genres: familiar conversation and exposition, in particular the examination of faith and justice. In both genres, one must take care that no passion be aroused, and that the discourse be conducted in a gentle and peaceful manner (mitis et placidus), full of benevolence and agreeableness, without any outrage.[9]

In addition, the mere repetition of Cicero's terms by Saint Ambrose does not mean semantic identity, inasmuch as the words he uses are loaded with a connotation proper to Judeo-Christian theology which decisively imprints theories of behavior, in particular because of the anthropological conception, proper to Christianity, of a human nature corrupted by the Fall.

This Christian horizon can, of course, go so far as to justify the prohibition of conversation: Since the original sin, human language is also corrupted and it might be better to be silent, a position sometimes defended, for example, by the Christian rigorist Lasne d'Aiguebelles[10], who, referring to both Saint Jacques and Saint

---

[7] Saint Ambrose 2007, p. 102. Livre I, Chaps. and ("If someone watches over all this, he becomes mild, gentle, moderate. For by watching over his mouth and restraining his tongue, and by not speaking before he questions, and examines and weighs his own words to see if he should say this, if he should say it against that one, if now is the time for this speech: this man assuredly practices moderation, calm and patience, so that he does not break out into speech in indignation and anger, that he does not reveal in his words any indication of passion, that he does not reveal in his speech the flames of ardent desire and the presence in his discourse of the goads of anger; he finally avoids that the speech which should make inner riches manifest, should reveal and display some fault in character")

[8] Cicero 1967, p. 160: "The word, whose importance is capital, has two uses: it serves for oratorical struggles and for conversation. […] The rules of the art of oratory apply to the first use of the word, there are none for conversation" (Cicero 2019, p. 114: "And since the power of speech is great, and it is twofold, one of contention, the other of conversation […] The precepts of the rhetoricians are for the former, there are none for the latter.").

[9] Saint Ambrose 2007, p. 144. Livre I, Chap 22, 99 ("The discourse is divided into two genres, into familiar conversation and into a treatise, a disputation on faith and justice. In both, let there be no disturbance: but let the discourse be conducted as mitis et placidus, and full of benevolence and grace, without any contumelia").

[10] For pragmatic reasons and because of the conscience he has of the weakness of man, he will nevertheless formulate many recommendations for conversation.

Paul, affirms "that he who does not sin by the tongue is a perfect man" and wants "the main conversation of a Christian to be in heaven."[11] The majority of theorists, however, do not privilege either the absence of relations or solitude, judging them too difficult for most, especially since in their eyes humans, because of the fundamental corruption and to compensate for it in part, are obliged to trade with each other. And this trade is aimed, *mutatis mutandis,* if not to restore, at least to simulate at first the interhuman relations as they existed before the Fall.[12] Indeed, the communication that conversation opens, by forcing humans to overcome the selfishness that the original sin has caused, allows it to strengthen social ties. As de Chalesmes writes:

> Everyone must agree that it is Conversation that contributes the most to making men sociable, & that it is she who does the greatest trade of life; so that one can say that we could not take too much care to make our conversation agreeable & useful.[13]

This idea that conversation must be accompanied by an agreement is also a continuation of the anthropological conceptions of the time. The corruption caused by the Fall led to giving of greater weight to sensitivity. And "if men are nose for Society [and if] one can say that it is the maintenance that makes their most ordinary link", as the Abbé de Bellegarde says, he is right to add that "[n]othing is more important for the trade of life than to please in Conversation".[14] This precept being valid for all interlocutors, it goes without saying that the conversation cannot be considered successful unless the pleasure it provides is reciprocal. And its purpose is to "obtain a mutual satisfaction, by mutually communicating our thoughts".[15]

It follows from the various rules governing the conversation, and which are based on several concepts: for Lasnes d'Aiguebelles, "[s]oftness, circumspection, ease, modesty, simplicity, precision & reticence are the main laws of conversation"[16]; According to Chicaneau de Neuville, "[t]he spirit of conversation consists mainly in attention, softness, cheerfulness & vivacity"[17]; According to Paradis de Moncrif, "[c] 'is in conversation that the spirit of softness has more frequent occasions to appear".[18] And the manuals of behavior quote personalities who perfectly

---

[11] Lasne d'Aiguebelles 1776, p. 220 (see Jc 3:2 and Ph 3,20).

[12] Despite a cultural horizon marked by a deep religious pessimism, we can guess the attitude of many authors who are voluntarists for whom the control of passions can contribute to overcome them: "By taking care not to fall into the defects that dominate us, we can overcome them" (Morvan de Bellegarde 1710, p. 30).

[13] Chalesmes 1671, p. 176.

[14] Morvan de Bellegarde 1743, p. 5.

[15] Buffier 1726, p. 130.

[16] Lasne d'Aiguebelles 1776 p. 217.

[17] Chicaneau de Neuville 1756, pp. 56–57.

[18] Paradis de Moncrif 1738, p. 51.

embodied this ideal, like François de Sales who "attracted more people by the sweetness of his conversations, than by the depth of his doctrine". He illustrated by his sweetness "that this virtue spreads a certain sweetness in the conversation, & that it is by her that one becomes graceful & agreeable".[19] And the Abbé Brémond, two centuries later, was quite right to say that "[w] hen one wants to summarize in a word the originality of Saint François de Sales, one does not know how to exclaim: "Sweetness! always sweetness!"[20]

In fact, the term "softness" can cover, as Bernard Spicq showed in a brilliant study[21], four terms used in the Septuagint. The first (ἠπιότης) refers to a softness reminiscent of courtesy and politeness. That it should not be reduced to a form of superficiality is obvious, if one thinks that this softness was that of Saint Paul in the exercise of his ministry, on the one hand, and that it is also related to the other forms of softness. This is how the second term (Πραὖτης) translates the softness of the "poor", this servant of God who abandons himself to his Providence, this person humble and affable in his speech, modest in his dress, refusing both indiscreet praise and anger. This softness, too, is a Christian virtue of which Saint Paul sees the origin in the Holy Spirit. Practicing it is also a way of imitating the master full of humility that was Christ. The third (Χρηστότης), which describes benevolence and beneficence, first refers to a divine quality applied to superiors. The softness that these latter must show is also a virtue that comes from the imitation of Jesus Christ and the condition for men to open themselves to the divine message. The last term, finally (ἐπιείκεια), refers to Clemency and Moderation, two characters—originally divine—which are extended to the Powerful to indicate the goodness that they testify to in the exercise of their power, meaning as well moderation and calm even in suffering (two qualities that Jesus showed during his Passion) as the will of reconciliation.

And even if some authors of behavior manuals use other terms that could translate the words used by the Septuagint, it is fundamentally to this ideal of softness[22] that all the precepts formulated in the 17th and 18th centuries formulate with regard to conversation can be related. External affability, beneficence and benignity, clemency and moderation, patience and humility, here, indeed, is all that softness contains. Girard de Villethierry, in *The Foreign Christian on Earth*, summarizes it well when he writes:

---

[19] Joly 1771, pp. 31–32. On the referral to Saint François de Sales, see also Claville 1734, p. 112, Destutt de Tracy 1770, p. 104 who gives him as an example of "the spirit of softness & affability "or Blanchard 1782, p. 178.

[20] Brémond 1923, p. 108.

[21] Spicq 1947 (see also Mennessier 1957).

[22] The importance of softness for behavior theory in the 17th and 18th centuries, of course, has already attracted the attention of researchers (see, for example, Huchon 2003, Jamain 2011, Mélouchan 2003 and 2006) but neither its biblical anchoring, nor its central position in the qualities of a good conversation have been systematically highlighted.

> He is truly gentle, say the holy Fathers, who adapts himself in all things to the temper of his neighbor; who bears the weaknesses and imperfections; who gives him no occasion to be angry, and who is not easily so himself; who willingly suppresses his own thoughts to preserve a holy union with his brethren; who is always ready to endure from them, who would not willingly grieve them in the least thing; who hears without being troubled, all the calumnies that are published against him; who, for the sake of peace, willingly renounces his own interests; who does not dispute for present goods; who sees himself dispossessed without impatience; who suffers with joy the greatest evils, and the most horrible persecutions. In a word, what can be called gentle and peaceable.[23]

And Chicaneau de Neuville, on the other hand

> gentleness is a fund of complacency that makes us defer to the will of others; it is a quality of temperament, which education and reflection strengthen. It makes us attentive and considerate in the society; it makes us conceal the offenses; it drives out the spirit of contradiction and the satirical spirit; it gives us this affectionate tone, this tone of feeling, which reconciles those who live with us; it inspires us with benevolence, gratitude and love of humanity.[24]

3 Gentleness and Affability

This first trait of sweetness is intended to govern the exterior of behavior. In the *New Treatise on Civility Practiced in France Among Gentlemen* (Paris 1671), a text that made its mark[25], Antoine de Courtin asserted that, in order to avoid startling his interlocutors, it is inadvisable to interrupt or to use a language that someone in the audience would not understand very well.[26] Similarly, Le Noble indicates how important it is to keep the voice "always in its natural state", that is, in accordance with the image one has of a natural voice, and therefore free of a nasal tone or babbling[27], two defects that must be corrected imperatively. It is also necessary to avoid that, by look or gesture, the interlocutor feels assaulted, which happens when someone gesticulates in the Italian manner[28], to ban all that, during conversations, recalls the presence of the body in its natural state[29] and to forbid any bodily contact[30], which leads to precepts that, as the famous domestication of bodies related to the process of civilization progressed, gradually disappeared and can now make us smile:

---

[23] Villethierry 1725, pp. 82–83.

[24] Chicaneau de Neuville 1756, p. 82.

[25] On the editorial history of this text, see Losfeld 2011, pp. 105–109.

[26] Courtin 1998, p. 65.

[27] Le Noble 1709, p. 121.

[28] Ibid., p. 134.

[29] See Courtin 1671, p. 45: "It is also very indecent in the company of ladies […] to take off his wig, or his justaucorps, to cut his nails, to gnaw them with his teeth, or to clean them, to scratch somewhere" (cited here from the 1679 edition, pp. 38, 39).

[30] See Ibid., 1672 edition, p. 27: "It is also a very great rudeness to pull by the cloak or by the dress a qualified person to whom you want to talk." Cited here from the 1679 edition, p. 24.

"It is also a very great rudeness to pull by the cloak or by the dress a qualified person to whom you want to talk" or "it is ridiculous when talking to a man, to take and pull his buttons, his tassels, his belt, his cloak, or to punch him in the stomach."[31]

It would not be less annoying to the interlocutors to impose their bad mood on them than to be "master of their mood"[32] and happy[33] (in return, the criticism of those who are sad in society and show "a dark & melancholy mind"[34] or only talk about themselves.[35] A repellent air or brusque words would prevent, indeed, that "the minds maintain between them a sort of union very useful to society for which men are made"[36]. The call not to shock the interlocutor by avoiding too brusque manners, too great physical proximity or too loud a voice or too insistent looks therefore directly results from gentleness, just as the injunction to be measured and moderate in any conversation.

4   Gentleness and Humility

But in the case of the call to be measured and moderate, gentleness is to be understood as humility, which implies the awareness of one's own limits, the place that has been assigned to each one in this world and the ability, therefore, to deliberately take a back seat.

Instead of hogging the conversation, everyone in a conversation should listen to their interlocutor attentively[37], as La Rochefoucauld already asserted in his 139th maxim[38] which Chicaneau de Neuville takes literally:

> One of the things that makes it so that one finds so few people who appear reasonable and likable in conversation is that there are almost no people who think more about what they want to say than about responding precisely to what is being said to them. The most skillful and the most accommodating are content to show only an attentive expression, at the

---

[31] See Ibid., 1672 edition, p. 27, 1671 edition, pp. 63–64. Cited here from the 1679 edition, p. 54.

[32] Morvan de Bellegarde 1743 p. 291. See also Callières 1665, p. 30.

[33] Caraccioli 1767, p. 338: "gaiety is the essence of conversation; I mean a moderate gaiety which does not consist in bursts of laughter, but in a smiling face; but in light talk, & sometimes banter".

[34] Borderlon 1692, p. 140. This precept can of course be varied according to the ranks of the people constituting the audience. The same individual can therefore be "a burden to his superiors, troublesome to his equals, unbearable to his inferiors; it makes conversation bitter, takes away its sweetness, & makes it quite unenjoyable" (p. 140).

[35] See Callières 1665, p. 30, Borderlon 1692, pp. 138–139, 139 Boutauld 1728, p. 191. Madame de Puisieux will give a sociological color to this general precept by inviting the powerful in particular not to talk about their ancestors in conversation because we know the great families of France quite well, so that the well-born people do not need to be shown (Puisieux 1750, p. 106).

[36] Callières 1695, p. 6.

[37] Borderlon 1692, p. 4.

[38] La Rochefoucauld 1976, p. 66.

same time that one sees in their eyes and in their minds a wandering for what is being said to them, and a haste to return to what they want to say; instead of considering that it is a bad way to please others or to persuade them, to seek so hard to please oneself, and that listening well and responding well is one of the greatest perfections that one can have in conversation.[39]

4.1 The Refusal of Contradiction

One of the adjacent precepts, based on the sweetness perceived as humility[40], is to avoid contradicting one's interlocutor. This does not mean that it is forbidden, in principle, to contradict, if the defense of a higher truth requires it. In the latter case, it is sometimes necessary to call into question the opinion of one's interlocutor if he is wrong, but, here again, one must nevertheless beware of any abuse and try at all costs to make him change his mind, if he does not want to, because it is better, as Buffier says, to let someone remain in error than to disturb the harmony of civil society[41]. And Lasnes d'Aiguebelles gives the following advice: "Do not argue stubbornly; give in modestly when you will not be able to persuade."[42]

What the authors of the manuals of behavior criticize without shame, is much more the spirit of contradiction:

> Do not be too opinionated to contradict in conversation, like those who, to show off their wit, or out of emulation, or out of whim, argue about everything without exception. It is an impertinence, a criminal vanity, & a rudeness of mind, which can attract the aversion of all to a man, & a thousand quarrels."[43]

If everyone complies with this precept and therefore ceases to consider conversation as "a fencing match"[44], everyone will be pleased with a conversation.[45]

---

[39] Chicaneau de Neuville 1756, p. 57. See also Lasnes d'Aiguebelles 1776, p. 217: It is necessary above all to know how to listen "if there is politeness in maintaining a conversation with the people with whom one is, there is even more in letting them speak in preference". There is obviously a link between the refusal of a monopoly on speech and the criticism of pedantry (see below), as attested by this remark by Chalesmes 1671, pp. 178–179: "however learned one might be, I do not know if one would be very good at demonstrating the eagerness to show off all one's learning. On the contrary, one must give the rest of the company the time to express their feelings".

[40] Lasnes d'Aiguebelles 1776, p. 217.

[41] Buffier 1726, p. 94.

[42] Lasnes d'Aiguebelles 1776, p. 218.

[43] Marmet de Valcroissant 1662, p. 213. See also Chalesmes 1671, p. 202, Paradis de Moncrif 1738, p. 62 Puisieux 1750, p. 42.

[44] Caraccioli 1767, p. 95.

[45] Boureau-Deslandes 1715: "The complacency that others have in listening to us talk must be paid for by reciprocal complacency: at least we must please them by an attentive look & studied applause"; Steele 1716, p. 146: "Everyone likes to be heard in turn & expects applause as much as anyone else. The one who wants to please in conversation must try to please everyone."

4.2 The Problem of Mockery

Just as the spirit of contradiction rejects the spirit of conversation by going against the respect of humility, mockery is in principle an offense against the rules of conversation. It implies, in fact, that the mocker sets himself up as superior, thereby ignoring the modesty that should arise from the awareness of his own imperfection.

This imperfection and the place occupied by passions in human nature after the Fall make mockery in conversation all too often inevitable.[46] Chalesmes, for example, in the tradition of Stefano Guazzo, welcomes its interest while warning against its excesses:

> It is certain that nothing animates conversation so much as mockery, & provided that it is honest & agreeable, far from being banned from conversation, one can say that it is a seasoning that prevents a discourse from becoming flat & languid. There are authors who have written that it made up the main part of what the ancient Romans called Urbanity, saying that this Urbanity, as the word expresses in some way, is proper to the air of action & speech of city-dwellers, who are so different, in all things, from people raised in the countryside, & who are called rustics for this reason. Others have believed that mockery is this Attic salt so renowned in the writings of both ancient & modern authors, & that it produces in conversation the same effect as ordinary salt in a ragout. So that we can say that too much mockery displeases the mind & pricks it, as too salty meat displeases the taste & hurts it. Mockery must therefore be fine & delicate, & one must use it rather to revive a conversation that is beginning to fall, than to offend the people who make up the assembly.[47]

This quote suggests that mockery is radically different from slander, "this vice so common in the world, & even in those who appear the most regular"[48], a vice not only stemming from a sin of pride, but also opposing the goal that conversation seeks: to strengthen ties between members of society. In and of itself, mockery can be licit to the extent that it participates in a desire to prune customs and proves to be "a clever & delicate wit, proper to make someone perceive subtly that one notices imperfections in them, that one does not want to reprove them directly"[49]. But the line is surely thin between such mockeries—which Boutauld

---

[46] Le Noble 1707, p. 163 "man, by his sin having made reason a slave to his senses, has allowed himself to be carried away by the torrent of his passions, & the excess of passion has led him into ridicule."

[47] Chalesmes 1671 De la Raillerie 180–182; Le Noble 1707, p. 160 "the compliment is […] the soul of affability" and mockery is its opposite.

[48] Lasnes d'Aiguebelles 1776, p. 222: "Love the truth, flee exaggeration. By speaking little, one can more easily be sincere & true, without offending anyone. Avoid above all, avoid slander."

[49] Crousaz 1722, p. 74.

called "modest & honest"[50]—and those which offend, such that, quite often, as Crousaz notes, "the spirit of mockery does not easily go hand in hand with that of politeness, which is undoubtedly one of the most necessary virtues in the business of life"[51]. And Marmet de Valcroissant also insisted on the ambiguity of mockery:

> It is said that mockery is the salt of conversation; but it is dangerous if it is stubborn, & if it goes too far. Do not engage in it, & use it only with your closest friends, if you are sure they understand it.[52]

Like Chalesmes, Marmet de Valcroissant therefore tolerates it insofar as it does not threaten the coherence of the group of peers in which conversation unfolds.

And this position will still hold in the last third of the eighteenth century: According to an anonymous writing, in conversation between equals banter is allowed, "which is nothing other than a playful and witty speech, which expresses something pleasant, without offending anyone, and without harming decency."[53] Under these conditions, indeed, it does not violate the laws of gentleness, because its good use presupposes a keen awareness of the rank and quality of the persons involved in the conversation and therefore a form of humility.

4.3 On the Necessity of Adapting to Circumstances

The conversation thus meets the same requirements as civility as a whole, which Antoine de Courtin defines as "the modesty & honesty that everyone must maintain according to their condition"[54] or as the "science that teaches us how to place what we have to do or say in its rightful place"[55]. In fact, "speaking with propriety

---

[50] Boutauld 1728, p. 194.

[51] Crousaz 1722, p. 68.

[52] Marmet de Valcroissant 1662, p. 246.

[53] Anonymous 1766, pp. 156 et seq. This banter "which should make the pleasure of conversation" is not the one that prevails generally in the world. Of course, one could here question the status of anonymity, which in the eighteenth century often served to protect the author of illicit thoughts. In the case of the text mentioned here, anonymity, far from having this meaning or serving to conceal plagiarism, is explained by the fact that the work is not original, simply repeating the precepts generally accepted on conversation, and which Dareau will repeat twenty years later by inscribing them, however, in a perspective Properly legal: "Those who enjoy sowing words in the public, of these words that we know can not spread without harming the person who is the subject, are therefore, strictly speaking, of these pests of society that everyone has in horror, & Justice can not spare. But speaking of rumors, let's make some grace to these stories that entertain the circles & the meals. These kinds of speeches, in the form of conversation, can hardly give rise to repair, unless they have taken place exactly with the intention of harming, & they were not brought by hazard & the circumstances. Apart from a clear intention, we should not be formalized, otherwise we would be exposed to a general inquisition, one against the other" (Dareau 1785, pp. 66–67).

[54] Courtin 1671, p. 2.

[55] Courtin 1998, p. 51.

means only saying those things that are appropriate to the times, places, the person speaking, & those who are listening."[56] Under these conditions,

> [t]he greatest secret to Conversation is to be in proportion to the character of the people one frequents: one must in some way take on their point & degree of wit, to lower or raise oneself according to the occasion, & to say things to them that are appropriate.[57]

This constant attention to circumstances means that the same behavior, depending on the place, can have a very different meaning:

> From equal to equal, if one knows each other well, familiarity is proper behavior; if one knows each other a little, it is impolite; & if one knows each other not at all, it can only be an act of frivolity.
> From inferior to superior, if one knows each other well, or if one knows each other a little (unless there is an express command), familiarity is presumptuousness: & if one knows each other not at all, it is insolence & brutality.
> From superior to inferior, familiarity is always proper behavior, & it is even obliging for the inferior, who receives it.[58]

Defined in this way, the general rules of conversation have the undeniable advantage of being able to integrate, in principle, the conception of a conversation proper to elites and aimed at distinction, a conception that does not call into question the essential purpose of conversation: to create sociality. On the one hand, the conversation practiced in accordance with the fine social distinctions cements the cohesion of elites. On the other hand, the attention paid to places and circumstances is by no means, as one might first think, to be interpreted as a restriction of the rights of the individual. On the contrary, in a society of states where the existence of a structural social inequality could lead, in some cases, to frustration, civility as it is expressed here makes it possible to compensate, to a greater or lesser extent, for the feeling of inequality and to avoid, precisely, the dissatisfaction and tensions that could arise from the awareness of their social inferiority. Much more: a certain familiarity gives rise, in the socially inferior person who benefits from it, to a feeling of gratitude. And such attention to circumstances, which will remain imperative until the end of the eighteenth century, contributes to making conversation a place reminiscent of human relations as they existed before the Fall.

4.4 Freedom in Conversation

This is all the more true because conversation, under certain conditions, can turn out to be the place where a certain freedom is expressed: When Nicolas Faret, in

---

[56] Morvan de Bellegarde 1743, p. 173.
[57] Morvan de Bellegarde 1719, p. 3.
[58] Courtin 1679, pp. 15–16.

his *Maximes générales de la conversation*, mentioning the "freedom that is found among honest people," for example, asserts that the honest man, among his peers, "will be able to let his natural inclination act freely and open his soul to the bottom, without fearing that these feelings will be offended," he is creating an obvious link between the freedom of conversation and friendship[59], he may only be painting the picture of relationships as they could have been originally woven. It would of course be wrong to understand, in this quotation, the reference to "natural inclination" as an invitation to respect no rules in conversation between honest people and therefore between peers. La Chetardye makes this quite clear when, in the rules on conversation between peers, he insists that it "must not be either eloquent or studied"[60] or when Marmet de Valcroissant invites friends to avoid the double pitfalls of excessive restraint or exaggerated freedom.[61] The former would prevent access to the high quality that exchanges between friends make possible and the second would, by violating sweetness, jar the interlocutor and make him insensitive to any desire to correct one of his faults, which is nevertheless one of the functions that conversation should also express, including the sweetness perceived as clemency.

5 Sweetness and Clemency

5.1 Discretion and Compliance

The awareness that everyone has of their own imperfection, combined with the desire to make use of the truth that the interlocutor has not yet reached or has forgotten, implies, in fact, an openness and magnanimity which are testified to by the precepts of discretion or compliance formulated in the treaties, addressed to the wisest. The former allows one to avoid putting in the full light or what has been entrusted under the seal of secrecy, or anything that could place one of the interlocutors in an embarrassing position.[62] If, therefore, one refrains from speaking discreetly in company, one cannot be considered a fool "except in those frivolous circles where the little masters set the tone."[63] As for the latter, it is neither servile obsequiousness nor "this bland & cowardly Compliance that Juvenal attributes to certain Greeks of his time, who courted Rome."[64] Well understood, on the other

---

[59] See, for example, Vassetz's remark in his *Traité du mérite* : "Conversation is the soul of friendship; it should therefore be frequent, free, easy, & full of those tender feelings that come from the heart" (Vassetz 1704, p. 224). On the link between the "sweetness of conversation and friendship," see Prévost 2017, pp. 204–205).

[60] La Chetardye 1683, p. 38.

[61] Marmet de Valcroissant 1662, p. 158.

[62] Boutauld 1728, p. 211, Morvan de Bellegarde 1743, p. 171.

[63] Lasnes d'Aiguebelles 1776, p. 218.

[64] Morvan de Bellegarde 1743, p. 73. He is obviously inspired here by a remark formulated by Chalesmes (1671, p. 166).

hand, it "makes the sweetness of Society; without it let us seek neither friendship among men, nor entertaining conversation in Companies, nor even any game, walk, or other pleasure."[65] And without it, any attempt to correct the errors of others would be threatened, Des Bans says it bluntly: "The sweetness in the dispute is a secret desire to defeat those against whom we dispute, it is an effect of the experience that we have that the heat of the disputes confuses the judgment."[66] This sweetness is as necessary to convince the other participants in the same orientation as the compliments.

5.2 Compliments and Flattery

These are not condemnable in themselves, because "tickling a little self-love" is not reprehensible since this self-love is one of the traits of man after the Fall.[67] Moreover, the compliment is able to reinforce social ties as a

> brief expression of esteem & friendship that we show to those we speak to, & the purpose of the Compliment is to make them believe that we feel in our heart what we say to them from our mouth, to encourage them to take confidence in us[68],

which is a prerequisite for any attempt to improve morals.

Like complacency, the compliment also has limits, limits that Lubières makes clear when he describes the "Genius of Flatterers":

> In all the best-policed Republics there is a class of man reared in falsehood, steeped in truth, their manners are soft, easy, convenient, their approach gracious & smiling, they all have the appearance of a good friend, at heart they only love themselves. They are not rare & important characters, their great pleasure is to show themselves, to present themselves, to introduce themselves into the best company; their conversation is all obliging, they do not know what it is to dispute; they applaud everything, they yield with pleasure, they sometimes make outbursts of approval which revive a dying conversation, with them one always thinks correctly, one expresses oneself with great purity of language, one has wit, merit, ability; one never lives with more honest or more regular people in keeping all proprieties, they are only content with themselves in proportion as others are content with them, their wit is of the mediocre kind, they shine at little expense, they have a remarkable talent for embracing, caressing with a tenderness of heart which is peculiar to them.[69]

---

[65] Morvan de Bellegarde 1743, p. 73.

[66] Des Bans 1702, p. 170. Despite its aggressive consonances, "defeat", as the quotation explicitly says, does not come from "the spirit of dispute".

[67] According to Paradis de Moncrif, putting oneself at the heart of the conversation is an "inclination of nature", but which should be kept, just as it should be all the more to praise oneself or one's family, as illustrious as it is (Paradis de Moncrif 1738, p. 55).

[68] Le Noble 1707, p. 151.

[69] Lubières 1706, pp. 152–153, Morvan de Bellegarde 1743, pp. 145–146.

The virulence of this diatribe is explained in that flattery, far from being a simple defect, calls into question all the foundations of conversation: the courtesy shown by the people criticized here when they praise others is a thousand miles from humility, since it ultimately serves them to "show themselves" and to take the lead. In addition, flatterers, "befuddled with the truth" do not "know what it is to contest" [70], even when it comes to correcting morals.

6 Sweetness and Benevolence

It is not a question, indeed, of giving in to all the fads of human nature, but of showing a "edifying gentleness," as Courtin says, based on Saint Paul: "Let your conversation [be] always accompanied by edifying gentleness." That it "be seasoned with the salt of discretion, so that you may know how to answer each person."[71] Beyond the simple phatic function, the communication that conversation makes possible implies the transmission and exchange of thoughts. It therefore also has, and this is a real topos, an obvious didactic dimension, as several authors remind us at the turn of the seventeenth and eighteenth centuries. This is how Bordelon, at the dawn of the latter, writes:

> Seek the conversation of people more skilled than you as much as possible. The mind is strengthened with true scholars, & weakens with those who know nothing. Without science, conversation is light. The conversation of good minds will make a school for you where you can learn with pleasure what they have learned with difficulty.[72]

---

[70] Of course, it is only a matter of contesting in order to spread the truth, and not of a spirit of contestation.

[71] Courtin 1671, p. 25 (see Col. 4, 6: Let your speech be always with grace, seasoned with salt, that ye may know how ye ought to answer every man).

[72] Bordelon 1693, p. 11. See also Angélique de Los Rios who, in response to the question of what opens up to knowledge, replies with these words: "It is experience that comes from use; it is the conversation of reasonable people; finally it is the study of Sciences, which teach what the world is" (Los Rios 1771, p. 130). For Lasnes d'Aiguebelles, "[i]t is a rather rare talent to know how to talk properly & as required with men. However, this is how the charms of friendship & the company of honest people are tasted, one can read in minds, penetrate into hearts & acquire useful knowledge" (Lasnes d'Aiguebelles 1776, pp. 216–217). And one could multiply these citations endlessly, referring to Vassetz, according to whom "[c]onversation makes one polite, gives good manners, & teaches in a short time" (Vassetz 1704, p. 41) or to the Abbé Marsollier: "However, since reason is the most essential & necessary quality for man, one should cultivate it. Nothing does it better than conversation; everyone contributes to it. One benefits from the mind of others, their lights increase ours, one begins, another perfects, another completes what was only sketched at first. Thus one becomes skilled at little expense, mind & morals are formed, reason extends, (so to speak) one gets used to speaking on the spot, & to speaking well, to being silent & to listening to others; finally to look at things from all the angles they can have" (Marsollier 1714, p. ix).

This conversation in search of a true culture allows us to deepen our knowledge, giving rise to thoughts that would otherwise not have seen the light of day.[73]

6.1 The Question of the Subjects Covered

In such a perspective, the selection of conversation topics cannot be left to chance, because it is on them that the balance, ultimately fragile, between the desire to instruct, the concern to educate and the aspiration to a improvement of morals depends. And the authors of treatises on behaviour do not fail to call for increased vigilance in the choice of conversation topics, as well as in the way they are treated. For Goussault, for example, "[a] to be good & useful, must be of moral, honest or Christian things, but it must be conversation of a company, & not of a crowd"[74]. Richard Steele makes a precise distinction between the different "societies" in which we converse:

> Nothing can be more useful in the course of a virtuous life than the company of wise people, whose conversation is animated by religion & by virtue. There is nothing more pernicious, on the contrary, than the company of people whose discourse revolves only around light-heartedness and banter. The gaiety may be apparent, but at bottom there is only impertinence & vanity. Civility does not require us to be fools: & what greater folly than to love a company where we cannot preserve our innocence, and where the joy & pleasure that charm us, corrupt our minds, & fill them with vanity or impurity, and all too often with both.[75]

This is in the same vein as the Abbé de Bellegarde, in his *Lettres curieuses de littérature et de morale* (Curious Letters of Literature and Morality), whose goal is to give women "something to occupy themselves with some sort of pleasure; so as not to be obliged to speak always of skirts & coats, of rain & fine weather, & of a thousand other frivolous things, which are neither worth saying, nor worth listening to"[76] and, a fortiori, to speak lightly of religious matters[77], which, in view of the moral pretension of conversation, cannot be acceptable.

In return, Bellegarde very well illustrates *in actu,* in his *Modèles de conversations pour les personnes polies,* (Models of Conversations for Polite People) which topics finally fall under such conversation, showing how a polite and

---

[73] "It is this exchange of thoughts, feelings, movements, that makes us enjoy conversation so much, & that we seek out with care those whose thoughts seem more beautiful to us, the feelings more intense, the movements more agreeable" (Callières 1695, pp. 7–8).

[74] Goussault 1692, pp. 68–69: "The Fine Arts, History, & everything that concerns the Sciences & the Arts, are also the subject of a very pleasant conversation, especially when it takes place with order & politeness, & not in a critical & pedantic manner."

[75] Steele 1716, p. 10.

[76] Morvan 1702, p. 5.

[77] Morvan de Bellegarde 1743, p. 309. See also Morelly 1743, p. 330 and Blanchard 1782, p. 164.

instructive dialogue can arise from the following topics: "passions, morality, politics, heroic virtues, commerce of women, reading of novels, studies, interests of princes, politics, historical facts, ecclesiastical matters." To converse profitably therefore requires preparation in order to acquire a solid foundation of knowledge, which gives memory an important role: "Memory can provide us with support, but it cannot give us back what we have lent it before. So we must work to enrich it with a great number of beautiful things, so that it can restore them to us when we need them," claims for example Chalesmes[78].

6.2 Neither Frivolity, nor Pedantry

If futility is to be avoided in conversation, pedantry must not be less so. Indeed, as Bellegarde continues, one must not "also be a scholar in conversation; those who prepare everything they have to say; these people steeped in phrases, & pretty expressions, often bore with their so sought-after turns."[79] And in his models of conversation, he takes care to specify, when he evokes a couple talking about passions, that "[t]he conversations they had together were neither studied nor premeditated; chance alone gave them birth" and that they were "without constraint."[80] To be true "monies for conversation"—an expression borrowed from Guyot de Pitaval[81]—the points one has in memory must be dispensed with sparingly to avoid "the abuse of memory"[82] and prevent, by doing so, the impression of pedantry, a fault criticized recurrently in manuals of behavior, to the extent that one must not be "too essential or too profound in polite society. Sweetness is more in place there than Science."[83]

This criticism of pedantry, to directly stem from the importance of gentleness in conversation, bears, it is important to recall, on the superfluous display of knowledge and not on the fact of possessing it. If such were the case, indeed, one would hardly understand the very laudatory portrait that Laurent Bordelon makes

---

[78] Chalesmes 1671, p. 176.

[79] Morvan de Bellegarde 1702, p. 5.

[80] Ibid., p. 3.

[81] Gayot de Pitaval 1728, p. 56: "these points are a currency for conversation."

[82] See the criticism formulated by Moncrif, for whom two faults harm conversation: vanity and "the abuse of memory." It must, for memory to be loved, that enlightened by a certain delicacy of mind, & by the attention not to offend the self-love of others, it does not occupy the only stage "(Paradis de Moncrif 1738, p. 59). He is thus part of a long tradition of which Chalesmes or Bellegarde are milestones („However necessary the [memory] aid may be, it is not enough to make us completely successful in Conversation, since Judgment must interfere, & regulate what we have to say ", Chalesmes 1671, p. 176," we must let ourselves go with the flow, & talk about what we say; without pulling the conversation by the hair, to make it roll on what we learned by heart ", Morvan de Bellegarde 1702, p. 6).

[83] Brillon-Deslandes 1715, p. 94.

of the mathematician Jacques Ozanam (1640–1718) in his *Caracteres naturels des hommes*. To master "in perfection the Algebra, the Geometry, the astronomy and finally what is more speculative in these sciences", "he is nevertheless very agreeable in conversation and [...] delights those who are lucky enough to be able to steal a little of his time in order to enjoy his company."[84] And it is the same for this mortar president whom Brillon paints the picture of: an honest magistrate who has benefited from the best education—and in particular "the commerce that he has taken pleasure in having with people distinguished by a deep erudition" -

> he professes gaiety, cheerfulness, good humor, speaks of everything that enters into an honest & gallant conversation, becomes familiar, tolerates that one is free with him, laughs then, & shows himself agreeable without ever losing the gravity necessary to a man of his rank.[85]

The whole art therefore consists in using to good purpose a vast and deep knowledge—of which many authors, precisely, deplore the absence in conversation of these idle companies which are no longer concerned with a founded knowledge, letting themselves be seduced by vain talkers who spread half-truths and gossip, favoring rumor and error—without harming the pleasure that conversation should bring. And as Goussault said as early as 1692: "The beautiful Letters, the History, & everything that concerns the Sciences & the Arts, are also the subject of a very agreeable conversation, especially when it takes place with order & politeness, & not in a critical & pedantic manner."[86]

6.3 Diversity and Spirit

The pleasure to which the conversation beyond its didactic dimension aims proceeds from several factors. The first is diversity, because conversation conducted according to the rules, "should not be the work of pedantry. We must vary the subjects, & enliven them with remarks as pleasant as interesting", as Marquis de Caraccioli writes [87], fitting into a tradition of which Bellegarde is obviously one of the major representatives: "It is variety that gives pleasure", a remark that he completes by saying that it is a "easy air and removed from all affectation, which never tires." [88] Such a concern for diversity justifies, according to Paradis de Moncrif,

---

[84] Bordelon 1692, p. 86
[85] Brillon 1696, p. 27.
[86] Goussault 1692, p. 69.
[87] Caraccioli 1767, p. 335. See also Marmet de Valcroissant 1662, p. 246.
[88] Morvan de Bellegarde 1743, p. 7.

the superiority of the art of speech over that of writing because "the man endowed with the spirit of conversation, pleases & renews itself constantly. He always delights in everything he meets." [89]

Such a concern goes hand in hand with both the refusal to imprison the conversation in a framework made up of memories[90] as well as with the insistence on the role that "spirit" should play. The recourse to this obscure term clearly shows the difficulty inherent in the art of conversation. Proof of this is both the definition given by the *Encyclopédie* which sees in it at the same time "judgement, genius, taste, talent, penetration, extent, grace, finesse; & it must derive all these merits"[91] than the one proposed by the Abbé Marsollier: "I have always believed that spirit is light, more or less extended, which gives a taste for well-thought-out and well-said things, which warms up the imagination, which gives vivid and brilliant ideas, which makes the conversation pleasant and light, in a word which pleases the one who speaks, & those who listen to him".[92]

6.4 Clarity of Language and Refusal of Ambiguity

For Le Noble, the priority is placed on the didactic aspect and the language must be therefore of a clear clarity:

> as we only speak to be heard, we must always use the clearest and most intelligible terms and expressions, without mixing in any of these obscure ambiguities, or these extraordinary terms that some people affect, in the imagination of appearing more capable, nor the low and popular expressions that smell too much of the mud.[93]

It is also necessary to avoid ambiguous terms, those that would not be honest and that could

---

[89] Paradis de Moncrif 1738, p. 64.

[90] The refusal of a conversation based solely on memory also stems from the ideal of nature that underlies the conversation and which is also found in the precepts concerning the epistolary genre: "Most Letters form a kind of conversation between people who cannot communicate with each other in any other way: thus they must have in their expressions the easy & natural air that we notice in Dialogues. The Ancients imitated in their Epistles the manner in which friends are accustomed to speak to each other" (Anonymous 1707, p. 1).

[91] Encyclopédie 1751, col. 973.

[92] Marsollier 1714, p. 27. The underlying semantic difficulty explains that under the pen of Boureau Deslandes, for example, the notion of mood is supplanted by that of spirit, of which it nevertheless takes over the attributes: "Mood pleases more in conversation than spirit. I'm not surprised. Mood offers oddities & naivety: it doesn't finish or perfect anything. Content to brush against what agitates it, it passes from one object to another with I don't know what lightness that one approves of in spite of oneself. & then it pursues:" Happy sallies enliven the conversation. They are usually the share of the Ladies. Born with less regularity of mind than men, but with more finesse, they sometimes stray: & one likes to stray with them. The coquetry which is the foundation of their mood, their accord to say many things that men would not dare to say, & which they collect with care" (Boureau Deslandes 1715, pp. 92–93).

[93] Le Noble 1707, p. 135. See also Buffier 1726, pp. 102–103.

offend their imagination; because for the words that hide a meaning that is not honest, they have never been for the people of the markets and the crossroads. This is not to say that we have entirely banished good words, many of our moderns have happily used them in conversation, & even in their writings.[94]

If it is less reason than mind that is at the heart of the conversation, a certain lightness is permissible. Boureau-Deslandes is right, then, to write that "a light banter must be the soul of the conversation. It sharpens the mind & only superficially occupies it. What makes us listen & respond appropriately."[95] The choice of language to be used in conversation depends largely on the context and conversation can, in this respect, turn out to be the place par excellence of the extension of good usage, the testing ground for new terms, and therefore of these "words that are only born" of which Bellegarde speaks[96]. Yet,

> one should never use bad words or bad phrases, because it is easy to get into the habit of speaking badly; & that one has all the trouble in the world to get rid of this bad habit. However, one should not be embarrassed in familiar conversation, or speak in phrases; these concerted speeches embarrass those who speak & those who listen; take away all the freedom, & all the pleasure of the conversation: there, one tolerates low, easy, familiar locutions which could not find their place, in a work of consequence; one can hazard the words that are only born, provided one does so without affectation, & without asking for applause for having said a new word. [97]

In either case, the freedom of language is not without limits, which remain subject to propriety.

It is therefore clear, in light of these reflections, that the precepts governing conversation in the 17th and 18th centuries forbid saying everything. To do so would, indeed, violate the fundamental principle of gentleness by putting oneself

---

[94] Chalesmes 1671, pp. 208–209.

[95] Boureau-Deslandes 1715, p. 95. For Tessin, one of the advantages of speech lies in the fact that it is "the art of ingeniously saying nothing. Art that without inconveniencing anyone, contributes infinitely to animating the conversation by the turn & the colors that one gives to the words. It is especially in the circles & in the company of the sex, that the mind is formed & polished, that it takes graces, & that it draws its sharp, salient & light ideas, without which the discourse is languid & is only suitable for inspiring disgust & boredom" (Tessin 1755, pp. 84–85).

[96] Bellegarde 1700, p. 300. See also Chalesmes 1671, p. 176–177: "It makes us take into account all the circumstances that we are obliged to observe; it forbids us to say gallantries to an old & austere Doctor, & to entertain young Ladies with any discourse of Geometry: because when a man spoke admirably of one & the other of these two subjects; he would not fail to give a lot of trouble to people whose humor was an enemy of such a conversation. So it is not enough just to say beautiful things, it is necessary that these beautiful things be well placed; & the eyes which are the brightest part of the face, would make them monstrous, if they were not in the places where nature destines them. So it is absolutely necessary to observe all the circumstances that can concern the people in front of whom we speak, the place where we are, & the subject of which we are talking."

[97] Bellegarde 1700, p. 301.

in the spotlight at the expense of others, by neglecting the role of guide that falls to anyone with broader knowledge and awareness of their place in the world, and finally, by renouncing clear language without which it is impossible to assume this role.

7 Anchoring and Limits of this Model

This is precisely where the "petty masters" fail, whose mockery contradicts the precepts of conversation, which can be seen as a sign of the elite's disarray in the face of a political and social system shaken by the crises of the 18th century. The "linguistic disorder" expressed by the petty masters' language "is in keeping with the confusion and uncertainty that now characterizes their social status."[98] And if conversation, as an instrument for constructing the elite, was far from implying the refusal to submit to rules that are valid for all, it became, for them, an ostentatious way of cutting themselves off from others.[99]

How can we be surprised, then, by the criticisms of which they are the target, from the 1730s onwards, in treatises on behaviour which incriminate them as representatives of a gilded youth "drunk with self-love, advantageous in its words, affected in its manners, & sought after in its adjustment"[100]? One reproaches, in fact, the small masters not only on their lightness, but their remarks of an incongruity which turns to obscenity. The little master whose portrait Gayot de Pitaval depicts, is thus

> a man who is an enemy of good manners and the duties of civil life, who considers them an inconvenient yoke that must be shaken off; a man whose wit consists of indiscreet jokes, off-color remarks, out-of-place abruptness, and extravagant dizziness: he takes a flaming fire for the fire of common sense, the false gleams of lies for the pure lights of truth, the vain flash of glitter for the splendor of gold [...]. Look at his mind, it is a jumble of ideas; look at his heart, it is a confusion of feelings. In a word, a little master does not think, does not speak, does not do anything like other men, not even the most indifferent actions. A little master, being but a runt of nature's caprice, is constantly himself the plaything of caprice. In the end their life will be filled only with exploits of bastard value. See them in the land of love, they attach themselves only to libertine women whom they rule over, & whom they put to work; they abandon them when they have pressed them to the dregs.[101]

In the Pitaval collection, which aims to collect "useful and pleasant traits for conversation", such a portrait is dirimant, to the extent that the dandy takes the exact opposite of the rules allowing for good conversation: not caring at all for

---

[98] Bourguinat 1998, p. 80.
[99] See Stewart 1973.
[100] Encyclopédie, 1751 Tome 12, p. 465.
[101] Gayot de Pitaval, 1728, pp. 13–135.

softness or benevolence, he despises both truth and the pruning of customs as much as a language that would allow them to spread. Knowing neither the softness that comes from humility, nor the one that leads to clemency, dandies abuse their neighbor after having dazzled him. And far from practicing the softness that is expressed in affability, they rush their surroundings. In one word, a thousand miles from seeking the cohesion of the community of men, they threaten it by putting distinction first. The link established by some authors of behavior manuals between dandies and libertines is very logical, under these conditions[102], because dandies are, in short, the expression of a world where the individual, having lost all form of reference, pushes freedom too far. What is more, "petty mastery" ends up destroying the very foundations of a conversation conducted with profit by subjugating:

> to his quirks Literature & Philosophy itself. As it is the fruit of refinement, & often of an presumption unable to produce beautiful things, it turns to the side of the frivolous & the wonderful. Thus she substituted the fussiness & the affectation for the natural beauties of Bossuet & Masillon [sic]; singularities for the energetic reasoning of Bacon & Montesquieu; will-o'-the-wisps, for the fire that animated & Corneille & Crébillon.[103]

The list of authors cited here is interesting in that it well summarizes the objectives of a conversation that, without ignoring the tragedy inherent in existence, strives to correct the faults of humanity by educating it both through science and through the fervent respect of faith. And that only makes the criticism leveled at dandies all the more acerbic.

Of course, it is probably complicated to say what part of the population these latter represented, but one is entitled to assume that they were only a minority presented as an example to a society accepting, at least in theory, the values of conversation as they have been presented above and that they were, therefore, "useful like these Spartan Slaves that one envied, to inspire in children the horror of drunkenness."[104] In fact, one can assume that the principles of a "good" conversation were, as an ideal, anchored in a large part of the population, if only because they were inculcated, from an early age (and for the illiterate even in adulthood), through these catechisms of which Jean de Viguerie has well highlighted the intention and scope as an "instrument of salvation" because they summarized, on the one hand, the essentials of faith in a small number of pages[105] and, on the other hand, had an obvious practical scope.[106]

---

[102] Claville 1734, pp. 31–32.

[103] Caraccioli 1776, pp. 332–333.

[104] Soret 1756, p. 91.

[105] Viguerie 2010, pp. 50–56.

[106] Viguerie 1996, p. 103. Without being a treatise on behavior *stricto sensu*, the catechism is, by some of these aspects, a real pedagogical work used deliberately in a process of improvement of customs.

It is therefore not surprising that some of these catechisms contain recommendations regarding conversation. In the *Dogmatic, Moral and Canonical Catechism* ... by Abbé de Fourcroy, republished at the dawn of the eighteenth century, an entire chapter is devoted to "fraternal correction" (an unconditional duty for everyone to help others overcome their shortcomings) and the conversation of Christians. The precepts given with regard to the latter are structured along three axes: the people with whom one must converse (essentially "virtuous people, for the great spiritual goods and advantages that result from it"[107]), the subjects to be addressed ("good things that lead to God") and the faults to be avoided ("discourses of mockery, slander, contention, impurity and vanity"[108] And the *Catechism of Faith and Christian Morals* by Charles-Louis de Lantage (which will be reprinted until the second half of the nineteenth century) insists on the importance of conversing on the one hand "with charity" with one's neighbor—to console, encourage and edify the people present—"without saying a word that harms anyone"—and, on the other hand, to do it "with annihilation" of oneself, that is to say, by refusing the movements of self-love and vanity "which lead us to act & speak in order to attract the esteem of creatures"[109]

These recommendations, at first glance, appear to be far below the rules of conversation exposed above, are nevertheless to be related to the prayer that the author devotes "to the sweetness of Our Lord Jesus Christ". The sweetness of the latter has several facets:

> That our Lord Jesus Christ bears witness in the Gospel to a great desire that all Christians have a meek spirit. He speaks of meekness and humility as the great lesson he came to teach them on earth […];
> One of the proofs of the "admirable sweetness" of Jesus is that, in spite of the difficulty the apostles had in understanding him at the beginning, "he always continued to instruct them with wonderful benignity […];

Far from punishing his persecutors, Jesus

> persists in having only kindness for them […];
> The kindness of Jesus is also very remarkable towards sinful souls […] These poor souls, being despised & rejected by everyone, found in Jesus a debonair welcome that filled them with consolation & courage.[110]

The kindness that Jesus shows thus reflects the four dimensions of this virtue: humility, beneficence, clemency & affability, all qualities that the Christian should strive to

---

[107] Fourcroy 1696, pp. 130–131. A conversation with "wicked" people is licit if it is "charitable", that is to say, to correct their faults (p. 131).

[108] Ibid. "Contention" does not obviously mean the application to inner life (a very present and often discussed motif in Christian spirituality), but the dispute and debate, which of course refers to the spirit of contradiction.

[109] Langage 1684, p. 505.

[110] Ibid., pp. 560, 557–558, 559 & 558.

achieve, for whom "it is an obligation to be as gentle as a Lamb & a Dove"[111], from which logically follows the invitation to "approach & welcome all sorts of people with a heart full of benevolence, gentle words, a pleasant countenance & a graceful bearing" & to "be kind, particularly towards those who provoke impatience"[112].

8 Conclusion

However, one must not sink into irenicism: Despite its coherence, the model of the good conversation based on gentleness, and the definition of the boundaries to be assigned to the right to say everything that emanates from it, has not been a very effective barrier against the practices of sociability favored by social elites. The insistent and persistent criticism of the dandies is an obvious indication of the limited scope of this model, despite its capacity for integration. It is not the place here to review the debates, especially after 1750, on the meaning of an improvement in behavior and, more precisely, on the increasingly radical attacks launched against a politeness that, more and more distant from the virtues it should have been the expression, is denounced as a mere mask.[113]

These attacks delivered the coup de grâce to the conception of a conversation that, nowadays, and in the absence now of a unique system of values, could not have the same form as before. Instead of complying with a "universally" valid code, those who participate in the conversation now have to work to reach, at the end of a process one could qualify as "democratic", to make common values emerge. Such an approach is not easy, however. In the horizon of a pluralistic world, the absolutization of the individual, the pretension of this, and the belief that those who immediately share his opinions have *a priori* the truth and the right that they arrogate to say everything makes impossible such a process and degrades, alas, the discussion into vain logomachy.[114]

It could seem paradoxical to look back on the conceptions of the conversation formulated at a time prior to the existence of democratic regimes, but is it really if we consider that, by rediscovering the ideal it was pursuing, we could perhaps find affability, clemency, benevolence and humility and, through this, a certain softness of the conversation.

---

[111] Ibid., p. 561. That being Christian means striving to imitate Christ is here evident, inasmuch as this "gentle Savior" (p. 559) appears in the form of a dove (p. 309) & is a gentle lamb (pp. 560, 561, 557, 206, 252). The beneficence of Christ appears finally in the Eucharist, for "[t]he divine Eucharist which Jesus feeds us with for eternity, has the effect of communicating to us the kindness of Jesus" (p. 561).

[112] Ibid., p. 561.

[113] On these debates, see Losfeld 2011.

[114] In fact, even those who oppose "the tyranny of the politically correct" to take up the title of a recent book (Chardon 2002) do so with such vehemence that a real conversation is impossible.

References

Sources

Anonyme : L'Art de bien écrire des lettres En toutes Matieres. Sur le Modèle de celles qui ont étés [sic] écrites par les Auteurs les plus polis de ce tems. Divisé en deux Parties. Bruxelles : J. B. de Leeneer 1707.

Anonyme : Regles De La Bienseance, Ou La Civilité, Qui Se Pratique Parmi Les Honnetes Gens : Avec la Maniere de faire des Complimens & des Maximes pour se conduire sagement dans le monde, Nouvelle Edition considérablement corrigée. Strasbourg : Amand König 1766.

Blanchard, Jean-Baptiste : L'école des mœurs ou réflexions morales et historiques sur les maximes de la sagesse, ouvrage utile aux jeunes gens et aux autres personnes, pour se bien conduire dans le monde. Lyon : Jean-Marie Bruyset 1784.

Bordelon, Laurent La belle éducation. Paris : Belley 1693.

Bordelon, Laurent : Caractères naturels des hommes en cent Dialogues. La Haye : Van Dole 1692.

Boureau-Deslandes, André François : L'Art de ne point s'ennuyer. Amsterdam : Steenhouwer & Uytwerf 1715.

Boutauld, Michel : Les Conseils de la Sagesse Ou le Recueil des Maximes de Salomon les plus nécessaires à l'homme pour se conduire sagement. Amsterdam : Janssons à Waesberge 1728 (Ed. originale 1677).

Braga, de Martin : Martini Episcopi Bracarensis Opera Omnia (éd. Claude W. Barlow). New Haven : Yale University Press, 1950.

Brillon, Jean-Jacques : Portraits sérieux galands et critiques. Paris : Brunet 1696.

Buffier, Claude : Traité de la société civile, et du moyen de se rendre heureux, en contribuant au bonheur des personnes avec qui l'on vit. 2 Tomes. Paris : F. Giffart 1726.

Callières, François de : Du Bel Esprit : ou sont examinez les sentimens qu'on a d'ordinaire dans le monde. Paris, Amsterdam : Brunel 1695.

Callieres, François de : La Fortune des gens de qualité et des gentil-hommes particuliers. Enseignant l'Art de vivre à la Cour, suivant les maximes de la politique & de la Morale. Paris : Estienne Loyson 1665.

Caraccioli, Louis-Antoine, Marquis : L'Europe françoise. Turin, Paris, Duchesne 1776.

Caraccioli, Louis-Antoine, Marquis : Lettres recréatives et morales, sur les mœurs du temps, Paris : Nyon 1767.

Chalesme, de : L'Homme de qualité, ou Les moyens de vivre en homme de bien, et en Homme du Monde. Amsterdam : Le Grand 1671.

Chicaneau de Neuville, D.-P. : Dictionnaire philosophique, ou Introduction à la connaissance de l'homme. Lyon : Bruyset 1756 (Ed. originale 1751).

Cicero : De officiis. Vom pflichtgemäßen Handeln. Reclam : Stuttgart 2019.

Ciceron: De la vieillesse, de l'amitié, des devoirs (éd. Charles Appuhn). Paris : GF 1967.

Claville, Charles-François-Nicolas Le Maître de : Traité du vrai mérite de l'homme, considéré dans tout les âges et dans toutes les conditions : avec des principes d'éducation, propres À former les jeunes gens à la vertu. Francfort : François Varrentrapp 1739.

Courtin, Antoine de : Nouveau traité de la civilité qui se pratique en France parmi les honnêtes gens (éd. Marie-Claire Grassi). Saint-Etienne : PU Saint-Etienne 1998 (Ed. originale 1671).

Courtin, Antoine de : Nouveau Traité de la civilité qui se pratique en France parmi les honnestes gens. Paris : Hélie Josset 1671.

Crousaz, Jean Pierre de : Traité de l'éducation des enfants. La Haye : Vaillant/Prevost 1722.

D'Alembert/Diderot (éd.): Encyclopédie, Tome 5, 1751.

Dareau, François : Traité des injures dans l'ordre judiciaire : ouvrage qui renferme particulièrement la jurisprudence du petit-criminel. Paris : Nyon 1785.
Des Bans, Louis : L'Art de connoistre les hommes. Amsterdam : Etienne Roger 1709 (Ed. originale 1702).
Destutt de Tracy, Bernard : Traité Des Devoirs De La Vie Chrétienne, A L'Usage De Tous Les Fideles ; Dédié A Monseigneur Le Dauphin. Ou Exposition des plus importantes obligations du Christianisme, par rapport à Dieu, à soi-même, au prochain & à son état : Avec Des Exercices De Piété. Paris : Tilliart 1770.
Fourcroy, Abbé de : Catéchisme dogmatique, moral et canonique, ou Abrégé méthodique pour apprendre facilement les principaux points de la doctrine et de la morale chrétienne et du droit canon, Paris : Edme Couterot 1696.
Gayot de Pitaval, François : L'Art d'orner l'esprit en l'amusant, ou nouveau choix de traits vifs saillans et legers, soit en vers, soit en prose, & de morceaux d'Histoires singulieres. Paris : Briasson 1728.
Joly, Pere J.-R. : Dictionnaire de morale philosophique. Paris : Didot l'aîné 1771.
La Chetardye : Instructions pour un jeune seigneur ou l'idée d'un galant homme. Paris : Girard 1683.
Lantage, Charles-Louis de Catéchisme de la foy, et des mœurs chrétiennes. Dressé particulièrement pour l'usage du diocèse du Puy. Le Puy : Delagarde 1684.
La Rochefoucauld : Maximes et Réflexions diverses (éd. Jean Lafond). Paris : Gallimard 1976 (édition originale 1678[5]).
Lasnes d'Aiguebelles : Testament spirituel, ou Derniers adieux d'un père mourant a ses enfans. Ouvrage posthume du Chev. de +++, auteur des Sentimens affectueux et de la Religion du cœur. Marseille : Mossy 1776.
Le Noble, Eustache Baron : L'Ecole du monde, ou instruction d'un père à son fils, touchant la manière dont il faut vivre dans le monde, divisée en entretiens. Amsterdam : Coup 1709 (Ed. originale 1695)
Los Rios, Angélique de : L'Encyclopédie enfantine ou Magasin pour les petits enfans. Dresde : George Conrad Walther 1770.
Marmet de Valcroissant, Melchior : Maximes pour vivre heureusement dans le monde, et pour former l'honneste homme. Paris : Charles de Sercy 1662.
Marsollier, Abbé Jacques : Entretiens sur les devoirs de la vie civile et sur plusieurs points importants de la vie chrétienne. Paris : F. Babuty 1714.
Morelly : Essai sur l'esprit humain ou principes naturels de l'éducation. Paris : Delespine 1743.
Morvan de Bellegarde, Abbé Jean-Baptiste : L'art de plaire dans la conversation, Nouvelle édition. La Haye : Antoine van Dole 1743.
Morvan de Bellegarde, Abbé Jean-Baptiste : Lettres curieuses de littérature et de morale. Paris : Jean et Michel Guignard 1702.
Morvan de Bellegarde, Jean-Baptiste : L'éducation parfaite, contenant les maniéres bienséantes aux jeunes Gens de qualité, & des Maximes, & des Réfléxions propres à avancer leur fortune. Amsterdam : Estienne Roger 1710.
Morvan de Bellegarde, Jean-Baptiste : Réflexions sur l'élégance et la politesse du stile. Trevoux : Palard 1700.
Morvan de Bellegarde, Jean-Baptiste, Abbé : Modèles de conversations pour les personnes polies., augmentée d'une Conversation sur les Modes. La Haye : Guillaume de Voys, 1719 (Ed. originale 1697).
Paradis de Moncrif, François-Augustin : Essais sur la nécessité et sur les moyens de plaire. Genève : Pellissari 1738.
Puisieux : Conseils à une amie. Paris : s.n. 1750.
Saint Ambroise : Les Devoirs (ed. Maurice Testard), Paris ; Les Belles lettres 2007.
Soret : Essais sur les mœurs. Bruxelles : s.n. 1756.
Steele, Richard : Bibliothèques des Dames contenant des Règles générales pour leur conduite, dans toutes les circonstances de la vie. Ecrite par une Dame, & publiée par Mr. le Chev. R. Steele. Amsterdam : Aux dépens de la compagnie 1716.

Tessin, Carl Gustav, Comte : Lettres à un jeune Prince, par un Ministre d'Etat, chargé de l'élever, de l'instruire, traduit du suédois. Londres : Harreveldt 1755 (Ed. originale 1753 sous le titre En äldre mans bref till en stadigare prins).
Vassetz, ... de : Traité du Mérite. La Haye : Guillaume de Voys 1704.
Villethierry, Jean Girard de : Le chrétien étranger sur la terre, ou les sentimens et les devoirs d'une âme fidèle qui se regarde comme étrangère en ce monde. Paris : Pralard 1725 (Ed. originale 1696).

Littérature critique

Bourguinat, Elisabeth : Le siècle du persiflage 1734 – 1789. Paris : PUF 1998.
Brémond, Henri : Histoire littéraire du sentiment religieux en France depuis la fin des guerres de religion jusqu'à nos jours. Tome I, Paris : Bloud et Gay 1923.
Chardon, Jean-Marc (éd.) : La Tyrannie des Bien-Pensants. Débat pour en finir. Paris : Economica 2001.
Craveri, Benedetta : L'Âge de la conversation. Paris : Gallimard 2001.
D'Amico, Juan Carlos : Castiglione, Erasme et Plutarque : Le "Prince parfait" et la "Patrie universelle" entre mythes et réalités, in : Paolo Grossi et Juan Carlos D'Amico (éd.) : De la politesse à la politique. Recherches sur les langages du "Livre du Courtisan". Actes du colloque international de l'Université de Caen Basse-Normandie (18 février 2000). Caen : Presses universitaires de Caen 2001, pp. 121–151.
Hübner, Helga : Stefano Guazzo *La Civil Conversazione* in der französischen Kultur des 16. und 17. Jahrhunderts. Frankfurt a. M. e. a. : Peter Lang 2012.
Jamain, Jean-Claude : La douceur de vivre : D'une esthétique de la grâce au XVIIIe siècle. Rennes : PUR 2011.
Losfeld, Christophe : Politesse, morale et construction sociale : pour une histoire des traités de comportements (1670–1788). Paris : Honoré Champion 2011.
Méchoulan, Eric : la douceur du politique, in : Marie-Hélène Prat et Pierre Servet : Le doux au XVIe et XVIIe siècle. Ecriture, esthétique, politique, spiritualité. Lyon : PUL 2003, pp. 221–238.
Méchoulan, Éric : Le pouvoir féerique, in : Féeries 3, 2006, pp. 43–57.
Mennessier, André-Ignace : Douceur, in : Dictionnaire de spiritualité ascétique et mystique, Tome 3, Paris : Beauchêne 1957, col 1674–1685.
Mireille Huchon : Le doux dans les rhétoriques et poétiques françaises du XVIe siècle », in : Marie-Hélène Prat et Pierre Servet, Pierre (éd.) : Le doux au XVIe et XVIIe siècle. Ecriture, esthétique, politique, spiritualité. Lyon : PUL 2003, pp. 9–28.
Montandon, Alain : Konversation und Gastlichkeit in der französischen Aufklärung : zur Konzeptualisation sozialer Interaktion zwischen Kontinuität und Umbruch, in : Jörn Garber et Thoma, Heinz (éd.) : Zwischen Empirisierung und Konstruktionsleistung : Anthropologie im 18. Jahrhundert. Tübingen : Niemeyer 2004, pp. 339–362.
Montandon, Alain : Conversation, in : Alain Montandon (éd.) : Dictionnaire raisonné de la politesse et du savoir-vivre : du Moyen Âge à nos jours, Éditions du Seuil, Paris, 1995, pp. 125–151.
Montandon, Alain : Les bienséances de la conversation, in : Bernard Bray, Bernard y Christoph Strosetzki (éd.) : Art de la lettre, art de la conversation : à l'époque classique en France. Paris : Klincksieck, Paris, 1995, pp. 61–79.
Prévost, Aurélie : L'Amitié en France au XVIe et XVIIe siècles. Histoire d'un sentiment. Louvain : UCL 2017.
Spicq Ceslas : Bénignité, Mansuétude, Douceur, Clémence, in : La Revue biblique 54, 1947, pp. 321–339.

Stewart, Philip : Le masque et la parole, le langage de l'amour au XVIIIe siècle. Paris : José Corti 1973.
Strosetzki, Christoph : Rhétorique de la conversation, sa dimension littéraire et linguistique dans la société française du XVIIe siècle. Paris, Seattle, Tübingen : PFSCL 1984.
Strosetzki, Christoph : Konversation als Sprachkultur. Elemente einer historischen Kommunikation. Berlin : Frank & Timme 2013.
Viguerie, Jean de : L'Eglise et l'éducation. Bouère : DMM 2010.
Viguerie, Jean de : Les catéchismes enseignés en France au XVIIIe siècle. Premier approche, in : Revue de l'histoire de l'Eglise de France 82, 1996, pp. 85–108.

Duties and Conventions of Conversation: Adolph Freiherr Knigge

Hans-Christian Riechers

Abstract

In his book *On Human Relations* (1788), Adolph Freiherr Knigge attempts to transform the social customs of the nobility into a system of etiquette for equals. To do this, he ties them, in the spirit of his time, to moral obligations. Courtly and bourgeois conversation culture play a significant role in this process. Knigge evaluates their conventions ambivalently, on the one hand as external accidents, on the other hand as aids in preserving the inner self in social interaction.

Keywords

Courtly Culture · Art of Conversation · French Revolution · Subject Constitution · Adolph Freiherr Knigge · Werther · Bourgeois Society · Noble Society · Ancien Régime

1 Courtly and Bourgeois Conversation

Adolph Freiherr Knigge is famous and is not. In the German-speaking countries, his name is known everywhere and appears on far more book titles than he has written books. This is mainly due to his best-known book, *Ueber den Umgang mit Menschen* from 1788, which was printed and translated several times in the first years after its appearance, but later developed a life of its own, as was not

H.-C. Riechers (✉)
Universität Basel, Basel, Switzerland
e-mail: hc.riechers@rocketmail.com

foreseeable in the lifetime of its author. This book has something else to it than the many advice books that still advertise with Knigge's name today.[1]

Born in 1752 in Bredenbeck near Hanover, died in 1796 in Bremen, Knigge was set on a path that left little room for personal fulfilment: From his early deceased parents he had inherited debts, and so he was dependent on the goodwill of the creditors, who paid him a pension from the proceeds of the family's property in the Calenberg Land. In Göttingen, Knigge studied law and 'Kameralistik', which pointed to a career in state administration. And indeed he took up an office at the Kassel court at the age of 19. The next ten years took him through various princely courts, such as Weimar or Kassel. After another ten years as a writer, editor, literary critic, pedagogue and secret society secretary in Frankfurt and Heidelberg, he took up a position as Oberhauptmann in Bremen in 1790, that is, as a representative of the Kingdom of Hanover in the Hanseatic city of Bremen. During this time he wrote a series of political-satirical novels, which, next to the *Umgang mit Menschen*, are his main work.

Knigge's life was characterized on the one hand by the conditions of the Ancien Régime, on the other hand by the hopes for a bourgeois society, inspired, like many other, by the French Revolution of 1789. His origin and the years he spent at courts made him an intimate connoisseur, but also an opponent of the court world. He openly sympathized with republican ideas and took the Hanseatic cities as a model for a possible bourgeois society in Germany.

He despised the power that was exerted on the individual at the courts he knew, and he got into several consequential conflicts there. For this power, the focal point of which was always the prince, was distributed officially over the various state offices, but just as much through informal channels among the courtiers and ladies-in-waiting.

> I was very young when I first stepped upon the theatre of the great world and the court. […] Grown up in a country where flattery, dissimulation and cringing are not much encouraged, I was indeed but little prepared for that pliancy I wanted to ensure success among utter strangers and in despotic states […][2]

What Knigge experienced as a young man and of which his book *Ueber den Umgang mit Menschen* bears eloquent testimony, was a conformist phalanx that

---

[1] Including publications that do not openly advertise with Knigge's name, but go into him in a more founded way, for example Axel Hacke's *Über den Anstand in schwierigen Zeiten und die Frage, wie wir miteinander umgehen*, which addresses the social disintegration caused by new ways of communication, and expressly refers to Knigge (cf. Hacke 2017, pp. 25–27).

[2] Knigge 1788, Introduction, p. 27 (cf. Knigge 1993, p. 26).—Where possible, I quote from the first edition of *On Human Relations*, which was published in 1788 by Schmidtsche Buchhandlung in Hanover (acronym: Knigge 1788). To make the quotes easier to find, I am additionally giving in brackets the edition of the *Selected Works* (Knigge 1993) which is based on the third edition of the book published in 1790 by Christian Ritscher in Hanover. Transl. by P. Will (Practical Philosophy of Social Life, or The Art of Conversing with Men. After the German of Baron Knigge. London: Cadell & Davies 1799); the translation is incomplete, which is why some quotes cannot follow it.

immediately punished any deviation from the social role, primarily through acts of communication about absent people such as slander or mockery. Hence comes Knigge's urgent advice: "Show, as much as you can, an always even, cheerful countenance!"[3] For where this does not succeed, trouble threatens: "As soon as your neighbor reads melancholy and despair on your countenance—then it is all over."[4] Knigge is therefore not aiming for a break with conventions, but for adaptation to them. What lies behind this?

Johann Wolfgang Goethe, who was temporarily at the Weimar court with Knigge in 1776, took the opposite path in life: coming from a wealthy bourgeois family, he was ennobled in 1782 and rose to the rank of minister. While Goethe's later views were partly opposed to those of Knigge—for example, in his assessment of the French Revolution[5]—the young Goethe shared with Knigge the dislike of the exclusionary mechanisms of court society. If the young Werther (1774) as a bourgeois man finds himself in an evening party with nobility, the Count's invitation that led him there is of no use to him, because it cannot prevent him from becoming the subject of conversation, the subject of gossip behind his back.

> I didn't notice that at the far end of the hall the women were whispering in one another's ears, that it then reached the men, that Frau von S. had a word with the Count (I had all this later from Fräulein B.) till finally he came over and drew me into the alcove of a window. – 'You are aware', he said, 'how bizarre our conventions are. I notice that the company ist not happy to see you here. I wouldn't for anything in the world —' I interrupted him. 'Your Excellency', I said, 'a thousand pardons, I should have thought of it before now and I know you will forgive me this lapse. I was about to take my leave a while ago, but' I added with a smile and a bow, 'some evil genius held me back.' — The Count pressed my hands with a feeling that said everything. I slipped quietly out of that respectable company, and drove in a cabriolet to M. and from the hill there watched the sun go down and read in my Homer the glorious episode in which Odysseus is given hospitality by the excellent swineherd. Then all was well.[6]

Werther bows and thus serves the etiquette, the valid rules of the game. This action is ambivalent, because on the one hand the form gives him the inner freedom to rise above the present with his defeat, on the other hand he has to submit to it externally. He performs his submission quite according to the rules of convention, even with the contradictory confession of guilt and even literally, physically, by bowing, while he is internally resisting. That he does this with a sardonic smile keeps a door of bourgeois self-confidence open to him, and that he finally keeps himself outside of society by reading Homer's hospitality on a hill alone strengthens the 'subjective inner life' of both author and reader by bringing the bourgeois Werther closer to the Homeric hero in a pleasant way and the image of knowledge

---

[3] Knigge 1788. First Part, p. 60 (cf. Knigge 1993, p. 46).

[4] Knigge 1788. First Part, p. 41 (cf. Knigge 1993, p. 33).

[5] For example, in his farce *Der Bürgergeneral*, see Hermes 2016.

[6] Goethe 1774, pp. 131–132. Transl. by David Constantine (Johann Wolfgang Goethe: The Sorrows of Young Werther. Oxford: Oxford UP 2012).

associated with it. But this does not help much in the social situation at the court; convention and freedom stand side by side. The bourgeois subject named Werther is constituted in this conflict.

The experience of Knigge is also richly filled with such ambivalence of action within the existing power structures, which are expressed in words and gestures, and is dealt with in the text of *Ueber den Umgang mit Menschen* once as an anecdote, then imperatively briefly, finally in the form of longer raisonnements and advice.

Unlike in Goethe's *Werther* however, Knigge is concerned with developing a different, integrative and ethically founded variant of the art of conversation from the negative diagnosis of court conversation, which includes individuals from different social groups: a basis for the conversation of the rising bourgeoisie. Of course, Knigge's book is non-fictional, unlike Goethe's *Werther*. It is a guide, but by no means the etiquette book that it is known to be. It is a moral-philosophical work, passages of which are proto-sociological, which formulates principles of social interaction, and. It differs from contributions from genuine school philosophy in that it deliberately avoids a philosophical systematization and instead emphasizes empirical legitimacy.

A key concept, by which *Ueber den Umgang mit Menschen* differs from ordinary etiquette books but is closest to moral philosophy, is the concept of duty, which Knigge prominently positioned in the preface to the third edition of 1790:

> If the rules of social interaction are not just rules of a conventional politeness [...] then they must be based on the teachings of the duties we owe to all kinds of people, and which they can in turn claim from us—[7]

Obligations are divided into two practical classes in Knigge: obligations towards others and obligations towards oneself, quite typical for the moral philosophy of the Enlightenment.[8] In addition to the perfectibility of the moral subject, as there, the second point of escape here is that of the self-assertion of the moral subject in an adverse environment. In contrast, obligations towards others are oriented towards a possible bourgeois conversation culture, which preserves the freedom and dignity of the individual without rank differences, but with respect for the differences of the milieus, whether they are shaped by status, region or the city-country difference. Those who do not take these differences into account in the rituals of conversation will fail like the old, "honest country gentleman",[9] who comes to the court:

> Now he approaches a circle of people who seem to be talking with interest and liveliness; He wishes to take part in this conversation; but everything he hears, subject, language, expression, turn, everything is foreign to him.[10]

---

[7] Knigge 1993, p. 405.
[8] Cf. Mihaylova 2015 as well as Pittrof 1989, p. 76: Knigge presupposes a corresponding "moral basic knowledge".
[9] Knigge 1788, Introduction, p. 18 (cf. Knigge 1993, p. 21).
[10] Knigge 1788, Introduction, p. 20 (cf. Knigge 1993, p. 22).

This phenomenon is not one-sided, and therein lies Knigge's sociological view, which understands class differences as a coexistence of lifestyles, not as a hierarchy, because just as the country gentleman fares, so does the fine courtier who comes to country people: "His compliments, which he really means well, are considered to be falsehoods"[11] etc. Without value, Knigge states: "So great is the difference in tone between two classes of people!"[12]

2 Obligation to Conversation

Conversational culture is an essential building block of a new society based on general principles, according to Knigge. Unlike the representatives of Sturm und Drang, who categorically reject conventional conversation, Knigge's goal is not to abolish, but to realign established conversational culture. Its rules should be based on the solid foundation of moral maxims that lead to a common point of reference: respect for the individual, regardless of origin.[13] Understood in this way, conversation is not intended to harm, but to protect individuality. However, this is precisely why the protective rules that stand in the way of "direct" communication must be observed, especially as long as the rules of the Estates Society apply (one should remember that Knigge's book was published in its first edition one year *before* the French Revolution), but also beyond. Like the whole *Umgang mit Menschen*, the rules of conversation also have the dual face of respectful communication among equals on the one hand and self-protection within the power structures of (estates) society on the other. The convention that had caused headaches for the stormers and drifters is, for him, an instrument that is not in and of itself wrong, but only needs the right basis. Then it applies:

> Do not despise everything that has only conventional value if you want to live comfortably in the great world […] but do not set any inner value on it […]. In your secret little room you may laugh heartily at all these follies; but do not do it loudly. In a word! Do not stand out too much among the people of the world with whom you have to live. It is not only a rule of prudence, no! but it is also a duty to adopt the customs of the estate one chooses, to be quite what one is, but, as one understands it, never at the expense of one's individuality.[14]

---

[11] Knigge 1788, Introduction, p. 21 (cf. Knigge 1993, p. 23).

[12] Knigge 1788, Introduction, pp. 21 f. (cf. Knigge 1993, p. 23).

[13] It should be expressly noted that Knigge's concept of equality has its limits. The denigration of Jews, to which Ruth Klüger (Klüger 1996) drew attention, must be mentioned here quite clearly. In *Umgang mit Menschen*, Jews appear in essentializing attributions and negatively evaluated in their socio-economic role as moneylenders, debt collectors and traders, and there is concern about the advancement of Jews into the bourgeoisie. See Gelbin and Gilman 2017, pp. 31 ff. In other works by Knigge, the connotations are sometimes much more drastic; see Rüllmann 2001.

[14] Knigge 1790, Second Part, p. 48 (cf. Knigge 1993, p. 318).

The "status" is, as mentioned in Knigge's understanding, not so much associated with social hierarchy, but rather designates the milieu in which one moves; it is less fixed by origin than by profession—which is restricted by origin, of course. Nor is social status the only consideration according to which he divides society, but he also names, for example, personal and family relationships, regional influences and individual temperaments that need to be considered. But one must move with skill and attention in particular in situations of social decline: "One is polite and friendly to those people who have not been thrown such a rich sum of meaningless temporal advantages by fortune as us, and honor the true merit, the true value of the human being, even in the lower class!"[15] Even if the conditions of the status society are present throughout Knigge's book, his positive orientation is above all about merits that determine social rank, not about inherited rank. In this respect, this book is a step towards the abolition of the status society from which it originates, and towards a meritocratic organization of society.[16] It is "the common mistake of the courtiers" that they "regarded their jargon as the only general language". But the "great art of dealing is […] to study the tone of each society and to be able to adopt it according to opportunity."[17]

Knigge's variant of social discipline therefore has a certain purpose, which does not exhaust itself in the choice of the path of least resistance, as may initially appear: He thinks of another moral order of society by replacing the hierarchical class differences, which form the backbone of the rules of etiquette of his time, with rules of respectful intercourse—and intercourse means above all conversation[18]—among equals. There are no statutory special rules for persons of different status with him, only rules of prudence that recommend taking certain considerations into account in dealing with persons of other status. However, what is decisive here is always that the duties towards oneself are not violated, that is, ultimately those of self-respect.

The courtly and bourgeois conversation, as Knigge describes it, is a highly conventionalized form of speech that is already immanently regulated, but Knigge is concerned with a level of metaregulation. The conversation is thus morally conceived as a whole, it is the subject of social duties.

For it is precisely in social intercourse "between persons of different status and education"[19] that the need for universally valid social maxims becomes apparent. There is therefore a duty to entertain. Knigge warns "for his own sake and for the sake of others" that one might underestimate the value of a conversation with a

---

[15] Knigge 1788, Second Part, p. 34 (cf. Knigge 1993, p. 306).

[16] "That the orders of the old status world had been broken and that the spirit of a new universalism had become apparent in the book of manners—there can be no doubt about that […]" Pittrof 1989, p. 82.

[17] Knigge 1788, Second Part, p. 37. (cf. Knigge 1993, pp. 307 f.).

[18] For example, the first English translator Peter Will translates the title with *Practical Philosophy of Social Life, or, The Art of Conversing with Men* (London 1799).

[19] Knigge 1788, Introduction, p. 17 (cf. Knigge 1993, p. 21).

person: "From all conversations one can gather some new experience, some material for reflection."[20] There is almost an imperative of conversation, because social intercourse is achieved through the conversations of all with all and the consideration of the universal rules of etiquette.

In general, one should be moderate in one's speech, not talk too much, and the negative and shocking image is delivered at the same time:

> There are people who without perceiving it, monopolise everywhere the conversation and were they in a company of more than fifty people would nevertheless find means to be the only speakers in the room.[21]

Knigge repeatedly returns to this duty of self-knowledge in conversation, and thus to equality in speech. Alongside the obligation to converse with others and to let them have their say, there is the very insistent advice that, if one takes the floor oneself, one should also entertain the others. To bore people is quite simply out of the question, as in the anecdote about a respected professor; this

> entertains a society which had looked forward to enjoying him, at dinner with a dissection of the new academic Credit Edict, or, if the wine gives the good man a jovial mood, with stories of amusing escapades from his student days.[22]

In short, boredom arises from the inability of the person speaking to awaken the interest of the others, by looking at themselves to some extent—in a way, a responsible way of being aware of their individuality. Knigge brings together a whole series of such examples:

> Above all things let us never forget that people want to be amused and entertained; that even the most instructive conversation at least becomes irksome to many if it be not seasoned by occasional sallies of wit and good humour; further, that nothing in the world appears to the generality wittier, wiser and more pleasant than what is saidto their praise and flatters their vanity; but that it also is beneath the dignity of a rational man to act the mean part of a jester, and unworthy of an honest man to flatter meanly.[23]

Nobody, least of all the weaker, should ever be excluded from the conversation or be made the object of it in a derogatory way: "Attempt never to render a person ridiculous in company how many defects soever he may have."[24] And an anecdote, which he only added in a later edition, tells of how he, "at the table of a friend" sat next to a "ugly old maid" and paid no attention to her for a long time. "When the desert was served up, the rudeness of my conduct suddenly struck me"—he turns

---

[20] Knigge 1788, First Part, p. 44 (cf. Knigge 1993, p. 68).
[21] Ibid.
[22] Knigge 1788, Introduction, p. 22 (cf. Knigge 1993, p. 23).
[23] Knigge 1788, First Part, pp. 59 ff. (cf. Knigge 1993, p. 45).
[24] Knigge 1788, First Part, p. 75 (cf. Knigge 1993, p. 44).

to the lady with a cheap compliment, which she receives with great pleasure, while she should "have despised me for that flattery". "How easily would it have been" for him to find "a subject that could have interested her", and it would have been his "duty" to think about it instead of neglecting her for the whole conversation.[25] The respectful conversation is, in this sense, a minimum of social interaction, and a practiced recognition of the dignity of the other person.

3 Limits of the Convention

Knigge judges social proximity, which is associated with conventionalized conversation, to be positive, provided it is based on the self-protection assumption. Thomas Pittrof therefore succinctly summarizes: "dealing with people" meant not letting them get too close.[26] For an admirer and translator[27] of Rousseau like Knigge, it can be assumed that he feels the pain that comes with the suspended intimacy of communication. After all, Rousseau had written in *Émile* that "all our customs" are "only submission, torture, coercion", in short, the "civilized man" is "bound by conventions" throughout his life.[28] However, Knigge prefers these bonds to the unprotected exposure, since the subjectivity he starts from in *Ueber den Umgang mit Menschen* is constituted within power relations that threaten it: From this perspective, an open-hearted communication, like unconventionality in general, is risky, and the subject cannot control the risks it takes.

There is also a second great benefit of the convention. Although Knigge warns against "taking such measures that put our inner value at stake."[29] However, this "inner value" is "like a treasure hidden underground" and while it remains gold if it is not raised, it can be used to the benefit of humanity "if it is brought to light and circulated by the stamp of convention."[30] In this way, the convention is given the value of a universally established speech that also mediates universally.

However, it is by no means exclusively positively connoted, as is clear from many passages, as in this one (which at the same time, through its metaphors, gives an indication of Knigge's constant efforts to prevent unauthorized reprints of his works):

> The conversation with children is highly interesting to a sensible man. Here neholds in them the book of nature in an uncorrupted edition. Children appear as they really are, He sees the true, simple original text, which one can often find with difficulty later on under

---

[25] Knigge 1993, pp. 47–48. The passage is not included in the first edition of 1788.

[26] Pittrof 1989, p. 52.

[27] Rousseau 1790. See Nübel 1999.

[28] Rousseau in *Émile*, quoted here according to Göttert 1995, p. 147.

[29] Knigge 1788, Second Part, p. 65 (cf. Knigge 1993, p. 324).

[30] Knigge 1788, Second Part, p. 65 (cf. Knigge 1993, p. 324).

the heap of foreign commentaries, embellishments and adornments; The disposition to originality in the characters, which later on, alas! is either entirely lost, or hidden behind the mask of finer manners and conventional considerations, lies still openly there [...][31]

There is thus a original character, an inner essence, which is hidden by conventions, a self-consciousness, which can be lost. Knigge's advice to adapt oneself outwardly in order to live agreeably thus entails the risk of not finding oneself again, because courtly conversation demands the "extirpation, grinding down of every characteristic peculiarity and originality".[32] Although it is advisable and right to inform oneself about the conventions of social intercourse, one should not deny the inner truth, the character, which is possible at all because the rules of prudence are bound to moral duties; thus the underlying, the moral subject, remains.

Similar to the dealing with children a special case—and in the book a complementary chapter to the dealing with courtiers—is the dealing among friends, from which "all dissimulation must be banished". "There all false shame, all constraint, which convenience, exaggerated friendliness and mistrust lay upon in common life, must fall away. Trust and sincerity must reign among intimate friends."[33] But even here there are rules which stand in the way of a quite immediate social intercourse; even here one should be cautious, after all there are very few really trustworthy friends, and even these should not be entrusted with everything. There is thus a quite fundamental reserve, which seems to be the basis of social intercourse for Knigge.

In terms of the ethics of conversation, Knigge wants to move beyond "a certain middle ground"[34] that is located at the border of the person between mere external conventions and inner nature. There should be no excessive flattery among people, but also no raw self-interest—it is better, however, to stick to one's own background and education in case of doubt, than to try to conform to completely foreign conventions.[35] The art of conversation mediates between these areas.

4 Conclusion

Knigge's book is on the threshold of the estates-based society and the meritocratic society. It is a project from the end of the Ancien Régime, from where the bourgeois society is not yet visible, but already foreseeable, and where Knigge provides rules for this foreseen possibility. In this respect, the project is similar to

---

[31] Knigge 1788, First Part, p. 98 (cf. Knigge 1993, p. 145).
[32] Knigge 1788, Second Part, p. 42 (cf. Knigge 1993, p. 311).
[33] Knigge 1788, First Part, p. 245 (cf. Knigge 1993, p. 211).
[34] Knigge 1788, First Part, p. 60 (cf. Knigge 1993, p. 45).
[35] Cf. Knigge 1788, Second Part, p. 7 (cf. Knigge 1993, p. 288): "Do not deny your principles, your status, your birth, your education; thus the high and the low will not be able to deny you their respect."

that of Friedrich Schiller's *Ästhetische Erziehung des Menschen* (1795), which, however, has already processed the experience of the reign of terror in revolutionary France and therefore proceeds from a consistently negative evaluation of the Revolution. Even more than Schiller, however, Knigge always sees the individual involved in a communicative event—the intercourse—and focuses his whole attention on it. What is one's own, the essence of a person, interests him insofar as it has to be protected from the risks of dealing with people. In dealing with others, however, this essence is never "in play", but only hints at it.

The culture of conversation is a fundamental element in the transformation of the estates-based society. Knigge evaluates the conventional values of this society ambivalently, because on the one hand the conventional values stand in contrast to the inner values as inferior, on the other hand the convention is a means of self-preservation and coping with others and even a way of the subject to objectify, that is, to be effective in society at all.

Knigge's book is an attempt to establish and assert individuality (one's own and others') in the midst of a highly conventionalized environment. Intercourse conventions are means to this end. In the course of its history of editions and reception in bourgeois society, that is, after Knigge's death, it became a mere handbook of the mere conventionalization of intercourse. In this respect, it is addressed to a future bourgeois society; however, after this society had actually arisen, it received the book differently, namely as a greeting from a courtly society to which the bourgeoisie, which had just emancipated itself to some extent, now wanted to join. Instead of the respectful, coordinated intercourse, the tone of the "so-called great world" prevails.[36] "Unfortunately!"—anticipating the fate of his own book—"this tone will be set and spread by princes and nobles [...] and imitated by all classes that claim some claim to fine living."[37]

References

Gelbin, Cathy S. und Gilman, Sander L.: Cosmopolitanisms and the Jews. Ann Arbor: University of Michigan Press 2017.

[Goethe, Johann Wolfgang]: Die Leiden des jungen Werthers. Zweyter Theil. Leipzig: Weygandsche Buchhandlung 1774.

Göttert, Karl-Heinz: Knigge, oder Von den Illusionen des anständigen Lebens. München: dtv 1995.

Hacke, Axel: Über den Anstand in schwierigen Zeiten und die Frage, wie wir miteinander umgehen. München: Kunstmann 2017.

Hermes, Stefan: Die Revolution als Posse. Politik und Komik in Goethes Lustspiel ‚Der Bürgergeneral' (1793), in: Ernest W. B. Hess-Lüttich, Carlotta von Maltzan und Kathleen Thorpe (Hg.): Gesellschaften in Bewegung. Literatur und Sprache in Krisen- und Umbruchzeiten. Frankfurt a.M u.a.: Lang 2016, S. 69–87.

Klüger, Ruth: Knigges *Umgang mit Menschen*. Eine Vorlesung. Göttingen: Wallstein 1996.

---

[36] Knigge 1788, Zweyter Theil, p. 43 (cf. Knigge 1993, p. 311).

[37] Knigge 1788, Zweyter Theil, p. 43 (cf. Knigge 1993, p. 311).

Knigge, Adolph Freiherr von: Ueber den Umgang mit Menschen. Hannover: Schmidtsche Buchhandlung 1788 (Reprint Hannover: Hahnsche Buchhandlung 1967).

Knigge, Adolph Freiherr: Über den Umgang mit Menschen (= Ausgewählte Werke, hg. von Wolfgang Fenner, Bd. 6). Hannover: Fackelträger 1993.

Mihaylova, Katerina: Gewissen als Pflicht gegen sich selbst. Zur Entwicklung des *forum internum* von Pufendorf bis Kant, in: Simon Bunke und Katerina Mihaylova (Hg.): Gewissen. Interdisziplinäre Perspektiven auf das 18. Jahrhundert. Würzburg: Königshausen & Neumann 2015, S. 53–70.

Nübel, Birgit: „jede Zeile von ihm mit dem wärmsten Interesse": Aspekte der Rousseau-Rezeption bei Knigge, in: Martin Rector (Hg.): Zwischen Weltklugheit und Moral: Der Aufklärer Adolph Freiherr Knigge. Göttingen: Wallstein 1999, S. 103–121.

Pittrof, Thomas: Knigges Aufklärung über den Umgang mit Menschen. München: Fink 1989.

[Rousseau, Jean-Jacques]: Fortsetzung der Bekenntnisse J. J. Rousseau's. Uebersetzt von Adolph Freyherrn Knigge. III.–IV. Theil, Berlin: Unger 1790.

Rüllmann, Almut: Adolph Freiherr Knigge und die Juden, in: Horst Gronke, Thomas Meyer und Barbara Neißer (Hg.): Antisemitismus bei Kant und anderen Denkern der Aufklärung. Würzburg: Königshausen & Neumann 2001, S. 153–242.

Back to Community. Criticism of Conversation in German-Language Reflexion on Conversation in the 20th Century

Simon Meier-Vieracker

Abstract

The normative discourse on conversation in the German-speaking world of the 20th century is characterized by a clear break with the ideal of sociable conversation, while the private-intimate dialogue experiences a significant valorisation. In dialogue philosophical and existentialist approaches as well as in sociological and, especially after the Second World War, pedagogical treatises, fundamental reservations are expressed against the traditional forms of sociability. The contribution examines this discourse in the methodological framework of a history of mentality of dialogue and contextualizes the devaluation of sociable conversation with emphatic theories of community, as they were developed in a culture critical motivation based on Tönnies' distinction between community and society. The contribution approaches the historicity of successful communication through the consideration of historically situated interpretations and normative loadings of communicative practice, the remote effects of which can still be seen in newer scientific approaches to (historical) conversation practices.

Keywords

Mental history of dialogical research · Conversation reflection · Discourse history · Community · Philosophy of dialogue · Existential philosophy

S. Meier-Vieracker (✉)
Technische Universität Dresden, Dresden, Germany
e-mail: simon.meier-vieracker@tu-dresden.de

© The Author(s), under exclusive license to Springer-Verlag GmbH, DE, part of Springer Nature 2023
C. Strosetzki (ed.), *The Value of Conversation*,
https://doi.org/10.1007/978-3-662-67200-6_7

1 Introduction

In Theodor Fontane's first novel, *Irrungen, Wirrungen*, published in 1887, there is a scene at the beginning in which Baron Botho von Rienäcker is visiting the seamstress Lene Nimptsch, whom he had previously met at a boating party, and is introducing her to the art of conversation. Lene had previously been impressed by Botho's ability to "start a conversation with so many foreign ladies [...] without a second thought", whereupon he offers to "give a demonstration of table talk".[1] In a sort of role-playing game, in which Lene takes on the role of a countess and the also present neighbour, the gardener Dörr, that of a baroness, the conversation then proceeds in loose order on the weather, travel plans, the advantages of Dresden and the Saxon Switzerland, and finally on a morel bed in a Polish castle. For, as Botho finally concludes,

> in reality it doesn't matter what one talks about. If it's not morels, it's mushrooms, and if it's not the red Polish castle, then it's Schlößchen Tegel or Saatwinkel or Valentinswerder. Or Italy or Paris, or the city railway, or whether the Panke should be filled in. It's all the same. You can always say something about each of them, and whether you like it or not. And "yes" is just as good as "no".[2]

This image, which Fontane allows his protagonist to draw, or rather: to caricature, of the art of conversation, well captures the basic outlines of the same and also its ideal and social location in late 19th century. In conversation, it is important to strike a casual tone in an informal atmosphere for purposeless, social exchange, in which the objects are not decisive in their factual content, but rather their suitability for pleasant conversation.[3] And even if the equality of the conversation topics is translated into an equality of the conversation partners, so that everyone can participate equally, the cultivation of this art remains reserved for the upper classes and can be used for social distinction.[4] This is precisely why the bourgeois Lene is so much impressed and intimidated at the same time by Botho's performance, from which she remains excluded: Botho speaks in the role play for the "little Countess" Lene, to whom only audience reactions are allowed.

However, the staging, which is clearly inscribed here in the conversation, already shows signs of ironic distance. The ideal of conversation, which Schleiermacher had still placed at the center of his normative social theory,[5] has become fragile. In this respect, the novel joins a whole series of texts of this time in which conversation is only mentioned as an ideal form of communication

---

[1] Fontane 1888, p. 34.

[2] Fontane 1888, p. 37.

[3] This idea is of course much older and can be traced back, for example, to 17th century France. See Schrott and Strosetzki 2020, p. 4.

[4] Linke 1996, p. 150.

[5] Schleiermacher 1984, pp. 165–84.

with certain reservations. As early as 1857, in an encyclopedia article on talk, social conversation was equated with "mere chatter".[6] In Moritz Lazarus' treatise *On Conversations*, which is commonly referred to as the earliest draft of a scientifically empirical conversation research, it is in line with Fontane's literary implementation that the "finest conversations" would be held "among complete strangers" and that it would be particularly important here to create "a mild excitement or to make quick transitions into distant areas possible through wit, paradoxes and anecdotes."[7] But even more valuable than these "loose [conversations] full of cheerfulness and wit" are, according to Lazarus, "those serious dialogues that thoughtful people have with each other in the deepest interest of what occupies them mentally"—constellations of talk that are incompatible with the requirements of sociable conversation in the semi-public of the dinner party and the salon. In the same year, Nietzsche characterizes the dialogue as "the perfect conversation", in contrast to which social conversation in a larger circle must "lose in individualizing finesse".[8] A little later, in his history of literature of the dialogue, Rudolf Hirzel strictly delimits it from conversation. The essence of the latter is the "colorful change of more or less witty remarks, the jumping of the conversation from one subject to the other", whereas the dialogue "is immersed in the objects to be discussed and therefore cannot flutter like a butterfly from one to the other".[9] Finally, in 1911, the sociologist Georg Simmel dedicated a monument to conversation in his *Sociology of Sociability*, in which he characterizes sociability, where "talking is a legitimate end in itself",[10] as a "form of socialization".[11] As such, it can compensate for the individuals overloaded with factual demands in modern society and can serve as a retreat and place of recreation. But it can hardly, as Schleiermacher had still defined it as the "free intercourse of reasonable men forming themselves into a society",[12] serve as a source of morality and knowledge.

It is by no means the case that conversation disappears from philosophy. On the contrary, something like a philosophy of dialogue emerges in the 19th century, which highlights the exclusive achievements of dialogue for subject constitution and truth finding.[13] In this fundamental philosophical sense, the dialogue enters into opposition on the one hand to monological thinking, but on the other hand also to social conversation, which must be ethically and aesthetically normed by

---

[6] Scheidler 1857, p. 331.

[7] Lazarus 1878, p. 244. Lazarus was personally well-known to Fontane, and the latter, who placed great value on the realistic portrayal of conversations in his literary works, is likely to be familiar with the treatise *On Conversation*.

[8] Nietzsche 1967, p. 267.

[9] Hirzel 1895, pp. 4–5.

[10] Simmel 1911, p. 12.

[11] Simmel 1911, p. 4.

[12] Schleiermacher 1984, p. 165.

[13] Heinrichs 1972, pp. 226–229.

rules of polite behavior.[14] With authors such as Humboldt or Feuerbach, who were later referred to as the founders of so-called dialogical philosophy, the conversation between I and You and thus the personal dialogue, which gives the normative measure. This continues in the configuration of philosophy of dialogue in the proper sense in the 20th century. Social conversation is often only used as a negative foil, against the background of which the "real" dialogue, which is always a highly personal dialogue, stands out all the clearer. The reflection on successful dialogue, which radiates from philosophy into adjacent disciplines in the German-speaking world in the 20th century, is thus decisively shaped by this.

In the following, I would like to trace this development in the period between 1918 and around 1960 from a perspective of history of concepts and discourse history and then ask what knowledge about conversation and the normative orders of the types of talk is expressed therein. To do this, I will first derive the methodological framework of this research question. I will then discuss approaches to dialogue of the 1920s and 1930s and contextualize the devaluation of social conversation observable therein with Tönnies' distinction between community and society, which serves as a discursive basic figure shaping the metapragmatic discourse of the time. I will then show how these motives are taken up again after the Second World War. Finally, I will discuss how this discourse still affects newer scientific perspectives on (historical) conversational practices.

2 Methodological framework: History of mentality of dialogue

Conversation research has a long tradition in linguistics. Karl Bühler, for example, anchors his theory of communication in the "living exchange conversation"[15] and Karl Vossler describes the conversation as the original form of existence of language.[16] Since the availability of tape recorders and corresponding recording and transcription methods made authentic conversations accessible to analysis in great detail from around 1950, conversation research then established itself as a sub-discipline of linguistics, whose basic concepts and methods also radiate to other areas of linguistics such as sociolinguistics.[17] Linguistic conversation research typically sees itself as an empirical and purely descriptive discipline, in which normative questions about the conditions for success or the value of certain forms of talk are only asked with great restraint.[18] Explicitly normative approaches, ranging from philosophy of dialogue to Habermas' theory of discourse without domination, are

---

[14] Meier 2020, p. 120.
[15] Bühler 1978, p. 93.
[16] Vossler 1923, pp. 665–79.
[17] Meier 2018, pp. 283–302.
[18] Deppermann 2007, p. 52; Gronke 2020.

usually viewed with suspicion in linguistic conversation research. The observation of the reality of talk in its empirical diversity would be too much obscured by the normative assumptions of these approaches, which rather should be captured and described without prejudice.

However, from a cultural studies perspective, the historicity of interpersonal communication has often been pointed out. This not only affects changes in certain conversation practices, such as greeting and address forms, but also essentially the normative reflection on communication and the changes observed here. In a cultural history of communication, as Linke outlines, for example, it is necessary to shed light on the values and mental dispositions that underlie and possibly also condition the historically located conversation practices.[19] Which forms of talk are framed as particularly valuable and desirable or rather problematic and how and with what reach are such framings possibly translated into directives, be it in moral-philosophical treatises or in directly normative contexts such as etiquette books or curricula? Just as the history of language places the history of language usage next to the history of language consciousness, in which "changes in communicative mentalities, attitudes and theories"[20] are to be captured, it is necessary, within the framework of a "history of communication consciousness"[21] also to ask about the changing idealising conceptions of communication. In somewhat different terminology, Kilian has outlined the history of mentality of dialogue as an important pillar of historical dialogue research, which is to reconstruct "the knowledge of people about communication and the normative order of contemporary worlds of communication"[22]. Different kinds of sources on communication are questioned in this research perspective on "the ideal—and sometimes ideological—dress that sorts and types of talk were put on by certain groups of speakers."[23]

Under these circumstances, normative concepts of communication and thus also philosophical theories of conversation return to linguistic conversation research—less as normative standards that would allow their evaluation in empirical analysis, but as objects of historical discourse analysis. In fact, the view to be thrown on theories of successful conversation in the following is a consistently historicizing one.[24] It is less about, how this is the case in most philosophical approaches, whether the respective normative statements about conversations

---

[19] Linke 2008a, p. 36. Here there are cross-references to the established term in Romance Studies of the discourse tradition, which describes historically located patterns and routines of communication that are considered appropriate by a speech community and thus normatively contoured, cf. Schrott 2020, p. 34.

[20] Mattheier 1995, p. 15.

[21] Meier 2014b, pp. 250–265.

[22] Kilian 2002, p. 46.

[23] Kilian 2005, p. 52.

[24] Schrott 2020, p. 48.

are plausible and justified and which of the normative concepts of communication should be adopted as a guideline. Rather, the interest is focused on why conversation was conceptualized in a certain epoch in this way and not otherwise. A suitable approach to these questions is provided by discourse-semantic analyses of the—more or less explicit—negotiations of meaning of the metadiscursive vocabulary, which has to be contextualized from a historical and social perspective. The questions of how this vocabulary is ordered, which words are set in opposition to each other, which semantic connection points are sought or avoided with related words and why can be instructive, especially in a historical comparative perspective.

3 The Idealization of the Dialogue in Philosophy

As stated in the introduction, the ideal of conversation already gets clear cracks in the late 19th century. Even if sociability and the demands placed on it are often thematized when reflecting on the achievements of the communication, affirmative representations of sociable conversation are hardly to be found anymore. In contrast, the private-intimate dialogue gains in radiance. But above all, after 1918 a whole series of texts appears, through which this turning away from the ideal of conversation in favor of an idealization of the dialogue runs like a leitmotif.

The outstanding work of this time is probably Martin Buber's *I and Thou*, in which he develops a comprehensive social ontology[25] which assigns a fundamental, almost constitutive role for the subject and its personality to the interpersonal relationship in full reciprocity. Buber justifies this position linguistically with reference to the—linguistically well-founded[26]—functional difference between the pronouns of the first and second person *I* and *you* on the one hand and those of the third person *it* on the other hand. Only in the reciprocal address, in which the pronouns *I* and *you* refer to the persons involved in the conversation, the human being comes to himself, as it were. Already the title *I and You* makes it clear that above all the dialogue—Buber himself uses the term "Zwiesprache"[27]—is the mode of the interpersonal, in which the human being comes to his "destiny"[28]. For this dialogue, Buber formulates a number of conditions for success, which revolve around the concept of "immediacy"[29]. One must face it "with the whole being"[30] and forego anticipations and purposeful actions as much as possible, and even the

---

[25] Theunissen 1977.
[26] Bühler 1999, p. 113.
[27] Buber 1962, p. 142.
[28] Buber 1962, p. 104.
[29] Buber 1962, p. 85.
[30] Buber 1962, p. 79.

understanding of a factual topic should ultimately be left behind in favor of personal "encounter"[31].

The apparent preference for purposeless forms of communication, in which even the topics of talk are secondary, can of course be traced back to earlier times and also underlies the idealization of conversation. However, the narrowing down to the dialogue clearly marks a break with the ideal of conversation. This becomes clear when *I and You* is contextualized with the present-day and cultural-critical essays that Buber had published in the years before. In these, Buber, who was a member of the life reformist *Neue Gemeinschaft,* had called for a comprehensive renewal of the forms of human coexistence, a "new and real becoming of the relationships between people"[32]. And already here Buber formulated quite explicitly a commandment of "immediacy"[33], which he sets in opposition to the conventional and institutionalized forms of social interaction of modern society. Unspoken, but still quite clearly recognizable as a counter-image, the semi-publicity of social conversation with its conventional forms of decency is here and later also in *I and You* shown to be incompatible with the requirements for successful conversations. This differentiation becomes quite clear in the essay *Zwiesprache,* published in 1930, in which Buber, in a typology of communication, on the one hand differentiates the "true [...] dialogue"[34] from mere factual agreement and on the other hand from a number of "pseudo-dialogues"[35], which, in addition to the debate primarily aimed at rhetorical effectiveness and friendly chat, also includes conversation. Because, as Buber formulated it, this is

> neither determined by the need to communicate something, nor by the need to find out something, nor by the desire to influence someone, nor by the desire to get in touch with someone, but only by the desire to confirm one's own self-esteem by reading the impression made or to stabilize oneself who has become unstable.

This representation, of course, exaggerates the dark side of conversation, which is thus easily condemned. Nevertheless, it is striking that its positive aspects as a source of morality or even cultivated pleasure do not come into view at all and that no attempt is made to derive such degenerate forms of conversation into a "good" conversation practice.[36] While by Simmel the opposition line was drawn between the purely economically motivated meetings on the one hand and the purposeless

---

[31] Buber 1962, p. 85.
[32] Buber 1919, p. 346.
[33] Buber 1953, p. 291.
[34] Buber 1962, p. 192.
[35] Buber 1962, 180.
[36] Negative representations of conversation practices are not a sign of the 20th century, but can be demonstrated for many epochs. But, unlike the texts dealt with here, they serve to make the requirements for a good conversation stand out even more clearly. See, for example, Linke 2008b, p. 119.

conversation on the other, now both are separated from the highly personal dialogue in which man finds his destiny. Even the exchange oriented towards factual knowledge and understanding, as it was mostly in focus in the philosophical conversation theories of the 19th century, plays a minor role in favour of the personal encounter in the dialogue.

Buber is not alone in this departure from traditional conversation ideals. Also worth mentioning is the dialogical philosophy of Ferdinand Ebner, which also opposes the factual agreement to the self-expression in dialogue,[37] as well as Siegfried Kracauer's theory of the productive dialogue, in which two partners experience a development of personality that is only possible together and with "the whole human being"[38] in "existential connectedness"[39]. While Simmel had pointed out that in conversation the "most personal thing in life" must be kept out of the conversation, it is now precisely this most personal concerns that are to be determinative of the dialogue. The idealization of the dialogue is also continued in the phenomenological tradition in the wake of Heidegger and his clear criticism of the "chatter" in public life,[40] when, for example, Karl Löwith states that "being together" is limited to "being two" under "exclusion of the public"[41] (55). Only "in private"[42] is meeting in full mutuality possible, in which the human being comes to him/herself. Communication far removed from all social typifications and practical purposes, which once characterized conversation as "form of socialization" according to Simmel, is now considered possible only in the most personal dialogue. Even Gadamer, who in his habilitation thesis *Plato's Dialectical Ethics* attaches much greater importance to factual agreement in conversation and sees the reduction to a "communication of oneself" (*Sichmitteilen*) typical of dialogical philosophy with skepticism,[43] it is still the dialogue away from the public that is particularly distinguished.

As another significant approach of this time, in which the dialogue is idealized, Karl Jaspers' theory of existential communication can finally be mentioned.[44] Quite comparable to the contemporary approaches of Buber or Löwith, Jaspers develops a detailed normative typology of communication, in which, in addition to the merely practical-utilitarian communication, the matter-of-factly argumentative argumentation and the ritualized communication with group identity-forming function appear to be deficient. Jaspers sets them against existential communication, in which the impersonality experienced in the other forms of communication is overcome. This existential communication must be "sought with

---

[37] Ebner 1980.
[38] Kracauer 1990, p. 224.
[39] Kracauer 1990, p. 225.
[40] Heidegger 2001, p. 167.
[41] Löwith 1928, p. 55.
[42] Löwith 1928, p. 55.
[43] Strosetzki 2020, pp. 14–15.
[44] Jaspers 1932.

the commitment of my whole being"[45] and require complete equality of the partners, which, however, in contrast to the conversation, which also assumes equality at least, must be accompanied by "absolute[r] openness"[46]. Tactful restraint, as required in social intercourse or, as Jaspers himself puts it, in "merely social intercourse"[47], precisely prevents the advances of existential communication, in which man alone comes to self-consciousness.

And so Jaspers' existential communication is also expressly limited to the dialogue "between two"[48]. If the goal in conversation is to include as many people as possible, this very demand for the whole self to be involved makes it impossible. Although sociability can create the prerequisite for existential communication in the form of "purposeless, playful [...] togetherness"[49], the social basic maxim of politeness, the orientation to the norms of propriety and tact, must be overcome in order for existential communication to take place:

> These world forms [of politeness, SMV] [...] remain superficial. Because they are meaningless, they are suitable for creating smoothness in interaction, but they are not able to bring people into communication. Sociable interaction as only this remains stuck in the Dasein situation; existential communication, however, takes place where no society penetrates. In it, the sociable forms are overcome by relativizing them.[50]

The attitude of unlimited openness demanded in existential communication is only possible "in contrast to sociability"[51]. Here, conversation has completely lost its normative power and now only serves as a negative foil against which successful communication is defined as a radically different form of togetherness.

4 The Dialogue of the Community and the Conversation of Society

In all of the approaches mentioned that take the private-intimate dialogue as an ideal, there is, despite the philosophical foundation that seems to address anthropological constants, an unmistakable critical reference to present time. The idealized image drawn of the dialogue as an encounter, becoming a person, or existential realization is always also a counter-image to the perceived conditions

---

[45] Jaspers 1932, p. 55.
[46] Jaspers 1932, p. 65.
[47] Jaspers 1932, p. 59.
[48] Jaspers 1932, p. 61.
[49] Jaspers 1932, p. 95.
[50] Jaspers 1932, p. 97.
[51] Jaspers 1932, p. 97.

of time, in which humanity appears to live in a state of alienation. In particular, Buber attributes a devastating "diminution of the human capacity for relationship"[52] to the modern society with its anonymous social apparatus of economy and politics, which is then to be healed, as it were, by the dialogue as a "living, incessantly renewed process of relating"[53].

This perspective and also its argumentative and metaphorical implementation find an important model in Ferdinand Tönnies' work *Community and Society*, which was published in a second edition in 1912 and had a great influence in a cultural-critical reading after the First World War. In reaction to the social change towards the industrial society, Tönnies uses this pair of terms to capture a historical development from community (of the village or the family) to the much more anonymous society with its contractually secured institutions. This is a normative distinction that Tönnies underlies with a metaphor of the organic-living in contrast to the mechanical-artificial:

> Community is the permanent and true living together, society only a temporary and apparent one. And according to this, community is to be understood as a living organism, society as a mechanical aggregate and artefact.[54]

A communication-theoretical flip side of this distinction, which is of great importance for further reception, is the juxtaposition of an understanding based on immediate participation to the purposively sought agreement by means of artificially created sign systems.[55]

Now it seems that the aforementioned designs that idealize the conversation are also joining this normative theory of community, which constructs the history of modern society as a history of decline of its communication forms. The pair of terms community and society turns out to be a discursive basic figure,[56] which fundamentally shapes the normative, reflexive discourse of that time. Buber's demand for a "renewal and authenticity of relationships between people", which leads to the "formation of ... new community cells"[57] is to be mentioned here, but also in *I and Thou* the metaphor of the "living, constantly renewed relationship process", which in modernity has "frozen" into civilization[58] is continued. Jaspers also describes existential communication as a "developing seed"[59] which can only thrive outside of society, and Albert Schweitzer diagnoses that the stunting of human communities in modern society is particularly evident in the forms

---

[52] Buber 1962, p. 106.
[53] Buber 1962, p. 114.
[54] Tönnies 2019, p. 126.
[55] Tönnies 2019, pp. 143f.
[56] Busse 1997, pp. 17–35.
[57] Buber 1919.
[58] Buber 1962, p. 114.
[59] Jaspers 1932, p. 60.

of sociability in which aloofness is legitimized as "worldly behavior"[60]. Finally, sociological approaches of this time also take up the communicative theory of community, when, for example, Pieper explains the contrast between community and society explicitly on the basis of the prevailing communication forms. The "communal dialogue" is the "most personal expression and a *'Speaking-out'* of the interlocutors"[61] and characterized by "closeness, intimacy, unreservedness"[62]. Pieper contrasts this with the "social conversation", which is determined by "social etiquette"[63] and find its expression in particular in sociability with its distancing forms of social interaction. The deep mistrust of traditional forms of social conversation expressed in all these texts thus fits into an emphatic concept of community, which is outlined as an antithesis to the alleged decline forms of modern society. In the 19th century, the term "good society" was used in the sense of a social gathering, in which, for example, the business-motivated roles of the participants were temporarily suspended.[64] But now this seems to have become a contradictory formula, and "good" can only be the society if it becomes a community.

A most informative source in this context is Helmuth Plessner's 1924 work *Grenzen der Gemeinschaft [Limits of Community]*, which subjects the community enthusiasm of the time after the First World War to a fundamental criticism. The book has hardly had any effect whatsoever in contemporary reception, but it throws light on the ruling discourse on conversation of the time by way of negation. Plessner reconstructs an "ethos of absolute unreservedness"[65] and the striving for "abolition of artificiality and life-alienation, of impersonality"[66] as the ideal framework of community enthusiasm. However, he rejects this on the basis of the anthropologically anchored need for recognition and shamefulness of humans, which endows the "abolition of the intimate sphere of the person"[67] demanded in the community with violent features. Therefore, Plessner sets out on a defense of society and of social customs, which he characterizes as follows:

> social behavior, mastery not only of written and codified conventions, but also of the virtuoso handling of the play-forms with which people come close to each other without hitting each other, with which they distance themselves from each other without wounding each other through indifference. The atmosphere is one of amiability, not of earnestness; the game and the observance of its rules are its moral code. The forced distance between

---

[60] Schweitzer 1923, p. 15.
[61] Pieper 1933, p. 71.
[62] Pieper 1933, p. 54.
[63] Pieper 1933, p. 49.
[64] Kieserling 2001, pp. 177–91.
[65] Plessner 1981, p. 58.
[66] Plessner 1981, p. 40.
[67] Plessner 1981, p. 45.

people is ennobled to become distance; the insulting indifference, coldness, brutality of living side by side are made ineffective by the forms of politeness, deference, and attentiveness, and too great closeness is countered by reserve.[68]

Here, motives from the traditional theory of conversation are taken up again, such as the sociability of play, which requires virtuoso handling of the forms, or the middle position between indifference and too much closeness through the forms of politeness. In particular, in social intercourse, an "art of not getting too close, of not offending" is required, which Plessner—like Simmel[69]—also calls tact:

> All explicit, every eruptive authenticity is avoided. Untruth, which spares, is still better than truth, which hurts. [...] In this sphere there should be neither good nor evil, neither truth nor falsehood, but only the values of benevolence, the hygiene of the greatest possible consideration.[70]

The explicit postponement of factual and content-related issues and truth claims in favor of benevolence, which at the same time comes with a command of restraint—all this is based on an ideal of conversation that can be traced back at least to the 17th century.[71] But the decisive counterpart to the sociable conversation is no longer the purpose-oriented sphere of business life, whose serious role commitments are then to be played down in conversation by an egalitarian conversation style.[72] The counterpart is rather that private-intimate dialogue in the community, which is mostly raised to the ideal by his contemporaries. Especially in Plessner's criticism of the emphatic concept of community, which only sees successful communication as possible through the renunciation of all forms of social behavior, the discursive figure of community and society shapes the normative reflection on the conversation.

5 Reflection on Conversation in the Post-War Period

After the Second World War, the democratization policy of the Allied occupation forces in the West German occupation zones or the Federal Republic of Germany as well as in Austria set new accents for the normative discourse on conversation. As a decisive instrument of democratization, discussion events in various manifestations were considered, since the discussion was conceptualized as the mode of

---

[68] Plessner 1981, p. 80.

[69] Simmel (1911, p. 5). A few decades later, Goffman (1955) will take this up, devoting special attention to the so-called *face-work* in his theory of interaction rituals: face-saving actions both in one's own behavior and in the treatment of others. Goffman calls the competence to exercise appropriate practices of face-work "tact" Goffman 1955, p. 217.

[70] Plessner 1981, p. 107.

[71] Accarino 2002, pp. 141–146.

[72] Kieserling 2001, p. 187.

public and participatory opinion-forming as democratic practice par excellence.[73] In particular, in pedagogical contexts there are numerous contributions in which the—often explicitly as 'American' or 'Anglo-Saxon' apostrophized—discussion methods are systematized and reflected in their achievements for the establishment and consolidation of a democratic society after the dictatorship.[74]

The almost euphoric reception of these methods in the early post-war years, which was certainly also promoted by the Allied control of the publishing industry, soon subsided, however, and the number of skeptical voices increased.[75] The discussion of American provenance is characterized by many authors as a foreign cultural practice and as a form of communication that must remain purely "technical"[76], thereby leaving a supposedly typical German need for conversations "about the last personal fundamental questions"[77] unsatisfied. "But our actual task", Müller-Schwefe formulated, referring explicitly to the German nation with the possessive pronoun *our*,[78] is "not the discussion, but the conversation [Gespräch]."[79] Here, conversation is not, as is common in recent linguistic approaches, an umbrella term for all forms of verbal interaction,[80] but takes a position in a consistently normative conversation typology, which is also translated into national demarcations.

This figure finds its theoretical justification in an explicit return to dialogical and existential approaches, the idealization of the most personal, private-intimate dialogue is now taken up and continued. The political relevance of conversation is not denied, but precisely dialogue is raised to the preferred "intimate [n] starting point"[81] of the political debate. Only such dialogus "connect from person to person, open up the respective cores of being" [82], while public discussion formats are characterized by a "too strong strain on the character of compromise" [83].

Thus, the—often nationalist-based—separation from the discussion as a practice mainly oriented towards factual arguments and, consequently, purpose-oriented, does not lead to an idealization of the purposeless conversation, which is in turn rejected as inadequate after the First World War. The often stated purposelessness of dialogue as a prerequisite does not bring sociable conversation into focus, but only the very personal dialogue. And even more: Wherever the conversation is

---

[73] Verheyen 2010.
[74] Meier 2013, pp. 167 ff.
[75] Meier 2014a, pp. 106–124.
[76] Müller 1954, p. 20.
[77] Müller 1954, p. 20.
[78] Müller 2009, pp. 377–423.
[79] Müller-Schwefe 1956, p. 10.
[80] Hess-Lüttich 2020, p. 9.
[81] Sieburg 1961, p. 177.
[82] Pöggeler 1964, p. 115.
[83] Pöggeler 1964, p. 118.

mentioned at all, it only serves as a contrast, against the background of which the requirements and achievements of the "real" dialogue become all the more clear. Willy Kramp's essay, head of the Evangelical Study Centre Villigst, is revealing in this respect, in which he firstly differentiates dialogue from discussion, since it "can also encompass the human depths, indeed the hopes, destinies, values of those involved in the conversation".[84] But even the "talk that we call conversation in a derogatory sense"—Kramp gives the "coffee house conversation", for example, as an example[85]—is a "stereotyped and externalized form of dialogue".[86] Even in a *dictionary of sociology*, it says in the entry for the term "Gespräch", which obviously takes up the antithesis of community and society again:

> In addition to the real dialogue in community relations, there is a very weakened form in modern "society". In the waiting room, in the railway compartment, next to the need to speak, a kind of obligation towards the situation partner often arises to engage in conversation.[87]

Linguistics is also involved in this reflexive discourse. The English scholar Wolfgang Schmidt-Hidding, for example, contrasts the word fields of *Gespräch* and *conversation* in German and English in a philological study. The latter he recognizes their ability to "practical and political areas", *Gespräch* is particularly "for mental contact and the discussion of issues relating to human existence"[88] and can only succed as "intimate dialogue"[89] succeed. The required for the conversation attitude Schmidt-Hidding describes with "self-irony, humor, willingness to compromise and tolerance"[90]. This grasps the 17th century ideal conversation quite well, but the author makes it clear that this form of communication, which ultimately deals with "the society itself"[91], but not with man, must remain incomplete. So he expressed elsewhere explicitly the opposition "conversation [Unterhaltung] —real conversation [echtes Gespräch]"[92], with authenticity being mainly linked to the latter. As after the First World War, conversation is thus not only denied moral potential and its determination is limited to the mere pleasure. Conversation with its demands on the external form is explicitly rejected as a practice and is said to be overcome. Only with Jürgen Habermas, who recognizes in

---

[84] Kramp 1956, p. 587.
[85] Kramp 1956, p. 586.
[86] Kramp 1956, p. 585.
[87] Wichmann 1955, p. 181.
[88] Schmidt-Hidding 1953, p. 397.
[89] Schmidt-Hidding 1953, p. 387.
[90] Schmidt-Hidding 1953, p. 396.
[91] Schmidt-Hidding 1953, p. 384.
[92] Schmidt-Hidding 1955, p. 199.

his work on the *structural transformation of the public* just in the table societies and salons and the "social conversation unfolded to criticism"[93] a regulatory also for contemporary communication relations, the conversation is—albeit in an idealized version—thus rehabilitated.

6 Conclusions

The historical reconstruction of the discourse on conversation has shown how and with what justification and motivation conversation in the German-speaking world has lost its normative function in the 20th century. Compared to the private-intimate and highly personal dialogue among two, which is considered as the primeval source and origin of both personal identity and successful community, sociable conversation must appear superficial. The egalitarian attitude demanded in conversation, the noble restraint and deferral of purely personal matters in favor of the inclusion of everyone in a cultivated conversation—all of this is not seen as an advantage in the texts of the time. And as can be seen in the post-war discourse, in which pedagogy was particularly involved in normative reflection on conversation and derived teaching formats from it in the sense of conversation education, such idealistic visions can have highly relevant regulative power. From the contemporary perspective of the authors treated here, it would have been contradictory to orient conversation education to conversation. And the concept of the dialogue of religions and cultures was developed primarily in reference to dialogical philosophical ideas and deliberately excluded conversation theories as a possible normative guiding idea.

This discourse may still be effective today. This would at least be one explanation for why affirmative representations of sociable conversation are actually still rather rare in German-speaking countries. Publications such as Stephen Miller's *Conversation. History of a declining art*[94] or Chantal Thomas *L'esprit de conversation*,[95] which explicitly recommend the traditional ideals of conversation as models for the communication culture of the present, are hardly available or only available in translation from English and French. The negative connotations of conversation as "mere" chatter typical of the German-speaking discourse are not found in this form here.

Another manifestation, in a way a remote effect of the discourse reconstructed here, can be found in Germanistic linguistic conversation analysis, where, for example, the question was discussed whether *Konversation* or *konversationell* are suitable partial translations for the English terms *conversation analysis* and *conversational*

---

[93] Habermas 1990, p. 90.
[94] Miller 2007.
[95] Thomas 2011.

implicatures.[96] Early *conversation analysis* was mainly concerned with telephone conversations in partly highly institutionalized contexts such as emergency call numbers and thus approached *conversation* as a neutral category in a way that is only partially compatible with the associations of the German expression *Konversation.*[97] However, there are occasionally normatively connoted definitions of the term *conversation* in English-language research. For example, Goffman states:

> Thus, conversation, restrictively defined, might be identified as the talk occuring when a small number of participants come together and settle into what they perceive to be a few moments cut off from (or carried on the side of) instrumental tasks; a period of idling felt to be an end in itself [...]; everyone is accorded the status of someone whose overall evaluation of the subject matter at hand – whose editorial comments, as it were – is to be encouraged and treated with respect.[98]

This understanding of *conversation* as an equal one is explicitly rejected in recent work in order to be able to apply the concept and the conversation analytical methodology to institutionalized or power-laden interaction.[99] In a German-language introductory work, in which the term *conversation analysis* is used specifically to align itself with the tradition of American *conversation analysis,* it is emphasized that "it is not about cultivated conversations, but about quite everyday conversations, such as those you have when shopping or having breakfast, in the doctor's office or at work."[100] Here it is the normative view of conversation practice as a whole that is rejected.

In contrast, and here we can go back to the initially mentioned literary example, literary studies draw an image of conversation which seems to be affected by reservations at times, which frame conversation as a false model. This becomes clear, for example, in Goetschel's essay *Causerie: Zur Funktion des Gesprächs in Fontanes 'Der Stechlin',* according to which the conversations set in scene in detail and artfully by Fontane "instead of real dialogues (in the sense of Buber) are in fact patterns of causeries and representations of 'pseudo-encounters'".[101] Only the conversations between the figures of Melusine and Lorenzen could be considered as an encounter in the full sense, all other conversations in the novel are "determined from the outside", and sociability remains in the realm of the aesthetic, which "can never advance to dialogue"[102] It is precisely in this metaphor of

---

[96] Polenz 2008, p. 310.

[97] Conversely, the disappointment with which, in my experience, those familiar with traditional conversation ideals react to the research questions, methods and findings of linguistic *conversation analysis* is probably due to this mismatch.

[98] Goffman 1981, p. 14.

[99] Sharrock and Button 2016, p. 34.

[100] Birkner et al. 2020, p. 3.

[101] Goetschel 1995, p. 116.

[102] Goetschel, p. 120; critically see Ernest W.B. Hess-Lüttich 2002, pp. 217–230.

the advance that shows how a normative conversation typology shapes the view of communication and only conceives it as an intermediary stage. Meuthen also characterizes the conversation staged in the novel as "certainly skillful, but ultimately futile, its goal […] failing to materialize". It shows "not the sense fulfilled in 'proper speech', but the experience of its disintegration in semantic polyvalence".[103] This may well capture the ambiguity and fragility with which Fontane also staged the conversation in the example cited at the beginning of *Irrungen, Wirrungen* as a practice in which, for example, claims to truth are completely subordinated to external form and lost in indifferent courtesy of external form. And yet, in the way Goetschel and Meuthen pick out this aspect and extend it into a dialogically based argumentation, one can see how effective the form of criticism of conversation that became established in the early 20th century is up to the present day.

References

Accarino, Bruno: Spuren des Hofstaates in Plessners ‚Grenzen der Gemeinschaft', in: Wolfgang Eßbach, Joachim Fischer und Helmut Lethen, (Hg.): Plessners „Grenzen der Gemeinschaft". Eine Debatte. Frankfurt a.M.: Suhrkamp 2002, S. 131–159.

Angela Schrott: Regeln, Traditionen, Urteile: Verbale Höflichkeit und wie sie gelingt, in: Angela Schrot und Christoph Strosetzki (Hg.): Gelungene Gespräche als Praxis der Gemeinschaftsbildung. Berlin, Boston: De Gruyter 2020. S. 23–54.

Birkner, Karin/Auer, Peter/Bauer, Angelika/Kotthoff Helga: Einführung in die Konversationsanalyse. Berlin, Boston: De Gruyter 2020.

Buber, Martin: Die Revolution und Wir, in: Der Jude 3, 1919, S. 345–64.

Buber, Martin: Was ist zu tun?, in: Martin Buber: Hinweise. Gesammelte Essays. Zürich: Manesse 1953. S. 290–293.

Buber, Martin: Werke. Erster Band: Schriften zur Philosophie. München: Kösel 1962.

Bühler, Karl: Die Krise der Psychologie. Frankfurt a.M. u. a.: Ullstein 1978.

Bühler, Karl: Sprachtheorie. Die Darstellungsfunktion der Sprache. Stuttgart: Lucius & Lucius 1999.

Busse, Dietrich: Das Eigene und das Fremde. Annotationen zu Funktion und Wirkung einer diskurssemantischen Grundfigur, in: Matthias Jung, Martin Wengeler und Karin Böke (Hg.): Die Sprache des Migrationsdiskurses. Das Reden über „Ausländer" in Medien, Politik und Alltag. Opladen: Westdeutscher Verlag 1997, S. 17–35.

Deppermann, Arnulf: Grammatik und Semantik aus gesprächsanalytischer Sicht. Grammatik und Semantik aus gesprächsanalytischer Sicht (= Linguistik – Impulse & Tendenzen 14). Berlin, Boston: De Gruyter 2007.

Ebner, Ferdinand: Das Wort und die geistigen Realitäten. Pneumatologische Fragmente. Frankfurt a.M.: Suhrkamp 1980.

Fontane, Theodor: Irrungen, Wirrungen. Leipzig: Steffens 1888, in: Deutsches Textarchiv, online unter https://www.deutschestextarchiv.de/fontane_irrungen_1888 (Zugriff am 31.05.2021)

Goetschel, Willi: Causerie: Zur Funktion Des Gesprächs in Fontanes Der Stechlin, in: The Germanic Review: Literature, Culture, Theory 70(3), 1995, S. 116–122.

Goffman, Erving: Forms of Talk. Pittsburgh: University of Pennsylvania Press 1981.

---

[103] Meuthen 1994, p. 165.

Goffman, Erving: On Face-Work, in: Psychiatry 18(3), 1955, S. 213–231.
Gronke, Horst: Gesprächsrhetorik in begriffssystematischer Perspektive, in: Ernest W. B. Hess-Lüttich (Hg.): Handbuch Gesprächsrhetorik. Berlin, Boston: De Gruyter 2020, S. 43–76.
Habermas, Jürgen: Strukturwandel der Öffentlichkeit: Untersuchungen zu einer Kategorie der bürgerlichen Gesellschaft. Mit einem Vorwort zur Neuauflage 1990. Frankfurt a.M.: Suhrkamp 1990.
Heidegger, Martin: Sein und Zeit. 18. Auflage. Tübingen: Niemeyer 2001.
Heinrichs, Johannes: Dialog, dialogisch, in: Joachim Ritter (Hg.): Historisches Wörterbuch der Philosophie. Band 2: D – F. Basel, Stuttgart: Schwabe 1972, S. 226–229.
Hess-Lüttich, Ernest W. B.: Rede und Gespräch, in: Ernest W. B. Hess-Lüttich (Hg.): Handbuch Gesprächsrhetorik. De Gruyter 2020, S. 1–40.
Hess-Lüttich, Ernest W. B.: 'Evil Tongues': The Rhetoric of Discreet Indiscretion in Fontane's L'Adultera, in: Language and Literature 11(3), 2002, S. 217–230.
Hirzel, Rudolf: Der Dialog. Ein literarhistorischer Versuch. Leipzig: Hirzel 1895.
Jaspers, Karl: Philosophie. Zweiter Band: Existenzerhellung. Berlin: Springer 1932.
Kieserling, André: Das Ende der guten Gesellschaft, in: Soziale Systeme 7(1), 2001, S. 177–191.
Kilian, Jörg: Historische Dialogforschung: Eine Einführung. Tübingen: Niemeyer 2005.
Kilian, Jörg: Lehrgespräch und Sprachgeschichte: Untersuchungen zur historischen Dialogforschung. Reihe Germanistische Linguistik 233. Tübingen: Niemeyer 2002.
Kracauer, Siegfried: Schriften. Bd. 5.1: Aufsätze 1915–1926. Frankfurt a.M.: Suhrkamp 1990.
Kramp, Willy: Der Raum des Gesprächs in unserer Zeit, in: Die Sammlung 11, 1956, S. 581–589.
Lazarus, Moritz: Ideale Fragen in Reden und Vorträgen. Berlin: Hofmann 1878.
Linke, Angelika: Kommunikation, Kultur und Vergesellschaftung: Überlegungen zu einer Kulturgeschichte der Kommunikation, in: Heidrun Kämper, Heidrun und Ludwig Eichinger (Hg.): Sprache – Kognition – Kultur. Berlin, Boston: De Gruyter 2008, S. 24–50.
Linke, Angelika: Sprachkultur und Bürgertum. Zur Mentalitätsgeschichte des 19. Jahrhunderts. Stuttgart: Metzler 1996.
Linke, Angelika: Zur Kulturalität und Historizität von Gesprächen und Gesprächsforschung, in: Gesprächsforschung 9, 2008, S. 115–28.
Löwith, Karl: Das Individuum in der Rolle des Mitmenschen. Ein Beitrag zur anthropologischen Grundlage der ethischen Probleme. München: Drei Masken 1928.
Mattheier, Klaus J.: Sprachgeschichte des Deutschen: Desiderate und Perspektiven, in: Andreas Gardt, Klaus J. Mattheier und Oskar Reichmann (Hg.): Sprachgeschichte des Neuhochdeutschen. Tübingen: Niemeyer 1995, S. 1–18.
Meier, Simon: Angelsächsische Diskussion und deutsches Gespräch? Zur nationalkulturellen Aufladung von Kommunikationsformen in der Nachkriegszeit, in: Simon Meier, Daniel H. Rellstab und Gesine Leonore Schiewer (Hg.): Dialog und (Inter-)Kulturalität. Theorien, Konzepte, empirische Befunde. Tübingen: Narr 2014, S. 105–124.
Meier, Simon: Gesprächsforschung zwischen Deskriptivität und Normativität. Ein Annäherungsversuch, in: Georg Albert, Georg und Sabine Diao-Klaeger (Hg.): Mündlicher Sprachgebrauch zwischen Normorientierung und pragmatischen Spielräumen. Stauffenburg Linguistik, Band 101. Tübingen: Stauffenburg 2018, S. 283–302.
Meier, Simon: Gesprächsideale. Normative Gesprächsreflexion im 20. Jahrhundert (= Studia linguistica Germanica 116). Berlin, Boston: De Gruyter 2013.
Meier, Simon: Gesprächsrhetorik im 19. und 20. Jahrhundert, in: Ernest W. B. Hess-Lüttich (Hg.): Handbuch Gesprächsrhetorik. Berlin, Boston: De Gruyter 2020, S. 117–139.
Meier, Simon: Kommunikationsbewusstseinsgeschichte des 20. Jahrhunderts. Gegenstände und Zugriffsweisen einer diskurshistorischen Dialogforschung, in: Vilmos ʼgel und Andreas Gardt (Hg.): Paradigmen der aktuellen Sprachgeschichtsforschung. Jahrbuch für Germanistische Sprachgeschichte 5. Berlin, Boston: De Gruyter 2014, S. 250–265.
Meuthen, Erich: Poesie des Nebensächlichen. Über Fontanes Stechlin und die Kunst der Rede, in: Jahrbuch der Deutschen Schiller-Gesellschaft 38, 1994, S. 147–170.

Miller, Stephen: Conversation – A History of a Declining Art. New Haven, London: Yale University Press 2007.
Müller, Eberhard: Die Kunst der Gesprächsführung. Ein Weg zum gemeinsamen Denken. Hamburg: Furche 1954.
Müller, Marcus: Die Grammatik der Zugehörigkeit. Possessivkonstruktionen und Gruppenidentitäten im Schreiben Über Kunst", in: Ekkehard Felder und Marcus Müller (Hg.): Wissen durch Sprache. Theorie, Praxis und Erkenntnisinteresse des Forschungsnetzwerkes „Sprache und Wissen". Berlin, New York: Walter de Gruyter 2009, S. 373–417.
Müller-Schwefe, Hans Rudolf: Die Stunde des Gesprächs. Wesen und Bedeutung des Dialogs in unserer Zeit. Hamburg: Furche 1956.
Nietzsche, Friedrich: Menschliches, Allzumenschliches. Ein Buch für freie Geister. Kritische Gesamtausgabe Bd. IV.2. Berlin, New York: De Gruyter 1967.
Pieper, Joseph: Grundformen sozialer Spielregeln. Eine soziologisch-ethische Untersuchung zur Grundlegung der Sozialpädagogik. Freiburg: Herder 1933.
Plessner, Helmuth: Macht und menschliche Natur. Frankfurt a.M.: Suhrkamp 1981.
Pöggeler, Franz: Methoden der Erwachsenenbildung. Freiburg: Herder 1964.
Polenz, Peter: Deutsche Satzsemantik, Grundbegriffe des Zwischen-den-Zeilen-Lesens. Berlin, Boston: De Gruyter 2008. https://doi.org/10.1515/9783110969832.
Scheidler, K.H.: Gespräch, in: Johann Samuel Ersch und Johann Gottfried Gruber (Hg.): Allgemeine Encyclopädie der Wissenschaften und Künste Bd. 64. Leipzig: Gleditsch 1857, S. 330–337.
Schleiermacher, Friedrich Daniel Ernst: Theorie des geselligen Betragens, in: Schleiermacher, Friedrich Daniel Ernst): Schriften aus der Berliner Zeit 1796–1799. Kritische Gesamtausgabe, I.2. Hg. v. Günther Meckenstock. Berlin, New York: De Gruyter 1984, S. 165–184.
Schmidt-Hidding, Wolfgang: Das Gespräch im Deutschen und Englischen, in: Die neueren Sprachen 2, 1953, S. 377–398.
Schmidt-Hidding, Wolfgang: Die Kultur-Zivilisations-Antithese, in: Sprachforum 1(3/4), 1955, S. 192–201.
Schrott, Angela und Strosetzki, Christoph: Einleitung, in: Angela Schrott, Angela und Christoph Strosetzki (Hg.): Gelungene Gespräche als Praxis der Gemeinschaftsbildung: Sprache, Literatur, Gesellschaft. Historische Dialogforschung 5. Berlin, Boston: De Gruyter 2020, S. 1–8.
Schweitzer, Albert: Verfall und Wiederaufbau der Kultur. München: Beck 1923.
Sharrock, Wes/Button, Graham: The Technical Operations of the Levers of Power, in: Stephen Hester und David Francis (Hg.): Orders of Ordinary Action. Aldershot: Ashgate 2016, S. 33–51.
Sieburg, Friedrich: Die Lust am Untergang. Selbstgespräche auf Bundesebene. 2. Aufl. Reinbek bei Hamburg: Rowohlt 1961.
Simmel, Georg: Soziologie der Geselligkeit, in: Verhandlungen des Ersten Deutschen Soziologentages 1911, S. 1–16.
Strosetzki, Christoph: Konversation als Spiel: Charles Sorel vs. Grice und Gadamer, in: Angela Schott und Christoph Strosetzki (Hg.): Gelungene Gespräche als Praxis der Gemeinschaftsbildung: Sprache, Literatur, Gesellschaft. Berlin, Boston: De Gruyter 2020, S. 11–21.
Theunissen, Michael: Der Andere: Studien zur Sozialontologie der Gegenwart. Berlin, New York: De Gruyter 1977.
Thomas, Chantal: L'esprit de conversation. Paris: Rivages 2011.
Tönnies, Ferdinand: Gemeinschaft und Gesellschaft. Gesamtausgabe. Berlin, Boston: De Gruyter 2019.
Verheyen, Nina: Diskussionslust: eine Kulturgeschichte des „besseren Arguments" in Westdeutschland. Göttingen: Vandenhoeck & Ruprecht 2010.

Vossler, Karl: Sprechen, Gespräch und Sprache, in: Deutsche Vierteljahrsschrift für Literaturwissenschaft und Geistesgeschichte 1(4), 1923, S. 665–79.

Wichmann, Günter: Gespräch, in: Wilhelm Bernsdorf und Friedrich Bülow (Hg.): Wörterbuch zur Soziologie. Stuttgart: Enke 1955, S. 180–182.

Contexts

Conversation in the Salon and Among Salonnières in 19th-Century Paris and Berlin

Petra Dollinger

Abstract

19th century salon conversation adapted to the changes of the age. There were not only restaurative, but also innovative tendencies and thus more diversity. A European pluralism replaced the old, primarily French-dominated salon landscape. The horizon of the aristocratic elite expanded, the influence of the bourgeois conversational sociability grew, salons of Jewish women made their appearance. In Berlin they were even at the very beginning of polished conversation in German. The ideas of Romanticism gave new impulses (poetry, sympoesie, etc.), the epoch of "world literature" made itself felt, international exchange increased. Salon conversations carried their value in themselves, but they could radiate on the cultural life of their time. Sources discussing Parisian and Berlin salons (partly normative, mostly descriptive, with memorable, vivid content) report a variety of cheerful and serious conversations in which the "bien-dire", the "savoir" and the "savoir-vivre" were inseparably linked. Up to the catastrophe of 1914, salon conversations enriched the culture of "Old Europe".

Keywords

Salons · Paris · Berlin · Restauration · Romanticism · Historism · Culture of "Old Europe" (Kultur des "Alten Europa")

P. Dollinger (✉)
Ludwig-Maximilians-Universität München, München, Germany
e-mail: petra.dollinger@edu.lmu.de

The crises of conversation and its important living space in the salons of the 19th century have already been frequently and competently investigated.[1] In this publication on the value of conversation, however, I would like to highlight another perspective: Examples of a then up-to-date, diverse, stimulating conversation culture in the Parisian and Berlin salons.[2] The social basis of refined conversation was expanded by the educated middle class, and there were new impulses, especially through Romanticism and Historism. The spread of mother tongue salons throughout Europe led to a lively personal and cultural exchange (internationality of salon culture, "epoch of world literature").[3] Here, the younger, more modest Berlin conversation culture, which is nevertheless extremely instructive for the history of ideas, is juxtaposed to the Parisian salon conversation of that time. In order not to let the topic get out of hand, the following will only deal with the conversation culture in "literary" salons run by women (where, pre-eminently, the "litterae" were cultivated in the broadest sense of the word).[4]

1 New Horizons Around 1800: Revolution, Restoration and Romanticism

In 1800, the *esprit de conversation* came alive again in the Parisian salons. Many emigrants had returned, and at the head of society, Joséphine Bonaparte, the wife of the First Consul and then Empress, made efforts to maintain the traditional values of conversational culture. In 1807, Princess Regent Pauline zur Lippe observed that, at a reception, the Empress spoke very friendly and "more individually" than the Emperor: "With great amiability, she understands the lovely art of saying something flattering to everyone, and with a study of kindness, she quite naturally treated those in a most welcoming way, whom the Emperor had neglected before."[5] In publications at the beginning of the century, above all the nostalgia for the old, pre-revolutionary conversational culture was given voice.[6] The year 1789 had opened up many opportunities to extend the concept of nobility of spirit, often invoked in salon conversation, to a broader social base (cf. the debate "de vera nobilitate" in Renaissance humanism). But at the same time, the very real ghost of ambitious and trivial imitations with questionable taste *(mondanité fausse)* arose.

---

[1] In detail see Fumaroli I 1992, pp. 717 ff.—Many social changes had a stressful effect (materialism, mass society, myth-making, etc.).

[2] Emmanuel Godo has rightly pointed to the will to survive and to the metamorphoses of 19th century conversation, which erroneously had been so often declared dead. Godo 2003, p. 260. Cf. For placement and history: Strosetzki 1978; Fumaroli 1992; Craveri 2002.

[3] Simanowski 1999; Dollinger 1999; Bohnenkamp 2008.

[4] The large area of brilliant *mondanité* in Paris must be left out. For the Parisian and Berlin salons see above all Martin-Fugier 2009 and 2011 as well as Wilhelmy 1989.

[5] Pauline zur Lippe 1990, p. 83 (01.11.1807).

[6] Godo 2003, pp. 203 ff., see there for the works of Morellet, Delille, Roederer, d'Abrantès, etc.

The true *mondanité* of the salons—the "spirit of the Hôtel de Rambouillet" (Anne Martin-Fugier)—, which was practiced in both modest and elegant contexts, was characterized by a love of conversation. It still tried to combine the "savoir" and the "savoir-vivre" in conversation, and found means to do so while both avoiding elegant superficiality and boring pedantry.[7]

While the socio-cultural context of *Ancien Régime* French salon conversation can be taken for granted in this publication, some preliminary remarks must be made on salon conversation in Germany, which was initially French, then German, but always retained the option of bilingualism or multilingualism. The early approaches to salon conversation in Berlin were in French; not least because of the Huguenot refugees who immigrated in the 17th century, one was familiar with the French tradition—an important basis for the future.[8] Frederick the Great, writing, of course, in French, complained about the variety of German dialects and added: "The upper class speaks French, and the few schoolboys and professors cannot give their mother tongue the smoothness and ease of movement that they can only acquire in good company."[9] For Immanuel Kant and Christian Garve, too, it was quite self-evident that the French tradition of conversation constituted a yardstick and a model, and the knowledge of French was present in all educated circles.[10] Henriette Herz took lessons in French stylistics from the famous writer Mme de Genlis, who was an emigrant in Berlin from 1798 to 1800.[11] The conversation of Princess Luise Radziwill (1770–1836), a niece of Frederick the Great in Berlin, was characterized as follows: "Endowed with the best talent for conversation, she often knew how to enliven a whole salon full of the most heterogeneous and sometimes not entertaining elements. She was perhaps the last woman of our country who knew how to make a *conversation de salon* of the old type: more by striking perception, liveliness of expression and presentation, than by dealing with deeper subjects."[12]

The fact that people in the German-speaking world had less talent and inclination for conversation than in France is partly due to historical factors. There was no single political and cultural center that set the tone, High German often remained a written language and was often overshadowed by local dialects in oral communication. Only slowly, also through the rise of the theater, the spoken word finally gained a certain polish, first sporadically in capitals and princely residences, in university and trading cities, then around 1800 in the salons of Weimar, Vienna and Berlin. More than the French, the Germans needed a subject matter of conversation, such as literature

---

[7] Martin-Fugier 2011, p. 233.—For the classification, delimitation and definition of "salon" etc.: Wilhelmy 1989; Seibert 1993; Lilti 2005; Wilhelmy-Dollinger 2001, 2008 and 2009; Martin-Fugier 2009 and 2011.

[8] For the francophone Berlin salons see Wilhelmy-Dollinger 2009, pp. 63 ff.

[9] Friedrich the Great 1913, vol. 8, p. 309 (to Voltaire, 24.07.1775).

[10] Kant 1923 (²1800), vol. 8, p. 207; Garve 1974 (1792). In 1796, Freiherr Knigge pointed to the "great diversity of conversation tones" in the German-speaking world. Knigge 1991, p. 15.

[11] This was also a discreet support. The Egeria of French literature, conversation culture and etiquette also frequented the new Berlin salon circles. Herz 1984, p. 94; Broglie 1985, pp. 300–309.

[12] Rochow 1908, p. 42 (before 1857).

and the arts, which could serve as a social catalyst. In his fragment "Attempt at a Theory of Sociable Conduct I" (1799), Friedrich Schleiermacher analyzed the ideal situation of free conversation about these topics among educated men and women. Literature would be a unifying topic of conversation, unburdened by professional and everyday worries, indeed a glimpse into other worlds.[13] Goethe's works were preferred reading. The poet himself attached great importance to the culture of conversation and expressed his views, inter alia, in the "Conversations of German Emigrants". His novel "Wilhelm Meister's Apprenticeship" contains many conversations and occupied the minds as a "novel of the artist" and an "education manual on the art of life".[14] Elisabeth Staegemann (1761–1835), a Königsberg salonnière from Kant's circle of friends, who moved to Berlin in 1805, wrote: "Reading weaves a new, social bond between fair and kindred souls, and becomes an interpreter of vague ideas and feelings."[15] At the same time, there were signs of progress in the social intercourse and conversation between educated members of different classes. Elisabeth Staegemann explained: "The citizen is as guilty as the nobility of the separation of the classes. The latter places too great a value on the external refinement of his education; the former remains too inflexible in the inner culture of the mind." And: "The man of the world gains when he becomes acquainted with the scholar, the scholar when he becomes acquainted with the man of the world [...]."[16]

In 1800, Berlin had barely 200,000 inhabitants; it could not aspire to a leading "society" or *mondanité* like in the Paris of the *Ancien Régime*. But the enlightened discourse, literature and arts were cultivated. Class barriers had not yet completely fallen, but there "was a complexly structured interacting culture of permeability and coexistence " (Conrad Wiedemann).[17] The Berlin philosopher Moses Mendelssohn formulated the creed that underlay the ideas of good conversation there: "A language achieves *Enlightenment* through the sciences, and *Culture* through social intercourse, poetry and eloquence. [...] Hail to the nation whose polish is the effect of culture and enlightenment; whose external gloss and finish has inner, solid authenticity as its foundation!"[18] In the age of the French Revolution and Early Romanticism, the Enlightenment received new impulses through revolutionary thought. The ideas of the Early Romantics about conversation revolved around a dynamic, creative concept of poetry. A dialogue between author and reader ("Sympoesie") was opened, the autonomy of art was proclaimed, literary norms were relativized, and an interest in medieval poetry and

---

[13] Schleiermacher 1913; also influenced by Schiller's letters "On the Aesthetic Education of Man".

[14] Schlegel 2018, pp. 261 ff. cConversation about poetry, 1800). Cf. Weithase 1949 and 1961.

[15] Staegemann 1846, vol. 2, p. 158 (around 1802).

[16] "The educated people in both classes will certainly know how to take their rightful place." Staegemann 1846, vol. 2, pp. 141–142 (around 1802).

[17] Wiedemann 2009, p. XXIII.

[18] Mendelssohn 1985, p. 81 (1784).

the diversity of literatures was aroused.[19] Friedrich Schlegel, who later married Mendelssohn's eldest daughter Brendel (Dorothea) Veit, wrote: "Poetry befriends and binds together with indissoluble bonds all minds that love it. They may otherwise seek the most dissimilar things in their own lives [...]; but in this region, by higher powers of magic, they are still united and at peace."[20]

Contemporaries regarded it as almost revolutionary that the early German culture of conversation in Vienna and Berlin was largely shaped by Jewish women. In Berlin, young women from the circle of Moses Mendelssohn were enthusiastic about literary conversations and, in the spirit of the Enlightenment and Haskala, made a contribution to the emergence of the German "Kulturnation" (cultural nation).[21] Schleiermacher's "Theory of Sociable Conductn" reflected his experiences in the salon of Henriette Herz (1764–1847), who later wrote that at that time "the mind" had been "a powerful equalizer."[22] Friendly intercourse (conversation) among similarly minded people created the basis for a salon culture of Jewish and Christian hostesses, in which for over a hundred years it made little difference to which religion one belonged. A talent for the bon mot related to the French tradition, which many salonnières and guests of Jewish origin possessed, was combined with the local wit of Vienna, Berlin or Paris. Géneviève Bizet-Straus (1849–1926), the widow of Georges Bizet, replied ironically and gracefully to an attempt to convert her, declaring that she had too little religion to change it.[23] Definitely, in the Parisian salons of the 19th century, hostesses and guests of Jewish origin played an important role.

The philosophical head among the salonnières was Rahel Levin-Varnhagen (1771–1833), whose conversation was characterized by love of humanity and uncompromising reflection: "Communicating, sympathetically participating, in every minute".[24] She met her guests with compliant understanding and employed all possible tolerance: "I only demand the [consideration] of social etiquette, because I cannot dispense with it."[25] She described the conversations in her salon around 1800 as "a constellation of beauty, grace, coquetry, inclination, love, wit, elegance, cordiality, the urge to develop ideas, honest earnestness, unpretentious approach and encounter, playful banter [...]."[26] There were also attempts in Berlin to resume the tradition of the "esprit Hôtel de Rambouillet", even though social life was still almost provincial compared to Paris. When Rahel met and conversed with the champion of French conversation, Anne Louise Germaine

---

[19] Schlegel 2018, p. 71 (Lyceum-Fragmente 112 and 117) and p. 91 f. (Athenaeum-Fragment 116). Art should not mirror life, but artistically reshape it. See Mainusch 1991, especially p. 148 ff.

[20] Schlegel 2018, p. 199 (Gespräch über Poesie). For a detailed discussion of Romanticism and "romantic poetry", see Matuschek 2021.

[21] Dollinger 2001.

[22] Herz 1984, p. 67.

[23] Gramont 2017, p. 188.

[24] Varnhagen 1983, vol. 2, p. 24 (08.03.1812).

[25] K. A. Varnhagen 1859, vol. 8, p. 592. See Dollinger 2001. She particularly appreciated the *Grand siècle* and the French moralists.

[26] Varnhagen 1983, vol. 2, p. 609 (30.11.1819).

Baroness de Staël-Holstein (1766–1817) in 1804, each woman was able to recognize the genius of the other, but there remained a biographically conditioned distance between them. I will be brief because Mme de Staël is treated in detail by Brunhilde Wehinger in this volume, but the little feud over German conversation culture, which was caused by a passage in Mme de Staël's book "De l'Allemagne" (1813), must be mentioned: The author claimed that German women would "very rarely have that mental agility which enlivens conversation [...]"—something like that could be found "only in the most stimulating and brilliant social circles of Paris".[27] In her slim volume "On German sociability in answer to the judgment of Madame de Staël" (1814) Caroline Baroness de la Motte-Fouqué (1773–1831) immediately pointed out that Mme de Staëlcould not really judge German sociability.[28] Fouqué's critical analysis was by no means satisfactory in detail, but found general approval. Rahel Varnhagen put it in a nutshell: "The dear Staël's book is nothing more to me than a lyrical sigh, [a symptom of] not being able to make conversation in Paris [...]."[29] However, Baroness Fouqué admitted their own shortcomings when she said that the Germans "wavered between affectation and uneducated nature". She therefore demanded for conversation a "poetry of life, which comes from the soul: kindness and love, [...] goodwill, empathy, willing concession and steadfast self-assertion" and emphasized: "[...] they alone allow grace free access and breathe soul into the rushing word."[30]

In the Berlin salons of the Biedermeier period, conversation flourished as a mixture of classical and romantic influences, both in elegant and rather modest salons. Discussions about the cultivation of mind and spirit and veneration for Goethe and his works often took center stage; the romantic "poetization" of life and the merging of genres was particularly discernable in the cultivation of song culture (including set poems), and one talked about natural performance and "bravura singing". Romantic conversation theory emphasized the spontaneous, dynamic and creative aspects of "poetry", but was not in opposition to the French tradition. In 1812, Adam Müller described the structures of good conversation with musical metaphors: Concurrent "ideas" and different "natures" developed like the interplay of a basic harmony and the modulations of different voices in music as endless variations. He refers to the model of French conversation in the 17th century (measure, tact). In this context he speaks of a "harmoniously structured basic disposition that characterizes the earlier French language, conversation, society and literature", and he claims that this could be just as favorable to the lightest fantasy as to the serious efforts of the mind. His diction suggests that he also had salon conversation in

---

[27] Staël o. J., p. 30. The undertone that even in Paris not everything met her requirements was overlooked.

[28] Fouqué 1814, pp. 11 ff.

[29] Varnhagen 1983, vol. 2, 218, cf. pp. 217 ff. (23.05.1814). Only Sara von Grotthuß (1763–1828) was willing to defend Mme de Staël against some points of criticism. Grotthuß 1911, p. 150–151 (To Goethe, 25.11.1814).

[30] Fouqué 1814, p. 29; Fouqué 1826, p. 44 ff., cf. p. 32 ff.

mind: Among the words of the French language, a relationship prevails which is just as "graceful" as between "persons in society"— Müller is convinced that the French language came about "from a live conversation".[31]

The restoration of the Parisian salon conversation after the restoration of the Bourbon dynasty in 1814/15 was complicated by the different political convictions within polite society. Even the leading legitimist salons represented a broad political spectrum. The fact that the time of "absolutism" in salon conversation (with the role of the salonnière as "directrice de l'opinion") was over, did not, indeed, have to be a disadvantage: As a matter of fact, salon conversation itself was, in principle, pluralistically structured. Through exile, foreign languages and travel, the horizon of aristocratic ladies had expanded considerably. Blanche Duchesse de Maillé (1787–1851) indicated that one no longer just lived in and for society, but switched from the salon to the writing desk.[32] Elegant conversation had become more serious, more content-related, but flexible. This was shown by the superior conversation of Armande de Richelieu, Marquise de Montcalm (1772–1832), which was basically oriented towards the classical patterns. She practiced the important principle of good causerie which decreed not to exclude anything from the conversation that could serve the entertainment; in the 19th century, with its thirst for knowledge, even serious conversations could be enjoyable. The elegance of her language and posture was still Rococo, but she kept up with the times and was prepared to judge progress fairly.[33] In the political salons, too, one tried to maintain a detached, considered attitude. This was notably achieved by the diplomat's daughter Adèle d'Osmond, Countess Boigne (1781–1866), a friend of Louis XVIII, who was a salonnière in favour of a liberal monarchy and, after the July Revolution in 1830, learned many details as an intimate of Queen Marie-Amélie and Chancellor Pasquier.[34] She entertained, inter alia, close social contacts with the salons of the Duchess Dorothea von Dino, Talleyrand and Sagan (1793–1862), Talleyrand's confidante, and the Princess Dorothea Lieven (1785–1857), Metternich's and Guizot's friend.

The new "égalité" of cultivated bourgeois women in the conversation of good society was personified by Juliette Récamier (1777–1849) during the heyday of her salon in the *Abbaye-aux-Bois*. After the early death of her friend Mme de Staël, she took over her social functions, but cultivated a different style of conversation. She led the classical "general conversation" in her own discreet, wise and humorous way (later hymns of praise by admirers often did her harm, she was ironically

---

[31] Müller 1967, pp. 54 and 57 ff., cf. p. 52 ff. ("On Conversation"). A similar assessment of the French conversation tradition of the 17th century can be found repeatedly in Rahel Varnhagen.

[32] Maillé 2012, p. 121.

[33] Maillé 2012, pp. 61–62.

[34] Compare Boigne 1999, vol. 2, p. 10 on the situation around 1820: "I saw people of all opinions. [...] We were the royalists of the King and not the royalists of Monsieur, the royalists of the Restoration and not the royalists of the Emigration, the royalists who, I believe, would have saved the throne if they had been listened to."

called a "Madonna of Conversation").[35] Mme Récamier stayed in the background, gave cues for replies and encouraged with looks and gestures. The "savoir-vivre" went hand in hand with the "bien-dire"—pretty phrases were presented like a work of art. The conversation apparently had the stimulating effect of a "mental cup of coffee" (Mary Clarke-Mohl).[36] Mme Récamier's dexterous move to have her friend Chateaubriand read from the manuscript of his "Mémoires d'outre tombe" not only saved him from the *ennui*, but also secured her salon a place in the literary history of French Romanticism. The echo among the listeners was mixed, but there was food for conversation.[37] At first, French Romanticism had a hard time. In 1828, Alfred de Vigny accused conversation in general of a triviality which left no chance for the poet and poetry. Bitingly, he wrote that the French loved neither literature, nor music and poetry, but just society, salons, *esprit* and prose. Nevertheless, people in Paris were soon interested in the feud between classicists and romantics and found a fair assessment of the new direction.[38] In Germany, on the other hand, where poetry was given free rein by the richness of the German vocabulary, there were frequent complaints about an undisciplined prose style. Polemically, Friedrich Nietzsche later accused German prose of lacking the "grace of good French writers". Nietzsche's criticism met with great interest in the late 19th century Berlin salon society, which was receptive to good style.[39] Around 1900, the poet Robert Comte de Montesquiou liked to talk to German guests about Goethe and said: "I like this romantic Germany."[40] Here it is ventured that the combination of French style and French formal perfection with (originally German or English) "poetry" and romantic art theory could particularly enrich the salon conversation.

2 Case Studies of European Conversation: Mrs. von Olfers and Mme Mohl as Salonnières in the Spirit of Romanticism and Historism

The 19th century was, despite its nationalist tendencies, also a time of mutual perception of European literatures, art, and science.[41] Culturally, Europe began to grow together, travel of the European salon society was facilitated by steamboats and

---

[35] Goncourt 1947, p. 142 (23.10.1864).

[36] Mohl 1862, pp. 1 ff. and pp. 100 ff.

[37] Dino 1909, vol. 3, pp. 25 ff. (15.02.1841).—See Godo 2003, pp. 215 ff. for Romanticism in France.

[38] Vigny 1928, p. 15 (1828). See Maillé 1984, pp. 307 ff.; Godo 2003, p. 216; Martin-Fugier 2011, pp. 224 f.

[39] Here there were were many Nietzsche scholars (Richard M. Meyer, Raoul Richter, Harry Graf Kessler, etc.). Nietzsche appreciated the French conversation tradition and commented on individual aspects of conversation in general in his aphorisms. Nietzsche 1980, vol. 1, pp. 343 ff. and vol. 2, pp. 241 ff. Cf. to the problems of the Germans in spirit and life caused by the contrast "of form and content, of inwardness and convention" also vol. 1, pp. 275 ff. (On the Use and Abuse of History …).

[40] Nostitz 1933, p. 63.

[41] Cf. Dollinger 1999.

railways. In 1827, Goethe considered the epoch of isolated national literatures to be over and proclaimed an international world of literature, indeed an epoch of "world literature."[42] The theory of salon conversation did not change fundamentally despite some modifications brought about by the romantic zeitgeist (special emphasis on spontaneity and creativity, etc.). It was adapted to the current needs and the respective style of the hostess, as had been the case before (one had always to pursue the ideal of perfect conversation under constantly changing conditions). Very important and new for the understanding of the art of conversation itself, however, was the perception of Romanticism as formulated by Friedrich Schlegel: "The theory of art is its history."[43] This meant for the art of salon conversation that the old normative principles were not made obsolete, but that one saw them—relativized—in their historical context. One asked questions about the historical development of the traditions of conversation. Some aspects of the theme indicated here can be illustrated by two salons, whose hostesses took over the legacy of Mme de Staël and Mme Récamier (Mme Mohl), and of Elisabeth Staegemann (Mrs. von Olfers).

A prime example of the cultivation of "romantic" conversation in Berlin is the salon of the literarily and artistically gifted bourgeois family (ennobled in 1816) of the State Councillor Friedrich August Staegemann. Elisabeth Staegemann's salon (in Berlin from 1805) existed for three generations and always retained a romantic imprint, which combined artistic creativity and individual culture of mind and spirit with the grace of pleasant social intercourse. A guest was Heinrich von Kleist, who used to speak of an electrical charging process at work in animated discussions, a view he shared with Mme de Staël. He explained: "The Frenchman says, *l'appétit vient en mangeant,* and this experience remains true if one parodies it and says, *l'idée vient en parlant*"[44] Something similar could be seen when Kleist read from his plays at Staegemann's. Their daughter Hedwig remembered: "[…] he usually started hesitantly, almost stammering, and only gradually did his performance become bolder and more fiery."[45] The early romantic conversation theory of Friedrich Schlegel, which emphasized the creative and sociable aspects of poetry in connection with the cultivation of an individual personality, was also reflected in the Staegemann salon conversation: "Reason is only one and the same in all", but, as Schlegel says, just as everyone has their own nature, so "everyone has their own poetry in them". In conversation, the poet can and must "strive to expand his poetry and his view of poetry forever […]. Actually, for the true poet

---

[42] Eckermann 1908, vol. 1, p. 329 f. (31.01.1827). See Bohnenkamp 2008 for a detailed account.—For Wilhelm von Humboldt, language was not only a cooperation of understanding, feeling, and shaping, but also a cultural link between the individual and all of humanity. Humboldt 1963a, vol. 3, p. 76 ff.

[43] Mainusch 1991, p. 122 ff., elaborates on this in detail and comments on the consequences.

[44] In the essay "On the gradual composition of thoughts while speaking" (1805) it is pointed out that a lively conversation can be electrically charged and lead a speaker to unexpected, even dramatic declarations (he names Mirabeau on 23. June 1789 as an example). Kleist 1952, vol. 2, p. 321 ff.

[45] H. v. Olfers, communication to Otto Brahm, 1884, in: Sembdner 1992, vol. 1, p. 397.

even the intercourse with those who only play on the colorful surface can be salutary and instructive. He is a sociable being." In Schlegel's opinion, the conversation between "poets and poetically minded people" about poetry is not only useful, but also attractive.[46] Due to the participation of numerous young people, there was often a spontaneous, semi-playful conversation in the literary circles and salons, which was partly left to its own dynamics. In view of the then flourishing enthusiasm about Shakespeare, one might call it a poetic "civil war of wits".[47]

Seventeen-year-old Hedwig von Staegemann (1799-1891) herself reported on an evening in autumn 1816, when the poet Clemens Brentano, a friend of her brother August, joined the circle of young people in the Staegemann salon. In her mother's stead, she was temporarily the lady of the house: "We were all sitting around a large round table, and lively, amusing conversations ensued. Eventually, the talk turned to Brentano. Some spoke in his favor, others against him. He was compared to [Ludwig] Tieck, and August cried: 'How can one compare Brentano's often one-sided humor with Tieck's grand spirit and good-natured wit?' And at that very moment, a black head of curls peeks through the door, and Brentano enters with the pointed, satyrical smile [...]. We girls giggled, and the young men pulled long faces. He spoke profusely and wittily, sat down on the sofa and began to play Bataille with August [...]." Then he pulled "a few manuscripts out of his pocket, which he promised to read to us. I was to choose between some Slavic poems [in German translation] and decide which one was to be included in [Friedrich] Förster's pocket book, which is to be printed soon. I forbade it and instead asked Brentano to read us the allegorical comedy he had recently written. He did so—in the meantime, mother came home, and about twenty people huddled together. I cannot describe to you how much this comedy amused us [...] Some of the songs he had composed himself and partly sang them to us. When we said goodbye, he said to me: 'Good night, Viktoria', after the heroine of his play."[48] Some conversations could be creative on the spot back then—poetry and verse-making were equally cultivated. From a poetic "writing game" of the "Thursday society of young people ["Donnerstag-Jugend"] " at Staegemann's, the Ur-Müllerlieder (poems by Wilhelm Müller, Hedwig Staegemann and Wilhelm and Luise Hensel) emerged in 1816, composed by Ludwig Berger. They were expanded by Wilhelm Müller into the cycle of "Müllerlieder", which later became famous in Schubert's setting.[49]

In 1823, Hedwig Staegemann married the diplomat Ignaz von Olfers. After several years in Naples and Bern, she took over her mother's salon in 1835. Soon, three daughters were able to assist her, in particular the poet and painter Marie von

---

[46] Schlegel 2018, p. 199 and 201 (Conversation about poetry).

[47] Shakespeare, Love's Labour's Lost, II, 1, 238. The conversations there almost seem like a premonition of conversations in the Hôtel de Rambouillet.

[48] Olfers 1914, vol. 2, p. 15 f. (17.10.1816). The mentioned comedy is "Viktoria und ihre Geschwister" (written in 1813, printed in 1817).

[49] Dollinger 2016 provides more detailed information.

Olfers (1826–1924).⁵⁰ The circle of guests was international, and since Ignaz von Olfers had been appointed director of the Royal Museums (1839), Hedwig von Olfers' salon was, at the special request of King Frederick William IV, also a meeting place for foreign artists. In 1847, the Munich painter Wilhelm von Kaulbach wrote: "[…] silken dresses rustled, and the conversation sounded in all languages […]". He complained about being served "[…] only tea, tea, tea, and very small, small butter sandwiches, but art conversations in abundance."⁵¹ However, one also discussed the classics and modern literature. In October 1855, a heated discussion began about the life and works of George Sand. Marie von Olfers took a clear stand for the poet: "[…] women have always had it bad in public […]. I should like to see the woman who would be forgiven disclosing her love-affairs like those which [happened] in Goethe's life, even if she had Goethe's quill to relate them." On the same evening, Heinrich Abeken, an intimate friend of the family, told them about an essay on Goethe and Mme de Staël in Cotta's "Morgenblatt". Central topic was the translation of the poem "The Fisherman" into French. As is well known, the fisherman lured the wards of the water nymph "hinauf in Todesgluth" ("up into death's glow"). Mme de Staël had translated "Todesgluth" with "air brulant", referring to the heat of the sun. Was that correct? All present were questioned. Finally, the solution was revealed: Goethe had corrected Mme de Staël and "told her that it was the coal glow in the kitchen in which the fish would be fried". This caused a disbelieving uproar among the guests. Only Friedrich Wilhelm Graf Redern had said "The kitchen fire" and correctly guessed Goethe's dictum (or he already knew the essay). One considered whether Goethe might have permitted himself a joke. Marie von Olfers was not convinced by the coal glow at all: "If he [Goethe], however, had really meant the kitchen fire, then his poem spoke better than he himself, because I don't think anyone else will come up with it."⁵² Even when the Olfers' social life was limited to the more intimate form of the literary tea table in the 1870s, the conversation remained extremely stimulating, and the close "romantic" connection and fusion of poetry, music and fine art remained. After the death of the 92–year-old Hedwig von Olfers (1891) Anna von Helmholtz wrote that with her, the "heroine of the Müller song", probably the last representative of the old literary Berlin of Romanticism had gone to her grave: "She was […] the kindest, prettiest, most beloved of all the old ladies. As delicate as Aunt [Mme Mohl], always ready for conversation, a graceful piece of femininity of past times and phenomena."⁵³

---

⁵⁰ Nina (1824–1901; Countess Yorck), Marie (1826–1924) and Hedwig (1829–1919; Geheimrätin Abeken). See Wilhelmy 1989, on the family's Russian relationships also Dollinger 2019. In 1847, Julius and Mary Mohl were also guests at the Olfers salon.

⁵¹ Quoted from Wilhelmy 1989, p. 176.

⁵² M. Olfers 1928, vol. 1, pp. 157–158 (14.10.1855). The essay was about notes from Karl August Böttiger's literary estate on Mme de Staël's metrical translation of the poem. Böttiger 1998, p. 386. For Goethe's own interpretation, see Eckermann 1908, vol. 2, p. 76 (3.11.1823).

⁵³ Helmholtz 1929, vol. 2, p. 40 (15.12.1891).

The most interesting Parisian example of international conversation in the spirit of Romanticism and Historism can be found in the salon of Mary Clarke-Mohl (1793–1883) from the 1840s to the 1870s. She had been a subtenant, friend and apprentice of Mme Récamier in the *Abbaye-aux-Bois*, but her temperament was more like Mme de Staël's. As a native Briton, long-time friend of Claude Fauriel, and wife of the German orientalist scholar Julius Mohl, Mary Clarke-Mohl embodied a synthesis of modern intellect, traditional French genius for conversation and Romantic spontaneity. Her brother-in-law, the Württemberg professor Robert (von) Mohl, wrote: "She speaks with wit and intelligence, is of astonishing liveliness and full of interest in intellectual and spiritual matters, has the tone of the best society and a fine understanding of the demands of the same, even though she permits herself many things that would never occur to a German or French woman. Her nature is a very peculiar mixture of Italian *disinvoltura,* French grace, and English, sound, and conscientious common sense."[54] She loved the theater as much as scientific lectures, campaigned for Shakespeare and the novels of Sir Walter Scott, and was a friend of Elizabeth Gaskell and Florence Nightingale. The wide horizon of her salon also included the literary history of the Middle Ages and the *Grand Siècle* (Fauriel, Jean-Jacques Ampère, Victor Cousin) and the poetry of the Orient. Julius Mohl (professor at the *Collège de France*) devoted his research primarily to the ancient Persian epic *Shahnameh* by Firdusi (Firdausi). An international elite of very different world views met here without pedantry or stiffness. Reason and politeness were important to Mme Mohl, other conventions and external elegance did not interest her (Guizot is said to have remarked that she and his Scottish terrier went to the same hairdresser).[55] When Leopold von Ranke visited her in 1852, Mme Mohl immediately engaged him in a "conversation about Rahel [Varnhagen]," in which the historian demonstrated his fabulous French.[56] Her young niece Anna Mohl lived with her in Paris for a while in 1852/53—as the wife of Hermann (von) Helmholtz, she later practiced conversation at the highest level in her Berlin salon.

Mme Mohl intensively explored the historical roots of conversational sociability and added a short history of French salons to her biography of Mme Récamier (1862).[57] As Claude Fauriel's literary estate administrator, she always emphasized the great civilizing role of French women since the chivalrous troubadour culture of Provence in the 11th and 12th centuries. She described how conversation in the circle of ladies finally became equal to festive culture and that in the Hôtel de Rambouillet the elegantly formulated exchange of thoughts and feelings was

---

[54] R. Mohl 1902, vol. 1, p. 36, vol. 2, p. 433.

[55] Lesser 1984, pp. 24f.

[56] Helmholtz 1929, vol. 1, p. 41 (25.10.1852).

[57] Mohl 1862. The work was also shaped by the historical understanding of her old friend Augustin Thierry.

elevated to a style of art in sociability.[58] Like Mme de Staël, the idol of her youth, Mme Mohl saw the most important inspiration of conversation in the interplay of mind, feeling and language. She explained this as follows: Real conversation is a conversation in which individual ideas are stimulated by the social situation and brought to the point by means of reason and imagination. Such exchange of ideas, in particular the translation of abstract thoughts into vivid language, are basic social needs and sometimes in conversation make people grow beyond themselves.[59] Vivid diction and personal involvement she considered the "soul" of lively conversation (in contrast to dry discourse).

Of course, conversation in Mme Mohl's salon—just as in the salons of the 17th/18th centuries—frequently focused on purity of speech and the deliberations of the *Académie Française*. Mme Mohl's French was excellent, with a slight flair of the 18th century.[60] Anna Mohl reported on a conversation with Prosper Mérimée (1853): "He spoke of the Académie Française and of their improvements to the French language. Aunt [Mohl] said that much of it degenerated into pedantry, but Mérimée rejected this. When I asked him whether all these refinements would benefit mankind or even be understood by the smallest part of it, he replied: first, only an infinitely small part of humanity has taste, and they must not be deprived of their pleasure because others do not appreciate it. How few people know how to judge a Madonna by Raphael and know its value; but this does not make it any less beautiful and perfect!"[61] In Mme Mohl's salon, conversations about the letter-writing and conversational culture of the *Grand Siècle,* about Mme de Sévigné and her daughter sometimes developed into an exchange of ideas that was both rational and emotional. Anna Mohl wrote about a visit by Victor Cousin: "Cousin came to speak about his hobby horse, Mme. de Longueville, and did so with an enthusiasm as if he had seen her every day. By the way, the ladies of the Fronde seem to have made a strong impression on him. He compares Madame de Chevreuse and Madame la Palatine to Mazarin and Retz in intelligence and ability. Mme de Sévigné he ranks in some respects lower than her daughter [Mme de Grignan], which greatly upset Uncle [Julius]. [...]."[62] Julius Mohl was an enthusiastic admirer of Mme de Sévigné.

---

[58] "[...] for when the habit of changing all thoughts and sentiments into words has become natural and easy, it offers so great a variety in itself that society needs no other." Mohl 1862, p. 191.

[59] Mohl 1862, pp. 191–192. "The most abstract thoughts may be made tangible by lively imagery,—the most complicated subjects may be simplified by the learned to obtain the approbation of an attentive listener [...]. Conversation is the mingling of mind with mind, and is the most complete exercise of the social faculty" (p. 192).

[60] O'Meara 1885, p. 37.

[61] Helmholtz 1929, vol. 1, p. 49 (09.01.1853). In Berlin, too, people talked a lot "about language and the way to speak", cf. Wilhelmy 1989, p. 129.

[62] Helmholtz 1929, vol. 1, p. 41 (18.10.1852).

3 Memory Culture, Science and Arts in the Salon Conversation of the Late 19th Century

Conversation was impaired by overcrowded, heterogeneous "high society" receptions. Even in the salon of the writer Countess Anastasie de Circourt (1808–1863) people eventually complained about a loud, "very eclectic, very full, very mixed [...] society"— the brothers Goncourt remarked that it had been "more of a numbness than an entertainment".[63] In salon circles, the hectic present tended to promote an "antiquarian" attitude towards history, in particular the cultivation of an often quite personally shaped memory culture.[64] This was frequently accompanied by a delight in storytelling and mythologizing. The painter and writer Virginie Ancelot (1792–1875), for example, wrote a comedy about the Hôtel de Rambouillet and dedicated it to Mme Récamier (1842). But Mme Ancelot could also analyze sharply and formulated an) accurate definition of conversation under socio-cultural aspects of urbanity (stimulated conversation and constant exchange of ideas in a familiar circle of acquaintances with similar values), which was closely related to Mme Mohl's ideas.[65]

A perspective intertwined with historical "monumentality" can be found in the salon of Princess Mathilde Bonaparte (1820–1904). The daughter of Jérôme Bonaparte and Catherine of Württemberg venerated her uncle Napoleon I and studied her family history, but kept out of day-to-day politics. Princess Mathilde's interesting childhood memoirs give us an idea of her vivid manner of speaking.[66] Sainte-Beuve helped her set up a literary salon that existed during the Second Empire and also during the Third Republic, with "freedom of thought and entertainment". The Goncourt brothers admired her as a woman who "by a confidential way of speaking, by the liveliness of everything that goes through her head [...], puts everyone in a good mood." Princess Mathilde was pleased with the Goncourt brothers' book "The Woman in the 18th Century" (1862), but regretted that modern women "no longer take an interest in artistic things, in the new publications of literature [...]." She claimed that she could enjoy a good conversation only with very few women.[67] Bourgeois salonnières and female writers tended to have historical interests as well. Since Judith Gautier (1845–1917), the daughter of Théophile Gautier and friend of Richard Wagner, had met many celebrities from literature and art and liked to tell her friends about them, Vincent Laisney explicitly characterized her salon as a "sociabilité du souvenir".[68]

---

[63] Goncourt 1947, p. 128 (27.09.1863).

[64] Nietzsche 1980, vol. 1, pp. 265 ff. (On the Use and Abuse of History).

[65] Ancelot 1858, pp. 15 ff. See also Fumaroli 1992, pp. 717 ff.

[66] Bonaparte 2019; see Picon 2005 for biography.

[67] Goncourt 1947, p. 108f. (13.12.1862). This was probably an exaggeration, later her guests included, inter alia, Julia Daudet. Mme Daudet reports a mixture of older and younger people, current topics and historical reminiscences. Daudet 1910, p. 73f.

[68] Laisney 2020, p. 56.

A similar culture of memory existed in the Berlin salons. It is striking how many echos of the French "Grand Siècle" were still kept alive in these circles. When Hildegard von Spitzemberg (1843–1914), an old friend of Bismarck's, occasionally mentioned internal details after his death, Harry Graf Kessler commented: "The conversation [was] something like if one could, while reading [...] Madame de Sévigné, ask Madame de Grignan a few questions [...]."[69] In the salon of Princess Marie Radziwill née de Castellane (1840–1915), the history of salon conversation overlapped considerably with that of her own ancestors. She was a granddaughter of the Duchess Dorothea von Dino, Talleyrand and Sagan and ran an elegant francophone salon in Berlin, well into the 20th century. Her house was visited by many politicians and diplomats.[70] Jules Cambon, 1907–1914 French ambassador in Berlin, expressed his highest admiration for the art of her conversation ("Elle avait à l'extrême le goût de la conversation et savait, d'un mot, provoquer et exciter les causeurs", in English: "She had the extreme taste of conversation and knew, with a word, to provoke and excite the talkers").[71] The princess liked to show her souvenirs of Talleyrand and had inherited much of the conversational talent of her grandmother, whose letters she published in 1909. She also liked to talk about the time of Louis XIV—the writer Marie von Bunsen (1860–1941) remembered: "We had excited debates about the Duke of St. Simon and Madame de Maintenon and agreed in our admiration of Madame de Sévigné, her ancestress."[72] Sometimes in salon-conversations, the memories of very old participants served as direct personal bridges which linked the past and the present. When in 1911 Walther Rathenau met Marie von Olfers and her sister Hedwig Abeken in the salon of Countess Babette Kalckreuth (1835–1916), he asked them to tell him about the late romantic Schinkel era, about Rahel Varnhagen, Bettine von Arnim, etc. He wrote that it had been something very special for him that he, the "electrician boy" (his father was the founder of AEG) had thus been able to touch once more the "magic ring of romanticism", even in the early 20th century.[73]

Traditional conversation and modern science met in the Berlin salon of Anna von Helmholtz née Mohl (1834–1899). Her "apprenticeship" in the salon of her aunt certainly contributed to the fact that she confidently rose to the top of Berlin

---

[69] Kessler 2004, vol. 3, p. 210f. (26.10.1898).

[70] At the beginning of this salonnière dynasty was the Duchess Dorothea of Courland (1761–1821), who for a few winters, around 1800 (until 1806), led a salon in Berlin. The tradition was continued by her youngest daughter Dorothea (Mme de Dino, Duchess of Talleyrand and Sagan), her granddaughter Pauline Marquise de Castellane (1820–1890) and by her great-granddaughter Marie Princess Radziwill.

[71] Radziwill 1931, p. V.

[72] Bunsen, 1932 p. 104, cf. Bunsen 1916, p. 100 f.

[73] Rathenau 2006, p. 1035 f.; cf. Rathenau 1967, p. 153 (both December 30, 1911).—An extreme case of oral tradition is reported from the court of Empress Eugénie, when a very old lady, the Duchess of Richelieu, mentioned in passing what Louis XIV had once said to her husband! ("Le roi Louis XIV avait prédit à mon mari …"). According to Martin-Fugier 2009, p. 10.

society in the Bismarck era, long before her husband, the great scholar Hermann Helmholtz, was ennobled[74] Court and salon circles, as well as an international elite from all branches of science and art, met at her house. In particular, medicine, natural sciences and technology were represented. In 1891, Hermann von Helmholtz emphasized: "Science and art are currently the only remaining bond of civilized nations [...]."[75] Anna von Helmholtz had no easy task in directing the conversation in her salon, but even at very large receptions she managed to get people talking, easily switching from German to French and English. Her style impressed even sophisticated French observers: "Of outstanding mind and finest education, she is also characterized by those polished manners which are rarely found in Berlin outside the circles of the aristocracy. She receives with an ease and casualness which the wife of many an ambassador might envy. Although very friendly with Empress Friedrich [a daughter of Queen Victoria] and in closest contact with the literary world, she is neither arrogant nor blue-stockinged [...]. Her salon is undoubtedly one of the most outstanding and intelligent in Berlin and free from any pedantry. Professors, officers, musicians, writers, Englishmen, Frenchmen, Russians meet there in a select circle. I have witnessed that the lady of the house, with her lightly ironical grace, conducted the conversation in French, in a manner a witty Parisian could not have surpassed."[76] Here—as with Mme Mohl in Paris—European conversation took place in the best sense of the word, that is, as a pan-European encounter of art, culture and science.

At the top of the Parisian art of conversation, the beautiful, highly gifted Élisabeth Countess Greffulhe (1860–1952) was committed to music, ballet, art and literature, but she also developed a preference for conversations with physicists and other natural scientists.[77] Unlike Anna von Helmholtz, the muse of Marcel Proust had no prior knowledge in this sphere, but this apparently did not detract from the mutual stimulation of ideas. Élisabeth de Gramont explained that the magic of Mme de Greffulhe's conversations lay in the fact that they represented a much more subtle phenomenon than direct comprehension.[78] As early as 1878, the Berlin psychologist and philosopher Moritz Lazarus had pointed out that in conversation "science" and "reality" could grow together if well-conducted dialogue filled abstract correlations with life.[79] Apparently Mme de Greffulhe's sincere enthusiasm and her curiosity were most fascinating, and the meeting of very different ways of thinking or the need for general explanation sometimes could even inspire the experts. One is

---

[74] Wilhelmy-Dollinger 2010.

[75] Helmholtz 1929, vol. 2, p. 39 (18.10.1891).

[76] Legras 1892, pp. 66–67.

[77] Like many intelligent women of her circle, Countess Greffulhe did not really feel comfortable in the hustle and bustle of the elegant world and suffered from the mental narrowness of her environment (she was criticized by her own family because she held "mixed" parties in her salon). See de Pange 2014, p. 95.

[78] Gramont 2018, p. 25.

[79] Lazarus 1878, pp. 258 ff., on the "collaborative work of spirits" in conversation on p. 262 f.; there are analogies to Mme Mohl's thoughts.

reminded of the interest 17th century Parisian salons developed for the natural sciences of that time. Mme de Greffulhe's conversation seems to have once more combined all the qualities of classical conversation and even carried them gracefully into the modern world.[80] A very personal female perspective had always played a special role in salon conversations. At the beginning of the 20th century, in view of the emancipation of women and their admission to university exams and degrees, the Berlin painter and salonnière Sabine Lepsius (1864–1942) explicitly warned against the pedantry of dry discussion. She argues that since the salons were a "creation of women", one must forego "dry matter-of-factness in conversation": The "*female woman*" sets "her pride in judging from a personal point of view, even in the assessment of factual questions. After all, objectivity excludes all intuition […]."[81]

In music, an international network of conversation for the works of Richard Wagner emerged through the interaction of large parts of the European salon society. Very early, in the Second French Empire, the wife of Austria-Hungary's ambassador in Paris, Princess Pauline Metternich (1836–1921), took up Wagner's cause and ensured that his "Tannhäuser" was performed there in 1861. In Berlin, the composer's followers met in the salon of Marie (Mimi) Freifrau (from 1879 Countess) von Schleinitz (1842–1912), a friend of Cosima Wagner. The Countess was cosmopolitan and an admirer of Goethe, "but her great passion was Wagnerian music".[82] After the death of her first husband she married Anton Graf Wolkenstein, who was Austrian ambassador to Paris in the 1890s; there she also cultivated music and knew how to "turn conversation into a work of art".[83] The whole network of the Wagner circle was dominated by Cosima Wagner, who often came to Berlin and occupied a sovereign social position there. Anna von Helmholtz appreciated her conversation and wrote in 1891 that the effect of her personality lay "in the calm, the height of all views, in the spell of the speech, which is never banal, general or impersonal, and expresses nothing but thoughts of her own in the greatest simplicity […]. I had a dinner of twenty people the other day—all learned gentlemen and unlearned ladies. After half an hour Cosima had enchanted them all. Mommsen and Dilthey, Virchow, Siemens […] and what is more, their wives too."[84] Of course, Cosima Wagner often ruthlessly exploited her dominance: Anna von Helmholtz once complained about the "Wahnfried-servitude" of Countess Schleinitz-Wolkenstein.[85] Cosima Wagner was downright ungrateful to Judith Gautier, who had campaigned for the Bayreuth

---

[80] During the Second World War, she had a small heated wooden cabin built in her icy salon so that she could continue her conversations with friends. Hillerin 2018, p. 493.

[81] Lepsius 1916, p. 37; cf. Simmel 1986, pp. 229 and 239 ff. The principle of complementarity was strongly emphasized by the sociology and philosophy of life of that time.

[82] Bunsen 1932, p. 66.

[83] Nostitz 1933, p. 27. Cf. Helmholtz 1929, vol. 2, p. 178, cf. p. 181 (13/24 February 1899).

[84] Helmholtz 1929, vol. 2, p. 35 (31 January 1891).—Harry Graf Kessler spoke of her "social genius". Kessler, vol. 3, p. 291 (15 March 1900) and p. 456 (30 January 1905). Cosima Wagner's art of conversation does not surprise in the daughter of Marie d'Agoult.

[85] Bunsen 1932, p. 66.

cause for decades. When in 1898 she came up with the attractive idea of privately performing Wagner's "Parsifal" as a puppet theatre with singing in her salon, for purely charitable purposes, Cosima Wagner intervened and threatened legal action.[86] The Countess Greffulhe was very successful in her efforts to have "Tristan" and "Götterdämmerung" performed in Paris in 1899 and 1902, respectively. Helene von Nostitz (1878–1944), a granddaughter of the German ambassador Georg Fürst Münster, wrote of Mme de Greffulhe: "It was always an event when she appeared in a salon. […] When she spoke, she produced an exceptionally well-formed language from her mouth, whose fine, curved lips always held ready a pointed repartee. […] With inimitable grace and culture, she often put herself at the service of mediation between France and Germany."[87]

A particularly important German-French connection in the fine arts was created by the Bernstein couple in Berlin; their cousin was Charles Ephrussi of the *Gazette des Beaux-Arts* in Paris. Professor Carl Bernstein, a lawyer, and his wife Felicie (1852–1908) brought the first impressionist paintings to Berlin as early as 1882; they were controversial at the time, but soon opened up a new horizon.[88] Debates at Bernsteins' helped to lay the groundwork for the later founding of the Berlin Secession: "Such conversations were not interrupted by the hostess, even if they took on a serious and passionate character, and yet she knew how to prevent them from degenerating into disputes."[89] In 1900, Cornelie Richter (1842–1922), the youngest daughter of Meyerbeer, opened the door to Art Nouveau in Berlin society. In her salon, in the spring of 1900, Henry van de Velde gave his revolutionary lectures on modern interior design. "Afterwards the pros and cons were discussed with […] closer friends. Sharp words rarely occurred in such a conversation, which mostly remained just a conversation […]."[90] The art of conversation enjoyed the important privilege of not needing to take immediate action.

4 Structures of Salon Conversation in the 19th Century: Framework, Mechanisms and Development of the Conversations

19th century salon conversation could take place in both modest and elegant settings, but a fundamental difference existed in the type of hospitality one chose, i.e. the decision of "table" or "tea". With conviviality around a table one was able to prepare a harmonious conversation through the selection of invited guests, if one understood the " composition-rules of society" and the guests were well

---

[86] Richardson 1987, pp. 138 ff. and 170 f.; Martin-Fugier 2009, pp. 341 ff., cf. p. 284 ff.

[87] Nostitz 1933, p. 13.

[88] Carl Bernstein also took care of the young poet Jules Laforgue when he was a reader for Empress Augusta in Berlin. See Wilhelmy-Dollinger 2021.

[89] Lepsius 1916, p. 42.

[90] Nostitz 1933, p. 50.

"counterpointed".[91] A pure conversational sociability with simple hospitality in the form of a tea (every evening or as a *jour fixe*) was open to all persons introduced in the house. Here the number and composition of the company was not predictable. Much had to be improvised, which could be attractive, but possibly also difficult. In Berlin, at first, the pure conversation salons predominated, later there were also additional frequent invitations to dinner. Often it was claimed that conversational culture had been suffocated by increasing table luxury, and in Paris as in Berlin, around 1900, the joke circulated that many a lady believed she was running a salon, but she only had a dining room. Connoisseurs rightly declared, however, that where conversation was really in the center, a good meal could not hurt.[92] Predominantly in Paris there was still a third variant: After a dinner with invited guests followed a tea party open to the whole circle of friends. This guaranteed a thriving conversation for the whole evening, even if only few or badly harmonizing random guests showed up.[93] Conversations late at night could indeed have the amusing function of a "conversation about conversation". Mme Mohl said: "I prefer catching my friends after they have left the grander balls or receptions. One hears then the remarks, the wit, the reason and the satire which they had been storing up during their evening of imposed silence."[94]—Music, poetry readings and the performance of dramatic scenes could at times complement salon conversation.

The old form of the "cercle", which was still widespread at the beginning of the century, was increasingly replaced by loosely arranged seating areas that invited conversation in small groups.[95] In Berlin, the "general" conversation at the tea table was often the center of the salon. Additional conversation circles had to be created for larger parties. In 1864, Marie von Olfers reported: "I founded all sorts of small colonies in the corners that thrived very well. In one [...] they argued about whom they liked better: the real Wallenstein—or Schiller's, the real Johanna—or Schiller'sn, in general: the poetic person or the real one! "Somewhere else someone said," Art is a monkey and originated from imitation [...]. I replied, it originated from the yearning for the ideal [...]. What they talked about in the third and fourth corner, I do not know, but it was an agitation and eagerness, as if something spectacular was going to be found out."[96] In a very directive, but highly successful way, Anna von Helmholtz dissolved boring groupings of old acquaintances or colleagues at very large parties in order to "reconnect them in conversations that were equally attractive to everyone, in a new order. With incomparable skill, she took up the short

---

[91] Bunsen 1929, pp. 158ff.

[92] Liebermann 1914, p. 50; Bunsen 1929, p. 186. Cf. Godo 2003, pp. 221ff.

[93] Bamberger 1898, pp. 94ff. In Berlin one usually avoided "to impose on one's friends that they only come after the table has been lifted, *en cure-dents*, as toothpicks, as is jokingly expressed in French [...]".

[94] Lesser 1984, p. 101 (report by Elizabeth Gaskell, 1854); cf. to the "soirée seconde" Godo 2003, pp. 237ff.

[95] Martin-Fugier 2011, pp. 217 ff.

[96] M. Olfers 1928, vol. 1, p. 297 (17.03.1864).

profile of well-being, the last journey or professional matters in order to move on as quickly and as unnoticed as possible to a conversation that went far beyond the usual social entertainment, even though she never disregarded the tone of "mondanité".[97] When, around 1900, some salons integrated parts of the bohemian scene into their company, the conversation might become a bit louder. The humorous Baroness Bertha von Arnswaldt (1850–1919) in Berlin had a small bronze bell with which she could call her circle to order.[98] A preferably uninterrupted continuity of the salon and its regular guests, a *stabilitas loci* as well as a harmonious ambience had a positive effect on the creative leisure and on conversation. The salon of old Marie von Olfers was praised as follows: "The whirlpool of the Berlin haste did not penetrate into these quiet rooms, where the Rauch busts and old Biedermeier furniture radiated the spiritual aura of the inhabitant. Here every hasty step was moderated, and the word soon found the connection with the inner experience in front of the calm, light blue eyes of the poetess."[99]

In conducting and shaping the conversation the hostess had to be able to listen, speak and give directions at the same time; she set the "tone" of a conversation. Mme de Maillé wrote that one should neither categorically reject "serious conversations" nor refuse "frivolous chatter"—the former being stupid, the latter pedantic. Only variety could banish boredom.[100] *Varietas delectat,* or, as Hedwig von Olfers quoted: "Tous les genres sont bons, hors le genre ennuyeux" (Voltaire).[101] There was also the general tone of polite society which characterized the style of an epoch. In the 1820s, for example, "light irony" was considered "the best social tone" in Berlin, so one had to "clothe one's best sides, and they are always the serious ones, in jest". But this could sometimes lead to affectation. It was observed that chiefly small and intimate gatherings enabled people to remain "quite natural" in conversation.[102] Such naturalness, however, required, just as in Mme de Sévigné's time, a certain amount of internalized values and forms, a style, a sense of decorum. As a desideratum of salon conversation, "esprit" is also mentioned again and again. The word is, however, ambiguous and misleading. For Mme de Maillé, French esprit was not primarily associated with amusing ideas, but with tact, a highly developed taste and a sensibility for the fine nuance.[103] Anne Martin-Fugier points out the important difference between "avoir de l'esprit" and "faire de l'esprit" in the sense of the 19th century. Both were needed, because just "having" esprit (education, intelligence) carried the danger of dry pedantry. On the other

---

[97] Lepsius 1916, p. 39.
[98] Schleich 1922, p. 318.
[99] Nostitz 1933, p. 60.
[100] Maillé 2012, pp. 61–62.
[101] Olfers 1914, vol. 2, p. 579 (22.7.1884).
[102] Olfers 1914, vol. 2, p. 85 (25.11.1825).
[103] "[…] this very fine sense of what should remain unsaid and what can be said", "this gift of choosing well". Maillé 2012, p. 432 (1850).

hand, "faire de l'esprit" could set off a sparkling fireworks of remarks and replies. It was a kind of communicative imagination or the ability to give suggestions and keywords and prepare cracking verbal stage-effects.[104] Mme de Maillé reports of Mme de Montcalm that she knew how to set and direct a general conversation masterfully—sometimes so well that she hardly had a chance to speak herself.[105] In Berlin, Bertha von Arnswaldt was considered an "Entflammerin" (inflamer, kindler) of conversations, and of Princess Marie Radziwill it was said that she could "challenge and get going" a conversation with "one word".[106] The writer and journalist Arthur Meyer wrote, particularly referring to the conversation skills of Countess Greffulhe, that a good hostess should, so to speak, present the tennis racket, but not swing at the ball herself.[107] If an observation by Mme de Circourt can be trusted, this could also have its drawbacks. Thinking of Princess Lieven, Mme de Circourt mentioned a kind of occupational disease that could affect important hostesses. They were so used to leading the conversation in their own salon—i.e. rather inciting others to speak than to speak themselves—that elsewhere, among a crowd, they sometimes seemed rather boring and indifferent.[108]

In certain talking situations, the hostess had to intervene more strongly than usual, for example when the conversation flagged. From time to time she had to discreetly give the conversation a different direction or correct platitudes, as Mme Récamier so tactfully understood: "[...] a charming, never offensive satire often brings salt and life to hackneyed subjects [...]."[109] Rahel Varnhagen's conversational skills included a special linguistic gift for expressing her observations in a vivid individual way: "[...] to grasp life; and sometimes baroque, in a comical or tragic guise, to name it what I saw."[110] Felicie Bernstein understood just as well how to tell refreshing anecdotes "from a higher perspective" and with humor: "She always experienced something curious: of course, the curious thing was not in the objective facts, but in her subjective perception of the experience. And in telling her experiences she was a master" (Max Liebermann).[111] Knowledge of the world, of men and manners were helpful: The brilliant art of conversation which characterized Mme Straus benefited from her intuitive insight into the thoughts and feelings of her conversation partners as well as from her "esprit de repartie".[112] Experienced salonnières were even allowed to address precarious topics. The Berliner Henriette von Crayen née Leveaux (1755–1832) had led a turbulent life, occasionally read

---

[104] Martin-Fugier 2011, pp. 226–228.

[105] Maillé 2012, pp. 61–62.

[106] Schleich 1922, pp. 314–315; Radziwill 1931, p. V.

[107] Meyer 1912, pp. 89–90, cf. p. 92, also in Martin-Fugier 2009, p. 133.

[108] Senior 1880, vol. 1, p. 303 (29.4.1861).

[109] Gans 1995, p. 150 (1835).

[110] Varnhagen 1983, vol. 2, p. 19 (27.2.1812).

[111] Liebermann 1914, p. 51.

[112] Gramont 2017, pp. 188 ff.

from letters of her "musée d'amour" and embodied the *esprit de conversation* of the Rococo even in the Biedermeier period.[113] Marie von Bunsen reports that old Hedwig von Olfers sometimes delighted her circle "with frank utterances concerning delicate questions" and Princess Radziwill possessed the "charming French ability" to "present very daring statements, such as those of her little respectable, but all the more witty nephew Boni de Castellane with ease and taste."[114] Since conversation was team work, it was desirable that as many guests as possible should have a sense of lighthearted causerie, literary allusions and bon mots. Of course, appropriate politeness and gallantry were also required. The individual was respected, as well as the peculiarities, and even the eccentricities of the interlocutors. However, wit and judgment should never be obtrusive. Prince Anton Radziwill, husband of Princess Louise and composer of an incidental music to Goethe's "Faust", used to speak of "parade oxen" if someone in conversation wanted to shine with paradoxes in a too self-satisfied way.[115] Herman Grimm wrote about Hedwig von Olfers: "What she said always had the appearance of an occasional utterance, and if she hit the nail on the head, she seemed to be the most surprised herself."[116]

German salon conversation at its best was quite similar to the French, but it had one peculiarity—it was always allowed to take on a little bit of dialect coloring, from the musical Viennese to the Low German expressions in Northern Germany. In Berlin, the popular patois was jokingly or emphatically interspersed in the conversation, and often colloquial phrases were used to avoid an unwanted pathos.[117] Even Princess Marie Radziwill sometimes adorned her French letters with blossoms of Berlin popular wit.[118] French expressions were also still in use. When in the summer of 1848 Marie von Olfers saw the democratic-minded Bettine von Arnim and an ultra-conservative acquaintance arm in arm on the street, she commented: "les extrêmes se touchent".[119] On the Seine, dialect phrases were not welcome in the salons, but there was the special Parisian metropolitan flair as a distinctive local color. Élisabeth de Gramont writes that Mme Straus, as a Jewish

---

[113] Wilhelmy 1989, pp. 118 ff. and 504. Theodor Fontane commemorated her as "Frau von Carayon" in his novel "Schach von Wuthenow". Like her, he was a jovial descendant of the Huguenots and a witty causeur.

[114] Bunsen 1916, p. 14, cf. Wilhelmy 1989, p. 419; Bunsen 1932, p. 107.

[115] Olfers 1914, vol. 2, p. 579 (7.8.1884).

[116] Grimm 1892, p. VI.

[117] In December of the revolutionary year 1848, Marie von Olfers related the saying of a shopkeeper: "Na, warten Sie man zu Weihnachten, da wird det Geschäft wieder janz jut, denn uff sone fürchterliche Traurigkeit, da machen sich die Menschen ne ordentliche Freude." ("Now, wait until Christmas, then the business will be quite good again, because on such terrible sadness, people make themselves a proper joy.") M. Olfers 1928, Vol. 1, p. 33. King Friedrich Wilhelm IV of Prussia, a master of wit in all nuances, also liked to talk in the Berlin patois.

[118] Compare, for example, Radziwill 1933, Vol. 1, p. 49 (3 December 1890), p. 115 (9/10 March 1892) and p. 131 (8/9 November 1892).

[119] M. Olfers 1928, vol. 1, p. 21 (10 August 1848).

Parisian, was a particularly convinced ("double") Parisian. Every nuance of the Parisian atmosphere was reflected in the salon of Mme Straus.[120]

Since this book is concerned with the value of conversation, we cannot go into the many forms of *mondanité fausse* and failed "salon conversation" here, like that which the Goncourt brothers complained about and sometimes experienced in the salon of the Paiva (1819–1884).[121] Only a few examples shall illustrate situations when the intervention of the hostess in everyday salon life was indispensable. In 1801 Rahel Levin-Varnhagen was forced to improvise spontaneously when someone had made an unsuitable joke and an embarrassing silence threatened. She defused the situation with the exclamation "I know dirty stories, too" and, after a coarse but harmless remark, quickly moved on to a French anecdote which she related gracefully, "swiftly and comically". "Everyone felt relieved and laughed from the bottom of their hearts […]."[122] Even in the rather relaxed early romantic salons appropriate manners were absolutely demanded. Slander could not be tolerated in good conversation: Although Mme Mohl sharply rejected the regime of Napoleon III, she defended Empress Eugénie's mother against malicious gossip in her salon.[123] In times of political tension, experienced salonnières could build bridges by their conversation. In Berlin they even tried to remain polite and diplomatic during the Revolution of 1848. When the royalist Hedwig von Olfers had a visit from the liberal Karl August Varnhagen in August 1848, she skilfully steered the conversation past many reefs. If necessary, digressions about the beautiful weather and the green trees could help: "If the conversation came to dangerous topics, it was quickly pulled back to the pastoral side again."[124] The Dreyfus Affair (1894–1906) was a heavy burden on Parisian salon conversation, which divided public opinion with its polemics and destroyed social relationships. Mme Straus defended Captain Dreyfus, and Countess Greffulhe also campaigned for a retrial. But even in conversations about serious matters there were sometimes light-hearted moments. Felicie Bernstein liked to tell how she had once been Émile Zola's neighbour at dinner. Incidentally, she knew nothing about the family circumstances of the author of the famous pamphlet "J'accuse". When she expressed her sympathy that he had been separated from his wife for so long during his exile in London (1898/99), he beamed at her: "[…] the time in London was the happiest time of my life."[125] Countess Greffulhe had friends and acquaintances in all political camps and was often able to intervene as a mediator through her conversation; she was therefore called the "Queen of Reconciliation between the old Aristocracy and the Third Republic" (Enrique Larreta).[126]

---

[120] Gramont 2017, p. 186.

[121] Goncourt 1947, pp. 162 ff. (24/31.5.1867). But see also p. 170 f. (Good Friday 1868).

[122] K. A. Varnhagen 1859a, vol. 8, pp. 580 f. It is said to have been an anecdote by Chamfort.

[123] Helmholtz 1929, vol. 1, pp. 50 ff. (26.1.1853). Mme Mohl knew through Prosper Mérimée that these were slanderous rumours.

[124] M. Olfers 1928, vol. 1, p. 26 (18.8.1848), cf. p. 20.

[125] Liebermann 1914, p. 51.

[126] Hillerin 2018, p. 181 ("une reine conciliatrice entre l'ancienne noblesse et la troisième République").

Directing salon conversation could be exhausting if you had difficult guests. Mrs. von Olfers once confessed to having been a "wretched hostess" at her last "Thursday": "There were various tête-à-têtes around that had got caught up in each other and could not get loose again out of embarrassment, but if someone had given me a kingdom for a phrase, I could not have delivered it, and always hoped that they would at last sail into the common harbor, too."[127] Mme Daudet had to learn that even at dinner parties with illustrious guests the conversation sometimes turned out to be disappointing. She concluded that one should not invite more than two great men together—too many tenors in an opera, too many virtuosos in an orchestra tended to cause problems.[128] Mrs. Mohl also warned against "celebrities" and regarded them as difficult guests if they had no social skills. "As celebrities, they are simply bores. Because a man has discovered a planet, it does not follow that he can converse agreeably, even on his own [research] subjects [...]."[129] Salon conversation always remained a little bit of an experiment and a risk. Mrs. von Olfers wrote: "You may possibly have a lot of wit in your salon, but if you are unlucky, it does not explode."[130]

Under good conditions, salon conversations, once started, often continued as an artistically managed "laissez-faire" that was attentively followed by the hostess, and only occasionally needed to be adjusted. In the free play of conversation, the salonnière was the referee. Mme Récamier's conversation was considered reserved, but she missed nothing. The Berlin legal scholar Eduard Gans viewed her in 1835 through the lens of Romanticism. Mme Récamier appears as a tournament queen who praised the eloquent "fighters when they fought bravely and well." "The conversation goes sharply back and forth: the combatants often touch each other with the tips of their arguments, but like fine and agile men, they do not wound each other."[131] Conversations unfolded, according to the topic, in a linear, varying, branching, or deepening manner. In April 1843, in a conversation at the Princess Lieven's in Paris, one could find a kind of transatlantic relay, from the politics of the United States of America via the earthquake in Guadeloupe (Caribbean, natural disaster) to the great comet of spring 1843 (natural phenomenon). The serious was flanked by the cheerful (appropriate anecdotes, caricatures).[132] At Mme de Boigne's salon, a sequence of conversation which may be described as revolving around a topic was initiated by some travellers' account of a trip to Rome and the Papal States. Finally, the memory of the late Cardinal Secretary of State Consalvi

---

[127] Olfers 1914, vol. 2, p. 335 (June 1854).

[128] Daudet 1910, p. 202 f. (August 1894).

[129] Lesser 1984, p. 101 (after Elizabeth Gaskell, 1854).

[130] Olfers 1914, vol. 2, p. 342 (1854). Cf. Friedrich Schlegel: "Wit is an explosion of bound spirit." Schlegel 2018, p. 66 (Lyceum Fragment No. 90).

[131] Gans 1995, p. 150. This was a controversial discussion about the death penalty. In the end, Mme Récamier gave a balanced verdict.

[132] Dino 1909, vol. 3, p. 247 f. (April 2, 1843).

was evoked, of whom Chancellor Pasquier had some stories to tell. Mme de Dino added an anecdote that showed the churchman as a politician with a dramatic talent: When Consalvi negotiated with Talleyrand at the Congress of Vienna for the restitution of territory of the Papal States, he declared, not without a hidden meaning, that Talleyrand would not lose anything by giving the Pope a few pieces of land back on earth—for in return, he would one day, above in heaven, get everything he wanted. Mme de Dino described how, with a grand gesture, Consalvi had raised his eyes and hands to heaven.[133] Of course, one did not always talk about politics, history, or literature. News of the day, such as sensational criminal cases, aroused lively interest everywhere. In 1891, Henri de Régnier criticized a conversation at Mme Straus's unfairly, saying that they had discussed the sensation of the day—the case of a poisoner—elegantly and with refinement, but really "as if in a concierge's lodge."[134] One could counter that the murder of the Duchess de Choiseuil-Praslin (1847) was also a topic in the best salons, and that the story of the poisoner Mme Voisin can even be found in Mme de Sévigné's letters (1680).

Salon conversation could and should be instructive, but not pedantic. Marie von Olfers wrote about the didactic side effects: "You learn more from a conversation than from all books and lessons. The peculiarity of the speaking person comes to help [...]."[135] The manner in which conversation promoted understanding had already been explained by Heinrich von Kleist. Building on the phenomenon of mental blockades suffered by examination candidates he wrote: "If these young people had been in a society where one had talked about the state or property for some time, they might have found the definition with ease, by comparison, separation and combination of concepts."[136] Since, long ago, the early salonnières had adapted the conversation theory of Renaissance humanism for their women's socializing, salon conversation traditionally allowed quite serious, even philosophical sequences. Some of Rahel Varnhagen's ideas remind us of Montaigne and Shaftesbury: "Whoever honestly asks and answers himself honestly is constantly busy with everything that happens to him in life, and constantly invents, even if it has been invented many times and for a long time before him."[137] She was, like Mme de Staël or Mme Mohl, considered a female Socrates and a midwife helping to bring forth the thoughts of her friends.[138] Rahel's method of open, dynamic questioning in order to promote understanding is closely related to

---

[133] Dino 1909, vol. 3, p. 250 f. (April 14, 1843).

[134] Quoted from Martin-Fugier 2009, p. 133 f.

[135] M. Olfers 1928, vol. 1, p. 58; see Lazarus 1878, p. 258 ff.

[136] Kleist 1952, vol. 2, p. 326.

[137] Varnhagen 1983, vol. 1, p. 267 (19.02.1805); see Dollinger 2001, p. 79 ff.

[138] It is reported that Mme Mohl quickly grasped the ideas and opinions of her conversation partners, viewed them from all sides, and often found more in them than they themselves suspected. O'Meara 1885, p. 146.

Schleiermacher's pluralistic hermeneutics, which cannot be elaborated here.[139] In doing so, she by no means came across as didactic. Rahel Varnhagen was particularly skilled in elegantly switching from one level of conversation to another and from current topics of the day to general matters. In March 1830 she explained the political character of the Biedermeier period, using the singer Henriette Sontag as an example. "Since 1815 the great and sublime has vanished, while the moderate and attractive has taken its place." In the political and social landscape of Europe, currently "a mixture of everything" was thought attractive, "agreeable behavior, pleasing elegance, virtuous restraint with appropriate liveliness." In the realm of art, this was embodied by Henriette Sontag, "and so she is," concluded Rahel, "an expression of the political and social eclecticism of our time, the artist exactly as our conditions produce her, carry her, allow her."[140] In the 19th century, outstanding conversation was still considered a work of art. In 1827, Frau von Olfers reported on a witty exchange between General Ernst von Pfuel and Wilhelm von Humboldt: "They know so well how to mix the jest into the significance of their speeches and thoughts that one sits there, as in front of a work of art, which, while light and pleasing in appearance, nevertheless shows us by its perfection that a calm wisdom has helped the playful imagination."[141]

The light art of the "causerie" in the salons often had a deeper dimension of experience and serene poise. This is shown by a conversation which, on the threshold of the 20th century, once again represented very much the spirit of classical conversation before the conversation culture of "Old Europe" collapsed in the catastrophe of 1914. It took place in January 1900 among the friends of Princess Marie Radziwill at a dinner in the Italian embassy in Berlin, the language was French. The just twenty-year-old Daniele Varè, who at that time was studying the violin with the famous Joseph Joachim and was still in doubt whether he should become a diplomat, describes this evening in his memoirs. After chatting about various other things, the older gentlemen took the young man under their wing. The Prussian General Julius von Verdy du Vernois advised him above all to be calm and humorous: "Laugh at successes, laugh at failures. Laugh about how our world is governed. Laugh at the others and above all: laugh at yourself!" The Princess Radziwill kindly added: "So you will have to create a new type […]. The

---

[139] "Friedrich Schleiermacher discovers […] as the basic situation of the pluralizing-literary hermeneutics the sociability of the *infinite conversation,* which lets everyone have a say without temporal limit and without pressure to reach agreement […]. The talking and letting talk of the infinite conversation includes reading and letting people read, and is devoted to living and letting live." Marquard 1984, p. 131.

[140] K. A. Varnhagen 1859b, pp. 615f. Rahel Varnhagen's goal was to make German conversation more flexible; she was confident because, just as with the French, "daily life is also my 'raw material.'" Varnhagen 1983, vol. 2, pp. 410f. (28.07.1816). Cf. Wilhelmy 1989, pp. 134f.

[141] Olfers 1914, vol. 2, p. 107 (conversation with Gabriele von Bülow née von Humboldt, early 1827). In his philosophy of language, Humboldt also emphasizes the aspect of "living" speech. Language develops "socially"; it is a dynamic "activity" or "energeia." Humboldt 1963b, p. 418 and p. 429.

Laughing Diplomat. Something like 'The Laughing Philosopher'." (Democritus is meant.) Ambassador Carlo Count Lanza di Busca advised him to be cautious and rather "laugh inwardly", while the painter Edoardo de Martino quoted the proverb: "The happy do not laugh, they smile." Now the princess invited the young man to come to her salon: "If you really want to become a diplomat [...], do look me up on the Pariser Platz. As you may know, I am a great-niece of Talleyrand. All diplomats come to me." She turned to Count Lanza: "Or not, Monsieur l'Ambassadeur?" With "old-fashioned gallantry", Varè concluded his story, the ambassador brought her hand to his lips and replied: "Should we indeed be surprised? [...] Diplomacy is in your blood. Next to you we are all amateurs."[142]

This cheerful and gallant scene elucidates quite plainly that the art of conversation in its best examples is much more than a witty interchange of words—namely kind compliance and human companionship, built on practical philosophy and the "grace of the heart" (Rahel Varnhagen).[143]

References

Ancelot, Virginie: Les Salons de Paris. Foyers éteints. Paris: Jules Tardieu 1858.
Bamberger, Ludwig: Über einige Formen des geselligen Verkehrs (1895), in: Ludwig Bamberger: Studien und Meditationen aus fünfunddreißig Jahren. Berlin: Rosenbaum & Hart 1898, S. 87–107.
Böttiger, Karl August: Literarische Zustände und Zeitgenossen. Begegnungen und Gespräche im klassischen Weimar. Hg. von Klaus Gerlach und René Sternke. Berlin: Aufbau Verlag 1998, 3. Aufl.
Bohnenkamp[-Renken], Anne: „Versucht's zusammen eine Strecke". Goethes Konzept einer ‚Weltliteratur' als Form europäischer Geselligkeit?, in: Susanne Schmid (Hg.): Einsamkeit und Geselligkeit um 1800. Heidelberg: Universitätsverlag Winter 2008, S. 177–191.
Boigne, Adèle Comtesse de: Mémoires de la Comtesse de Boigne née Osmond. Récits d'une tante. Édition présentée et annotée par Jean-Claude Berchet. Bd. 1: Du règne de Louis XVI à 1820, Bd. 2: De 1820 à 1848. Paris: Mercure de France 1999, 1. Aufl. 1971.
Bonaparte, Mathilde [Princesse]: Mémoires inédits. Édition établie et annotée par Carole Blumenfeld. Préface de Philippe Costamagna. Paris: Bernard Grasset 2019.
Broglie, Gabriel de: Madame de Genlis. Paris: Librairie Académique Perrin 1985.
Bunsen, Marie von: Die Frau und die Gesellschaft. Leipzig: Seemann & Co. o.J. [1916].
Bunsen, Marie von: Die Welt in der ich lebte. Erinnerungen aus glücklichen Jahren, 1860–1912. Leipzig: Koehler & Amelang 1929, 3. Aufl.
Bunsen, Marie von: Zeitgenossen, die ich erlebte, 1900–1930. Leipzig: Koehler & Amelang 1932.
Craveri, Benedetta: L'Age de la Conversation. Traduit de l'Italien par Eliane Deschamps-Pria. Paris: Gallimard 2002.
Daudet, [Julia] Mme Alphonse: Souvenirs d'une groupe littéraire. Paris: Bibliothèque Charpentier Eugène Fasquelle 1910.

---

[142] Varè 1940, pp. 16f. Here only an excerpt from the conversation described in detail by Varè could be quoted. Previously, the turn of the century (1900 or 1901) had been mentioned, the German Kaiser, painting, the "Laughing Cavalier" by Frans Hals, etc.
[143] Varnhagen 1983, vol. 2, p. 24 (08.03.1812).

Dino, [Dorothée] Duchesse de (puis Duchesse de Talleyrand et de Sagan): Chronique de 1831 à 1862. Publiée avec des annotations et un Index biographique par la Princesse [Marie] Radziwill née Castellane. 4 Bde., Paris: Librairie Plon 1909.

Dollinger, Petra: Die internationale Vernetzung der deutschen Salons (1750–1914), in: Roberto Simanowski, Horst Turk und Thomas Schmidt (Hg.): Europa – ein Salon? Beiträge zur Internationalität des literarischen Salons. Göttingen: Wallstein Verlag 1999, S. 40–65.

Dollinger, Petra: Die jüdische Salontradition in Berlin. Vom späten 18. Jahrhundert bis zum Ersten Weltkrieg, in: Christof Römer (Hg.): Mitteldeutsches Jahrbuch für Kultur und Geschichte. Bd. 8, Köln, Weimar, Wien: Böhlau 2001, S. 75–102.

Dollinger, Petra: Wilhelm Müller, die „Ur-Müllerlieder" und sein Freundeskreis in Berlin, in: Mitteilungen des Vereins für Anhaltische Landeskunde 25, 2016, S. 9–37.

Dollinger, Petra: Verborgene Erinnerungsräume. Historische Fußnoten zu Vladimir Nabokovs „Speak, Memory" und deutsch-russische Begegnungen im Bannkreis der europäischen Romantik, in: Alexander Bierich, Thomas Bruns und Henrieke Stahl (Hg.): Gedächtnisraum Literatur – Gedächtnisraum Sprache: Europäische Dimensionen slavischer Geschichte und Kultur. Festschrift für Svetlana und Gerhard Ressel. Berlin, Bern: Peter Lang 2019, S. 453–475.

Eckermann, Johann Peter: Goethes Gespräche mit J.P. Eckermann. Neu hg. und eingeleitet von Franz Deibel. 2 Bde., Leipzig: Insel-Verlag 1908.

Fouqué, Karoline [sic] de la Motte: Ueber deutsche Geselligkeit in Antwort auf das Urtheil der Frau von Staël. Berlin: L.W. Wittich 1814.

Fouqué, Caroline Baronin de la Motte: Die Frauen in der großen Welt. Bildungsbuch bei'm Eintritt in das gesellige Leben. Berlin: Schlesinger 1826.

[Friedrich der Große:] Die Werke Friedrichs des Großen. Bd. 8: Philosophische Schriften. Hg. von Gustav Berthold Volz, deutsch von Friedrich v. Oppeln-Bronikowski. Berlin: Verlag von Reimar Hobbing 1913.

Fumaroli, Marc: La conversation, in: Pierre Nora (Hg.): Les lieux de mémoire, III, 2. Traditions. Paris: Gallimard 1992, S. 679–743 (III. Le XIXe Siècle, S. 717–743).

Gans, Eduard: Der Salon der Madame Recamier (1835), in: Eduard Gans: Rückblicke auf Personen und Zustände. Hg., kommentiert und mit einer Einleitung versehen von Norbert Waszek. Stuttgart-Bad Cannstatt: Frommann-Holzboog 1995, S. 147–163, Ndr. der Ausg. Berlin 1836.

Garve, Christian: Über die Maxime Rochefoucaults: das bürgerliche Air verliehrt sich zuweilen bey der Armee, niemals am Hofe [1792], in: Christian Garve: Popularphilosophische Schriften über literarische, ästhetische und gesellschaftliche Gegenstände. Im Faksimiledruck hg. von Kurt Wölfel. Bd. 1, Stuttgart: J.B. Metzlersche Verlagsbuchhandlung 1974, S. 295–452 [S. 559–716].

Gersal, Luc: Siehe Legras, Jules.

Godo, Emmanuel: Une histoire de la conversation. Paris: Presses Univ. de France 2003.

Goncourt, Jules und Edmond de: Tagebuch der Brüder Goncourt. Aus dem Französischen übertragen und hg. von [Hermann] Uhde-Bernays. München: Verlag Kurt Desch 1947.

Gramont, Élisabeth de: Au Temps des Équipages. Mémoires [Bd. 1]. Paris: Bernard Grasset 2017.

Gramont, Élisabeth de: Les Marronniers en fleurs. Mémoires [Bd. 2]. Paris: Bernard Grasset 2018.

Grimm, Herman: Hedwig von Olfers [Nachruf], in: Hedwig von Olfers: Gedichte. Berlin: Verlag Wilhelm Hertz 1892, S. I–X.

Grotthus [Grotthuß], Sara von: Briefe von Sara von Grotthus und Marianne von Eybenberg, in: Goethe und seine Freunde im Briefwechsel. Hg. und eingeleitet von Richard M. Meyer. Bd. 3, Berlin: Georg Bondi 1911, Sp. 141–176.

Helmholtz, Anna von: Ein Lebensbild in Briefen. Hg. von Ellen von Siemens-Helmholtz. 2 Bde., Berlin: Verlag für Kulturpolitik 1929.

Herz, Henriette: Henriette Herz in Erinnerungen, Briefen und Zeugnissen. Hg. von Rainer Schmitz. Frankfurt a.M.: Insel Verlag 1984, Lizenzausgabe des Verlags Gustav Kiepenheuer, Leipzig und Weimar.
Hillerin, Laure: La comtesse Greffulhe. La vraie vie de la muse de Proust. Édition revue et augmenté. Paris: Flammarion/Libres champs 2018.
Humboldt, Wilhelm von: Ueber den Nationalcharakter der Sprachen (Bruchstück), in: Wilhelm von Humboldt, Werke in fünf Bänden. Hg. von Andreas Flitner und Klaus Giel. Bd. III: Schriften zur Sprachphilosophie. Darmstadt: Wissenschaftliche Buchgesellschaft 1963, S. 64–81.
Humboldt, Wilhelm von: Ueber die Verschiedenheit des menschlichen Sprachbaues und ihren Einfluss auf die geistige Entwicklung des Menschengeschlechts (1830–1835), in: Wilhelm von Humboldt, Werke in fünf Bänden. Hg. von Andreas Flitner und Klaus Giel. Bd. III: Schriften zur Sprachphilosophie, Darmstadt: Wissenschaftliche Buchgesellschaft 1963, S. 368–756.
Kant, Immanuel: Anthropologie in pragmatischer Hinsicht [2. verb. Aufl., Königsberg 1800], in: Immanuel Kants Werke. Hg. von Ernst Cassirer. Bd. 8: Anthropologie. Hg. von Otto Schöndorfer. Berlin: Bruno Cassirer 1923, S. 1–228.
Kessler, Harry Graf: Das Tagebuch 1880–1937. Bd. 3: 1897–1905. Hg. von Carina Schäfer und Gabriele Biedermann, Stuttgart: Cotta 2004.
Kleist, Heinrich von: Über die allmähliche Verfertigung der Gedanken beim Reden (1805), in: Heinrich von Kleist: Sämtliche Werke und Briefe. Hg. von Helmut Sembdner. Bd. 2, München: Carl Hanser Verlag 1952, S. 321–327.
Knigge, Adolph Freiherr: Über den Umgang mit Menschen. Hg. von Karl-Heinz Göttert. Stuttgart: Reclam 1991.
Laisney, Vincent: Le Temple des Souvenirs/Témoignages sur le „Salon" de Judith Gautier, in: Yvain Daniel, Martine Lavaud (Hg.): Judith Gautier. Rennes: Presses Universitaires 2020, S. 53–73.
Lazarus, Moritz: Ueber Gespräche. Vortrag, im wissenschaftlichen Verein der Singakademie gehalten am 24. Februar 1876, in: Moritz Lazarus., Ideale Fragen, in Reden und Vorträgen behandelt. Berlin: A. Hofmann & Comp. 1878, S. 237–265.
Lesser, Margaret: Clarkey. A Portrait in Letters of Mary Clarke Mohl (1793–1883). Oxford: Oxford University Press 1984.
Lilti, Antoine: Le monde des salons. Sociabilité et mondanité à Paris au XVIIIe siècle. Paris: Arthème Fayard 2005.
Legras, Jules: Spree-Athen. Berliner Skizzen von einem Böotier. Leipzig: Carl Reißner 1892.
Lepsius, Sabine: Vom deutschen Lebensstil. Leipzig: Seemann & Co. o.J. [1916].
Liebermann, Max: Meine Erinnerungen an die Familie Bernstein, in: Carl und Felicie Bernstein. Erinnerungen ihrer Freunde. Dresden: Wilhelm und Bertha v. Baensch Stiftung 1914, S. 47–52.
Maillé, Duchesse de: Souvenirs des deux Restaurations. Journal inédit présenté par Xavier de La Fournière. Paris: Librairie Académique Perrin 1984.
Maillé, Duchesse de: Mémoires. Un regard sur le monde 1832–1851. Introduction, revue et corrigée, et notes de Frédéric d'Agay. Paris: Lacurne 2012, 1. Aufl. Paris: Librairie Académique Perrin 1989.
Mainusch, Herbert: Skeptische Ästhetik. Plädoyer für eine Gesellschaft von Künstlern. Stuttgart: Metzler 1991.
Martin-Fugier, Anne: La vie élégante, ou la formation du Tout-Paris, 1815–1848. Paris: Perrin 2011, 1. Aufl. Paris: Arthème Fayard 1990.
Martin-Fugier, Anne: Les salons de la IIIe République. Art, littérature, politique. Paris: Perrin 2009, 1. Aufl. Paris: Perrin 2003.
Marquard, Odo: Frage nach der Frage, auf die die Hermeneutik die Antwort ist, in: Odo Marquard: Abschied vom Prinzipiellen. Philosophische Studien. Stuttgart: Philipp Reclam junior 1984, S. 117–146.

Matuschek, Stefan: Der gedichtete Himmel. Eine Geschichte der Romantik. München: Verlag C. H. Beck 2021.

Mendelssohn, Moses: Über die Frage: was heißt aufklären?, in: Friedrich Gedike, Johann Erich Biester (Hg.): Berlinische Monatsschrift (1783–1796). Auswahl, hg. mit einer Studie „Die Berlinische Monatsschrift als Organ der Aufklärung" von Peter Weber. Leipzig: Verlag Philipp Reclam jun. 1985, S. 80–84.

Meyer, Arthur: Ce que je peux dire. Paris: Librairie Plon 1912.

M[ohl], Madame [Mary]: Madame Récamier. With a Sketch of the History of Society in France. London: Chapman and Hall 1862.

[Mohl, Mary:] Clarkey. A Portrait in Letters of Mary Clarke Mohl (1793–1883), see above: Margaret Lesser.

Mohl, Robert von: Lebens-Erinnerungen 1799–1875. 2 Bde., Stuttgart, Leipzig: Deutsche Verlags-Anstalt 1902.

Müller, Adam: Zwölf Reden über die Beredsamkeit und deren Verfall in Deutschland. Gehalten zu Wien im Frühlinge 1812. Mit Einleitung und Nachwort von Walter Jens. Frankfurt a.M.: Insel-Verlag 1976.

Nietzsche, Friedrich: Sämtliche Werke. Kritische Studienausgabe in 15 Bänden. Hg. von Giorgio Colli und Mazzino Montinari. Bd. 1 [u.a. Unzeitgemäße Betrachtungen] und Bd. 2 [Menschliches, Allzumenschliches]. München: dtv/Berlin: Walter de Gruyter 1980.

Nostitz, Helene [von]: Aus dem alten Europa. Menschen und Städte. Berlin: Kurt Wolff 1933, 4. erw. Aufl.

Olfers, Hedwig von: Mitteilung an Otto Brahm, 1884, in: Helmut Sembdner (Hg.), Heinrich von Kleists Lebensspuren. Dokumente und Berichte von Zeitgenossen. Erweiterte Neuausgabe. Dokumente zu Kleist. Bd. 1, Frankfurt a.M., Leipzig: Insel Verlag 1992, Nr. 504, S. 397, 1. Aufl. 1952.

Olfers, Hedwig von: Hedwig v. Olfers geb. von Staegemann, 1799–1891. Ein Lebenslauf. Hg. von Hedwig Abeken. 2 Bde., Berlin: Ernst Siegfried Mittler und Sohn 1908–1914.

Olfers, Marie von: Briefe und Tagebücher. Hg. von Margarete von Olfers. 2 Bde., Berlin: E. S. Mittler und Sohn 1928–1930.

O'Meara, Kathleen (Pseud. Grace Ramsay): Madame Mohl: Her Salon and her Friends. A Study of Social Life in Paris. London: R. Bentley & Son 1885.

Pange, [Pauline] Comtesse Jean de: Comment j'ai vu 1900 [Bd. 1]. Paris: Bernard Grasset 1962.

Pange, Pauline [Comtesse Jean] de: Confidences d'une jeune fille. Comment j'ai vu 1900 [Bd. 2]. Paris: Bernard Grasset 2014.

[Pauline Fürstin zur Lippe:] Eine Fürstin unterwegs. Reisetagebücher der Fürstin Pauline zur Lippe 1799–1818. Bearb. von Hermann Niebuhr. Detmold: Lippische Geschichtsquellen 1990.

Picon, Jérôme: Mathilde, Princesse Bonaparte. Paris: Flammarion 2005.

Radziwill, Marie Fürstin: Une Française à la Cour de Prusse. Souvenirs de la Princesse Antoine Radziwill (née Castellane), 1840–1873. Publiés par les Comtesses Élisabeth et Hélène Potocka. Préface de M. Jules Cambon, de l'Académie Française. Paris: Librairie Plon 1931.

Radziwill, Marie Fürstin: Une Grande Dame d'Avant Guerre. Lettres de la Princesse Radziwill au Général de Robilant, 1889–1914. 4 Bde., Bologna: Nicola Zanichelli 1933–1934.

Rathenau, Walther: Tagebuch 1907–1922. Hg. und kommentiert von Hartmut Pogge-v. Strandmann, mit einem Beitrag von James Joll und einem Geleitwort von Fritz Fischer. Düsseldorf: Droste Verlag 1967.

Rathenau, Walther: Briefe, Teilband 1: 1871–1913. Hg. von Alexander Jaser, Clemens Picht und Ernst Schulin. Düsseldorf: Droste Verlag 2006.

Richardson, Joanna: Judith Gautier. A Biography. New York: Franklin Watts 1987.

Rochow, Caroline von: Vom Leben am preußischen Hofe 1815–1852. Aufzeichnungen von Caroline v. Rochow geb. v. d. Marwitz und Marie de la Motte-Fouqué. Bearbeitet von Luise v. d. Marwitz. Berlin: Ernst Siegfried Mittler und Sohn 1908.

Schlegel, Friedrich: „Athenaeum"-Fragmente und andere frühromantische Schriften. Edition, Kommentar und Nachwort von Johannes Endres. Stuttgart: Reclam 2018.
Schleich, Carl Ludwig: Besonnte Vergangenheit. Lebenserinnerungen (1859–1919). Berlin: Ernst Rowohlt Verlag 1922.
Schleiermacher, Friedrich Daniel Ernst: Versuch einer Theorie des geselligen Betragens, in: Otto Braun (Hg.) Schleiermachers Werke. Auswahl in vier Bänden. Bd. 2: Entwürfe zu einem System der Sittenlehre. Leipzig: Meiner 1913, S. 1–32.
Seibert, Peter: Der literarische Salon. Literatur und Geselligkeit zwischen Aufklärung und Vormärz. Stuttgart, Weimar: Metzler 1993.
Senior, William Nassau: Conversations with Distinguished Persons during the Second Empire from 1860 to 1863. Edited by his daughter M.C.M. Simpson. 2 Bde., London: Hurst and Blackett 1880.
Simanowski, Roberto, Horst Turk und Thomas Schmidt (Hg.): Europa – ein Salon? Beiträge zur Internationalität des literarischen Salons. Göttingen: Wallstein Verlag 1999.
Simmel, Georg: Weibliche Kultur, in: Philosophische Kultur. Über das Abenteuer, die Geschlechter und die Krise der Moderne. Gesammelte Essais. Mit einem Vorwort von Jürgen Habermas. Berlin: Verlag Klaus Wagenbach 1986, S. 219–253, 1. Aufl. Potsdam 1923.
Staegemann, Elisabeth von: Fragmente in Stunden der Muße niedergeschrieben. Angebinde einer deutschen Mutter für ihre Tochter, zu ihrem siebzehnten Geburtstage, in: Dies., Erinnerungen für edle Frauen. Nebst Lebensnachrichten über die Verfasserin und einem Anhange von Briefen. Hg v. Wilhelm Dorow. Bd. 2, Leipzig: J.C. Hinrich 1846, S. 109–164.
Staël-Holstein, Anne Louise Germaine de: Über Deutschland. Aus dem Französischen übertragen und mit einem Nachwort sowie Anmerkungen versehen von Robert Habs. München: Verlag Robert Borowsky o.J., nach der Ausgabe Leipzig 1882.
Strosetzki, Christoph: Konversation. Ein Kapitel gesellschaftlicher und literarischer Pragmatik im Frankreich des 17. Jahrhunderts. Frankfurt a.M., Bern: Peter Lang 1978.
Varè, Daniele: Der Lachende Diplomat. Berlin, Wien, Leipzig: Paul Zsolnay Verlag 1940.
Varnhagen von Ense, Karl August: Rahel Levin und ihre Gesellschaft. Gegen Ende des Jahres 1801. (Aus den Papieren des Grafen S*** [Salm-Reifferscheidt]), in: Karl August Varnhagen von Ense: Denkwürdigkeiten und vermischte Schriften. Hg. von Ludmilla Assing. Bd. 8, Leipzig: F.A. Brockhaus 1859, S. 564–594.
Varnhagen von Ense, Karl August: Der Salon der Frau von Varnhagen. Berlin, im März 1830, in: Karl August Varnhagen von Ense: Denkwürdigkeiten und vermischte Schriften. Hg. von Ludmilla Assing. Bd. 8, Leipzig: F.A. Brockhaus 1859, S. 595–630.
Varnhagen von Ense, Rahel: Gesammelte Werke. Hg. von Konrad Feilchenfeldt, Uwe Schweikert und Rahel E. Steiner. 10 Bde., München: Matthes & Seitz Verlag 1983.
Vigny, Alfred de: Journal d'un poète. Nouvelle édition, revue et augmentée par Fernand Baldensperger. London: The Scholartis Press 1928.
Weithase, Irmgard: Goethe als Sprecher und Sprecherzieher. Weimar: Hermann Böhlaus Nachfolger 1949.
Weithase, Irmgard: Zur Geschichte der gesprochenen deutschen Sprache. 2 Bde., Tübingen: Max Niemeyer Verlag 1961.
Wiedemann, Conrad: Das Archiv, die Stadt und die „Wonne des Lernens". Annäherungsversuche an einen Berliner Vereinsnachlass der klassischen Zeit, in: Uta Motschmann: Schule des Geistes, des Geschmacks und der Geselligkeit. Die Gesellschaft der Freunde (1799–1861). Hannover: Wehrhahn Verlag 2009, S. XI–XXVI.
Wilhelmy, Petra: Der Berliner Salon im 19. Jahrhundert (1780–1914). Berlin, New York: Walter de Gruyter 1989.
Wilhelmy-Dollinger, Petra: „Salon" und „Tusculum". Urbane und ländliche Gesellgkeit in Brandenburg-Preußen um 1800, in: Susanne Schmid (Hg.): Einsamkeit und Gesellschaft um 1800. Heidelberg: Universitätsverlag Winter 2008, S. 67–94.
Wilhelmy-Dollinger, Petra: „Häuser ohne Frauen sind Verse ohne Poesie" – Berliner Salons vor und um 1800, in: Bärbel Holtz und Wolfgang Neugebauer (Hg. im Auftrag der

Berlin-Brandenburgischen Akademie der Wissenschaften): Kennen Sie Preußen – wirklich? Das Zentrum „Preußen – Berlin" stellt sich vor. Berlin: AkademieVerlag 2009, S. 59–90.

Wilhelmy-Dollinger, Petra: Der Salon der Anna von Helmholtz (1834–1899). Die Begegnung von alter Salontradition und moderner Naturwissenschaft im Berlin der Bismarckzeit, in: Harro Kieser und Gerlinde Schlenker (Hg. für die Stiftung Mitteldeutscher Kulturrat): Mitteldeutsches Jahrbuch für Kultur und Geschichte. Bd. 17, Bonn: Monumente Publikationen 2010, S. 120–140.

Wilhelmy-Dollinger, Petra: Felicie Bernstein. September 7, 1850 – June 11, 1908, in: Alice Shalvi/Paula Hyman: The Shalvi/Hyman Encyclopedia of Jewish Women. Last updated June 23, 2021, online: Jewish Women's Archive, https://jwa.org/encyclopedia/article/bernstein-felicie (abgerufen 1.9.2021).

On Luther's Table Talks

Thomas Pittrof

> When a dear man speaks a word in his time, that is indeed like a golden apple or beautiful pomegranate and lemon in a silver bowl, as the wise King Solomon says, and is difficult to forget among good people, as the honest deeds of great people should be justly praised from time to time. So now help us the Son of God with his spirit, that I as a grateful pupil of my dear preceptor's good sayings and blessed works may speak something useful and funny.

Abstract

The guests and listeners at Luther's table were so convinced of the "value of conversation" that they began during the Reformer's lifetime to make conversation records and then transcriptions, which were first printed in collected form in 1566. But what exactly is this label of the "table talk" of Luther? The following article serves as an introduction to both the complex internal structure of this text corpus of over 7000 notations and—to a limited extent—to basic problems of table talk research. It becomes clear: Despite valuable individual studies on the linguistic form of the table talk, the complicated editorial relationships or their placement in a literary history of sociability and conversation, much is still only outlined; We seem to know very little about their concrete history of reception.

T. Pittrof (✉)
Katholische Universität Eichstätt-Ingolstadt, Eichstätt, Germany
e-mail: thomas.Pittrof@ku.de

Keywords

Luther's table talk · Performance · Mediality · Conversation culture ·
Apophthegmatics · Facet · Extra-theological reception

In his "Luther's Table Talks", which his first Protestant biographer Johannes Mathesius mentioned at the beginning of the 13th of his sermons dedicated to Luther's life and work,[1] he paid tribute to the collection of conversations started in 1529[2] and continued by various eyewitnesses until Luther's death year 1546, which were initially transmitted in writing by various collectors, also those who were not present on site, then printed for the first time in 1566[3]. Many of the conversations that took place during the meals of Luther and his table society in the Black Cloister in Wittenberg were recorded in writing, in which the reformer lived with a fluctuating and growing household community of family, servants, boarders and scholars from 1522 onwards.[4] They were probably held mostly in the former refectory, less often in other rooms of the building.[5] The toilet has recently been mentioned as a special *locus conversationis*, so that in addition to the table talks, the existence of "toilet talks" is also conceivable.[6] but some of it has also been expressed on other occasions and in other places, such as on the Koburg,[7]

---

[1] Mathesius 1566/1883, p. 250.

[2] This is the dating according to Beyer, 2017, p. 393; differing from the otherwise usual one from 1531.

[3] Aurifaber 1566/1981.

[4] On March 6 of this year, Luther returned from the Wartburg to Wittenberg and moved back into the monastery, which, however, "emptied out visibly due to his criticism of the vows—in autumn 1523 only one other convent member was living there. […] Since his marriage [on June 13, 1525] Luther received a princely professor's salary. In addition, since the Elector made the former Augustinian monastery available to him as a residence in 1532, he even transferred it to him, it could become the "Lutherhaus" under the direction of Katharina Luther. The familiar environment remained the center of Luther's life […] Six children were born from the marriage, four of whom reached adulthood […] Guests, relatives and refugees filled the house, in addition to the students living there" (Zschoch 2017, pp. 112 f.); according to Stolt 2014, p. 136, one must imagine the whole thing as a kind of "boarding school or guesthouse for scholars". According to a note in the Weimar edition (WA) to Table Talk No. 261, Luther built a bowling alley in the Black Cloister for his sons and students.

[5] Junghans 2000, p. 36.

[6] Mecklenburg 2019. This discovery—Mecklenburg builds on a FAZ report from spring 2015, which had the excavation of a stone seat with drainage to the subject, "the latrine Martin Luther's" (ibid., p. 135)—has not increased the text content of the table talks, but has, by quoting from No. 5537 of the Weimar edition, newly pointed out: "It is, as I often said: I am the ripe shit, so the world is the wide asshole; Therefore, we should be able to separate." (Ibid., p. 148). For the rest, the essay is the playful counterpart to the material-, knowledge- and ascetic monograph of the same author (Mecklenburg 2016).

[7] Junghans 2000, p. 36.

on trips to Torgau and Eisleben,[8] or from sermons, letters[9] and other writings[10] Luther flowed. In the history of the mediated Luther-*memoria* the table talks have, probably in connection with the testimonies of the fine arts—print graphics and painting—Luther imagology, played a certain role. They confirmed in the intra-Protestant disputes after Luther's death the memory of the "dear man" (Mathesius) and stabilized, after they had found their scientifically decisive edition in the Weimar edition[11] had found, in selection editions that were intended for the wider book market, the 'popular' Luther image of the Germans over the empire and the Weimar Republic into the "Third Reich"[12] into it. While the non-specialist contemporary interest in the table talks is difficult to assess,[13] since Kroker's edition

---

[8] Ibid.

[9] Stolt 2014, Sp. 136; Volz 1966, p. 722, Sp. 2. Good introductions to the table talk complex are Junghans 2000, repeated in Junghans 2001; Bartmuss 2015 and Beyer 2017. Volz/Orth 2009 is the strongly shortened and supplemented by the indication of newer literature version of Volz 1966, also a very useful overview, whose author was unfortunately also the very infamous co-author of a book *We walk through the National Socialist Berlin: A guide to the memorials of the struggle for the Reich capital* (Munich: Eher 1937)—'Topography of [self-produced] terror' and Martyrology from the typewriter of a convinced National Socialist. Whether these (and other party publications on the history of the NSDAP) have in any way affected Volz's work after 1945 is not clear from his dedicated Wikipedia article; He was at least employed as a full-time employee to continue the WA in 1950 and, in addition to a teaching position from 1954 to 1972, had the leadership of the Göttingen WA office, which was newly founded there in 1959, from 1959 to 1976 (Köpf 2000, p. 18). He died in 1978.

[10] See, for example, the compilation of excerpts from Mathesius 1566/1883 below at No. (13).

[11] 6 Bde., 1912–1921, this again 2000 in a (used here) special edition with an accompanying booklet hg. from U. Köpf; Additions due to recent findings in WA 48, 371-719 and WA 59, 729-746 as well as a bibliography of the [independent] table talks editions [16th-18th centuries] in WA 59, 747–780 (information according to Beyer, 2017, p. 398) That the history of the table talks editions is not yet complete, shows the discussion about a planned (digital) new edition by Wilhelm 2013 and Glaser 2013.

[12] Cf. the editions by H.H. Borcherdt and W. Rehm 1925, H. Mulert 1935 and R. Buchwald 1938. The latter two reflect in the introductions of their editors a remarkable distance to the brown zeitgeist—Mulert, one of the best-known 'liberal' evangelical university theologians and editor-in-chief of the Christliche Welt, had requested his dismissal from state service in 1935 because of his opposition to the NS; the later by his Schiller biography (2 Bde., Leipzig 1937, neubearb. Edition 1953–54, 4. neubearb. Aufl. 1959) become known R. Buchwald was active in the adult education movement and was also far from the NSDAP (no party member). Cf. about him Reimers 2003.

[13] In bookstores, the table speeches are indeed well represented. Available are each a selection edition at Insel, Reclam and from the Evangelical Publishing House (for this edition Kritisches bei Stolt 2014, p. 138 ff.), in addition two more single volumes within the ten-volume edition "Luther Deutsch" by K. Aland (ed.) at utb and the eight-volume Bonn edition by O. Clemen (ed.) at de Gruyter as well as an audiobook version with Uwe Ochsenknecht at Herder, but bpsw. in the Reformation Jubilee Year 2017 the table speeches have found no special attention. The (instructive!) Contribution by Treu 2016 for example, the question of the popularity of the Luther image exclusively on the basis of visual (and occasionally commercial) evidence. The editions by W. Sparn 1983 and J. Henkys ²2003 are out of print.

in the Weimar edition, research has developed a number of questions that are partly due to the problem of their object due to the origin and transmission history, partly to its multidimensionality a) at the transition from oral to written; b) in its mixed German-Latin composition; [14] c) in the editorial mixture between the *ipsissima vox Lutheri* and what is content-wise and linguistically an addition, omission or editing of their utterances; and finally d) as a multi-referentiality of the table speeches within the variety of genres of a literary system, the common ground of which is the conviction of the "value of conversation".

Aurifaber was the first to discover this multiplicity or even variety of table talk in terms of their content. The "Register or Index / of the main parts / which are contained in this Tomo of the table talk of Doctor Martini Luther" of the 1566 edition contains the entries

> Of the Word of God / or the Holy Scriptures.—Of the Works of God.—Of Creation.—Of the World and its Art.—Of Idolatry.—Of the Holy Trinity.—Of the Lord Christ.—Of the Holy Spirit.—Of Sin.—Of Free Will.—Of the Holy Catechism.—Of the Law and the Gospel.—That Faith in Christ Alone Makes God Just.—Of Good Works.—Of Prayer.—Of the Confession of Doctrine and Perseverance.—Of Holy Baptism.—Of Confession of the Ear.—Of the Sacrament of the Altar / of the True Body and Blood of Christ.—Of the Christian Church.—Of Excommunication and Bann / or the Jurisdiction of the Church.—Of the Preaching Office or Church Servants.—Of Angels.—Of the Devil and his Works.—Of Sorcery.—Of Temptation and Temptation.—Of Antichrist or Pope.—Of the Opponents / who have written against Dr. M. L.—Of Monks / their Lives and Good Days.—Of Cardinals and Bishops.—Of Papal or Spiritual Law.—Of Human Traditions.—Of Ceremonies.—Of the Mass.—Of the Purgatory.—Of Schwermern / Mobs and Sects / which have been laid against D. M. L.—Of Christians and a Christian Life.—Of Hypocrites and False Brethren.—Of Sophistry.—Of Annoyance.—Of the Right Worship.—Of the Marriage State.—Of the Authority and Princes.—Of Kings / Princes and Lords.—Of Unanimity.—Of Sickness / and its Causes.—Of Death.—Of the Dead Resurrection and the Eternal Life.—Of Damnation and Hell.—Of the Last Day.—Of Allegories / and Spiritual Interpretation of the Scriptures / and how to Deal with it.—Of Legends of the Saints.—Of Councils.—Of Reichstages and Conuenten / or Assemblies in Religious Affairs.—Of Spiritual or Church Goods.—Of the Books of the Veter in the Church.—Of SchoolTheologians.—Of the Books of the Old and New Testaments / D. M. L. Judgment.—Of Patriarchs and Prophets.—Of the Apostles and Disciples of Christ.—Of Wars.—Of Outstanding Warriors and Heroes.—Of the Counter and Defense.—Of Noblemen.—Of Jurists.—Of Schools / Universities / and Good Arts.—Of Music.—Of Languages.—Of Astronomy / Star Art and Astrology.—Of Signs and Weather.—Of Studies.—Of Scholars.—Of the Jews and their Büberery.—Of the Turk.—Of Countries and Cities.—Of the City of Rome.—Of Profession.—Of Drunkenness.—Of the Court Life.

As "discharged locos", also *loci communes* Aurifaber has referred to this sequence of topics[15] and has given them an eclectic systematics, which begins with the biblical foundations of the Christian faith, spans over focal points of Luther's theology,

---

[14] To this day, Stolt 1964 has not been outdated.

[15] In an addition to this list: "Also many other table talks of D. M. Luther partly belonging to the obgesetzte Locos / of all sorts of things / gathered together from some written books."

questions of spiritual and worldly government and various groups of people of the Estates society up to their ways of life and knowledge as well as with the last section "Of Court Life" naming a communicative environment, the description and precepts of which in the temporal environment of Luther had become the subject of its own body of writing and a "literature of 'good taste'"[16] through Castiglione's *Cortegiano* (1528), Casa's *Galateus* (1539) and Guazzo's *La civil conversazione* (1574). This opens up a range of questions which must remain unanswered by Aurifaber because his catalogue of topics cannot reflect the colloquial element of table talk. They concern, on the one hand, the [above mentioned under (d)] placement of their transcription in the history of conversation literature, on the other hand their communicative form. So what did the culture of conversation of the entertainment look like? What did the modes and models of communicative socialization look like at the table in the Black Cloister? Do we know anything about the atmosphere? An older essay by H.O. Burger, for example, has shown which conclusions about Luther's personality the conversation records allow – this is the melancholic Luther;[17] but did this basic feature of his character also lower the conversation atmosphere? How was it with the cheerful, the witty, the facets; also the crude, which we have already encountered? Was it allowed to laugh at the table? Were there explicit or implicit norms – conversation maxims, conversation regulatives – of a more restrictive character or, on the contrary, something like role models of a communicative competence interpretable as 'courtly' and 'urban'; such that the table talk could be placed in a history of "communication ideals" as K.H. Göttert 1988 presented in his "Investigations into European Conversation Theory"[18]?

It should be noted in advance that the table conversations, which took place in the former Black Cloister after all, broke with a basic rule of monastic life that Luther himself had still practiced: silence at the table. Johann Mathesius, who has already been mentioned and to whom we owe the classic description of an opening conversation and the subsequent course of the conversation, recalled this fact:

> But whether our Doctor often took heavy and deep thoughts to the table with him, and sometimes kept the whole meal in his old cloister silence, so that no word fell at the table, yet he let himself be heard very pleasantly from time to time, as we used to call his speeches condimenta mensae (table spices), which we liked better than all spices and delicious food.
> When he wanted to win us over to talk, he used to make an accusation: "What's new?" We let the first admonition pass; when he stopped again, "you prelates, what's new in the country?" then the old men at the table began to speak. D. Wolf Severus, who had been preceptor to the Roman royal majesty, sat at the top, if no one else was present, as a wandering courtier.

---

[16] Verweyen 1970, p. 77.

[17] Burger 1973, p. 388: "A main topic of the table talk are the temptations (*tentationes*), i.e. inner troubles, depressions"; "The air seems to be temporarily charged with depressions as in the waiting room of a psychiatrist" (ibid., p. 400)!

[18] Munich 1988; Pittrof 1993, pp. 80–84.

When the chatter[19] went on with due decorum and respect, sometimes others also shot their part, until they approached the Doctor; often they put good questions from the scriptures, which he solved very briefly and roundly, and as one held a part, he could also endure it and refute it skillfully with a suitable answer. Often honest people came from the university, also from foreign places, to the table; there were very beautiful speeches and stories. I will mention some here shortly, perhaps they will all come together once, as it would be a very beautiful and useful work to write Noctes et dies Albiacas, or Miscellanea D. Lutheri.[20]

Once again, the versatility of Luther's table talks is also evident in the three sections of this description. The first of these, with its initial reference to the "old monastic silence", points to a religious world of origin from which the table talks both depart and, as they remain present in the thought-provoking silence of the reformer, are inspired by a "metaphor of biblical hermeneutics"[21]. For Mathesius, Luther's speeches proclaim salvation-relevant content to such an extent that here the recitative completely gives way to religious didactics, sometimes even to prophetic speech.

In contrast, the second section, with the question "What's new?", introduces a moment of *curiositas* into the game, which may have been open to secular matters, especially in the political sphere of the Reformation history, but above all calls for a basic category of novellist oral tradition like writing: the new, still unknown, like the "unheard" in the transferred sense, as something (norm-violating) entertaining, the scale of which ranges from the changeable to the scandalous to the monstrous. And with "D. Wolf Severus" finally, in the conversation circle, that type of communicatively experienced informant speaks up who, as a "sophisticated courtier", is rarely at a loss for an answer and enriches every conversation because he moves in the great interwoven contexts of a world of society rich in ideas and variety, which is more unkown to the theologian in the lecture hall and in his study than to hardly any other scholar.

The last section of Mathesius' conversation report deals with the addition of these university scholars, with two important expansions. Firstly, the fact that they know of any news, especially when it "comes from foreign places", gives rise to "beautiful speeches and stories". But stories want to be told; which is why, at Luther's table, not only was "reasonably spoken" (Goethe) and learnedly disputed, but also, presumably even lively and certainly impressively[22], told, so that "telling

---

[19] "Gedöber, n.: gesprech or gedöber [...] *a verb* döbern *gives* WEIGAND (1873 1,332) *in the meaning to talk earnestly, also in Wetterauisch* gedibber (1, 529), *borrowed from Judendeutsch* [...]*in Ostfriesland*. Gedibber, *eager chatter* [...]" DWB Bd. 4, Sp. 2030.

[20] Mathesius 1566/1883, p. 227.

[21] Lange 1966.

[22] Read only the pieces No. 6933 "History, how adultery has been punished", No. 6935 "Stories that the Lord Doctor Martin Luther told at that time, how cruel God punished adultery" and the following numbers 6936–6939—all gruesome punishment stories, which end in vain request for forgiveness, expulsion and despair, murder and manslaughter.

at table" has become the topic of research into Luther's table talk[23] and with it both the variety of small forms of oral storytelling such as fable, jest and anecdote as well as their communicative condensation into the proverbial, pointed speaking, apophthegmatic and sententious. But Mathesius has this in view too: both in the preserved content of Luther's sayings and in their variety of themes and linguistic conciseness, it is justified if, according to him, "it would be a very beautiful and useful work to write Noctes et dies Albiacias, or Miscellanea D. Lutheri". With which, by looking at the transition from the oral nature of table talk to its written form and referring to Aulus Gellius' *Attic Nights and Days* for this purpose, Mathesius at the same time names a genre model to which the "Wittenberg Nights and Days D. Lutheri" or his (so M.) "Nights and Days on the Elbe" would have had to be the Christian counterfaction, if they had not found their own form, differing from Gellius, in Aurifaber's edition of the table talk. But the table talk are not "compilation literature" in the sense that the *Attic Nights and Days* are— Gellius' material was drawn from very different source areas, while the transmission strands brought together in Aurifaber's collection, despite the certainly compilatory character of their compilation, all went back to Luther and his table society. But in this they not only had their common "source ground"[24]; from it, as the reservoir of traditionary value, they also drew that of the *memoria* Luther serving task of tradition formation, which plays hardly any role in Aulus Gellius' work, which is directed at the transmission of educational knowledge.

Despite the reinsurance or self-anchoring of the table talk edition Aurifabers as a site of tradition[25] the question of performance remains; the question of how to imagine the 'how' of the spoken word in its outcome. A complete answer would require the reading of all 7000 table talks. We must be content with a few samples on the following keywords: Luther as a conversation partner; value of the conversation; dialogical dressing; "Telling at the table"; facets and aphorisms, and begin with a quotation from Matthesius:

> (1) The man [Luther] could adjust his histories and speeches to the market and use them so skillfully that one received joy and comfort from them. (p. 229)
> (2) [On the date of the Last Day, which no one can know:] "But I believe that all the signs that are supposed to go before the Last Day have already happened." (p. 229)
> (3) Our dear prophet was in the habit of holding such speeches with his own people before and after the meal, which I cannot all relate here. (p. 231)
> (4) When great jurists and courtiers and his good and trusted friends were around him and held discussions and spoke of great potentates, courts and servants, he listened to them very reasonably as an experienced man [...] (p. 232)
> (5) As long as I have been around him, I have not heard an immodest word from his mouth. When one sometimes told stories, he could cut them off politely and subtly, as he also did with proverbs that were just as loud in German [...] (p. 234)

---

[23] Wachinger 1993.

[24] Beyer 2017, S. 391 and S. 392.

[25] Already recognizable in the Bible quotation at the end of the title page of the Aurifabers edition: "John. 6. Chapter Gather the remaining pieces / so that nothing is lost."

(6) Otherwise, wise speeches would fall from time to time. The man was full of grace and the Holy Spirit, so everyone who sought advice from him as from a prophet of God found what they wanted. (p. 235)

(7) I must also remember some table talks that took place at other times [...] (p. 236)

(8) But whether this man [L.] was good at speeches and could present his case elegantly and richly, as he proves in his books and especially in the Psalm and the Jews' writings, he nevertheless liked to hear round and short speeches [followed by an example] [...] Great people like to express their things with few and clear words and do not like to hear long and wide speeches, nor do they like to read fat letters. (236 f.)

(9) The short and beautiful speeches that were made at the table, which he often used in his books, are also worth mentioning [follow examples, including this one:] He also said once: "The Bible is a beautiful forest, in which there is no tree that I have not knocked on with my hand." (p. 237 ff.)

(10) Of the Christian holy cross he made much more beautiful and comforting speeches at the table [follow examples]. (p. 238)

(11) He also often thought of D. Staupitz's good speeches [follow examples] (p. 239), including the following: Staupitz wants to recite the birth register of Jesus Christ from Matthew 1 by heart in a sermon, but loses the thread with the 14 princes of the tribe of Judah and is then asked at the court table by the two old Electors of Saxony how it went with him in the Gospel today ?: "Gracious Prince," says Staupitz, "I had three different masters in my Gospel, the patriarchs were pious people, with whom it was necessary to get along; item, the old kings let themselves be talked about; but when I came among the princes, they were strange people, they confused me in the Gospel." (p. 240)

(12) We come back to our Doctor [L.] "On bad and sad thoughts a good and cheerful little song and friendly conversations," he often says.

(13) He also liked to say good German rhymes at the table and from the pulpit, as I wrote some of them down from his little Psalter: Do you know what, be quiet. Are you well, stay. Do you have something, hold on. Misfortune with its broad foot comes soon. Item: Eat what is done, drink what is clear, speak what is true; item: Be quiet, suffer, avoid and endure, your need no one complains; do not despair of God; your help comes every day.

(14) There were really a lot of good speeches that often showed and comforted me later, when all kinds of questions and disputes arose [follow examples]. (p. 240)

(15) Let's finish this time, God will one day wake up someone who will read this dear man's sayings, parables, proverbs, rhymes, stories and other accidents and good reports together, as it would be a very beautiful book for the Germans, if in particular our emperor, kings, princes and lords wise and reasonable sayings came along. (!)

(16) I will briefly report on his daily life and behavior to young people now; for the example and life of great and holy men gives young people good teaching and instruction. (p. 241)

(17) He also sometimes went to collation with good and foreign people, and was according to the occasion cheerful and of good sayings over the meal [follows an example]. (p. 242)

(18) A doctor from Wittenberg asks him [Luther] to sit down at the table with others. Now he brought heavy thoughts to the table, so everyone was quiet. When they were done eating, Mr. Philippus [Melanchthon], who could behave in the doctor's manner very well, wanted to make a move; the host asked if they would stay with him for another hour. In the meantime, someone else takes the bench away; but when our doctor stayed, the host wanted to sit down again and fell lengthwise on his back; that gave a good polite laugh. Dr. Luther said: "We have an unfriendly host who serves the best dish last." Then everyone became cheerful and happy and stayed in good spirits with each other for a while. (p. 242 f.)

(19) Once a messenger of a great potentate came to the Elector to Wittenberg; Dr. Luther was also invited as a guest. The messenger wanted to win him over: "My dear doctor," he

says courteously, "what do you think of the priests who offer the same and both kinds of shape on an altar?" Gracious sir, says Dr. Luther, they are boys. Not long after, Dr. Luther puts a question to the messenger again: "Gracious sir, what does your grace think of those who drive the people away or imprison them because of both shapes?" Because the legate was not interested in answering this question, he turned to a prince at the table. "Sir," he says, "your grace must be old now, we have known each other for a long time." Then the Elector says to the host: "The gentleman is a cavalryman; he can throw a horseshoe;" for according to reasonable court etiquette, not every question is to be answered; lucky is the one who can hold out with Glimpf[26] or dismiss them, the wise say. (p. 243)

(20) He also came home from a collation and brought a good drink of joy. "I must and must be happy today, because I have heard bad times; nothing serves better against that than a strong Our Father and good courage; that annoys the melancholy devil that one still wants to be happy." (p. 243)

(21) Above and after the table, D. Luther also sang from time to time, as he was also a lutenist. I have sung with him; between the singing, he brought good speeches with him [follows an example]. (p. 244)

(22) One of his table companions gave him 100 beautiful oranges at a time. (p. 244)

(23) At a time he had some from the valley as guests, who let their children be deposited [...]. (p. 244)

(24) [Luther quotes:] "A fish is nowhere better than in the water, and a thief on the gallows." (p. 246)

(25) In addition to his sufficient heart and gentle hands, he had a true and disciplined mouth; what he promised and agreed, he always kept and spoke, also spoke badly of people, as he was the enemy of those who thought badly of him in his absence [follows a related statement of L.]. (p. 246 f.)

(26) What his housekeeping was, he kept his children a private tutor, let them pray and read before meals, and often gave them arguments himself. He admonished his servants not to cause him annoyance in the house. (p. 247)

(27) Mr. Philippus provided that all Slisteners in the college stood up when D. Luther came and wanted to read; although this is an old and honorable school discipline, the humble doctor did not like it [follows the quotation of a defensive speech of L., inter alia with the rhyming verse Doxa, doxa est magna noxa]. (p. 247)

(28) He was earnestly sometimes in his sermons and let himself be heard with violent temper if one angered him [...] We must not only have gentle and mild rain and velvet breezes, but also storm winds and downpours, as our Doctor from Brenz and Philippus are used to saying, when leaves and grass, trees and stems are to be entangled and sprout. (p. 248)

(29) One is just as hard in office with other gentleness and meekness as with hot zeal and violence, as one notices in Saul and Aaron. I have heard D. Luther warn more than once that we should hold the royal road and continue according to the rule, and not easily set off across the field; special riders are needed for this. (p. 249)

---

[26] There is a comprehensive entry in DWB Bd. 8, pp. 101–109, relevant to this: "3GLIMPF, m., verbal substantive to the strong verb 1 glimpfen [...] 1. 'behavior' [...] a) primarily of human behavior, in the sense of 'behavior', at first indifferent [...] [,] with positive attributive values: [...] with fine glimpf [...]; also as much as 'custom' [...] [;] b) in objective correspondence 'honor, reputation, good reputation' [...] [;] c) with a special meaning nuance 'pretext', 'appropriate justification' " (pp. 103–106)—used in exactly this meaning here.

Luther's (implicit) conversation theory is that of a "dietetics of the soul."[27] Just as music, singing (12, 21) and playing the lute (21), have long been proven remedies against melancholy, so are "friendly conversations" (12), as well as eating and drinking (20). Despite that dark foundation of his mind, the words of the reformer provide "joy and comfort" (1), are "beautiful" and "consoling" (10), and have often "instructed and comforted" Matthesius (14). Luther is "our dear prophet" (3). Matthesius has never heard "an immodest word" (5) from him, nor has he ever spoken "evil" (25) about people—a remarkable statement in light of Luther's well-known invectives. In conversation with "great jurists and courtiers" (4), he has let himself be heard as a (in court affairs! see [29] and [19]) "experienced and reasonable man." Although he has proven in his writings that he can develop his themes "elegantly and richly," i.e. bring their wealth of aspects to light in the splendor *(ornatus)* of the figures of speech through detailed *amplificatio*[28], he nevertheless (like all great men) loves "round and short speeches" (8); such brevity[29] not only predisposes him for the concise word, but also for the pictorial-concise speech, the apt comparison (9). The preference for the "saying in use,"[30] here for use at "table and on the pulpit" (13), often in connection with a rhyming verse easy on the ear, is attested to several times (13 offers a whole nest of them, 24); the quick-witted reply also makes use of such form (27). It would therefore be a "very beautiful book" if someone were to take the trouble to once publish in a Florilegium "this dear man's sayings, parables, proverbs, rhymes, stories and other *casus* and good reports" together with "our emperor's, kings', princes' and lords' wise and reasonable sayings;" it should be added: that would be a basic book of the Germans!—Remarkably: Luther is no apocalyptist, he does not see himself at the end of time. But still, "all the signs that are supposed to go before the last day, [...] have already happened." (2).

Of casual cheerfulness, which does not have to be sought as a remedy against melancholy, Mathesius reports only once (18). The "well-mannered laughter" that rises above the physical misfortune of the host, who was not (that would be a motif of a joke) intentionally pulled away from the bank, but still did not notice that it was carried away, corresponds to Luther with a joke formed from the report of the wedding of Cana[31]: "We have an unfriendly host who serves the best dish last." He has, so to speak, served the social laughter to himself, and with the laughter at his expense "everyone is cheerful and happy"—it is obviously not always the "language" that functions as the "basis of sociability" (J. Burckhardt).

---

[27] Burger 1973, p. 401.
[28] On Luther's rhetoric, see Stolt 2000.
[29] On the *brevitas*-ideal see Kallendorf 1994.
[30] See Dicke 1994.
[31] "But when the headwaiter tasted the wine that had become water, and did not know where it came from—the servants, however, knew it, who had drawn the water -, the headwaiter called the bridegroom and said to him: Everyone serves the good wine first and, when they are drunk, the inferior one; but you have kept the good wine until now." Joh 2, 9 f.

If one compares Mathesius' accounts with those in the first volume of the "Table Talks" in the Weimar edition, much is confirmed. In contrast to the genre of the "conversation books", the formulas of conversation dressing should not be a later added ingredient that only imitates the oral character of the conversations, but rather represent the communication situation of the actually spoken word: "When someone asked what the cause was or how twins were conceived, he replied: There are two nails in one heat forge."[32] Some conversations are dated.[33] Sometimes an utterance reflects its context of origin in its referential reference: In view of his little dog, which begs for meat at the table ("When Luther's puppy happened to be at the table [...]"), Luther exclaims: "O, that I could beg like the dog can see the meat!" (No. 274) Proverbs, perhaps only ad hoc sententiously uttered, sometimes with a wavering tone and misogynistic tendency[34], are often found: "If you fall out of the ship at the front or back, you lie in the water" (No. 313); "A lie is like a snowball; the longer you roll it, the bigger it gets" (No. 340); "Equal makes good runners" (No. 304). Once the "[i]ronic invitation to the eager copyists"[35] "Hoc scribite et notate!" (No. 246) is found. The following conversation record offers practical life wisdom with current application relevance (No. 360):

> Once our mayor asked me: "Is it against God to use medicine? Because Doct. Carlstadt had preached publicly: Whoever is sick should not use any medicine, but give the matter back to God and pray that His will be done, etc. I asked him in turn: Do you also eat when you are hungry?" "Yes," he said. So I said to him: "You may well use medicine, which is just as much a creature of God as food, drink and other things we need to maintain this life."

What is hardly visible in Mathesius is Luther's strong belief in the devil. When he enters into negotiations with the Zwickau Anabaptist Markus Thomä Stübner in April 1522, he "talked with the devil in person, [...] just as when I saw him bodily in Coburg in the form of a serpent and a star" (No. 362). With regard to his temptations and spiritual sadness during his time as a monk, the words are attributed to him: "It is said, and it is true: where the head is melancholic, there the devil has a

---

[32] No. 260; other examples: "When someone asked about Moses, he said: [...]" (No. 291); "Another asked if they [i.e. deformed children] had souls? He replied: I do not know, I have not asked God about it" (No. 323); "When someone asked M. L. if the sacrament should be worshipped, he replied: [...]" (No. 344), etc.

[33] "He was sitting at the table on the same day, 28 June 1532, deep in thought. Finally he said: I am now thinking about the Turk and thinking: [...]" (No. 289).

[34] Of a woman who had lost her virginity and was married to another as a virgin, Luther said: "That's called eating the cherries and putting the basket around someone's neck!" (No. 268).

[35] Editor's note to the passage.

prepared bath" (No. 122), known remedies are "the company and conversation of godly and Christian people".[36] And even today "it is" with him

> like this: When I wake up at night, the devil comes soon and disputes with me and makes all kinds of strange thoughts to me, until I encourage myself and say: "Kiss my ass! God is not angry, as you say" (No. 141; cf. 248).

This much from Mathesius and Luther on the topics of 'Luther as a conversation partner', 'value of the conversation', 'dialogical introduction'. How does it stand with the other three keywords on our list, 'storytelling at the table', 'facet' and 'aphoristic' (apophthegmata)? Here in research there is still much in flux. The judgments on the apophthegmata of the table talk differ particularly widely. Th. Verweyen wanted to recognize in them at most examples—he actually only gives one—"of what is adjacent to the apophthegma".[37] This is also related to the fact that he generally assigned the testimonies of the 16th century to the "prehistory"[38] of the genre in Germany according to the subtitle of his book. In contrast, the latest and most important study on the topic has recently pleaded for a radical revision of the genre designation to the effect that "the [entire, TP] manuscript tradition should be referred to as 'Apophthegmata Lutheri' or the individual 'saying' found there as 'apophthegma'.[39] However, since Klitzsch himself admits that "the 'table talk' is to be understood as a genre in the sense of a multi-perspective tradition stream"[40] and we have to expect a variety of 'small forms', "anecdotes, legends, reworkings, expansions and the incorporation of foreign motives, compilations such as the creation of 'milieus'"[41] this terminological fixation of the 'table talk' as "apophthegmata Lutheri"[42] appears to be a rather violent narrowing of the tradition stream.[43]

B. Wachinger 1993 has characterized the desiderata of the 'table talk' as follows:

> The narrative material in Luther's "Table Talks" has not yet been systematically recorded. The registers of the Weimar edition only help a little bit. Luther's high esteem for the Aesopian tradition of fables is clearly visible. Legends are mentioned in a positive as well

---

[36] Not the implementation of the rhyming couplet wrongly attributed to Johann Heinrich Voß by Luther: "Who does not love women, wine and song, / He remains a fool all his life"; "In fact, this anacreontic saying […] cannot be traced back to the historical Luther at all" (Mecklenburg 2016, p. 78; Burger 1973, p. 386).

[37] Verweyen 1970, p. 117.

[38] The title of the subchapter, ibid., p. 108–119.

[39] Klitzsch 2020, p. 70.

[40] Ibid., p. 557.

[41] Ibid., p. 59.

[42] Ibid., p. 559.

[43] "This name is unlikely to prevail", Stolt 2014, p. 142, suspects with reference to a similar proposal by Barbara Müller (Müller 2013, p. 76).

as in a negative light. Also, the farces that occur in the Table Talks need to be collected and examined; I only mention one variant of the "Monk as Love Messenger", which Luther tells with reference to a book "The Florentine Women" (Boccaccio?) [...] Only for the devil stories there is a modern, complete register [...] In addition to these tendentially closed narrative forms, of course, current news was of high importance for the conversations, and occasionally Luther may have also come to autobiographical narration. [...][44]

How it [...] came to telling or quoting stories can not always be seen from the fragmentary records. Sometimes Luther may have started a topic himself with his previous activity, perhaps even with the intention of teaching. "On another occasion, Doctor brought with him the Saxon Renckfuchs [...] he praises him for a really good poem and a living contrafacture of court life", Matthesius reports [...]; with such a demonstration, Luther must have read or re-told without doubt. In other cases, one could probably be content with just alluding to the familiar. So in the following report of Matthesius two episodes of the Aeneid by Vergil, the historical news of the death of Antonius and three biblical episodes are present, without the need to tell them [...]

Sometimes an external occasion gives the impetus to tell. When a boy brought a sparrow to the table, [Luther told] [...] the anecdote of how a Dominican and a Franciscan quarreled with each other in the image of a swallow and a sparrow. And this in turn prompted D. Severus to tell another anti-monastic anecdote (No. 5098). The conspicuous introduction of Luther, reproduced by Aurifaber with the words "I wish that one of these fables would once declaim", is certainly to be understood as a modesty formula of the narrator, who crudely brings what would probably be worth a more artful representation.

The integration of a Schwankerzählung in the report of Luther's reaction to two bad news in June 1540 (No. 5096) is particularly enlightening. [...] Overall, Luther's reaction to the devastating news is not only typical of him in its mixture of theology, educational science and Grobianism, but above all in its cheerful confidence in faith, which is particularly strengthened when only God can help. [...][45]

G. Dicke has determined the presence of the facet in Luther's table talks to be fundamental. His central reference text are the WA-numbers 2965a and b:

Diligendus est, qui sua humana facetia laetificare potest melancholicos; in qua arte excellit Christoff Groß, homo admodum facetus.
Quamvis christianus sermone cautus esse debet, ne quem offendat, attamen recreationis gratia inter amicos festivus sermo conceditur. Lepidus, facetus, festivus sunt eadem, et est virtus. Dicax, qui est inmodicus in facetiis, qui aspergit nigrum salem, machet es bisweilen tölpisch; scurra, qui dicit aut facit obscoena, illepida, iniusta. Ideo Christophorus de Gross homo facetus, cuius conversatio placida fuit inter amicos; er kann allerley melancholicos frolich machen urbanitate facetissima. Est enim eloquens, facetus et expertus. Hat den bapst drey jar getragen, fuit Hierosolymis, linguas omnes mutare potuit. Der spricht, er hette alle stende versucht, alleine er möchte gern wissen, wie eynem witwer tzu mut were, quia habebat vetulam.

Finally, the moment of recreation, which has been so neglected up to this point, is given attention in the quotation of this utterance—conversations are also held in order to relax! In Christoph Gross/Groß, that "dietetics of the soul" (Burger)

---

[44] Wachinger 1993, pp. 279–280.
[45] Ibid., pp. 280–286.

already mentioned turns out to be a—pre-modern—"physiology of laughter"[46]: Experienced in the world and linguistically skilled, Groß "excels" in the art of pleasing every conversation society with the well-crafted joke and thus making "each melancholic happy"; the fazete *dictum* handed down here, however, goes back at the expense of—his—wife. We conclude this section with Dicke's excellent analysis:

> Christoph Gross, who is introduced in the table talks on various occasions as *homo prudentissimus et facundus* and quoted with various bon mots, was a Wittenberg magistrate who had studied in Bologna and, so to speak, had attended the High School of Fazeten as a Vatican servant. That Luther measures him as *homo facetus* at the humanist ideal, the quoted table talks show just as clearly as the clear concept that the reformer also testifies elsewhere of the task and value of 'fazetieren'. Paraphrasingly summarized, it is up to Luther as *ars* and *virtus* to be able to drive melancholy away with human wit, just as the incomparable Christoph Gross. But whoever *in facetiis* makes others sick, misses the right measure and mixes bitter mockery or obscenity into the *conversatio placida*, is a fool. Gross, on the other hand, is entertaining, knowledgeable, well-traveled, eloquent and polyglott—a cosmopolitan. And now Luther lets a sample of Gross's fazetie follow as a quotation and in German: He, who is experienced in all walks of life, would still like to try the widower's, because he is married to an old woman! At the beginning, Luther had still emphasized that the Christian should not cause any offense to anyone in the cheerful conversation among friends. Shortly thereafter, he let the exemplary fazetie Gross make a rather black-humored joke at the expense of his own wife [...], which does not care about the Christian commandment (... *ne quem offendat*) as little as about the admonished renunciation of the *sal niger*. For a punch line or the equivalent of general amusement, Gross thus 'sacrifices' his own wife and lets himself—of course playfully—be held responsible for wishing her death or at least deriving something positive from it. [...]—This is one of the rare examples in German for the fazetie *in situ*, in the conversational, even if its performance conditions are not further documented, and probably also an indication for its there hidden function. Because only in conversation does its agonistic moment come to the fore, also its suitability for teasing, for the initially playful settlement of played or actual rivalries or animosities, and therefore the conversation comment introduced by Luther demands not to strike over the socio-ethical strands. [...] Just as with Boccaccio and Pontanus, the moral index finger is first raised and emphasized that the 'fazetieren' have limits of decency that oblige them to self-censorship, but here too practice shows that their violation is even more fun. The joke takes the freedom to ignore the communication rules imposed on it, and Luther also takes this freedom.[47]

"In cultural memory, hardly any work by Martin Luther is as well known as the Table Talks," assure the editors of a collection that appeared a few years ago.[48] But how secure is this finding really? The—not raised here—print runs of their modern selection editions should provide the proof, because if you look at the evidence for the non-literary reception of the 'Table Talks' recorded by N. Mecklenburg,

---

[46] See Schmitz 1972, from part C: "Moral and immoral laughter—The Ars iocandi and the theologians' dialectic" pp. 184 ff. with repeated reference to Luther.
[47] Dicke 2005, p. 180 f.
[48] Bärenfänger et al. 2013, p. 1.

their number is quite low[49] and hardly allows any conclusions to be drawn about something like a continuity of the non-literary 'Table Talks' reception. "When Goethe learned of Luther's Table Talks in 1805, he was repelled by his tendency to constant damnation, and later added a critical excursus on Martin Luther to his *History of Color Theory* [...]"[50] Of Zacharias Werner's drama *The Consecration of Power*, Jean Paul wrote that Luther would have "thrown his genuine volume of Table Talks at the dramatist's head"[51] Joseph Popper-Lynkeus published a small humorous story *A Table Talk with Martin Luther* in 1899 between the reformer, Melanchthon and a rabbi[52], 1916 Gerhart Hauptmann read in the Table Talks,[53] 1981 Stefan Heym lets Luther "present a just as naive teleological as authentic (WA TR 3, 302) Table Talk creation praise" in his *Ahasver* novel.[54] But otherwise?

Of course, one thinks of Thomas Mann. Personally, he "would not have liked to be Luther's table guest," he wrote in 1945 in his essay *Germany and the Germans*, "I would probably have felt at home with him like in the cozy home of an ogre and I am convinced that I would have got along much better with Leo X., Giovanni de' Medici, the friendly humanist whom Luther called 'the devil's sow, the pope.'"[55] But two of his novel's characters remember her, namely Lotte in Weimar during the "patriarchal monologuing of the presiding head of the household"[56] and, in *Doctor Faustus*, Serenus Zeitblom, who notices of Kumpf's "versatile expectorations" that the latter thereby "unmistakably imitated Luther's table talk"[57] This would lead to the conclusion that Thomas Mann had also drawn from a table talk source while working on the novel. But the GKFA commentary on the passage says otherwise: "In spite of the popular opinion, Luther's table talk in particular did not have a direct impact on *Doctor Faustus*. The Luther German of

---

[49] Aland 1973 is not mentioned at all.

[50] Mecklenburg 2016, p. 85, with quotation of the Goethe passage.

[51] Ibid., p. 95, see also p. 88.

[52] Ibid., p. 168.

[53] Ibid., p. 153.

[54] Ibid., p. 272.

[55] Hamacher 1996, pp. 58 ff.; see also p. 75 ff. Thomas Mann on Luther, quoted in GW XI, p. 1132 ff. also by Aland 1973, p. 344. As the reason for Thomas Mann's aversion to the Luther of the 'table talks', Hamacher (p. 83) cites the latter's increasing affinity for Erasmus, his "self-stylization as a modern Erasmus" (ibid., p. 87).

[56] "An old word association and dark memory came to her mind and persisted in her. 'Luther's table talks', she thought, and defended the impression against all physiognomic inconsistencies." GKFA Vol. 9.1, p. 403; quoted in Hamacher 1996, p. 49. The term "table talk" for his table talks comes from F. W. Riemers' *Mitteilungen über Goethe* – the editor of the commentary volume to *Lotte in Weimar* does not rule out that "Carlotte Kestner might have remembered them" during her visit (GKFA Vol. 9.2, p. 114).

[57] Hamacher 1996, p. 64; GKFA Vol. 10.1, p. 145 line 19.

the novel is mostly derived from Luther's letters."[58] – But then does the uncanny "Weistu was so schweig", which is repeatedly quoted in the devil's conversation in the Palestrina chapter[59], not betray traces of Thomas Mann's table talk reading? For we have already encountered this admonition in the quotation by Mathesius (above under no. 13), and in vol. 6 of the Weimar edition it can be found under number 7048. But the GKFA commentary refers to another source for this as well, namely chapter 65 of the Volksbuch vom *D. Faustus*.[60] The author of this in turn drew on his knowledge from Mathesius, as Thomas Mann was able to ascertain from the modern commentary of the edition of the Volksbuch he used;[61] which finally raises a certain problem that may concern the reception of the Tischreden as a whole: it lies in the discrepancy between their claimed popularity as a whole (which in any case, with the exception of special cases such as the Catholic Luther biography or the anti-Protestant polemical literature[62] could be claimed for the Protestant readership) and their concretely demonstrable knowledge in individual cases.

References

Aland, Kurt: Martin Luther in der modernen Literatur. Ein kritischer Dokumentarbericht. Witten [u. a.]: Eckart 1973.

Aurifaber, Johann: Tischreden Oder Colloqvia Doct. Mart. Luthers: So er in vielen Jaren, gegen gelarten Leuten, auch frembden Gesten, und seinen Tischgenossen gefüret, nach den Heubtstücken unserer Christlichen Lere, zusammen getragen. Faks. der Orig.-Ausg. Eisleben 1566 [VD 16 L 6748] Leipzig: Edition Leipzig 1981.

Bärenfänger, Katharina, Volker Leppin und Stefan Michel: Martin Luthers Tischreden. Neuansätze der Forschung. Tübingen: Mohr Siebeck 2013.

Bartmuss, Alexander: Tischreden, in: Volker Leppin und Gury Schneider-Ludorff (Hg.): Das Luther-Lexikon. 2. unver. Aufl. Regensburg: Bückle & Böhm 2015, S. 688–696.

Beyer, Michael: Tischreden, in: Albrecht Beutel (Hg.): Luther Handbuch. 3., neu bearbeitete und erweiterte Auflage Tübingen: Mohr Siebeck 2017, S. 391–398.

Borcherdt, Hans Henrich und Walther Rehm (Hg.): Martin Luther: Tischreden. München: Georg Müller 1925. (= Martin Luther: Ausgewählte Werke. Unter Mitwirkung von Hermann Barge, Georg Buchwald, Paul Joachimsen, Paul Kalkoff, Gustav Roethe, Friedrich Wilhelm Schmidt, Wolfgang Stammler, Henry Thode (†) hg. von Hans Heinrich Borcherdt. Achter [= letzter] Band.)

---

[58] GKFA Vol. 10.2 [Commentary on *Doctor Faustus*], p. 354; on "Weib Wein und Gesang" ibid., p. 355.

[59] GKFA Vol. 10.1, pp. 324, 325 and 333.

[60] GFKA Bd. 10.2, p. 533 ff.

[61] Ibid.

[62] Thus, the Jesuit theologian and later Cardinal Bellarmin, in his *Disputationes de controversiis christianae fidei adversus nostri temporis haereticos* (3 vols., Ingolstadt 1586, 1588, 1593), repeatedly refers to Luther's sayings at table in his discussion of the canon of Scripture [...] with regard to Job [...], Ecclesiastes [...] and the Gospel of John. Walter 2016, p. 45.

Buchwald, Reinhard (Hg.): Luther im Gespräch. Aufzeichnungen seiner Freunde und Tischgenossen. Nach den Urtexten der „Tischreden" zum erstenmal übertragen von R. B. Stuttgart: Alfred Kröner [1938].

Burger, Heinz Otto: Luther im Spiegel seiner Tischreden, in: Germanisch-Romanische Monatsschrift N.F. 23, 1973, S. 385–403.

Dicke, Gerd: „Mich wundert, das ich so frölich pin". Ein Spruch im Gebrauch, in: Walter Haug (Hg.): Kleinstformen der Literatur. Tübingen: Niemeyer 1994, S. 56–90.

Dicke, Gerd: Fazetieren. Ein Konversationstyp der italienischen Renaissance und seine deutsche Rezeption im 15. und 16. Jahrhundert. In: Eckart Conrad Lutz, Johanna Thali und René Wetzel (Hg.): Literatur und Wandmalerei II. Konventionalität und Konversation. Tübingen: Niemeyer 2005, S. 155–188.

Glaser, Margrit: Zur Editionsphilologie, in: Bärenfänger et al. 2013, S. 249–258.

Göttert, Karl-Heinz: Kommunikationsideale. Untersuchungen zur europäischen Konversationstheorie. München: Iudicium 1988.

Hamacher, Bernd: Thomas Manns letzter Werkplan „Luthers Hochzeit": Edition, Vorgeschichte und Kontexte. Frankfurt a. M.: Klostermann 1996.

Henkys, Jürgen (Hg.): Luthers Tischreden. Hamburg: Hansisches Druck- und Verlagshaus Edition Chrismon ²2003.

Junghans, Helmar: Die Tischreden Martin Luthers, in: D. Martin Luthers Werke. Sonderedition der kritischen Weimarer Ausgabe. Begleitheft zu den Tischreden. Weimar: Hermann Böhlau Nachfolger 2000, S. 25–50. Durchges. Wiederabdruck in Ders.: Spätmittelalter, Luthers Reformation, Kirche in Sachsen. Ausgewählte Aufsätze, hg. von Micchael Beyer u. Günther Wartenberg. Leipzig: Evangelische Verlagsanstalt 2001, S. 154–176.

Kallendorf, Craig: [Art.] Brevitas, in: Gert Ueding (Hg.): Historisches Wörterbuch der Rhetorik. Bd. 2. Tübingen: Niemeyer 1994, Sp. 53–60.

Klitzsch, Ingo: Redaktion und Memoria. Die Lutherbilder der „Tischreden". Tübingen: Mohr Siebeck 2020.

Köpf, Ulrich: Kurze Geschichte der Weimarer Luther-Ausgabe, in: D. Martin Luthers Werke. Sonderedition der kritischen Weimarer Ausgabe. Begleitheft zu den Tischreden. Weimar: Hermann Böhlau Nachfolger 2000, S. 1–24.

Lange, Klaus: Geistliche Speise. Untersuchungen zur Metaphorik der Bibelhermeneutik, in: Zeitschrift für deutsches Altertum und deutsche Literatur 95, 1966, S. 81–122.

Luther, Martin: Tischreden. Unveränderter Nachdruck in 6 Bänden (Sonderedition) der Kritischen Gesamtausgabe (Weimarer Ausgabe). Weimar: Verlag Hermann Böhlaus Nachfolger 2000.

Mann, Thomas: Doktor Faustus. Das Leben des deutschen Tonsetzers Adrian Leverkühn, erzählt von einem Freunde. Hg. und textkritisch durchgesehen von Ruprecht Wimmer unter Mitarbeit von Stephan Stachorski. Große kommentierte Frankfurter Ausgabe [GKFA] Bd. 10.1 [Text] und 10.2. [Kommentar]. Frankfurt a. M.: S. Fischer 2007.

Mann, Thomas: Lotte in Weimar. Hg. und textkritisch durchgesehen von Werner Frizen. GKFA Bd. 9.1 [Text] und 9.2 [Kommentar]. Frankfurt a. M.: S. Fischer 2003.

Mathesius, Johann: Dr. Martin Luthers Leben. In siebenzhen Predigten dargestellt. Mit einem Vorworte von D. Büchsel. Nachdruck der Ausgabe Berlin 1883. Markkleeberg: Johannes-Mathesius-Verlag 2017.

Mecklenburg, Norbert: Der Prophet der Deutschen. Martin Luther im Spiegel der Literatur. Stuttgart: Metzler 2016.

Mecklenburg, Norbert: Sakramente und Exkremente. Martin Luthers Abtrittsreden, in: Walter Hömberg (Hg.): Marginalistik. Almanach für Freunde fröhlicher Wissenschaft. München: Allitera Verlag 2019, S. 135–148.

Müller, Barbara: Die Tradition der Tischgespräche von der Antike bis in die Renaissance, in: Bärenfänger, Katharina, Volker Leppin und Stefan Michel: Martin Luthers Tischreden. Neuansätze der Forschung. Tübingen: Mohr Siebeck 2013, S. 63–78.

Mulert, Hermann (Hg.): Luther lebt! Seine Tischgespräche ausgewählt für unsere Zeit. Berlin: Propyläen Verlag 1935.
Pittrof, Thomas: Umgangsliteratur in neuerer Sicht: Zum Aufriß eines Forschungsfeldes, in: Internationales Archiv für Sozialgeschichte der deutschen Literatur. 3. Sonderheft: Forschungsreferate, 2. Folge. Tübingen: Niemeyer 1993, S. 63–112.
Reimers, Bettina: [Art.] Buchwald, Ernst Reinhard, in: Christoph König (Hg.): Internationales Germanistenlexikon 1800–1950. Bd. 1, Berlin / New York: de Gruyter 2003, S. 287–289.
Schmitz, Heinz-Günter: Physiologie des Scherzes. Bedeutung und Rechtfertigung der Ars Iocandi im 16. Jahrhundert. Hildesheim / New York: Georg Olms Verlag 1972.
Sparn, Walter (Hg.:) Martin Luther: Lektüre für Augenblicke. Gedanken aus seinen Schriften, Briefen und Tischreden. Frankfurt a. M.: Insel Verlag 1983.
Stolt, Birgit: Die Sprachmischung in Luthers Tischreden. Studien zum Problem der Zweisprachigkeit. Stockhom [u. a.]: Almqvist & Wiksell 1964.
Stolt, Birgit: Martin Luthers Rhetorik des Herzens. Tübingen: Mohr Siebeck 2000.
Stolt, Birgit: Luthers beliebte Tischreden und Probleme ihrer Neuausgabe, in: Theologische Literaturzeitung 139, 2014, S. 136–145.
Treu, Martin: Luther zwischen Kunst und Krempel. Wie populär war und ist ein populäres Lutherbild?, in: Martin Luther: Monument, Ketzer, Mensch. Lutherbilder, Lutherprojektionen und ein ökumenischer Luther. Hg. von Andreas Holzem und Volker Leppin unter Mitwirkung von Claus Arnold und Norbert Haag. Freiburg [u. a.]: Herder [2016], S. 407–448.
Verweyen, Theodor: Apophthegma und Scherzrede. Die Geschichte einer einfachen Gattungsform und ihrer Entfaltung im 17. Jahrhundert. Bad Homburg v.d.H. / Berlin / Zürich: Verlag Gehlen 1970.
Volz, Hans: [Art.] Tischreden oder Colloquia Doct. Mart. Luthers […], in: Walter Jens (Hg.): Kindlers Neues Literatur Lexikon (Studienausgabe), Bd. 10, München: Kindler 1996, S. 721–724.
Volz, Hans und Gottfried Orth: [Art.] Tischreden oder Colloquia Doct. Mart. Luthers […], in: Heinz Ludwig Arnold (Hg.): Kindlers Literatur-Lexikon. 3., völlig neu bearb. Aufl. Bd. 10, Stuttgart; Weimar: Metzler 2009, S. 391 f.
Wachinger, Burghart: Convivium fabulosum. Erzählen bei Tisch im 15. und 16. Jahrhundert, besonders in der ‚Mensa philosophica' und bei Erasmus und Luther, in: Walter Haug und Burghart Wachinger (Hg.): Kleinere Erzählformen des 15. und 16. Jahrhunderts. Tübingen: Niemeyer 1993, S. 256–286.
Walter, Peter: Der Ketzer Luther. Robert Bellamin und die Kontroversliteratur, in: Martin Luther: Monument, Ketzer, Mensch. Lutherbilder, Lutherprojektionen und ein ökumenischer Luther. Hg. von Andreas Holzem und Volker Leppin unter Mitwirkung von Claus Arnold und Norbert Haag. Freiburg [u. a.]: Herder [2016], S. 37–62.
Wilhelm, Thomas: Vorüberlegungen zu einer möglichen Edition von Luthers Tischreden, in: Bärenfänger, Katharina, Volker Leppin und Stefan Michel: Martin Luthers Tischreden. Neuansätze der Forschung. Tübingen: Mohr Siebeck 2013, S. 241–247.
Zschoch, Helmut: Lebenslauf, in: Albrecht Beutel (Hg.): Luther Handbuch. 3., neu bearbeitete und erweiterte Auflage Tübingen: Mohr Siebeck 2017, S. 106–115.

Texts

Conversation Between Knowledge Transmission and Enjoyment: Georg Philipp Harsdörffer's Conversation Games *Gesprächspiele*

Rosmarie Zeller

Abstract

This article once again presents the role Georg Philipp Harsdörffer played in the transmission of the conversation culture of Romania, but especially Italy. In his eight-volume work *Women's Room Conversation Games* he practically shows the art of conversation, but also lets his characters discuss the conditions for a successful conversation. Use and entertainment are cornerstones between which topics should move that are to be adapted to society. Following the example of Italian conversation games, Harsdörffer also introduced women as conversation partners. A short analysis of the addressees shows that the work was mainly received in aristocratic circles.

Keywords

Georg Philipp Harsdörffer · Use and entertainment · Knowledge transfer · Addressees · Women · Game

In a book on conversation, the great mediator of Italian and to a lesser extent French conversation culture to Germany, the Nuremberg patrician Georg Philipp Harsdörffer (1607–1658), must not be missing. Harsdörffer's *Frauenzimmer Gesprächspiele* or *Gesprächspiele* as they are called from the third volume

R. Zeller (✉)
Universität Basel, Basel, Switzerland
e-mail: rosmarie.zeller@unibas.ch

onwards, were published in 8 volumes between 1641 and 1649.[1] They deal with the tension between *prodesse* and *delectare* or between utility and pleasure at numerous points, as Harsdörffer says.

In the introduction to the first volume, Harsdörffer explains that he wrote this work in order to give a guide on "wie bey Ehr- und Tugendliebenden Gesellschaften freund- und fruchtbarliche Gespreche aufzubringen / und nach Beschaffenheit aus eines jeden Sinnreichen Vermögen fortzusetzen" (how to bring up and continue fruitful and pleasant conversations in honorable and virtuous companies according to each one's ingenious ability) (FZG 1, 17). If the adjective "freundlich" refers to the social interaction, then "fruchbarlich" refers to the knowledge that is to be imparted in the conversations and to the effect that the conversations are to have, namely to promote virtue. It is not just advertising when Harsdörffer emphasizes the novelty of his enterprise. This also makes his work interesting because he can and must deal with many things that are already introduced in the Romance cultures and therefore self-evident. Thus, in the first conversation game, the old man Vespasian recalls that in his youth he passed his time with conversation games in France and Italy. These consisted "in kurtzweiligen als nützlichen Gesprechen in Fragen und Antworten." (in amusing and useful conversations in questions and answers.) (FZG I, 25) The *Gesprächspiele* move between utility and amusement. Already in the second volume, an emblem with the motto "Es nutzet und behagt" (It is useful and pleasing) is printed at the beginning of the volume. In addition to a garden and a sundial, the play staff, which is surrounded by so-called English or Italian beans, shimmering in many colors, which Harsdörffer received when he was admitted to the Fruchtbringende Gesellschaft together with the motto "auff manche Art", can also be seen on the emblem. All elements of this emblem are interpreted in relation to the motto: the flowers are useful as medicine and please the senses and mind. Angelica sums up: "Es nutzet alles den Verstand / und behagt den Augen; massen in dem Nutzen die Belustigung / und / wie in allen Tugendwercken in der Belustigung den Nutzen enthalten." (Everything is useful to the mind and pleases the eyes; as much as in the use the recreation and as in all virtuous works in the recreation the utility is contained.) (FZG II, 21) At the same time, Harsdörffer's personal emblem refers to the diversity and variety that is characteristic of this type of entertainment.

---

[1] There is a second edition (1644 and 1647) of the first two volumes, which appeared in octavo format in 1641 and 1642) in the same oblong octavo format as the volumes from volume 3. In the first part of the first edition there were only four people who carried on the conversation. I quote the *Frauenzimmer Gesprächspiele* below with the abbreviation FZG and the page number of the reprint (Harsdörffer 1968–1968). In recent years, Harsdörffer research has focused primarily on Harsdörffer's narrative work. The conversation games are noticed as an encyclopedia but not in their own right as a conversation.

1 Harsdörffer's Role Models

Harsdörffer's model for the *Gesprächspiele* are the conversations as they were conducted in the Italian academies, which he probably learned about on his grand tour of Italy.[2] He addresses this reference multiple times in the *Gesprächspiele* (FZG III, 121, 142 f.), explicitly in the preface to the fifth part, where he adopts the statutes of the Academia degli Intronati and adapts them to the German situation (FZG V, 97 f.). In the academies, the focus was not on conveying specific knowledge as in universities, but on acquiring as diverse a range of knowledge as possible in many areas, including those that were not taught at universities such as heraldry, palmistry, physiognomy, emblematics, animal characteristics, and similar topics. In the preface to the fifth part, he calls the *Gesprächspiele* a "new teaching method," "vermittelst welcher alles leichtvernemlich / kunstmercklich und spielartig vorgestellet wird" (through which everything is easily heard artfully and playfully represented.) (FZG V, 100 f.) Since these conversations take place in the vernacular, they are also associated with a certain expansion of the vocabulary in the vernacular. In their "advertisement," the Fruchtbringende Gesellschaft writes that "der Verfasser dieser Gespräch-Spiele sich umb unsere vielgeltende reine Teutsche Landes-Sprache nicht wenig verdient gemacht." (the author of these conversation games has earned our great esteem for our many-faceted pure German national language.) (FZG II, 14).

In 16th century Italy, a real discourse developed around this type of entertainment, which was both a conversation and a form of knowledge transfer. "Knowledge begins in conversation and ends in conversation," writes Stefano Guazzo in his 1574 work *Civil conversazione*,[3] and he is convinced that science can only develop if the educated person can assure himself of his knowledge in conversation, in dealing with other educated people, if he can conversate and discuss with them and thus test his knowledge.[4] Guazzo emphasizes that conversation is more useful than reading books alone, because one learns better through the ears than through the eyes, because the living voice is better imprinted in the memory. The loneliness, when reading books, makes one melancholic and arrogant. Moreover, one can never ask a book if it is incomprehensible, so that one leaves it dissatisfied. The company of the living is much more useful than that of the dead.[5] Similar things can be read in Harsdörffer:

---

[2] On Italian academies in general: Quondam 1982. The Fruchtbringende Gesellschaft itself is modeled after the Academia della Crusca.

[3] """'l sapere comincia dal conversare e finisce nel conversare." (Guazzo 1993, 30)("It is plain then that learning is both begun and perfected by conversation.* (Guazzo 1738, p.25)) Guazzo's book was also translated into German (Guazzo 1626) and in English (The art of conversation in three parts. London 1738. On Guazzo in Germany, but not from the perspective of knowledge, see Bonfatti 1979.

[4] "non può il letterato assicurarsi del suo sapere, infin che non viene ad accozzarsi con altri letterati, con i quali discorrendo, e disputando, si certifica del suo valore;" (Guazzo 1993, p. 30). "so neither can the Man of letters be thoroughly satisfied, that his Learning is of the right Stamp, till by reasoning and discoursing with others, he has tried it sufficiently." (Guazzo 1738, p. 25)

[5] "E voglio dirvi di più, che sarebbe errore il credere, che la dottrina s'acquisti più nella solitudine fra i libri, che nella conversazione fra gli uomini dotti, perciocché la prova ci dimostra, che meglio s'apprende la dottrina per le orecchie, che per gli occhi [...] e riceer per l'orecchie quella viva voce, laquale con mirabil forza s'imprime nella mente. Oltre

"dann gewiß das Lesen ein Vnterricht / so von den verstorbenen / als getreuen Lehrmeistern / herrühret: Das Gespräch aber die beste Schul / in welcher wir bey den Lebendigen das erlernte üben / und zu Werk bringen können [...]." (Then certainly reading is a lesson that comes from deceased as well as from faithful teachers: But conversation is the best school in which we can practice what we have learned from the living and put it into practice [...]) (FZG I, 85). Elsewhere, Harsdörffer takes the argument in favor of the living conversation and brings it back with an *argumentum ad antiquitatem* to the Hebrews and Greeks:

> Die Art in den Gesprächen zu unterweisen / ist von Anfang der Wissenschaften / zu Zeit der Hebreer und Griechen bekant gewesen / und deswegen füglicher als keine andere / weil man allerhand Aufgaben / nicht nur mit ja / und nein / sondern auf so vielerley Weise / als der Gesellschafter / oder Gesprächgenossen sind / beantworten kan: Zu geschweigen des Nachdrukks der lebendigen Stimme / der anmuhtigen Geberden / der vielmögenden Bewegungen der Lippen / der holden Mitwürkung der Augen / vnd beschäfftigen Händen [...]. (The way of teaching in conversation has been known from the beginning of knowledge, in the time of the Hebrews and Greeks, and therefore more suitable than any other, because one can answer all kinds of tasks not only with yes and no, but in as many ways as the companion or conversation partner is: not to mention the emphasis of the living voice, the amiable gestures, the powerful movements of the lips, the lovely cooperation of the eyes and the busy hands [...].)(FZG VI, 104)

The variation of answers is an argument that recurs again and again in favor of social conversation, to which facial expression and gestures also belong. It is also seen as a deficiency of *Gesprächspiele* that the "holdseligen Geberden" cannot be reproduced in print (FZG II, 43), which the title cupper try to compensate.

From the beginning, this type of entertainment has been associated with the concept of the game, as the titles of Italian treatises show.[6] 1551 Innocenzio Ringhieri from Bologna published *Cento giuochi liberali et d'ingegno,* which he dedicated to Catherine de Medici. The expression "ingegno", which can be translated as "wit", indicates that these games are intended for the mind and not for the body.[7] Fifty of the games were 1555 published in French, with the title *Jeus divers d'honnete*

---

che abbattendovi nel leggere in qualche oscura difficoltà, non potete pregare il libro che ve la dichiari, e vi conviene tal' ora partirvi da lui malcontento [...]. Dal che potete riconoscere quanto più util cosa sia il parlar coi vivi, che coi morti. (Guazzo 1993, p. 30) "And therefore I will aver it is a gross Error to suppose, that learning is better atteined by a solitary Acquaintance with Books than in the Company of learned and ingenious Men. For it is an undoubted Maxim in Philosophy and Experience confirm it, that Learning is more easily acquired by the Ears than by the Eyes. [...] Since the Hearing of the natural Voice leaves a deeper Impression on the Mind than the closest Reading can possibly do. But farther, if you happen to light on some difficult and obscure Passage in your reading, you cannot perswade the Book to expound it to you, but you must of Neccessity leave it just as you find it; and therefore it is much more instructive to talk with the Living than with the Dead." (GUazzo 1738, p. 26).).

[6] See Zeller 2010 for this.

[7] This distinction between conversation games and physical games is also repeatedly discussed by Harsdörffer. It is about a cultural program that is supposed to replace the usual games of nobility such as ball games, riding, etc. with mental games.

entretien establishing a clearer connection to conversation than the Italian.[8] 1572 *Il Dialogo de' giuochi che nelle vegghie senesi si usano di fare* by Girolamo Bargagli appears,[9] which is dedicated to the cultivated Isabella de Medici Orsiana, Duchessa da Braciano. Girolamo's brother Scipione Bargagli published 1587 *I Trattenimenti dove da vaghe Donne e da giovani Huomini rapresentati sono honesti e dilettevoli Giuochi, narrate Novelle, e cantate alcune amorose Canzonette.* This title suggests an interesting variant of this type of entertainment, namely that it can also include story-telling, and even singing. Stories will also play an important role for Harsdörffer, even so much so that he published whole volumes of such short stories, which can be seen as an addition to the conversation games, serving the conversation with the moral questions they raise.[10] It is also noteworthy that these italian conversation-books are dedicated to noblewomen or mention women in their title. Harsdörffer also justifies the introduction of women with reference to the Italian authors: "Das Frauenzimmer ist bey diesen Gesprächspielen eingeführet / zu Folg / der offt angezogenen Italiänischen Scribenten / welcher Erfindungen sonderlich dahin zielen / wie in dergleichen Zusammenkunfften die Zeit mit nützlicher Kurtzweil zugebracht werden möge." (The ladies are introduced in these conversation games for the following reason often referred to by Italian writers, whose inventions are particularly aimed how time can be spent usefully in such gatherings.) (FZG III, 15)[11] We will came back to this aspect.

The not self-evident, extensive equating of conversation and game, as shown in these titles, still needs explanation. Charles Sorel, who imitates the Italian games with his *Maison des Jeux,* equates the Platonic dialogues with games:

> On peut soustenir que tous les Ouurages de Platon ne sont proprement que des Ieux; Car d'introduire des personnes diuerses que l'on fait parler de plusieurs choses selon leur fantaisie, à dessein de rapporter differentes opinions des hommes, c'est vne espece de Ieu. (It can be argued that all of Plato's works are nothing but games; For to introduce different

---

[8] Charles Sorel mentions Ringhieri as a predecessor in his *Maison des Jeux* (1642). See F. Lecercle 1982, p. 195 ff.

[9] Bargagli 1982. There were further editions in 1574, 1575, 1581, 1591, 1592, 1598, 1609.

[10] See, for example, FZG II, 117: "Dieses Spiel ist im Ende nichts anders / als eine Erzehlung einer Mähr / mit welcher Art Gesprächen sich die Spanier / Italianer und Frantzosen so sehr belustigen." (This game is in the end nothing other than a story-telling with which the Spaniards Italians and French enjoy themselves so much.) For "Mähr" on the margin: "il novellare." See Zeller 2006, p. 193.

[11] He refers in the margin to Scipione Bargagli's *Delle lodi delle Accademie* (1569). Elsewhere, Reymund points out that "the Senesians of nobility" had come together to practice the conversation games, which they had set up so that "they might be suitable for women." (FZG III, 152) In Part VIII, Degenwert says: "Den Anfang der Gesprächspiele und derselben Erfindungen / haben wir dem Italienischen Frauenvolk zu danken / denen sie zu Ehren ersonnen worden [...]." (We owe the beginning of the conversation games and their inventions to the Italian women's people to whom they were invented [...].) (FZG VIII, 117). For Harsdörffer and the Italian academies, see also Battafarano 1994.

people who speak of different things according to their fancy, in order to report different opinions of men, is a kind of game).[12]

As with Harsdörffer, we also have here the idea of the different people who represent different opinions. It is interesting that Sorel uses the expression "rapporter differentes opinions", which indicates that one does not have to represent one's own opinion, but can report what one has read or heard. Reading books plays an important role in connection with the conversation. With regard to the equation of play and conversation, Sorel probably took this statement from Sperone Speroni, who in his *Apologia dei dialoghi* equates dialogues with games.[13] Traces of this discourse can also be found in Harsdörffer when he lets Vespasian say:

> Auf so angeneme Arten haben die Alten anderen die Weißheit eingegossen / und vieleicht daher die Schulen Ludos geheissen. Wie auch auß Platonis Gastung zu sehen / daß die verständigsten Gedancken / und tieffsinnigsten Lehren / unter einem freundlichen Gespräch eingeführet werden. (In such pleasant ways have the ancients poured wisdom into others and perhaps for this reason they called the schools Ludos. As can be seen from Plato's feast, that the most understanding thoughts and the deepest teachings are introduced under a friendly conversation.) (FZG III, 54)

Compared to the Italian games, what was new with Harsdörffer was that he let his persons play the games and did not just publish a kind of user's manual like the Italians. Of course, this requires that he introduces characters with names, while observing the rule of diversity, which makes such a society attractive. His personal includes three male and three female figures of different ages and status: the two noble virgins Angelica von Keuschewitz and Cassandra Schönlebin represent two different variants of young ladies, one characterized by her chastity and wit, as the name suggests, the other by her inclination to entertainment and beauty. The two ladies are accompanied by the "gereist- und belesene Student" (traveled and knowledgeable student) Reymund Discretin and the "verständige und gelehrte Soldat" (reasonable and learned soldier" Degenwert von Ruhmeck. The older generation is represented by the "kluge Matron" (wise matron) Julia von Freudenstein and the "alte Hofmann" (old courtier) Vespasian von Lustgau. Julia and Vespasian have been at court in their youth and know the conversation games from their own experience (FZG I, 24). Sorel sells exactly this staging in his *Maison de Jeux* as a novelty: "Il n'y a point eu [...] d'Autheurs [...] qui les ayent fait pratiquer à vne Compagnie, comme l'on fait en ce lieu-cy."[14] Since the first volume of Harsdörffer's conversation games came out in 1641 and the *Maison des Jeux* not before 1642, the German author probably deserves the credit for introducing a

---

[12] Sorel 1977, p. 477. Harsdörffer writes: "Vnsre Gesprächspiele sind von den Italianern abgesehen/ welche auch die Frantzosen nachgeahmet [...]." (Our conversation games are based on the Italians who also imitate the French [...].) On the margin a reference to *La Maison des jeux*, imprimés à Paris 1643 (FZG VIII, 85). For the *Maison des Jeux* see Strosetzki 2020.

[13] For this connection between dialogue and play, see Silke Segler-Messer 2002, pp. 48 and 66.

[14] Sorel 1977, Advertissement au lecteur.

new literary form. Harsdörffer knew the *Maison des Jeux* and also other works by Sorel, but it is unlikely that Sorel knew the work of his German colleague.

This staging of the game requires that it is spatially located. Harsdörffer gives each of his elaborate editions of his conversation games a copperplate which shows the society in the most diverse situations: in a room of a country house, in a room when viewing tapestries, in front of the country house when viewing the night sky, on a boat trip, in a garden or arbor, etc. The room often has something of a theater set, at any rate it is cut off from everyday reality, a property that it shares, for example, with Boccaccio's *Decameron* but also with the game, whose character it is to suspend reality - in Harsdörffer's case also that of the Thirty Years' War -. The entertainment of the *Maison des Jeux* also takes place in the countryside.[15]

2 Successful Conversation

A prerequisite for a successful conversation is a pleasant, not too numerous society: "Es ist zu anderer Zeit Meldung beschehen / daß zu den Gesprächspielen zum wenigsten drey / zum meinsten neun Vnterredner seyn sollen." (It has been reported at other times, that for conversation games at least three should be at most nine participants).[16] Harsdörffer repeatedly emphasizes that this society must be "einmütig" (unanimous) (FZG III, 155).[17] The diversity of the conversation partners also guarantees the fulfillment of the second criterion, the diversity of topics and answers, because the peculiarity of such conversations is that questions are raised which cannot be answered with yes or no, but which give rise to different opinions (FZG IV, 473): Questions which "etwas nutzliches / und zugleich auch anmutiges in sich haben / benebens unterschiedliche Meinungen leiden / können für solche Gesprächspiele [...] wol vorgebracht werden." (have something useful and at the same time also pleasing next to them suffer from different opinions can be raised for such conversation games [...] very well.) (FZG I, 199). In another place he says: "das Gesprächspiel [ist] eine artige Aufgab / so zu nutzlicher Belustigung einer einmütigen Geselschaft beliebet / und auf manche Art beantwortet werden kan." (The conversation game [is] a pleasant task so that a unanimous society can be pleased and answered in many ways.) (FZG III, 155).

Furthermore, consideration must be given to the conversation partners, a principle that is well known from rhetoric: "Es ist aber sonderlich die Zeit / das Ort und die Personen / so sich anwesend befinden / in acht zu nemen [...] / daß nemlich die Fragen erwähnten Umständen gemäß." (But it is particularly the time the place and the people who are present to take care of [...] that the questions mentioned in

---

[15] For the place of conversation, see Strosetzki 1988, pp. 17–30.

[16] FZG IV, 472. Harsdörffer here adopts a definition by Guazzo, according to which the number of participants should be no less than the number of Muses and no more than the number of Graces (after Fumaroli 1992, p. 13).

[17] Guazzo says that the society must be harmonious like organ pipes (after Fumaroli 1992, p. 13).

the circumstances)(FZG I, 199f.).[18] The Estates Clause also echoes when he says: "Geringe Spiele gehören nicht unter grosse Leute / wie auch die Sinnreichen sich übel zu den Blöden schiken." (Small games do not belong to great people as the sensible people are badly suited to the stupid.) (FZG III, 359) The game master plays an important role here, he must suggest the topics and questions suitable for the present.[19] This adaptation to the current situation is also the reason why Italian games are not as widespread, because they would not always be suitable "nach unserer Landesart" (according to our national customs)(FZG III, 121). In Part VIII there is a conversation game of the "Ungebräuchliche Spiele" (Unusual Games), in which many games by Ringhieri are mentioned (FZG VIII, 456 ff.).[20] Part of the difficulty of using Italian games in Germany is also due to the different cultural conditions. Vespasian says once, that Italian games would not be suitable in Germany, "weil unser Frauenzimmer in Weltlichen Schriften nicht so belesen / als in Welschland vnd Frankreich" (because our women are not as learned in worldly writings as in Italy and France) (III, 121 f.). The women themselves confirm this when they complain that there are so few German writings, while the "Frantzösische / Italiänische und Niederländische Frauenvolk fast alles / so man sonsten auf hohen Schulen erlernet / in ihrer Sprache zu lesen pflegen." (French / Italian and Dutch women can read in their language almost everything as one otherwise learns on high schools.) (FZG III, 364) So it is not surprising that these women can talk quite differently: "In Frankreich und Italien weiß alles Jungfernvolk von der Schönheit / von dem Reichthum / von der Keuschheit / und Tugend so schikklich zu reden / weil sie dergleichen Stükke der Sittenlehre aus den Büchern ihrer Muttersprache erlernet haben." (In France and Italy, every virgin can talk about beauty about wealth about chastity and virtue so properly because they have learned such pieces of moral education from the books in their mother tongue.) (FZG VIII, 118) It is no coincidence that, among other things, the moral education is mentioned here, which is another criterion why certain Italian games are considered inappropriate, such as the love sermon, which consists in "aus einem Poeten einen Text zu nemen / und eine Predigt darüber zu machen" (taking a text from a poet and make a sermon about it" (FZG VIII, 458) or the love confession. Significantly, when they speak on books to be translated, Mrs. Julia mentions the already translated *L'honneste Femme* by Jacques

---

[18] Similar FZG III, 118.

[19] „so solle solcher Regent / sich mit den Aufgaben der Gesprächspiele / nach der anwesenden Geselschaft richten / niemand fragen / was derselbe nicht zu beantworten weiß: jedem das / was er kan und wol verstehet / zu erweisen auferlegen." (So should such a master of game be related to the tasks of the conversation games according to the present company. No one ask what he can not answer: everyone, what he can and wants to understand to be imposed.) (FZG III, 168) See also FZG I, 305; II, 240, IV, 471.

[20] As early as Part III, it is suggested that he has „umb die Zahl [100] zu erfüllen / viel wunderliche und wie gedacht / unübliche Sachen fürgebracht [...]." (about the number [100] to fulfill many strange and, as it were, unusual things brought [...].) (FZG III, 142).

Du Bosc (FZG I, 291) and not a novel; only the men talk about novels.[21] In general, one must take care not to embarrass the women who should not be put in an awkward position: "Zu merken ist auch / daß man das Frauenzimmer nicht solle fragen von Sachen / so ihnen frey zu beantworten übel anstehen […]." (It should also be noted that one should not ask the ladies about things that they might have to answer badly […].) (FZG III, 171) In this context, society makes fun of inappropriate topics such as the suggestion of a cavalry captain to tell chivalrous deeds to which the women can not contribute (FZG IV, 472).[22]

It is clear from the foregoing that the material for the conversation comes from the books. one must be well-read to participate, in addition, one must be familiar with what Fumaroli calls the "la sagesse des nations", the clichés in a positive sense.[23] In connection with a discussion of books to be translated, Reymund says that it is not a lack of books, "sondern an jungen Leuten / die selbe zu lesen Belieben tragen." (but of young people who like to read them.) (FZG I, 291) This is another indication of the cultural lag in the german speaking countries. Angelica asks then: "Was für Bücher aber können zu Behuf der Gesprächspiel dienen." (What kind of books can be used for the conversation game.) Reymund replies: "Alle und jede / weil nichts in den Wissenschaften begriffen so zu den Gesprächspielen nicht solte gezogen werden können." (All and everyone because nothing should be included in the sciences to the conversation games.) (FZG I, 291)[24] In Part VIII, Vespasian summarizes the "sources" of the conversation games: "I. Von den Künsten / Handwerken allerley Ständen und ihrem Thun und Lassen […]. II. Von gewisser Begebenheit / Geschichten / Erzehlungen / Fragen und Antworten / etc. […] III. Von den Sachen / welche wir für Augen sehen […]." (I. From the arts, crafts of all kinds of professions and their doing and letting […]. II. From certain events, stories, narratives, questions and answers, etc. […] III. From the things we see […].) (FZG VIII, 460) Harsdörffer demonstrates all this in the course of the eight volumes, when he lets the persons talk about the jargon of hunting, music or painting, when he lets tell them stories or talk about the night sky or the arrangement of the garden in which they are staying.

Although one can talk about everything, it must be entertaining and enjoyable: "Das ist der Gesprächspiele rechte Art / solche Sachen auf die Bahn zubringen / darvon man Vrsach nehmen kan / mit Verstand kurtzweilige Reden zuführen."

---

[21] This is the translation of Jacques Du Bosc: *L'honneste Femme* (1632). German: *Die Tugendsame Frau. Das ist Außführlicher Wegweiser, wie sich eine Tugendsame Fraw verhalten möge*. Cassel: Schütz 1636. Strosetzki (Konversation 2014, p. 194 and 219) points out that in France in the first half of the 17th century, moral and religious components made up the *honnêteté*.

[22] Cf. also FZG I, 200.

[23] Fumaroli 1992, p. 11. See also Ann Moss 2002 for the Lieux communs.

[24] Similarly, „Alle Wissenschaften / welche benebens dem Nutzen / sonderliches Belusten bringen / (als die Betrachtung der Sterne ist) können auf dergleichen Gesprächart Spielweiß erlernet werden." (All sciences that, in addition to the benefit, are particularly pleasing, can be learned on such a conversation game.) (FZG III, 53).

(This is the right way to bring such things to the table to take them up with understanding to lead entertaining and enjoyable conversations." (FZG I, 195). Now the women come into play, because, as research in Romance languages, and above all Christoph Strosetzki, has long shown, they act as a kind of judge who intervene when the rules are not followed.[25] At one point, the gentlemen begin to mix foreign words like *diskuriren, perdoniren* into their speech, to which Julia protests: "Wollen die Herrn haben daß wir ihnen sollen zuhören / so geruhen sie zu reden / daß wirs allerseits verstehen können.* (If the gentlemen want us to listen to them so they deign to speak that we can all understand.) (FZG II, 55) The enemy of good entertainment are the "Schulfüchse", which have brought the dignity of art and science into disrepute with their "ungeschlachten und unartigen Sitten an Fürstenhöfen" (uncouth and unmannerly customs at princely courts) (FZG II, 56).

It is important that there is a balance between benefit and pleasure. If everything can become the subjet of a conversation game, then not every transmission of knowledge is already a conversation game. In a game about describing the celestial sphere,[26] Cassandra objects that this is "hard to keep". Vespasian believes that everyone can only remember two celestial lines. Angelica then objects: "Solche Vnterweisung aber ist noch kein Spiel nicht." (But such instruction is not yet a game.)Cassandra replies: "Der Herr wird es wissen in einen Spielmodel zu giessen." (The Lord will know how to pour it into a game model.) (III, 53) To "pour into a game model" means to transmit difficult things in a pleasant way or, as it is said elsewhere, "nach Art der Gesprächspiele verhandeln" (negotiate in the manner of conversation games) that is "von hohen Dingen einfältig reden" (talk straightforward about difficult things) (FZG III, 79). What is not explicitly discussed but always implied is variation and also a certain brevity. A topic should not be discussed to the end and above all it is not about finding a final, correct answer. "Die kürzesten Spiele sind mehrmals die allerlustigsten / weil die Veränderung und Abwechslung angenem." (The shortest games are the most enjoyable several times because of the change and variety pleasant.) (FZG VIII, 461). If everything can become the subject of conversation games, it is still limited by the fact that the matter must be enjoyable (FZG VIII, 84), which explains why Harsdörffer's *Gesprächspiele* have a preference for the arts and for the strange and the curious. This is nicely illustrated by the questions compiled in a register in Part VI, which cover very different areas, aesthetic with the question "Was von der Bilder Wirkung zu halten?" (What to think of the effect of the pictures?), natural magic: "Wie die Waffensalbe zu machen?" (How to make the powder of sympathy?), natural history, mythology: "Ob die Delphinen jemals einen Menschen bey dem Leben erhalten?" (Whether the dolphins ever kept a person alive?) or ethical-religious: "Ob es Christen gezieme Heydnische Gedichte auf dem Schauplatz vorzustellen" (Whether it is appropriate for Christians to represent

---

[25] See Strosetzki 2014, especially pp. 203 ff.

[26] The celestial sphere was thought as analogue to the earth's sphere with a north and south pole, an equator and meridian, as well as different lines crossing the constellations.

pagan poems on the stage) and similar (FZG VI, 624ff.). In the appendix to Part VIII there are "XXV. Merkwürdige Fragen aus der Naturkündigung und Sitten- oder Tugendlehre" (XXV. Remarkable questions from natural history and morality or virtue), which contain very different areas such as the effect of magnets, ebb and flow, but also ethical questions such as "Warum uns nach verbottnen Sachen gelüste?" (Why do we have desire for forbidden things?) (FZG VIII, 574).

Other compilatory works by Harsdörffer such as his *Philosophischen und Mathematischen Erquickstunden* (1651, 1653) and his translations of French story collections are to be seen in this context as a supply of material for useful and enjoyable entertainment.[27]

Harsdörffer advocates with his ideal of conversation games, which are to be both useful and entertaining, neither too learned nor too specialized nor too simple, a widespread norm of social interaction.[28]

In conclusion, it should also be noted that Harsdörffer not only deserves the credit for introducing Italian conversation literature to Germany, but also for introducing women as conversation partners. Harsdörffer was quite aware of this innovation when he writes in the preface to Part 1: "Sprichst du / solche Kurtzweil ist Teutschem Frauenzimmer zu schwer / ungewont und verdrieslich: So bitte Jch / du wollest von derselben hohen Verstand nicht urtheilen: sondern bedenken / was jederzeit für übertreffliches und Tugendberühmtes Frauenvolk in allen Historien belobet / und noch heut zu Tag aller Orten sich befindet […]." (If you such entertainment is too difficult unusual and tedious for German women: So I ask you not to judge them by the same high standards: but to consider what an excellent and virtuous women's folk has always been praised in all histories and what can still be found today in all places […].) (FZG I, 17 f.). Although Zesen also introduced a woman in his *Rosen-mând*, she is only allowed to ask questions and listen to the more or less long explanations.[29] In Rist's *Monatsgesprächen*, which are most comparable to Harsdörffer's *Gesprächspiele*, only men appear.[30] Harsdörffer founded the still existing Pegnesischer Blumenorden together with Johann Klaj, which was the only such society that also admitted women.

Finally, it should be noted that Harsdörffer's *Gesprächspiele* were also aimed at the culture of the nobility, at the "princely courts", as he calls them. Judging from the paratexts, it seems to have succeeded to some extent, especially to penetrate the aristocratic circles of the Protestant north. In the preface to Part VI he writes that these games are now common in many places "und sonderlich an einem vornemen Fürsten Hof / der jungen Herrschaft zu nutzlicher Kurtzweil / täglichs nach gehaltener Tafel ein Spiel daraus vorgegeben" (and especially at a prominent

---

[27] Above all the story collections:. *Der Grosse Schauplatz jämerlicher Mordgeschichte* (1649/50). *Der Grosse Schauplatz Lust- und Lehrreicher Geschichte* (1648). (

[28] Bonfatti 1979, p. 64. Strosetzki 1997.

[29] See Zeller 2013, pp. 240 f.

[30] See Zeller 2013, p. 242.

princely court the young lordship is given a game from it after the meal every day) (FZG VI, 105).[31] It has been assumed that this court is the one in Wolfenbüttel, where Justus Georg Schottel and Sigmund von Birken worked as preceptors. Harsdörffer also dedicated some volumes to noblemen who were also members of the Fruchtbringende Gesellschaft. Part 4 is dedicated to the Befreyende, that is, Duke Augustus of Brunswick-Wolfenbüttel, who expanded the library in Wolfenbüttel. Part 5 is dedicated to the Befreyendinn, meaning the highly educated wife of Duke Augustus, Sophie Elizabeth. Since the Fruchtbringende Gesellschaft did not admit women, Harsdörffer gave her the feminine form of her husband's name and dedicated the volume at the same time to the woman who perhaps contributed to the fact that at her court the young people practiced conversation games.[32] Part VI is dedicated to Wilhelm IV of Saxony-Weimar, who "und wegen der folgenden [Bände] (wie ich glaubwürdig berichtet worden) nachzufragen gnädigst geruhet" (most graciously deigned to inquire about the following [volumes]) after having read the five parts of the conversation games (FZG VI, 14). Part VIII and the last part are finally dedicated to Christian of Anhalt, who admonished him to continue the work.[33] A pretty testimony can then be found in the copy of the Herzog August-Bibliothek in Wolfenbüttel. Part I has a handwritten entry according to which Christine von Braunschweig-Lüneburg-Bevern, née von Hessen-Eschwege, the wife of Ferdinand Albrecht von Braunschweig-Lüneburg-Bevern, inherited the book from her mother Eleonora Katharina von Pfalz-Zweibrücken-Kleeburg, married von Hessen-Eschwege (1626–1692) in 1692 and gave it to her daughter Sophie Eleonore von Braunschweig-Lüneburg (1674–1711) as a name day present in 1695.[34] On the title page she has also added a poem that begins

---

[31] In the "Schutzschrift für Die Teutsche Spracharbeit" published as an appendix to Part I, he also talks about how the conversation games are "von etlichen hochgeborenen Fürstinnen und Fräulein mit gnädiger Gewogenheit beliebet und geübet werden." (favored and practiced by many noble princesses and young ladies with gracious approval.)(FZG I, 391).

[32] Her stepson Anton Ulrich will have the society play conversation games several times in his novel *Die syrische Aramena*. See Zeller 1997, pp. 539ff.

[33] „Weil aber E. Fürstl. Gn. diese geringe Arbeit gnädigst beliebet / mich zu deroselben Fortsetzung ermahnet / und ihre hohe Gewogenheit mir auf viel Wege bezeuget / habe / zu Beglauben schuldiger Dankwilligkeit E. Fürstl. Gnaden / ich derselben diesen letzten und vollständigsten Theil zuzueignen nicht unterlassen sollen."(But since His Serene Highness has graciously favored this small work admonished me to continue it and shown me his high favor in many ways I have not failed to dedicate this last and complete part to him out of my duty of gratefulness.) (FZG VIII, 11).

[34] The copy of Harsdörffer's *Philosophischen und Mathematischen Erquickstunden* (Part 2) preserved in Wolfenbüttel also belonged to a woman, Duchess Elisabeth Sophie Marie von Braunschweig-Lüneburg-Wolfenbüttel (1683–1767).

with: "Lebe vergnüget liebste Leonora | Ergehe dich öfters in diesem Buch" (Live happily dear Leonora | Enjoy yourself often in this book).[35] Although the book is located in Wolfenbüttel, it originally did not come from the library of Wolfenbüttel, which indicates that it was more widespread than one might think.

References

Bargagli, Girolamo: Dialogi de' Giuochi che nelle vegghie senesi si usano di fare. A cura di Patrizia d'Incalci Ermini. Introduzione Riccardo Bruscagli. Siena 1982.
Bargagli, Scipio: I Trattenimenti dove da vaghe Donne e da giovani Huomini rapresentati sono honesti e dilettevoli Giuochi, narrate Novelle, e cantate alcune amorose Canzonette. Venezia: Giunti 1587.
Battafarano, Michele: Die Frau als Subjekt der Literatur. Harsdörffer auf den Spuren der Intronati, Incogniti, Oziosi, in: M. B.: Glanz des Barock. Bern: Lang 1994, S. 117–136.
Bonfatti, Emilio: La "civil conversazione" in Germania: letteratura del comportamento da Stefano Guazzo a Adolph Knigge: 1571–1788. Udine: Del Bianco Editore, 1979.
Fumaroli, Marc: Le genre des genres français. La conversation. Oxford: Clarendon Press 1992.
Guazzo, Stefano: De Civili Conversatione, Das ist/ Von dem Bürgerlichen Wandel und zierlichen Sitten [...]. Frankfurt a. M.: Aubrius und Schleich 1626.
Guazzo, Stefano: La civil conversazione. Testo e appendice a cura di Amedeo Quondam. Modena: Panini 1993.
Harsdörffer, Georg Philipp: Frauenzimmer Gesprächspiele. Hg. von I. Böttcher. 8 Teile. Tübingen 1968–1969.
Lecercle, François: La culture en jeu. Innocenzo Ringhieri et le Pétrarquisme, in: Philippe Ariès und Jean-Claude Margolin (Hg.): Les Jeux à la Renaissance. Paris 1982, S. 185–200.
Moss, Ann: Les recueils de lieux communs. Apprendre à penser à la Renaissance. Genf: Droz 2002.
Quondam, Amadeo: L'Accademia, in: Letteratura italiana, Vol. I: Il letterato e le istituzioni. Torino: Einaudi 1982, S. 822–896.
Ringhieri, Innocenzio: Cento giuochi liberali et d'ingegno. Bologna: Giacarelli 1551, weitere Auflagen 1553, 1580.
Ringhier, Innocent: Cinquante Jeus divers d'honnête entretien. Lyon: Pesnot 1555.
Segler-Meßner, Silke: Der Dialog als Raum spielerischer Selbstentfaltung: Baldessar Castiglione, Stefano Guazzo, Moderata Fonte, in: Klaus Hempfer und Helmut Pfeiffer (Hgg.): Spielwelten. Performanz und Inszenierung in der Renaissance. Stuttgart: Franz Steiner 2002, S. 47–66.
Sorel, Charles: La Maison des Jeux. [Reprint der Ausgabe 1658] Avec introduction, un commentaire, une bibliographie et un index par Daniel-A. Gajda. Genf: Slatkine 1977.

---

[35] Christine von Braunschweig-Lüneburg was the wife of August Ferdinand von Braunschweig-Lüneburg-Bevern, a half-brother of Anton Ulrich. The dedication reads: "Dießes Buch habe geErbet von Meiner Hoch-Selligen Frau Mutter 1692 und verehre daß selbe mit allen seinen Theillen an unser hoch gelibte Tochter Sophie Eleonora auff ihren Nahmens Tag Eleonora. Bevern 1695 des 21. Febr." (This book was inherited from my highly respected mother in 1692 and I dedicate it with all its parts to our beloved daughter Sophie Eleonora on her name day Eleonora. Bevern 1695 21 February.) On the facing empty page, the recipient writes: „Dieses Buch sambt noch folgenden Theile habe ich von meiner höchst geehrten lieben Mama in Bevern bekommen. Anno 1695 Sophie Eleonora." (I received this book along with the following parts from my highly esteemed and dear Mama in Bevern. Anno 1695 Sophie Eleonora.) An example of the appreciation of the work with its many valuable copperplates.

Strosetzki, Christoph: Konversation und Literatur. Zu Regeln der Rhetorik und Rezeption in Spanien und Frankreich. Frankfurt a. M. u. a.: Lang 1988.
Strosetzki, Christoph: Die Norm und ihre Alternative in der Geselligkeitskultur des absolutistischen Frankreich, in: Wolfgang Adam u. a. (Hg.): Geselligkeit und Gesellschaft im Barockzeitalter, Teil 1, Wiesbaden: Harassowitz 1997, S. 135–153.
Strosetzki, Christoph: Konversation als Sprachkultur. Elemente einer historischen Kommunikationspragmatik. Berlin: Frank & Timme ²2014.
Strosetzki, Christoph: Konversation als Spiel: Charles Sorel vs. Grice und Gadamer, in: Angela Schrott und Christoph Strosetzki (Hg.): Gelungene Gespräche als Praxis der Gemeinschaftsbildung. Literatur, Sprache, Gesellschaft. Berlin: de Gruyter 2020, S. 11–23.
Zeller, Rosmarie: Die Rolle der Frauen im Gesprächspiel und in der Konversation, in: Wolfgang Adam u. a. (Hg.): Geselligkeit und Gesellschaft im Barockzeitalter. Wiesbaden: Harrassowitz 1997, S. 531–541.
Zeller, Rosmarie: Harsdörffers Mordgeschichten in der Tradition der *Histoires tragiques*, in: Hans-Joachim Jakob und Hermann Korte (Hg.): Harsdörffer-Studien. Mit einer Bibliographie zur Forschungsliteratur. Frankfurt a. M.: Lang 2006, S. 177–194.
Zeller, Rosmarie: Spiel mit Wissen, Spiel als gebildete Unterhaltung in der Frühen Neuzeit, in: Bernhard Jahn und Michael Schilling (Hg.): Literatur und Spiel. Zur Poetologie literarischer Spielszenen. Stuttgart: Hirzel 2010, S. 97–111.
Zeller, Rosmarie: Das Gespräch als Medium der Wissensvermittlung, in: Thorsten Burkard u. a. (Hg.): Natur – Religion – Medien. Transformationen frühneuzeitlichen Wissens. Berlin: Akademie-Verlag 2013, S. 229–247.

"Here Are Some Fine Advisements and Conversations"—Forms of Courtly Conversation in Brantôme's *Les Dames galantes*

Wolfgang Adam

Abstract The Early Modern period's courtly conversation is only sketchily reconstructable due to its ephemeral presentation form; the historian's direct access to the "réalité concrète de la langue parlée" ("concrete reality of spoken language") (Landy- Houillon) remains closed. Brantôme's Le Recueil des Dames II—better known by the sensationalist title Les vies des Dames galantes ("The Lives of the Gallant Ladies") chosen by the book printer Jean Sambix—at least offers a rudimentary access to the forms and types of courtly sociability, of which conversation is to be considered a substantial component. Pierre de Bourdeille, l'abbé commendentaire de Brantôme (1539/1542–1614) knows the practice of courtly life as a "gentilhomme de la cour" ("gentleman of the court"). As a confidant of high-ranking personalities such as Catherine i de Médicis or Marguerite de Valois, he records conversations and actions in his memories as an eyewitness. The "chronique scandaleuse" ("scandalous chronicle"), written after a serious accident in 1564, deals with affairs and gallant anecdotes at different European courts in several discourses. The principle of conversation becomes the composition principle of his work. In a narrative conglomerate that is difficult to disentangle, Brantôme presents stories that he himself experienced, that were told to him, or that he read in contemporary authors. In essence, according to this source, almost anything can be said in the courtly milieu, with the exception of explosive political topics, blasphemous derailments, or obscene stories that expose powerful actors.

W. Adam (✉)
Universität Osnabrück, Osnabrück, Germany
e-mail: wadam@uni-osnabrueck.de

Keywords

Brantôme · Montaigne · Catherine de Médicis · Marguerite de Valois ·
Courtly Conversation · Gallant Anecdotes · Women's Image ·
Voyeur Perspective · Licenses and Limits of Courtly Sociability

The conversation of early modernity[1] belongs to the ephemeral acts of courtly sociability,[2] which—like the baroque festival—are connected to the moment of presentation.[3] With the passing of the action, the event disappears from memory, unless it is recorded in a more dry and brittle way: descriptions that are rarely, or actually never, able to convey the fleeting charm of a performance. Of course, the participants in a word exchange, the central themes of a conversation can be recorded, but the inner mechanics of a conversation, how and when the points are set in detail, which themes are allowed and which are avoided, the facial expressions and body language of the discussants, these constitutive elements of every past conversation situation are hardly to be grasped in the later transcription of oral communication.

Texts that stage conversations, such as Georg Philipp Harsdörffer's *Frauenzimmer Gesprächspiele,* give important insights into the values and mental state of noble sociability.[4] Treatises and instructions on proper behavior at court make past worlds of life appear in outlines, but these literary witnesses of an intentionally stylized meta-level only grant access to the real practice to a limited extent. And the protocoling of a casual conversation in a pedantic way, like statements in court or in diplomatic negotiations, contradicts the fundamental idea of a conversation committed to the principles of *grazia* and *sprezzatura* that Baldassar Castiglione postulates in *Libro del Cortegiano*.[5] In general, as Isabelle Landy-Houillon emphatically points out in her article *Lettre et oralité*, we are cut off from the "réalité concrète de la langue parlée"[6] of the Early Modern period due to the lack of technical recording possibilities for conversations in past epochs. There are no tape or video recordings of Early Modern conversation!

The awareness of the difficulties, indeed the insurmountable barriers to the reconstruction of historical conversation situations should not lead to resignation or abandonment of the central theme of our colloquium "Should one talk? And if so, about what?"

---

[1] Strosetzki, 2013, pp. 11 ff. with overview of research; Albert 2005; Adam and Fauser 2005; Till 2003; Peter 1999; Hellegourach 1997; Beetz 1997; Bray and Strosetzki (eds.) 1995; Montandon 1995; Beetz 1990; Göttert 1988; Fauser 1991; Strosetzki 1978; Henn-Schmölders 1975.

[2] Adam et al. 1997, pp. 1–16; Göttert 1996; Chartier 1986; Im Hof 1982.

[3] Alewyn and Sälzle 1959.

[4] Zeller 1974, 1997; Becker-Cantarino 1997.

[5] Castiglione, *Il libro del Cortegiano*, ed. Quondam et Longo 2000, Introduzione, p. XIII f; Lib. I, XV, p. 43; Lib. I, XXVII, p. 61 ff.

[6] Landy-Houillon 1995, p. 81.

One possible way to answer this question, with regard to the Early Modern period, is a new reading of non-fictional texts that oscillate between the genre characteristics of memoir literature, historical representation and the newly emerging essayistic genre. For such an experiment, the text by Brantôme *Le Recueil des Dames II* - better known under the title *Les vies des Dames galantes*—offers itself, in which a multitude of "de beaux advis et entretiens"[7] can be found. In the Gallimard edition edited by Pascal Pia, the reader is presented with a vast repertoire of *causeries* and *discours* that were held at the various courts in France, Italy, Spain and England in the 16th century.

First, I will give some basic information about the exciting life of the author and the exciting oeuvre that is still being read today not only in Romance language seminars. In France, Brantôme's writings are also part of the cultural memory due to their spatial and thematic proximity to Montaigne, as documented, inter alia, by their presence in the *Bibliothèque de la Pléiade*.[8] In Germany, there was a reprint of a translation of the *Dames galantes* ten years ago, where the curiosity about delicate or pornographic stories probably outweighed the philological interest. This is at least suggested by the publication in the series "Erotic Literature".[9] Afterwards I would like to show characteristics of social conversation in the narrative macrostructure of the text and finally, with a view to the theoretical guidelines of contemporary pattern books on lifestyle and conversation such as the *Cortegiano* or the *Art de plaire dans la conversation*, prove to what extent the individual episodes told by Brantôme follow the established customs of courtly communication.

Pierre de Bourdeille,[10] l'abbé commendataire de Brantôme,[11] was born in the Perigord as the third child of a respected noble family between 1539 and 1542. For generations, the family had been in close contact with the court of Navarre. His grandmother, Louise de Daillon, and his mother Anne de Vivonne served as *dames d'honneur* to Marguerite d'Angoulême, the sister of Francis I.[12] Both women were directly involved in the creation of the *Heptaméron;* Anne de Vivonne could be identified as an *Ennasuite* in the cycle of novellas.[13] A great influence in this "trinité féminine".[14] had also his "aunt Dampierre",[15] Jeanne de Vivonne, the sister of Anne, who

---

[7] Brantôme 1981, p. 102, nach dieser Ausgabe wird zitiert.

[8] Brantôme 1991.

[9] Brantôme 2010.

[10] For the biography of Brantôme, see Lalanne 1896; Cocula-Vaillières 1986; Lazard 1995.

[11] For the meaning of "commende" in this context: «Administration temporaire d' un bénéfice ecclésiastique confiée à une séculier». Centre National de Ressources Textuelles et Lexicales (*CNRTL* online 2021). Lazard, S. 7: «Lui-même (Brantôme) ne se qualifia jamais d'abbé mais, de seigneur de Brantôme.»

[12] Balsamo 2007, p 147; Cocula-Vaillières 1986, p. 30 ff.

[13] Vaucheret 2010, p. 9 f.; Cocula-Vaillières 1986, p. 32; Marguerite de Navarre 2000.

[14] Vaucheret 2010, p. 47.

[15] Cocula-Vaillières 1986, p. 30.

belonged to the circle of friends of Marguerite de Valois, the first wife of Henry IV., and who became a "vray registre de la Court" for the later memoirist Brantôme.[16] His first years were spent at the court of Navarre until the death of Marguerite d'Angoulême, from 1550 he was a pupil at a college in Paris, after his studies in Poitiers he made his first journey to Italy at the end of 1558,[17] politically he joined the influential clan of the Guise, an important power factor in the France agitated by the religious wars. In 1561 he was part of the embassy that accompanied Mary Stuart to Scotland.[18] During his stay on the British Isles he also met Elizabeth I. Later military and diplomatic missions took him back to Italy, Malta, North Africa, Portugal and Spain. Brantôme, who spoke perfect Spanish, won the trust of Queen Elizabeth, the daughter of Catherine i de Médicis. In Spain he was one of the interlocutors of Duke Alba, and even Philip II paid attention to him. The court of the Valois became his preferred place of work for many years until the break with Henry III.[19] In 1567 Brantôme was appointed "gentilhomme de la chambre du roi", he was one of the confidants of Catherine de Médicis, to whose anti-chambre he had access and whom he accompanied on many trips. Brantôme knew the ladies-in-waiting of the widow Henry II, with at least one of the "dames d'escadron volant" he had fallen in love.[20] His connection to François, Monsieur duc d'Alençon, the youngest son of Catherine, to whom he dedicated his work *Les Dames galantes*, was particularly close.

His attachment to Marguerite de Valois, daughter of Catherine, was even stronger. His admiration was so intense that one of his modern biographers has rightly called him "le sigisbée de Marguerite".[21] The author of the *Vies des Dames galantes* proudly reports the absolute trust he enjoyed with this influential and power-conscious personality: "j'estois de ses bon amis, et (elle) ne se cachoit point de moy."[22] Brantôme dedicated the first volume of the *Recueil des Dames* to Marguerite de Valois, whom he praised as "la plus belle, la plus noble, la plus grande, la plus genereuse, la plus magnanime et la plus accomplie Princesse du monde »[23] and whose laudatio forms the sole subject of the fifth Discours.[24] Marguerite reciprocates by thanking the panegyrical author, whom she counts

---

[16] Brantôme: Recueil des Dames, I, 1, p. 25.

[17] De Piaggi 1966, pp. 79–116.

[18] Lazard 1995, pp. 69 ff.

[19] Henry III did not keep his promise to transfer the office of *Sénéchal de Perigord*, which became vacant after the death of his brother, to Brantôme. For Brantôme's reaction, see Jouanna 1998, p. 739: «il marque son «malcontentement» par un geste spectaculaire en jetant dans la Seine la clef d'or de la chambre du roi».

[20] Vauchert 2010, pp. 10 f.; Cocula-Vaillières 1986, pp. 78 f.

[21] Vauchert 2010, pp. 59 ff.

[22] Brantôme 1981, p. 206.

[23] Brantôme 1991, Preface to the second redaction of Brantôme, p. 3.

[24] Brantôme 1991, I, 5: Discours sur la reyne de France et de Navarre, Marguerite, fille unique maintenant restée et seule de la noble maison de France, pp. 119 ff.

among "de mes plus anciens amis"[25] in the *Dédicace à Brantôme,* with which she now opens her memoirs.[26]

This versatile career of a courtier, which has experienced highs and lows, was brutally interrupted in 1584 by a fall from a horse, which left Brantôme paralyzed in bed for several years.[27] In this phase he began to write his memories continuously:

> «Sur mon lit assaily d'infinies langueurs.
> Je discours, à part moy, de ma vie passée;»[28]

This is how he himself describes the crisis that forced him to exchange the quill for the sword. Now, far from the court where a new generation under Henry IV, whom Brantôme incidentally revered,[29] was setting the tone, the noble author lived writing his memories in the Abbay de Brantôme or later in the Château de Richemont, where he died on 5 July 1614.

Before I go on to the central text for my study, the *Vies des Dames galantes*, a word on the connection, or rather the lack of connection, between Brantôme and his contemporary and countryman Montaigne.[30] The relationship between the two, whose centres of life were only about 60 km apart—La Tour de Montaigne and the noble seats of Brantôme—and who probably met each other in person in Bordeaux, at court or during the siege of La Rochelle, was tense. Brantôme, as a proud representative of the "noblesse d'épée", looked down condescendingly on Montaigne, a member of the "noblesse de robe". He spoke of the author with full mockery: "whose profession it was better to continue his quill writing his *Essays* than to change it with a sword that did not suit him so well."[31] Brantôme never forgot that he was passed over for the "ordre de Saint-Michel" by Henry III, while the mayor of Bordeaux was honoured with it.[32] Conversely, Montaigne does not mention the writing neighbour even once in the more than thousand pages of his *Essais*, although—as will be shown shortly—there are certain affinities between the two works despite all the major differences. Montaigne and Brantôme sometimes

---

[25] Brantome quotes in the *Recueil des Dames* I, 5, p. 156 *Sur la reyne de France et de Navarre, Marguerite* from a letter by Marguerite to him, in which this formulation can be found.

[26] Marguerite de Valois 1971 and 1986, p. 39.

[27] Jouanna 1998, p. 739: «(1584) the accident that changes the course of his life occurs: a bad fall from a horse leaves him unable to pursue a military career.»

[28] Brantome, Œuvres complètes, éd. Lalanne, 1881, tome, X, p. 451.

[29] Brantôme speaks of "our great king of today, Henri IV", Brantôme, Oeuvres complètes, IV, p. 372; Cocula-Vaillières 1986, p. 426.

[30] See Dumoulin de Laplante 1974; Vaucheret 1996; Balsamo 2007 for this much-discussed relationship.

[31] Brantôme, Oeuvres complètes, tome V, p. 93; Desan, Montaigne 2014, p. 234.

[32] Jouanna 2017, p. 154; Balsamo 2007, p. 148; Vaucheret 1996, p. 87; Cocula-Vallières 1986, p. 410; Lalanne 1896, p. 221.

tell the same anecdotes,[33] they refer to the same ancient and modern sources, and at least between the first two books of Montaigne's *Essais* and Brantôme's Memoires there are similarities in the writing style and structure of the texts.[34]

The 'chronique scandaleuse' Brantômes—*Les Vies des Dames galantes* – is mainly written in the years after the accident. Brantôme mostly dictated his memories to his secretary Mathaud and then corrected them by hand;[35] the majority of the original manuscript is lost, some chapters of the first draft are kept in the *Bibliothèque Nationale* in Paris; in its entirety, the work is only preserved in mediocre copies.[36] It was printed for the first time in 1666, more than fifty years after the author's death in Leyden by Jean Sambix le jeune, who chose the attention-grabbing title *Les vies des Dames galantes,* which does not go back to Brantôme.[37] Brantôme always spoke only of the second volume of his *Recueil des Dames.* The extensive work is divided into seven discourses by the author himself, which deal with such amusing subjects as *sur les dames qui font l'amour et leurs maris cocus, sur la beauté de la belle jambe et la vertu qu'elle a;* there is also a section *sur l'amour des dames vieilles et comme aucunes l'ayment autant que les jeunes und* a particularly bizarre discourse speaks *sur ce que les belles et honnestes dames ayment les vaillans hommes, et les braves hommes ayment les dames courageuses.*[38] Already the subdivision into discourses in the *Recueil* shows the proximity to oral communication, Robert Duane Cottrell was quite right to speak of the "conversational nature" of the text.[39]

This proximity to the form of conversation pervades the entire work, and the phenomenon of genesis from the spirit of courtly sociability is just as expressly thematized in the dedication to François, duc d'Alençon, which Brantôme wrote before the prince's death, as he explains to the reader in the *Regrets sur la mort du Duc d'Alençon* after the first dedication letter.[40] Brantôme thanks his patron for the many intimate conversations he was able to have with him at court:

---

[33] There are affinities, for example, to some passages in Montaigne's *Essais*, I, 19 *Que Philosopher, c'est apprendre à mourir* and *Essais* II,3 *Coustume de l'Isle de Cea*, Montaigne, *Les Essais*, ed. Balsamo et al. 2007; see Balsamo 2007, p. 148; see also n. 154.

[34] According to Reichenberger (1989, p. 48), there is a "distant similarity" in structure between the *Vies des Dames Galantes* and Montaigne's early *Essais*.

[35] Cocula-Vallières 1986, p. 7.

[36] Omont 1904; Vaucheret 1991, p. CXXXIf.

[37] Cottrell 1970, p. 13: «The title, *Dames galantes,* was a concession to popular taste and had not the slightest autorization by Brantôme, who called the work variously *Deuxième volume des dames, Second livre des dames, Le traité des dames faict en second lieu, Le second volume que j'ay faict des dames et dédié à M. le duc d'Alençon»;* Grewe 2002, p. 115.

[38] Brantôme 1981, p. 27 ff., 289 ff., 311 ff., 353 ff.; Recueil des Dames, p. 237 ff., 439 ff., 586 ff., 662 ff.

[39] Cottrell 1970, p. 36; Vaucheret 2010, S. 115.

[40] Brantôme 1991, p. 25: "I HAD dedicated this 2nd book of Women to my lord of Alençon, while he was alive, as much as he honored me by loving me and talking to me very privately, and was curious to know good accounts."

> "MY LORD, as much as you have honored me often at the court to talk to me very privately about several good words and stories, which are so familiar and assiduous to you that one would say they are born at sight in your mouth (…)".[41]

With witty ideas and gallant anecdotes, Brantôme entertained the court society,[42] with causeries he drove the prince's boredom and helped him to pass the time pleasantly, "passer le temps."[43] Brantôme stylizes himself right at the beginning of the dedication as the ideal "gentleman of the court,"[44] who, in the spirit of the postulate in *Cortegiano*, knows how to "turn and dance, play and converse under the sign of grace."[45] Brantôme knew[46]—just like Montaigne[47]—the work that was created at the court of Urbino, which had already become the "classic of European literature" by the 16th century.[48]

The principle of conversation becomes the composition principle of his work: "je mes suis mis à composer ces discours."[49] The implementation of the originally oral presentation in written form is reflected in both the macrostructure of the *Recueil* and the smallest particles with which the stories are integrated into the discourses. Again and again one comes across formulations such as "J'ay ouy parler d'une fort belle et honneste dame,"[50] "et m'en a bien conté, à mon avis, nom par nom;"[51] "pour en parler franchement,"[52] "j'ay ouy parler d'femme françoise,"[53] or "j'ay ouy conter à un honneste gentilhomme."[54] These stories receive a special legitimacy when Brantôme emphasizes his eyewitness "comme de vray, en ma vie, j'ay veu force belles femmes toutes bonnes."[55] or relies on the testimony of

---

[41] Brantôme 1981, p. 23.

[42] A fitting characterization of the author can be found in Perche 1963, p. 47: "Brantôme is essentially a storyteller. The verve, the abundance, the pleasure of speaking and even the pleasure of listening to oneself speak, the ability to push the anecdote, one will not take anything away from him."

[43] Brantôme 1981, p. 23.

[44] Brantôme 1981, p. 23.

[45] Quondam, p. XV; for the outstanding importance of dance in courtly social life, see Mourey 2020.

[46] Cocula-Vallières 1986, pp. 172 ff.

[47] Cavallini 2003, p. 161.

[48] Ouondam, Introduzione, p. VIII.

[49] Brantôme 1981, p. 23.

[50] Brantôme 1981, p. 29.

[51] Brantôme 1981, p. 30.

[52] Brantôme 1981, p. 42.

[53] Brantôme 1981, p. 58.

[54] Brantôme 1981, p. 60, p. 118.

[55] Brantôme 1981, p. 56.

high-ranking personalities: "C'est pourquoy un grand prince que je sçay disoit."[56] Brantôme attaches great importance to the reliability of his sources, the serious guarantors include his grandmother and mother, both of whom have learned the scandalous stories told at the court of Marguerite de Navarre from first-hand.[57]

An methodological difficulty for the interpreter is thereby the fact that Brantôme does not always clearly mark what he owes to oral tradition, what he himself has experienced and observed, or what he has taken over from written sources. The author presents a hybrid text, in which autobiographical experiences,[58] third-person narratives, and the fruits of reading from ancient and contemporary authors offer an often inextricable conglomerate.[59] Preferred reference authors, where the loans are relatively easy to trace for the philologist because of the familiarity of the templates, are in antiquity Ovid, Livius, Sueton, Plutarch, in the modern age "the venerable and docte Bocasse"[60], Bandello,[61] 'Ariost[62], Aretino[63], Ronsard,[64] Rabelais[65], Théodore de Bèze[66] and Marguerite de Navarre.[67]

In order to evaluate *Les Vies des Dames galantes* under the focus of our question, it is therefore advisable to check the status of the tradition of a scene/anecdote *en détail* in each individual case.

Regardless of this aspect of the sources, it can be said that—as in real conversation and in the *Essais* by Montaigne—the speaking subject / author is allowed to digress and make mental excursions in order to loosen up the conversation: "Si faut-il que je face cette digression d'une femme mariée, belle et honneste."[68] Sometimes he calls himself to order when, with all the narrative insertions, he is

---

[56] Brantôme 1981, p. 42.

[57] Brantôme 1981, p. 89: "J'ay ouy faire ce compte à ma grand-mere, qui la disoit de bonne maison et belle femme"; p. 227: "à ce que j'ay dire à ma mère, qui estoit à la reine de Navarre et qui en sçavoit quelques secrets de ses Nouvelles s et qu'elle en estoit l'une des devisantes (= sous le nom d'Ennasuite, S. 227, Anm. 1),"; Marguerite de Navarre, L'Heptaméron, ed. Cazauran, Lefèvre 2000, cf. nouvelles IV, XIX, XXVII etc.; Lazard 1995, pp. 34 ff.

[58] Cf. Brantôme 1981, p. 147: "La premiere fois que fus en Italie"; see also p. 149, 151, etc.

[59] Balsamo 2007a, p. 148: "il combinait le fruit de nombreuses lectures, une large culture antique et moderne, la matière d'innombrables conversations et la connaissance directe ou par oui-dire des personnages évoquées."

[60] Brantôme 1981, p. 510.

[61] Brantôme 1981, p. 188.

[62] Brantôme 1981, p. 244.

[63] Brantôme 1981, pp. 64, 67, etc.

[64] Brantôme 1981, p. 243.

[65] Brantôme 1981, pp. 254, 642, etc.

[66] Brantôme 1981, p. 185.

[67] In the *Premier discours sur les dames qui font l'amour et leurs maris cocus* Brantôme takes over a delicate anecdote from the 48th novella of the collection of *Cent Nouvelles* (Les Dames galantes, p. 167).

[68] Brantôme 1981, p. 72.

in danger of losing the thread and fears that he may rightly be accused: "que je suis trop grand faiseur de digressions."[69] And almost reminiscent of the "alleure poétique, à sauts et à gambades" in the essay *De la vanité* by Montaigne, in which Montaigne confesses, «mon stile, et mon esprit, vont vagabondant de mesmes,»[70] Brantôme also uses the metaphor of the journey to characterize his way of representing: «Je me suis un peu là perdu et desvoyé; mais puisque ç'a esté à propos, il n'y a point de mal, et retourne à mon chemin.»[71]

It is a sophisticated conversation that Brantôme is having with the reader in written form. The author skillfully uses the possibilities of presenting thoughts discursively. Not everything has to be said, in delicate matters the gaps remain that the imagination of the recipient can fill in for itself. So Brantôme concludes a rather embarrassing histoire d'alcôve for the husband with the remark: "Ce conte est meilleur à se l'imaginer et representer qu'á l'escrire".[72] As in face-to-face communication, the speaker leaves it to the interlocutor to assess the facts: "Je vous laisse à penser si elle en devoit avoir blasme,"[73] Brantôme comments after a crude and future husband-injuring answer by a woman in a marital dispute. Sometimes the court chronicler doubts whether he is not talking too much, whether the somewhat delicate stories are not damaging his social reputation: "J'eusse fait ce discours plus ample de plusieurs exemples, mais je craignois que, pour estre trop lascif, j'en eusse encouru mauvaise reputation."[74]

Brantôme does not always say everything he knows: Out of consideration for the reputation of high-ranking personalities, he sometimes withholds the names of actors and locations.[75] He shows the utmost restraint in particular when it comes to members of the royal family, well aware[76] that for "les grands", the great ones, it is mainly important that scandals, which have indeed taken place, must under no circumstances be spread by gossip.[77] The courtier must know when and where to keep his mouth shut, solely for self-protection in the dangerous and mine-ridden milieu of the court, where one word too many can decide the career, or even the life, of the gentleman.[78]

---

[69] Brantôme 1981, p. 627.

[70] Montaigne 2007, De la vanité, Essais, III, 9, 1040 ff.

[71] Brantôme 1981, p. 543.

[72] Brantôme 1981, p. 75.

[73] Brantôme 1981, p. 109.

[74] Brantôme 1981, p. 287.

[75] Brantôme 1981, p. 91, 98, 153. A typical formulation can be found on p. 174: «J'ay ouy conter qu'en quelque endroit du monde (je ne le veux pas nommer), il y eut un mary …»

[76] Brantôme 1981, p. 96, 98 et al.

[77] Brantôme 1981, p. 123; on p. 442 Brantôme criticizes the widespread gossiping that prevails at the French royal court.

[78] "A lucky throw can lead to high esteem, a mistake can ruin the esteem—and with it the nobleman himself." Strosetzki 1978, p. 107.

Discretion and the ability to *dissimulatio*[79] are indispensable qualities that a courtier should possess. Brantôme perfectly masters the code of conduct of self-control and secrecy demanded in the sociable treatises on the court, which he skillfully adapts to his role as the all-knowing narrator in the text: "J'en sçay une milliasse de contes, mais je n'aurois jamais fait."[80] The author almost coquettishly confesses that he has such a wealth of amusing and daring stories at his disposal that he can no longer find his way out of this great narrative labyrinth.[81]

Brantôme is proud of his close contacts with the powerful people of his time. He knew all the French kings personally since the regency of Francis I., from Henry II., over Francis II., Charles IX., Henry III. and Henry IV. He enjoyed the sympathy of the "trois belles Marguerites"[82] and belonged to the closest circle of Catherine de Médicis. He went in and out of the room and antechamber of the queen and later the influential queen widow.[83] He accompanied the "Reine blanche" on her travels and particularly likes to remember intimate encounters, such as the private visit to the court painter Claude Corneille in Lyon[84] or the joint boat trip on the Gironde from Blaye to Bourg.[85] In the *Vies des Dames galantes* there is also the later often circulated story of the "fessée" of the court ladies, which Catherine applied herself.[86] In general, the memoir writer assesses the behavior of the queen rather mildly and understanding,[87] he defends numerous of her actions, which are still controversial among historians today, and absolves her from responsibility for the massacre of the Bartholomew's Night.[88]

---

[79] Cf. Strosetzki 1997, p. 145.

[80] Brantôme 1981, p. 107, p. 122.

[81] Brantôme 1981, p. 181: «Il est temps que je m' arreste dans ce grand discours du cocuage: car enfin mes longues paroles, tournoyées dans ces profondes eaux et ces grands torrents, seroyent noyées; et n' aurois jamais fait, n'y n'en sçaurois jamais sortir, non plus que d'un grand labyrinthe qui fut autresfois, encor j'eusse le plus long fillet du monde pour guide et sage conduite.»

[82] Ronsard plays in the «Bergerie» (Edition Paris 1565, S. 29v) on Marguerite d'Angoulême (or de Navarre), Marguerite de France (Tochter Francois I) and Marguerite de Valois an:
«Que dirons nous encor France de tes merites?
C'est toy qui as nourry trois belles Marguerites.»
In the later Edition 1584 he corrects the passage in: "C'est toy qui a nourry deux belles Marguerites". Vgl. Ronsard *Ouevres complètes* II 1994, S. 163; Kommentar, S. 1352: «Les trois Marguerites de 1565 sont devenues deux: Ronsard corrige l 'erreur de la première version où Margot (Marguerite de Valois) faisait son propre éloge à la troisième personne!»

[83] Brantôme, dedicates Catherine the second Discours in the *Recueil des Dames,Sur la reyne, mere de nos roys derniers*, Catherine de Médicis, p. 27 ff.; Lazard 1995, S. 273 ff.

[84] Brantôme 1991, I, 2, p. 34; Cocula-Vallières, p. 328.

[85] Brantôme 1991, I, 2, S. 56.

[86] Brantôme 1981, S. 269.

[87] Brantôme 1981, S. 222.

[88] Vgl. das Kapitel XV Regard de Brantôme sur la Saint-Barthélemy, Vaucheret 2010, pp. 235–245, p. 239; Lazard 1995, p. 131 ff.

Brantôme was present at many significant events of the epoch: At the death of Charles IX he was also in Vincennes,[89] he took part in the siege of La Rochelle,[90] Coligny, the leader of the Huguenots, stayed in his abbey.[91] Although he had been entrusted with important diplomatic missions, he did not belong to the first rank of political actors, and his self-image as a "petit compagnon"[92] probably hits the nail on the head: he was more observer than actor on the political stage of his time. However, the wealth of impressions, conversations and encounters at court made him "un peintre remarquable des moeurs de son temps"[93] Not without reason has Brantôme been characterized as a "petit Saint-Simon du XVIe siècle"[94].

It is a dark picture of the court of the Valois, which Brantôme draws in the *Vies des Dames galantes*;[95] even for the modern reader it becomes clear which brutality lies hidden under the varnish of courtoise. Intrigues, slander, rape, murder are omnipresent—the highest representatives of the state participate in incredible acts of violence, of which the "noces vermeilles"[96] on 24 and 25 August 1572 in Paris are only the best known events.[97] It is enough to remember what happened in December 1588: On the day before Christmas, Henri de Guise is murdered in the royal apartments in Blois on the orders of Henry III.,[98] and his body is burned in the fireplace, the next day his brother Cardinal Louis II de Guise is stabbed to death in prison. Henri de Navarre, the future King Henry IV., describes this oppressive atmosphere in January 1576 in an impressive way:

> "The court is the strangest you have ever seen. We are almost always ready to cut each other's throats. We carry daggers, breastplates and often the cuirass under the cape."[99]

---

[89] Lazard 1995, p. 149: "The king died on May 30, 1574, Pentecost Day. Brantôme speaks as an eyewitness."

[90] Brantôme 1981, p. 626: "at La Rochelle, the first time we entered the ditch". Lazard 1995, pp. 135 ff.

[91] Lalanne 1896, p. 151.

[92] Brantôme speaks of himself in the formulation "Nous autres petitz compaignons" in: Œuvres complètes, tom. VII, p. 76; Lalanne 1896, p. 226; Cocula-Vaillières 1986 p. 336.

[93] Vaucheret 2010, p. 16.

[94] Perche 1963, p. 62.

[95] Lazard 1995, pp. 145 ff. (Chapter XI: Brantôme at the court of the Valois).

[96] Erlanger 1960, p. 130.

[97] Brantôme 1981, pp. 58, 557, 559, pp. 620 et seq.

[98] Montaigne enters this event in his copy of the *Ephemeris historica* by Michael Beuther on 23 December. Legros 2010, p. 98.

[99] Henri IV to my Cousin Monsieur de Miossens, January 1576, Recueil, 1843, p. 81.

Brantôme is a careful chronicler of these events, which he meticulously and often amusingly records, while at the same time trying not to expose himself too much as a person. Cautious and discreet, he keeps out of controversial controversies; several times he emphasizes that one does not know which position is the right one. The initially told adultery story of a foreign prince told in the style of *Decameron* culminated in the murder of the faithless wife. The question of the guilt of the murderer leaves Brantôme open and closes the comedy, which, according to his words, ends in a tragedy,[100] with the remark: "Others will excuse him, others will accuse him; there are many pieces and reasons to report about this:"[101] True to the promise of objectivity, which he gave at the beginning of the *Receuil* he also notes: "I rely on the moods and speeches that those of the one and the other party can hold in this."[102] Through the often comprehensible dating and the precise localization of the piquant anecdotes, which took place in the room escapes of the Louvre, in hidden boudoirs, in inconspicuous, remote places in front of the fireplace or windows in the apartments of the kings, in the alleys of the parks, the authenticity of what is reported is emphasized and the stories gain in color and the reader more fascinating liveliness.

In his portrayal of the "mysteries of the court,"[103] the memoirist[104] addresses recipients who are familiar with the customs of court life. With the remark, "Ceux qui entendent l'histoire m'entendent bien,"[105] he concludes his report on a private performance à huis clos in the Louvre, at which high-ranking members of the court had participated. He addresses himself expressly to the "lecteur curieux,"[106] the curious reader of unusual stories. The female readers form the preferred target group.[107] At the end of the *Recueils*, next to the beginning pages of a text the exposed position in the semiotics of the book, which once again concentratedly stimulates the attention of the recipients, Brantôme addresses his female readers with the following words:

> "Now, ladies, I am finished; and excuse me if I have said anything that offends you. I was never born or raised to offend or displease you."[108]

---

[100] Brantôme 1981, p. 95: "Ce qu'ayant bien au vray cogneu, tourna et changea sa commedie en tragedie."

[101] Brantôme 1981, p. 95.

[102] Brantôme 1981, p. 29.

[103] Montaigne, De la vanité, Essais, III, 9, p. 1032.

[104] Jouanna 2013, p. 88; also Vaucheret 2010, p. 44.

[105] Brantôme 1981, p. 519.

[106] Brantôme 1981, p. 223.

[107] Bauschatz 2003.

[108] Brantôme 1981, p. 674.

Although the author tells very lewd and suggestive anecdotes in the *Vies des Dames galantes* and is not averse to detailed descriptions of normally hidden female body parts, he still spare the chaste ears of his female readers from obscene or dirty stories: "Il m'en fit un autre compte, le plus plaisant qu'il est possible,... mais, d'autant qu'il est trop sallaud, je m'en tairay, de peur d'offenser les oreilles chastes"[109]. If the punchline of a story could not avoid mentioning repulsive sexual practices "contre l'ordre de nature"[110], the author would switch to Latin and translate the offensive passages—"toutes ces formes et postures odieuses à Dieu"[111]— not: "J'ay mis cecy en latin sans le traduire en françois, car il sonne très-mal à les oreilles bien honnestes et chastes. Abominables qu'ilz sont!"[112]

The phenomenon of sexuality in almost all its variations takes up a large, indeed disproportionate, amount of space in Brantôme's stories.[113] The chronicler's attitude to this topic is ambivalent, on the one hand he vehemently defends the court at Paris against the accusation of being a den of iniquity[114] and goes so far as to claim that at the court of our kings, "(à) la cour de nos rois ... la vertu y habite aussi bien, voir mieux, qu'en tous autres lieux".[115] On the other hand, he praises almost enthusiastically "cette belle liberté françoise"[116], which knows hardly any limits. Starting from the self-evident premise for the mentality of the early modern nobility itself that the great ones at court—and only their behavior interests the author[117]—more is allowed than the members of the lower classes,[118] adultery stories are spread out in detail with pleasure from the perspective of the voyeur. The view through the keyhole, through the hole drilled in the wall, is the preferred narrator's perspective.[119] The first discourse is devoted exclusively to the

---

[109] Brantôme 1981, p. 79, this is a story told by the chevalier de Sanzay, who was known for his obscene stories; see also passages on p. 192 and p. 219.

[110] Brantôme 1981, p. 176.

[111] Brantôme 1981, p. 67.

[112] Brantôme 1981, p. 176.

[113] With some justification, Lazard 1995, p. 219 ff. speaks of the "Le rapport Kinsey du XVIe siecle."

[114] Brantôme 1981, p. 177 ff.: "Or il faut que je die une mauvaise opinion que plusieurs ont eue et ont encore de la cour de nos rois."

[115] Brantôme 1981, p. 178.

[116] Brantôme 1981, p. 186: "Moreover, this beautiful French freedom, which is more to be valued than anything."

[117] Brantôme 1981, p. 219; Lalanne 1896, p. 250.

[118] Brantôme 1981, p. 658 "I do not want to talk about vile people, nor about fields, nor about cities, because such was not my intention to write about, but about the great, for whom my pen is full."

[119] Cocula-Vaillières 1986, p. 365: "Everything is good to pass the time. The holes that are made through partitions and doors to catch conversations or surprise the antics of others."

"maris cocus". Under the leading perspective of our conference, to analyze what is actually sayable in early modern sociability, one can state that actually almost everything is sayable in this "vieille Cour", as already the sociability theorists of a later epoch—for example Ortigue de Vaumorière[120]—called the court of the Valois distantly. There are more than clear references to the "mignons" in the circle of friends of Henry III.,[121] it is openly spoken of the love "donna con donna"[122], there are obscene comments on the *genital parts* of both sexes[123] and maliciously it is reported from the results of a search of the luggage of her ladies-in-waiting ordered by Catherine for hidden weapons, in which instead of pistols and daggers were found to the mockery of the court several Godemichés. To increase the scandalous effect of the report even further, Brantôme dryly remarks: "I cognois the damoiselle; je croy qu'elle vit encores, mai elle n'eut jamais bon visage.[124] There are always subtle signals of rejection of sodomy;[125] with clear words incest is—"l'amour illicite de ses proches"[126]—rejected as inadmissible.

Without a doubt one can speak of a "manière quelque peu salace"[127] when faced with the lewd formulations with which Brantôme describes a particularly repulsive experiment with which a high representative of the royal family—"un prince de par le monde"[128]—delights the male spectators in his company. The prince, probably the Duc d'Alençon, the great patron of our author, possessed a valuable drinking cup made of gilded silver, on which a goldsmith had engraved the sex positions according to Arentino on the inside and outside. As an eyewitness, Brantôme then reports:

> «Quand ce prince festinoit les dames et filles de la cour, comme souvent il les convioit, ses sommelliers ne failloyent jamais, par son commandement, de leur bailler à boire dedans.»[129]

The girls were forced to drink from this cup, and then minutely Brantôme describes their reactions, which ranged from embarrassment, shy blushing, coquettish agreement to the frivolous participation in this obscene 'social game'. All

---

[120] Ortigue de Vaumorière 1668, p. 21.

[121] Brantôme 1981, p. S. 353; Cocula-Vallières 1986, p. 373.

[122] Brantôme 1981, p. 187: "and doing what they say donna con donna (imitating the learned Sappho lesbian)."

[123] Brantôme 1981, p. 256, p. 542.

[124] Brantôme 1981, p. 196.

[125] Brantôme 1981, p. 175 f.

[126] Brantôme 1981, p. 101.

[127] Vaucheret 2010, p. 261.

[128] Brantôme 1981, p. 62 ff.

[129] Brantôme 1981, p. 63.

these "sallaudaries"[130] took place to the amusement of the completely uninhibited spectators—by the way of both sexes "gentilhommes et dames ainsi à table,"[131]-. Over several pages Brantôme indulges in this experimental arrangement and shares his voyeuristic impressions with the readers and readerines:

> "as I have seen, that it was a very pleasant frolic, and something to see and hear; but above all, to my taste, the best and most was to contemplate these innocent girls, or who pretended to be, and other ladies newly arrived, to hold their cold, smiling countenance, or to constrain themselves and make hypocrites, as many ladies did likewise."[132]

Pietro Aretino's works[133] form, next to Boccaccio's *Decameron* and the *Heptaméron* of Marguerite de Navarre[134] the main source for burlesque-obscene stories in the *Vies des Dames galantes*. In spicy anecdotes Brantôme describes the seductive effects of the "figures de l'Aretin"[135] and he even names the name of the Venetian bookseller—Bernardin Turissan a relative of the famous Aldus Manutius—in the Rue Saint-Jacques in Paris, where you could buy the *Sonetti lussuriosi*.[136] Sufficiently, he quotes the information of the Italian, that single and married men, yes, even women belonged to the buyers of the book, which was immediately forbidden by the papal censorship after its appearance, and he finds it particularly noteworthy that three noble and well-known ladies of the court "trois de par le monde, grandes, que je nommeray point" had procured this erotic cult book of the Renaissance.[137] Brantôme knows of the danger that arises for female readers from reading pornographic books, the stimulating effect of which is increased by illustrations. Over several pages, he describes in the sixth discourse how the joint reading and viewing of works in the style of *Ragionamenti* leads court ladies into ecstasy, which can even end in a "terrible esvanouissement".[138] The dangers are vividly portrayed that can arise for young girls when reading Ovid's *Ars amandi* or the Amadis novels: "Combien de filles estudiantes se sont perdues lisant ceste histoire".[139] Brantôme warns particularly impressively—no

---

[130] Brantôme 1981, p. 63.
[131] Brantôme 1981, p. 64.
[132] Brantôme 1981, p. 64.
[133] Brantôme 1981, pp. 60 ff.
[134] Brantôme 1981, p. 97, p. 174, 658; p. 500: "the venerable and docte Bocasse"; p. 516: "According to the order of Boccace, our guide in this discourse (= II, 4 Discourse on married women, widows and daughters)"
[135] Brantôme 1981, p. 61.
[136] Brantôme 1981, p. 67.
[137] Brantôme 1981, p. 67.
[138] Brantôme 1981, p. 487.
[139] Brantôme 1981, p. 534 f.

doubt with Abelard's well-known case in mind—of the potential seducers who, by profession, come close to the young girls, the teachers or readers, and illustrates his admonition with a story of an "faiseur de leçons" seduced "grande dame" at the court of Henry III.[140]

The alterity of early modern mentality to modern concepts is nowhere as pronounced as in the representation of women. The chosen metaphors to characterize the physical charms or deficiencies of a lady are clearly chosen from the male perspective. Noblewomen are compared to racehorses or mares,[141] depending on their age they remind one of green or dried up vegetation.[142] The following folly by Brantôme is quoted affirmatively:

> "And, as an honest man said, that a woman resembled several animals, and primarily a monkey, when in bed all she does is move and stir around."[143]

Women are fortresses that need to be stormed.[144] Word games that equate the female body with buildings are very popular: Just as in architecture, beautiful columns usually have magnificent cornices, so, in the case of Madame de Fontaine-Chalandray, "belles jambes, beaux visages" are promised.[145] The physical attractiveness of older ladies below "de la ceinture"[146] is obscenely compared to ancient ruins, on which new buildings can be erected,[147] just as tasteless is the explanation that one can tack new and magnificent galley ships onto the wreck of a ship's hull.[148] Comparisons of women with culinary delights are not uncommon, they are *un bon morceau, une sauce, une bonne viande, une friandise*[149] etc.

Even today, one of the most disgusting events during wartime is the crime of rape. Plundering and rape were commonplace during the religious wars in France: several passages show that Brantôme considered these excesses to be obviously unavoidable and did not condemn them, on the contrary, he even reports them with an unbearable irony.[150] It is not comprehensible for a modern reader how the victim of rape, told by Brantôme without emotion or compassion, reacted. After the

---

[140] Brantôme 1981, p. 536 f.

[141] Brantôme 1981, p. 51, p. 330; Cocula-Vaillières 1986, p. 459.

[142] Brantôme 1981, p. 547.

[143] Brantôme 1981, p. 52.

[144] Brantôme 1981, p. 93.

[145] Brantôme 1981, p. 300. This refers to Claude Blosset, daughter of Jean Blosset and Anne de Cugnac, "dite la belle Torcy," p. 258, n. 1.

[146] Brantôme 1981, p. 311.

[147] Brantôme 1981, p. 324.

[148] Brantôme 1981, p. 324: "I have often seen beautiful galleys and ships being built and rebuilt on old bodies and old keels."

[149] Brantôme 1981, p. 528; further evidence can be found in Cottrell 1970, p. 54.

[150] Cocula-Vaillières 1986, p. 63.

violatio, the victim asks a priest whether she has sinned; when he grants her absolution, the victim states quite calmly: "Dieu donc soit loué, que je m'en suis une fois en ma vie saoulée, sans pecher ni offencer Dieu."[151] Montaigne tells the same story with the almost identical quote of the woman in the famous essay *Coustume de l'´sle de Cea*.[152] It is now highly enlightening for the different positions of both authors that in Montaigne's case the event is commented on in a distancing way: «A la verité ces cruautez ne sont pas dignes de la douceur Françoise.»[153]

The main goal of the Causeries is to entertain the court society through the telling of such daring stories,[154] mercilessly reported on the misfortune of the wretches who lose their reputation at court. Like the gallant of the mistress of Francis I, who, in order to save his life, hid himself in the fireplace when the Regent unexpectedly appeared. The "poor lover" has to watch silently, "that the king had done his business with the lady" and endure that the king then used the fireplace as a toilet.[155] One sees the "causer librement"[156] included in Brantôme's depiction of Rabelaisian coarseness; in the *Vies des dames galantes* sexual talk is not yet restricted and domesticated by norms and etiquette, which will discipline life at the court of Louis XIV a few generations later. Brantôme's *Recueil* shows that the *Gentilhomme* can actually talk about all topics, even daring anecdotes, in order to achieve cheerfulness and laughter at court—as long as they do not offend the sovereign. However, there are still limits in the field of politics and religion that must not be exceeded. Already in the *Cortegiano* the playing fields are marked out: Anecdotes without slipping into the ordinary are allowed "to recreate the minds of the audience, and induce them to feast and laughter,[157] but "faceti with little reverence for God" are taboo.[158]

---

[151] Brantôme 1981, p. 58.

[152] Montaigne Essais, II, 3, p. 376: «Dieu soit loué, disoit-elle, qu'au moins une fois en ma vie, je m'en suis soulée sans peché.»

[153] Montaigne Essais, II, 3, p. 376.

[154] Lazard 1995, pp. 177 ff.: "Avoid boredom, that was the great concern of all this Court society, and conversation was one of the best ways to escape it."

[155] Brantôme 1981, pp. 660 ff.

[156] Brantôme 1981, p. 347: "to keep company with the Frenchwoman, to laugh, dance, play, talk freely."

[157] Quondam, p. XVIII. See the comments on the use of the Fazetien in the courtly conversation in the *Cortegiano* II,42, p. 182: "how we are to use the facetiae of which you have just made mention, and show the art that belongs to all this kind of pleasant talk, in order to induce laughter and feast with a gentle manner, because in truth it seems to me that it matters a lot and very much befits the courtier."

[158] *Il Cortegiano* II, 68, p. 217: "And therefore these people, who want to show that they are faceti with little reverence for God, deserve to be driven out of the company of every gentleman."

Even for the French theorists of behaviorism, blasphemous narratives form an absolute taboo. Especially in the extremely tense atmosphere of the religious war, which reaches its fearful climax in the "massacre de la Sainct-Barthelemy"[159], they are not allowed to blaspheme or mock religious topics. Brantôme, who—like Montaigne—always understood himself as a loyal follower of "de 'Église Catholique Apostolique et Romaine"[160], does not conceal his aversion to the new religion—"la relligion refformée"[161]—which, in his eyes, endangers the state order.[162] The nobleman from the Perigord, who also counts Protestant personalities among his friends,[163] refrains from the then customary hatred speeches against the Huguenots. The partisan of the Guise never rose to the level of extermination fantasies like Henry III., who once promised to "exterminate this miserable religion that does us so much harm."[164] Brantôme rarely takes part in the dissemination of evil rumors against the followers of Calvin and Luther in this time full of aggressive pamphlets. This reserve is clearly visible in an episode related in the first discourse. Since the time of the first Christians, it has been part of the popular technique of defamation to accuse the members of the new faith of sexual excesses during their cult. Brantôme also spreads such a story when he reports about nocturnal Huguenot services in Paris in the Rue Saint-Jacques at the time of Henry II., which allegedly ended in the physical devotion of the brothers and sisters after the extinguishing of the candles. However, the author does not seem to be convinced of the truthfulness of these orgies himself, because he concludes the report with the rather distancing remark: "ce que je n'oserois bonnement asseurer, encor qu' on m'asseurast qu'il estoit vray; mais possible que cela est pur mensonge et imposture."[165]

Christoph Strosetzki has established in his dissertation that "politics in absolutist systems is a delicate conversation topic"[166]. This is especially true for the time of the civil wars, "les troubles,"[167] in which the events sometimes overlapped in monthly cycles and main protagonists suddenly changed positions. Very quickly, the courtier could find himself on the wrong side, so it was advisable to hold

---

[159] Brantôme 1981, p. 58.

[160] Montaigne, Des prieres, Essais I, 56, p. 335.

[161] Brantôme 1981, p. 633.

[162] Brantôme 1981, pp. 558 f.

[163] Brantôme was friends with François de Noue and with Charles de Théligny, Coligny's son-in-law. (Cocula-Vaillières 1986, pp. 251 f.)

[164] Marguerite de Valois quotes in her memories (1971 and 1986, p. 107) a passage from a conversation with her brother, Henry III.: "Je veux faire la guerre aux huguenots, et exterminer cette miserable religion qui nous fait tant de mal.»

[165] Brantôme 1981, p. 161.

[166] Strosetzki 1978, p. 46.

[167] Brantôme speaks of the religious wars as "les troubles" like Montaigne. Les Dames galantes, p. 367; Montaigne, *Journal de voyage*, ed. Rigolot 1992, p. 3.

back on political statements in conversation. Even at the end of the 17th century, in the meantime prevailing pacification of the conditions, a certain helplessness of the conversation theorists can be felt, as when Ortigue de Vaumorière in *L'art de plaire dans la conversation* lets the protagonist Lisidor ask somewhat helplessly what one could still talk about at the court, since apparently conversations about science, social life, military events or politics in general were not desired.[168] Scandals at the court, which are generally known, are only mentioned in a veiled way in the *Vies des Dames galantes*. Great excitement was caused in 1575 by the murder of Louis de Berenger, Sieur du Guast, one of the favorites of Henry III., by Baron de Viteaux.[169] It was an open secret that the perpetrator acted on the orders of Marguerite de Valois. None of this background is mentioned by Brantôme; he speaks of the deceased Herr von Guast in a downplaying way when he mentions the many adventures he spent together with his friend.[170]

The attempt at camouflage is clearly visible in the report on the unfortunate end of Joseph de Boniface, seigneur de La Molle, and Annibal, comte de Coconato, the two lovers of Marguerite de Valois and the Duchesse de Nevers, who were decapitated on the Place de Grève on April 30, 1574, on suspicion of conspiracy against the Duc d'Anjou.[171] When Brantôme describes the excessive grief of the lovesick princesses, who had the bodies of the executed transported in their coaches and had the heads embalmed[172], he mentions, without naming them, "two beautiful and honest ladies, who, having lost their servants in a war fortune."[173] Given the prominence of the affected ladies, it was more opportune to speak of noblemen fallen in war than of rebels beheaded. Although Brantôme assures us that it is his intention to tell stories "in all truth and without dissimulation"[174], the reader repeatedly comes across such camouflage of delicate events, about which one better not speak at court.

In the *Vies des Dames galantes* we at least catch a glimpse and in fragmentary form the course of the conversation in the centers of power at the time of the Valois. Brantôme moves with great caution in this confusing and dangerous

---

[168] Ortigue de Vaumoriére: On the question of Lisidor: "Quoy, Monsieur, it is not necessary to talk about Science, nor about what concerns the Palace, War, or Politics in the Conversations that we hear?" Dorante answers rather evasively: "Far from banning the matters you say, they serve to sustain the Conversation, & to make it more instructive. The Palace itself has Causes of éclat that provide entertainment for the best Companies. There are great substitutions, contested marriages, & separations whose subjects make many people moralize, & say pleasantries by many others. However, one became importunate, if, in order to be admired, one entered into the detail of an important subject, & that one did not want to talk about anything else all day." p. 6.

[169] Lazard 1995, pp. 162-163.

[170] Brantôme 1981, p. 119: "Feu M. de Gua".

[171] Lazard 1995, pp. 148 ff.

[172] Lazard 1995, p. 148.

[173] Brantôme 1981, p. 127.

[174] Brantôme 1981, p. 643.

environment between *violence* and *plaisir*,[175] in which the only constant is the inconstant. This feeling of insecurity—the "branle public"[176] with the words of Montaigne—decisively shapes the form of the conversation, depending on the awareness of the conversation partners, what, when, where and in which company can be said. Not surprisingly, one of the outstanding actresses of this epoch, Marguerite de Valois, compares the court to Proteus, the mythical figure who, like hardly any other, stands for unpredictable change and surprising transformation: "as the court is a Prothée who changes shape at every hour, always arriving there with new things."[177]

References

Quellen

Brantôme, Pierre Bourdeille de: Œuvres complètes de Pierre de Bourdeille, seigneur de Brantôme, publiées d'après les manuscrits avec variantes et fragments inédits pour la Société de l'histoire de France par Ludovic Lalanne. Paris: Jules Renouard 1864–1882.

Brantôme, Pierre Bourdeille de: Les Dames galantes. Texte établi et annoté par Pascal Pia. Préface de Paul Morand. Paris: Gallimard 1981 (= Collection folio classique).

Brantôme, Pierre Bourdeille de: Recueil des Dames, poésies et tombeaux. Édition établie, présentée et annotée par Étienne Vaucheret. Paris: Gallimard 1991 (= Bibliothèque de la Pléiade).

Pierre Bourdeille de Brantôme: Das Leben der galanten Damen. Grimma 1850, Repr. Berlin: Contumax 2010.

Castiglione, Baldassar: Il libro del Cortegiano. Introduzione di Amedeo Quondam. Note di Nicola Longo. Milano: Garzanti 2000.

Marguerite de Navarre: L'Heptaméron des nouvelles. Édition présentée et annotée par Nicole Cazauran. Texte établi par Sylvie Lefèvre. Paris: Gallimard 2000 (= Collection folio classique).

Marguerite de Valois; Mémoires et autres écrits. La reine Margot. Édition établie, présentée et annotée par Yves Cazaux. Paris: Mercure de France 1971 et 1986.

Montaigne, Michel de: Journal de voyage. Édition présentée, établie et annotée par François Rigolot. Paris: Presses universitaires de France 1992.

Montaigne, Michel de: Les Essais. Édition établie par Jean Balsamo, Michel Magnien et Catherine Magnien-Simonin. Édition des «Notes de Lectures» et des «Sentences peintes» établie par Alain Legros. Paris: Gallimard 2007 (= Bibliothèque de la Pléiade).

Ortigue de Vaumorière, P. de: L'art de plaire dans la conversation, Paris 1688.

Recueil des Lettres missives de Henri IV publié par. M. Berger de Xivrey, Tome I, 1562–1584. Paris: Imprimerie Royale 1843.

Ronsard: Elegies, mascarades et bergerie... A Paris, Chez Gabriel Buon, au clos Bruneau à l'enseigne S. Claude. 1565.

---

[175] So succinctly Cocula-Vaillières, p. 357: "in a court where violence and pleasure are combined."

[176] Montaigne: Du repentir. Essais III, 2, p. 844.

[177] Marguerite de Valois 1971 and 1986, p. 134.

Ronsard: Œuvres complètes II. Édition établie, présentée et annotée par Jean Céard, Daniel Ménager et Michel Simonin. Paris: Gallimard 1994 (= Bibliothèque de la Pléiade).

Forschungsliteratur

Adam, Wolfgang (Hg.) zus. mit Knut Kiesant, Winfried Schulze und Christoph Strosetzki: Geselligkeit und Gesellschaft im Barockzeitalter. 2 Bände. Wiesbaden: Harrasowitz 1997 (= Wolfenbütteler Arbeiten zur Barockforschung 28).
Adam, Wolfgang und Markus Fauser in Verb. mit Ute Pott: Geselligkeit und Bibliothek. Lesekultur im 18. Jahrhundert. Göttingen: Wallstein 2005 (= Schriften des Gleimhauses 4).
Albert, Mechthild: Unterhaltung, Gespräch, in: Karlheinz Barck, Martin Funtius et al.: Ästhetische Grundbegriffe. Stuttgart und Weimar: Metzler 2005, Bd. 6, S. 260–281.
Alewyn, Richard und Karl Sälzle: Das große Welttheater. Die Epoche der höfischen Feste in Dokument und Deutung. Reinbeck: Rowohlt 1959.
Balsamo, Jean 2007 Brantôme (Pierre de Bourdeille, abbé de) in: Philippe Desan Eds Dictionnaire de Montaigne, Nouvelle édition revue, corrigée et augmentée Honoré Champion Éditeur Paris p. 147f
Bauschatz, Cathleen, M.: «Le plaisir du texte» dans les Dames galantes de Brantôme, in: Isabelle Brouard-Arends (Hg.), Lectrices d'Ancien Régime (online). Rennes: Presses universitaires de Rennes 2003.
Becker-Cantarino, Barbara: Frauenzimmer Gesprächspiele. Geselligkeit, Frauen und Literatur im Barockzeitalter, in: Wolfgang Adam et al.: Geselligkeit und Barockzeitalter, t. I, p. 17–41.
Beetz, Manfred: Frühmoderne Höflichkeit. Komplimentierkunst und Gesellschaftsrituale im altdeutschen Sprachraum. Stuttgart: Metzler 1990.
Beetz, Manfred: Leitlinien und Regeln der Höflichkeit für Konversation, in: Wolfgang Adam et al.: Geselligkeit und Gesellschaft im Barockzeitalter, t. II, pp. 563–579.
Bray, Bernard und Christoph Strosetzki: Art de la lettre. Art de la conversation à l'époque classique en France. Paris: Klincksieck 1995.
Chartier, Roger: Civilité, in: Handbuch politisch-sozialer Grundbegriffe in Frankreich, 1680–1820. Heft 4, München: Oldenburg 1986, p. 1–50.
Cavallini, Concetta: L'Italianisme de Michel de Montaigne. Préface de Giovani Dotoli. Fasano, Paris: Schena Editore, Presses de l'Université Paris-Sorbonne 2003.
Cocula-Vallières, Anne-Marie: Brantôme. Amour et gloire au temps de Valois. Paris: Albin Michel 1986.
Cottrell, Robert Druan: Brantôme. The writer as Portraitist of his age. Genf: Librairie Droz 1970.
De Piaggi, Giorgio: Les Voyages de Brantôme en Italie, in: Annales de la Faculté des lettres et sciences humaines d'Aix-en-Provence 40, 1966, p. 79–116.
Desan, Philippe: Montaigne. Une biographie politique. Paris: Odile Jacob 2014.
Dumoulin de Laplante P.: Brantôme et Montaigne, in: BSAM 9, 1974, p. 47–56.
Erlanger, Philippe: Le massacre de la Saint-Barthélemy. Paris: Gallimard 1960.
Fauser, Markus: Das Gespräch im 18. Jahrhundert. Rhetorik und Geselligkeit in Deutschland. Stuttgart: M und P, Verlag für Wissenschaft und Forschung 1991.
Göttert, Karl-Heinz: Kommunikationsideale. Untersuchungen zur europäischen Konversationstheorie. München: Fink 1988.
Grewe, Andrea: L'historiographie des femmes. L'exemple de Brantôme, in: L'histoire en marge à la Renaissance. Cahier V.L. 19 Saulnier 19, 2002, p. 113–127.
Hellegouarc'h, Isabelle: L'art de la conversation. Paris: Garnier 1997.
Henn-Schmölders, Claudia: Ars conversationis. Zur Geschichte des sprachlichen Umgangs, in: Arcadia 10, 1975, p. 15–33.
Im Hof, Ulrich: Das gesellige Jahrhundert. Gesellschaft und Gesellschaften im Zeitalter der Aufklärung. München: Beck 1982.

Jouanna, Arlette: Brantôme, in: Arlette Jouanna et al.: Histoire et Dictionnaire des Guerres de Religion. Paris: Robert Laffont 1998, p. 738–740.
Jouanna, Arlette: Montaigne. Paris: Gallimard 2017.
Lalanne, Ludovic: Brantôme. Sa vie et ses écrits. Paris: Librairie Renouard 1896.
Landy-Houillon, Isabelle: Lettre et oralité, in: Bray und Strosetzki: Art de la lettre, p. 81–91.
Lazard, Madeleine: Pierre de Bourdeille, Seigneur de Brantôme. Paris: Fayard 1995.
Legros, Alain: Montaigne manuscrit. Paris: Classiques Garnier 2010.
Montandon, Alain: Les bienséances de la conversation, in: Bray und Strosetzki; Art de la lettre, p. 61–79.
Mourey, Marie-Thérèse: Le corps en spectacle. Danser dans le Saint-Empire (XVIe-XVIIIe siècle). Berlin: Frank & Timme 2020 (= Cadences—Schriften zur Tanz- und Musikgeschichte 4).
Omont, Henri: Notice sur les manuscrits originaux et autographes des Œuvres de Brantôme. Conservés à la Bibliothèque Nationale, in: Bibliothèque de l'école des chartes 65, 1904, p. 5–54.
Perche, Louis: Brantôme. XXe siècle. Textes choisis et commentés. Limoges: Rougerie 1963.
Peter, Emanuel: Geselligkeiten. Literatur, Gruppenbildung und kultureller Wandel im 18. Jahrhundert. Tübingen: Max Niemeyer Verlag 1999 (=Studien zur deutschen Literatur 153).
Reichenberger, Kurt: Pierre de Bourdeille, Sieur de Brantôme, in: Walter Jens (Hg.): Kindlers Neues Literaturlexikon. München: Kindler 1989, t. 3, p. 48 f.
Strosetzki, Christoph: Konversation als Sprachkultur. Elemente einer historischen Kommunikationspraxis. Berlin: Frank & Timme 2013.
Strosetzki, Christoph: Die Norm und ihre Alternative in der Geselligkeitskultur des absolutistischen Frankreich, in: Wolfgang Adam et al.: Geselligkeit und Barockzeitalter, t. I, p. 135–153.
Strosetzki, Christoph: Konversation. Ein Kapitel gesellschaftlicher und literarischer Pragmatik im Frankreich des 17. Jahrhunderts. Frankfurt a .M. u. a.: Peter Lang 1978 (= Studia Romanica et Lingustica 7).
Till, Dietmar: Unterhaltung. 2. Gespräch, Konversation, in Reallexikon der deutschen Literaturwissenschaft. Hg. von Georg Braungart et al. Berlin, New York: De Gruyter 2003, t. 3, p. 730–733.
Vaucheret, Etienne: Montaigne, Brantôme et leur conception du `point d'honneur´, in: Montaigne et Henri IV (1595–1995). Textes réunis par Claude-Gilbert Dubois, Biarritz: Terres et Hommes du Sud 1996, p. 87–99.
Vaucheret, Etienne: Brantôme. Mémoraliste et conteur. Paris: Honoré Champion Éditeur 2010 (= Bibliothèque de la Renaissance 81).
Zeller, Rosmarie: Spiel und Konversation im Barock. Untersuchungen zu Harsdörffers Gesprächspielen. Berlin, New York: De Gruyter 1974 (= Quellen und Forschungen zur Sprach- und Kulturgeschichte der germanischen Völker 58).
Zeller, Rosmarie: Die Rolle der Frauen im Gesprächspiel und in der Konversation, in: Wolfgang Adam et al.: Geselligkeit und Gesellschaft im Barockzeitalter, I, p. 531–541.

"Et Lors Se Metent En Autres Paroles..." Changes of Subject in Literary Conversation

Corinne Denoyelle

Abstract

Literary dialogues, a fortiori in medieval literature, do not resemble our real conversations, in which we jump from one subject to another. Synthetic, usually organized around a single theme sequence, they aim for narrative efficiency rather than for any semblance of reality. Yet some texts give greater importance to a form of conversational sociability expressed through greater variability of conversation topics. In two 13th-century prose romances (Prose Lancelot and Prose Tristan), we observe how subjects are introduced and then changed. These two romances demonstrate remarkable awareness of such pragmatic questions and create dialogue stylistics that give a clear impression of liveliness and highlight the effects of the meaning at play in them.

Jumping from one subject to another, talking about this and that... such everyday expressions say a great deal about the flexibility with which theme sequences follow one another in ordinary conversations, according to participants' fancy or the agenda's requirements. Pragmatists define conversations as co-constructed verbal interactions composed of sequences of varying nature and organization. A sequence is "a series of exchanges connected by their semantic and/or pragmatic

---

This article takes up and develops ideas briefly touched upon in my thesis, Denoyelle 2010, pp. 110–126. This work was supported by the FFI2017-84404-P research Project "Enunciation and marks of orality in the diachrony of French" initiated by the Ministerio de Ciencia, Innovación y Universidades, Spain.

C. Denoyelle (✉)
Univ. Grenoble Alpes, CNRS, Litt & Arts, Grenoble, France
e-mail: Corinne.Denoyelle@univ-grenoble-alpes.fr

© The Author(s), under exclusive license to Springer-Verlag GmbH, DE, part of Springer Nature 2023
C. Strosetzki (ed.), *The Value of Conversation*,
https://doi.org/10.1007/978-3-662-67200-6_12

coherence".[1] It is therefore characterized by its semantic unity insofar as the exchanges that make it up refer to the same topic and its pragmatic unity in that they refer to a single transactional purpose, even if it is sometimes difficult for analysts to distinguish the limits of each sequence in a real conversation. A verbal interaction includes several sequences: at least one opening sequence, one or more sequences forming the body of the interaction, and a closing sequence. The two opening and closing sequences, which we will call *phatic,* are highly ritualized and aim to initiate contact between speakers and then make it socially acceptable. In contrast, the one or more specifically interactional sequences are characterized by their great freedom of form, length, and function. Hence, several sequences can follow each another in a conversation and present different topics, different forms of exchange and different concerns, providing participants with different discourse roles and modifying their hierarchical positions with respect to each other. Management of these sequences involves socially acquired conversational skills: introduction of the topic into the conversation, its negotiated evolution and its closure are all stages that require a capacity for judgment as to its pertinence in relation to the situational context (the time and place of utterance), cognitive context (the knowledge shared by the participants), discursive context (the conversation's co-text) and social context.[2]

Transposed to a literary dialogue, identification and analysis of the various conversation sequences can also be highly instructive in terms of the dialogues' design and relationships between characters. In literature, Sylvie Durrer[3] has shown that, most of the time, novel dialogues are only "fragments of interaction", presenting only one thematic sequence, or even only one exchange, in which discourse roles are maintained. Narrative constraints remodel the conversation's structure into a dialogue subject to the story's dramatic framework, in which it must have a function, either by engaging the characters in an action or by illustrating a situation. The phatic opening and closing exchanges are generally omitted unless the author is trying to highlight the significance of the social ritual underlying them or resemanticize them at an affective level. A single transactional sequence, focusing on one goal and one theme, generally constitutes the essential part of the dialogue. It is very rare for two conversation themes, i.e. two sequences, to follow one another.

Yet, as early as the Middle Ages, authors were sensitive to what was happening between individuals during and through conversation, and sought to represent more than its strictly informational content. The *Prose Lancelot* and the *Prose Tristan*, two lengthy 13th-century Arthurian romances recounting the loves, adventures, and encounters of King Arthur's knights in the forests of Logres and Cornwall, pay particular attention to human interactions as manifested in conversations. These two romances, and above all the *Tristan*, which Jean Larmat

---

[1] Kerbrat-Orecchioni 1998, p. 218.
[2] Berthoud et Mondada 1995, p. 205–228.
[3] Durrer 1994, p. 95.

described as "a manual of courtesy",[4] testify to their authors' awareness of the subtlety of the stakes at play in conversations, which they use in order to create likeable, nuanced characters. Although they usually use dialogues to engage the characters in action, (what, in pragmatic terms, we may refer to as conversations with external purposes), they also provide accounts of conversations with internal purposes, i.e. which have no other purpose than to please their participants. Reunions, vigils, discussion during a journey... the characters in these two romances are often portrayed laughing, joking, and playing conversation games. The authors are happy to present a generally peaceful, courteous, and joyful sociability, manifested in countless dialogues. These "internal purpose conversations" can also have important narrative functions, advancing the story, characterizing this or that character, amusing or moving the reader, or constructing the story's meaning, but such functions are played within a scene which, as far as the characters are concerned, has no other purpose than to share time together.

Although not sufficient to reflect the endless mutability characteristic of real conversations, the contrast between external purpose and internal purpose conversations is practical enough in literature when it comes to determining what drives a character to start speaking in the first place. External purpose conversations are used to "act in the affairs of the world"[5]; they are the type most commonly found in literature. They are oriented towards action both as regards their themes (in our medieval texts where war, jousts and politics predominate) and in their purpose: whether it is an enquiry, an order, or a request for information, what drives the characters to speak is essentially the need to act in the world and make others act. In contrast, as they are essentially gratuitous, internal purpose conversations have a much wider range of possible topics, at least in theory. As they are not constrained by the necessities of immediate action, they can wander from topic to topic at the characters' fancy. In medieval literature, internal purpose conversations do not generally amount to dialogue and are not considered worthy of dramatic interest. At best, they are relegated to the sidelines of narrative discourse or simply evoked from a distance, as is the case with Gauvain and Tristan conversing peacefully *"de joie et de soulas, d'aventures et de merveilles"*[6] *[of joy and solace, of adventures and marvels...],* usually without the reader knowing exactly what they are saying. But here, the great Arthurian prose cycles that are my subject of study shift their focus to the dialogues themselves, giving them a role at the romance's ideological and emotional level and providing their characters with an additional level of subtlety in order to develop their psychology. Seeking to represent interactional dynamics as fully as possible, these stories present dialogues that are as much about what is said as what remains unsaid and that show as much as they

---

[4] Larmat 1979.
[5] Coltier 1989.
[6] *Tristan* 2, p. 208.

tell. Not only do they describe the dialogues' conceptual and psychological framework, they also include it in the very fabric of conversational discourse.

Their narrative interest is manifested in consideration of the many instances of tension and negotiation that can take place within an interaction. The authors play on the metaconversational replies that aim to regulate exchanges: by introducing them into a literary dialogue modeled on a real conversation whose dynamics they try to reproduce, they show their sensitivity to perlocutionary effects, revealing the power relationships between the characters and making their dialogues seem natural. Use of pragmatic concepts will enable us to show the authors' stylistic and narrative choices. Their management of topics reveals interpersonal relationships as they structurally and narratively shape dialogical discourse. We shall observe it first of all with regard to the introduction of a topic and then for changes of topic.

1 Introducing the Topic

Selection and introduction of a topic depend on a clear understanding of cognitive, contextual, and social conditions. At cognitive and contextual level, the speaker who wishes to introduce a subject must weigh the subject's acceptability in relation to the knowledge shared by the various speakers and its relevance in the context. At social level, it is not everyone's place to take the initiative in introducing a subject, above all in a society as hierarchical as medieval feudal society: it requires undisputed discursive authority.

At court, it is obviously the king who introduces the conversation's subject and keeps it flowing by giving the floor to his various knights or guests. Only his greatest barons can take the initiative of introducing a topic. However, such authority does not allow the king to start the conversation in any way he happens to choose, as we can see in the extract from *Lancelot* below: the precautions he seems to take before he asks the Lady of Malehaut the reasons for her visit show that he takes account of the rules of politeness (preserving the territories of the self, the interlocutor's negative face). As the text makes clear, the lady has made a long journey to come to court. It also stresses the king's patience before questioning her. He only asks her the reasons for her visit indirectly, a delicacy that shows that his authority is not sufficient to enable him to address just any subject. The imperatives of polite behavior are taken fully into account in the work.

(1) Mout fist li rois de la dame grant feste, et la reine. Et la nuit, aprés soper, se furent asis an une couche, et dit li rois a la dame:

«Certes, dame, mout vos iestes efforciee, qui si loig de vostre terre iestes venue. Or voi ge bien que ce n'est mie sanz beoign car costumiere n'iestes vos mie de vostre païs si esloignier

– Certes, sire, fet ele, sanz besoig n'est ce mie, ainz est granz li affaires et si lo vos dira…»[7]

---

[7] *Lancelot* 1, p. 788.

> [The king and the queen welcomed the lady warmly. And that night, after supper, as they sat on a couch, the king said to the lady,
>
> "Certainly, my lady, you have made a great effort, you who have come so far away from your land. I can see that this is not without reason, because you are not used to being so far from your country
>
> – Certainly, my lord, it is not without reason. On the contrary, it is a matter of great concern and if I tell it to you…"]

Without the text needing to specify the fact, we sense that King Arthur is taking care not to address the matter of the lady's visit too early or too directly. Rather than asking her outright why she has come to court, he points out that her visit is exceptional and, implicitly, that it must therefore be motivated by an exceptional reason. The lady confirms the importance of her journey via an introductory sentence preliminary to her explanation, but such royal discretion favors her designs as she does not want to reveal the true motive behind her journey.

Likewise, at contextual level, the noble Galehaut waits for the right spatio-temporal framework before approaching the clerics King Arthur has sent to him on a subject close to his heart. He takes care not to be impolite by not asking any burning questions too soon:

> (2) Si est Galehoz plus liez qu'il ne fu mais puis qu'il antra an sa terre, car or set il bien qu'il a tex genz avoc lui qui bien li savront dire la verité de ce dont il estoit a malaise. Mais il nes en velt encor metre a raison, por ce que trop est tost, et crient que il l'an tenissent por vilain. Si suefre ansi tant que vint aprés mengier. Et quant les tables furent ostees, Galehoz se lieve et prant Lancelot par la main. Puis apele les clers toz, si les en maine an sa chambre et dit…[8]
>
> [If Galehaut is happier than he was before he entered his land, it is because now he knows that he has good people with him who can tell him the truth about what worries him. But he does not want to address it yet, because it is too early, and he fears that they will take him for a villain. So he waits patiently for them to finish eating. And when the tables are removed, Galehaut gets up and takes Lancelot by the hand. Then he calls all the clerics and takes them to his room and says…]

Galehaut invites the clerics in and lodges them with him; he holds a great feast for them but feels obliged to wait until the end of the meal before addressing the truly important subject in a more intimate setting.

Furthermore, at cognitive level, the speaker who introduces a subject must make sure that their addressee has the means to answer them. Dialogues therefore often begin with a brief negotiation in which a character explains why they are proposing this particular topic in this context and waits for their addressee to accept it. In this extract, for example, Guerrehet introduces a topic of conversation with a young woman by linking it to a previous conversation:

> (3) Lors resgarde la damoisele et li dist:
>
> "Damoisele, vos souvient il de la derrienne parole que vos me deistes?
>
> – Sire, fait ele, mes por quoi le dites vos?

---

[8] *Lancelot* 2, p. 603.

> – Jel di, fait il, por ce que se Diex me donnoit trover celui por cui la parole fu dite, je ne lairoie por le millor chastel que li rois mes oncles ait que je ne vos en fusse bon message."[9]

[So he looks at the damsel and says:

"Damsel, do you remember the last word you told to me?

– Sire, she says, but why do you say that?

– I ask it, he says, because if God allowed me to meet the one for whom this word was spoken, I would rather lose the best castle the king my uncle has than not be a messenger to you."]

This preliminary statement is challenged by the damsel, who questions its relevance in their situational context: "mes por quoi le dites vos?" [but why do you say that?]. Having to justify the topic, Guerrehet expands his statement, emphasizing it by doing so. In contrast, in the extract below, taken this time from the *Prose Tristan*, Brunor, the Knight with the Slashed Coat, takes malicious pleasure in linking his statement to their conversation history incompletely, so forcing his interlocutor, the Slanderous Damsel, to ask twice before she understands how it concerns her. He mocks her viciousness to Lancelot, who accompanied them incognito for a while:

> (4) Cil a la Cote Mautaillie, ki savoit tout certainnement que ce avoit esté Lanselos ki avoec aus avoit cevaucié et ki si durement s'aloit envers aus celant, parole et dist a la damoisele: "Damoisele, fait il, grant merveille est comment langhe de damoisele emprent sour soi si fol hardement qu'ele dist onques vilonie a cevalier qu'ele ne connoisse !
>
> – Por coi, fait ele, le dites vous ? L'avés vous dit pour vous ?
>
> – En non Dieu, damoisele, fait il, pour moi nel di je mie, anchois le di pour le meillour cevalier du monde, a qui vous desistes, n'a mie encore granment de tans, honte et vilonnie, plus que on ne deüst dire a un garchon. [...]
>
> – Quant fu ce, fait ele, que je ting parlement au meillor cevalier du monde ?
>
> – Dont ne vous souvient il, fait cil a la Cote Maltaillie, du cevalier ki avant ier cevaucha avoec nous, celui meïsmes ki faisoit son escu porter couvert d'une houce vermeille?
>
> – De celui, fait ele, me souvient il bien. Onques en toute ma vie ne vi un si vilain cevalier com il est ne si mesdisant. De la soie compaingnie me gart Diex, car je ne fui onques sans courous tant con je fui avoec lui! Mais pour coi le m'avés vous mis ore avant ?
>
> – Por ce, fait cil a la Cote Mautaillie, que je voel bien que vous sachiés que cil meïsmes de qui vous alés orendroit si durement mesdisant est li mieudres cevaliers du monde.[10]

---

[9] *Lancelot* 4, Micha, p. 23.
[10] *Tristan* 1, p. 105.

> [He, who knows for certain that it was Lancelot who rode with them and who were hiding his identity from them, says to the damsel,
>
> "Damsel", he says, "it is a great wonder how a damsel can hold such a foolish grudge against a knight she has never even met!"
>
> – Why do you say that? she says. Do you say it for yourself?
>
> – No, by God, damsel, he says, I do not say it for myself, I say it for the best knight in the all world, to whom you have said, not long ago, shameful and wicked things, more than one should say to a boy. […]
>
> – When was it, she says, that I spoke ill of the best knight in the world?
>
> – Don't you remember, he says to the damsel, the knight who rode with us yesterday, the very same one whose shield was covered with a red sleeve?
>
> – I remember him well. I have never in my life seen such a vile knight or one who speaks so badly. May God keep me from such company, for I was never without shame as long as I was with him! But why do you remind him of me now?
>
> – Because, he says to the damsel, I want you to know that the very one you were speaking so ill of is the best knight in the world."]

Brunor opens the conversation with a completely decontextualized gnomic statement. His assertion's impertinence in the conversational context pushes the damsel to ask for justification: "Por coi, fait ele, le dites vous ? L'avés vous dit pour vous ? [Why do you say that? she asks, Do you say it for yourself?]. He answers her by referring to their common conversational history, but in too vague a way for the reminder to situate the reference. When she asks for the third time, his answer is a little more specific, although he takes malicious pleasure in confusing her by never giving complete answers.

Speakers' rhetorical precautions testify to a necessary pragmatic consideration of their addressees: the person who is about to introduce a subject takes care not to offend their interlocutor with too direct, impertinent, or inappropriate questions in the context. Preliminary statements to the subject also not only make it possible to highlight the information that will follow but also to explain why it fits the social, cognitive, or situational context. These first examples show the narrators' attention to the conversational plausibility of their dialogues. Introduction of such questions and metaconversational statements constitutes as many "effects of reality" that also play on the relationships between characters.

Accepting the Proposed Subject
Although it is hard to imagine a character refusing a topic that King Arthur imposes on them, it can also be a delicate matter to propose a subject of conversation among peers. Any of the characters may have their topic refused by their interlocutor. Such refusal can lead to more insistent repetition, as in the example below where a young lady explains to Lancelot that she was subjected to violence by her husband because she refused to answer him when he asked her why she was staring at Lancelot:

(5) « Dame, molt avez anuit resgardé mon signor Lancelot. Se Diex vos aïst, dites moi qu'il vos en semble.

– Sire, fis je, no ferai, car vos m'en savriez mau gré.

– No ferai, fist il, vraiment le sachiez vos.»

Tant m'engoissa que je li respondi par courrouz:

« Certes, sire, puis qu'il vos plaist a oïr ce dont vos m'angoissiez, je le vos dirai par couvent que vous me façiez seur que mal ne m'en vendra.»

Il me creanta que no feroit il et le me fiança, et je estoie moult correcie de ce qu'il me tenoit si corte, si dis:

« Sire, volez vos que je die qu'il me samble de ce seingnor?

– Oïl, fait il.

– Certes, fis je, il me semble qu'il ait en lui tant de bien com il a an vos de mal ne qu'il ne devroit avoir tant d'onor com vos devez de honte. »[11]

["Lady, you have looked a great deal at my lord Lancelot at night. If God is with you, tell me what you think of him.

– Sire, I said, I will not, because you would be angry with me.

– I will not, he said, you know > I will not.

I was so worried that I answered him angrily,

"Certainly, sire, since it pleases you to hear what worries me, I will tell you if you swear that no harm will come to me."

He swore that he would do me no harm and pressed me, and I was so angry at his hurrying me that I said,

"Sire, do you want me to say what I think of this lord?

– Yes, he said.

– Certainly, I said, it seems to me that he has in him as much good as there is in you of evil and that he should not have as much honor as you should have of shame."]

In this extract, a young wife, caught in the act of gazing at the handsome Lancelot, refuses to talk about him to her husband: "Sire, fis je, no ferai, car vos m'en savriez mau gré." [I will not, because you would be angry with me], which forces him to repeat his order. She only agrees to talk about it if he swears not to harm her for what she says: "je le vos dirai par couvent que vous me façiez seur que mal ne m'en vendra." [I will tell you if you swear that no harm will come to me], a promise that he will, of course, not keep.

In other cases, the speaker can simply abandon the conversation: two squires are curtly rebuffed by a knight when they ask him why he is weeping.

---

[11] *Lancelot* 4, Micha, p. 26.

(6) Li vallet le roi March, ki gardoient lour chevaux auques en sus de la, quant il oïrent chele plaainte, quidoient tout chertainnement que che fust li rois March ki ensi se plainsist. Et pour che s'en viennent il chele part et li demandent:

« Sire, que avés vous, ki si durement vous plaingniés ?

– Et vous, ki estes, fait Lamorat, ki me demandés pour coi je me plaing ? » [...]

Si dient : Sire, nous quidiom que che fust un autre que vous.

– Conment ? fait Lamorat, A il donc chi autre que moi ? »

Et il se taisent.[12]

[King Mark's valets, who were also guarding their horses there, when they heard his plaints, thought for certain that it was King Mark who was lamenting so. And so they came to that place and asked him:

"My lord, what's the matter, why are you are weeping so bitterly?"

"And you, who are you?" says Lamorak. "Who are you to ask me why I'm lamenting?" [...]

They say, "Sire, we thought that it was someone other than you."

"How so?" says Lamorak. "Is there someone else here besides me?"

And they fall silent].

Impressed by Lamorak's sharp response (they had taken him for King Mark, their lord), the squires are reduced to silence. Lamorak starts by challenging the legitimacy of their speaking to him by asking who they are and goes on to question the relevance of their addressing him. Similarly, in the extract below, which brings peers together this time, two knights refuse to answer their interlocutor after questioning his right to ask them questions:

(7) Quant il voit les deus cevaliers ki s'estoient aresté devant la fontainne, il s'en vient vers aus et lour dist:

« Signeur cevalier, veïstes vous par ci passer la Beste Glatissant?

– Et vous, ki estes, fait Breüs, ki de la Beste Glatissant demandés?

– Je sui, fait il, uns cevaliers errans ki voi en un mien afaire. Mais de ce que je vous demant m'asenés se vous le savés faire!»

Mesire Tristrans, ki tout certainnement connissoit que ce estoit Palamidés ki a aus parloit en tel guise, respont pour oïr k'il en dira :

« Nous ne vous en dirom ore pas tout ce que nous en savom, car de cachier la Beste Glatissant sommes nous aussi desirant qe vous estes.»[13]

[When he sees the two knights who had stopped in front of the fountain, he comes towards them and says to them:

"Sire knights, have you seen the Questing Beast pass by here?"

---

[12] *Tristan* 4, pp. 83–84.

[13] *Tristan* 5, pp. 80–81.

– And who are you, says Brehu, who asks about the Questing Beast?

– I am, he says, a wandering knight who goes about my own business. But tell me if you are able!" Sire Tristan, who knows for sure that it is Palamedes who is addressing them in such a way, answers so as to hear what he will say:

"We will not tell you all that we know about it now, because we are as eager to hunt the

Questing Beast as you are."]

By asking the knight who questions them to reveal who he is, Brehu ascertains whether or not he has the authority to require an answer from them. However, we do not know how he would have taken Palamedes' somewhat vague answer, because Tristan, who had already recognized him, intervenes in their exchange, and refuses to join in on the conversation, which he does not consider justified in the context of chivalrous competition. Although he expresses his hostility towards Palamedes, his favorite enemy, at this point, he shows a measure of tact (at least apparently) a little later on, before accepting a topic that might seem sensitive to another of his companions:

(8) Quand [Palamidés] ot son conte finé, il se taist et puis redist a chief de piece:

«Mesire Tristran, or vous ai conté de ma aventures teles com eles m'avinrent puis que je me parti de vous. Or vous voeil je proiier que vous me contés des vostres ki ci en dedens vous sont avenues puis que je de vous me parti.»

Adonc conmence mesire Tristrans a rire, puis regarde Dynadant et dist:

«Dynadant, volés vous que nous contom a Palamidés de nos aventures qui nous sont avenues puis k'il se departi de nous?

– Mesire Tristrans, fait Dynadans, mout estes tost apareilliés de conter de nos aventures ! Diex doinst que je vous voie encore en tel lieu que je vous puisse aussi gaber com vous faites ore moi, car trop vous gabés volentiers de moi, se Diex me saut!»

Mesire Tristrans conmence mout fort a rire, et aussi fait Gaheriés. Et Palamidés, ki bien voit k'il i a avenue aucune risee des œuvres Dynadant, parole adonc et dist:

« Ha! Sire, pour Dieu, contés ce de coi Dynadans se courece si fort ne nel laissiés mie por lui s'il vous plaist quar, tout aussi com il veut savoir de nos aventures, est il bien raisons, ce m'est avis, que nous saçom aucune cose des soies et des vostres.

– Certes, fait mesire Tristrans, vous dites boine raison ! Et puis que vous en volés savoir, je vous en conterai tout maintenant.»[14]

[When [Palamedes] has finished his story, he falls silent and then says after a while:

"Sire Tristan, I have told you of the adventures that have happened to me since I left you. Now I want you to tell me of those that have happened to you since I left you."

Sire Tristan begins to laugh then looks at Dinadan and says:

"Dynadan, do you want us to tell Palamedes about the adventures that have happened to us since he left us?

---

[14] *Tristan* 5, p. 214.

> – Sire Tristan," says Dynadan, "you are always ready to talk about our adventures! May God allow me to go somewhere where I can mock you as much as you do me because you make fun of me too much, God bless me!"
>
> Sir Tristan begins to laugh very loudly and so does Gaheris. And Palamedes, who sees clearly enough that there has been laughter at Dynadan's doings, speaks up and says:
>
> "Sire, for God's sake, tell us what Dynadan is so angry about and don't leave anything out, please, because, just as he wants to know about our adventures, it is quite reasonable, it seems to me, that we should know something about yours."
>
> "Certainly," says Sir Tristan, "you speak good sense! And since you want to know, I will tell you all now."]

This excerpt is typical of internal-purpose conversations, which do not usually get beyond the stage of narrative discourse in literature. Yet in this romance, such moments of relaxation are rendered in direct speech. The knights errant, who met during their adventures, tell each other what has happened to them. The good humor evident in these scenes helps create a chivalrous society, presented as ideal, and the exchanges contribute to the reputation of the knights, who seek to "improve their rank" in the hierarchy of knight-errantry, which is under constant discussion. In this specific discursive framework, Palamedes clearly indicates that he has finished talking about what has happened to him and naturally cedes the floor to his companions. The change of topic structures the dialogue. It is implicitly evident that each of them must tell of his adventures. Tristan pretends to hesitate to say what has happened to himself and Dynadan and asks his companion's permission. We may suppose that his request mainly serves to highlight the story to follow and give it greater importance. However, it is worth noting that Tristan makes it and that his request is supported by Palamedes, who insists on the necessary reciprocity of their stories. Such inclusions in the dialogues illustrate the author's attention to the unwritten rules of conversation. He uses these metaconversational replies to structure the dialogue and give it a turn which, if not mimetic, is at least plausible from a psychological point of view. Hence, this literary game has several functions: it acts as an effect of reality and so participates in the creation of a world in which interactions are credible and subtle.

2 Changing the Subject

The close attention paid to dialogues leads to the eventual development of several conversational sequences. The authors can highlight such thematic discontinuity or let the conversation evolve "naturally". Dialogues, above all when they take the form of external purpose conversations, usually evolve from a request for information to a commitment to action.[15] We transit from description of a negative,

---

[15] See for example *Lancelot* 1, p.804. Lancelot asks the Lady of Malehaut about Gawain's health. She then agrees to his request to go and fight alongside King Arthur in order to make up for the absence of the king's nephew in battle.

dysphoric, or surprising situation to an action, a commitment to remedy it as far as possible. In an internal purpose conversation, the change of topic is more arbitrary, working by metonymy, association of ideas and reciprocity:

(9) [Li rois retient Lanselot, si le mainne as feniestres de la sale, et la royne fu aveuk eulx, et messire Gauwains et Boors li essiliés, ki mout ont grant joie de Lanselot. Li rois conjoïst mout Lanselot et si li commande sor son sairement k'il diche oiant tous les aventures ki li sont avenues puis ke il se parti de laiens, et il l'en conte pluisours et pluisours l'en çoille, sy les oÿ mout volentiers li rois et la royne. [...] Et lors demanda Lanselos nouvielles de Lyoniel.

« Chiertes, fait li rois, bien a .i. an k'il ne vous fina de querre, si nel veismes onkes puis, car on disoit ke vous estiés mors.

– Ha ! Diex, fait Lanselos, ou ke il soit, vous en soiés garde!»

Lors li conte li rois en queil maniere Boors estoit venus a court et les proueces ke il fist encontre cheus de sa maison [...]. De ceste nouvielle se rist Lanselos et fait a Boort grant joie et le baise mout doucement, car grant piece avoit k'il ne l'avoit veu, si li dist:

« Biaus dous cousins, or gardés ke vous fachiés tant ke tous li mons parolt de vous de chi en avant aussi comme il font orendroit. [...]»

Et il li creante loiaument ke si fera il. A tel joie et a tel fieste tint li rois Artu Lanselot toute la semainne.[16]

[The king keeps Lancelot with him, sitting with him and looking out of the hall's window. The queen is with them, and Sir Gawain and Bors the Exiled, who are delighted to see Lancelot. The king is very fond of Lancelot and asks him to tell of all the adventures that have befallen him since he left the court. He tells him many and more, and the king and queen listen very willingly. [...] Then Lancelot asks news of Lionel.

"Truly, sire," says the king, "it is more than a year since he went away in search of you, and we have never seen him since, for it was said that you were dead."

"Ah! God," says Lancelot, "wherever he may be, may you protect him!"

Then the king tells him how Bors came to court and of the deeds he did against those of his household [...]. At this news Lancelot laughs and embraces Bors, kissing him tenderly, for it is a long time since he has seen him, and he says to him:

"Dear beloved cousin, now take care that you do so many deeds that all the world will talk about you from now on as they do now. [...]"

And he promises him faithfully that he will do so.

And with much such joy and feasting, King Arthur stays with Lancelot all that week.]

In this conversation between Lancelot and Arthur, the hero tells of his adventures and inquires about his cousin Lionel, King Bors' eldest son. By association of ideas, without formalizing the change of subject, the king also gives him news of Bors the younger, Lionel's Brother, a new knight, destined for a great future to which his older cousin commits him. The dialogue ends with these edifying

---

[16] *Lancelot* 5, p. 266.

words, which puts the two cousins in parallel, one as the head of the lineage and at the height of his knightly power, and the other at his dawning. Although the transition of the hero's conversation to his cousin Lionel and of the cousin's to his brother Bors may seem relatively logical in this case, some changes of conversation show neater continuity solutions.

2.1   Form and Nature of Topic Changers

Although very rarely, changes of subject are occasionally announced explicitly. Such thematic ruptures may be heavily emphasized by the narrator, as in the three examples below, from *Tristan:*

> (10)   Ensi vont entr'aus parlant du roiaume de Cornuaille, et puis retournent a parler sour lour afaire, che est sor la queste k'il ne pueent oublier.
>
> « Mesire Lanselot, fait Gaheriet, que volés vous que nous façom?»[17]
>
> [Then they go on talking about the kingdom of Cornwall, and then return to talking about their business, the quest they cannot forget.
>
> "My lord Lancelot," says Gaheris, "what do you want us to do?"]
>
> (11)   Li compaignon demandent a Gyrflet dont il vient ne u il vait et il dist k'il venoit d'une besoigne u li rois Artus meïsmes l'avoit mandé avant ier; or s'en revait a la court droit. «Aussi i alom nous a la court, ce dient li autre. Or nous en irom nous donc ensamble.
>
> – Ce me plaist mout, che dist Gyrflés.»
>
> Quant il orent grant pieche parlé de la court, il tournent lour paroles sour autres coses. Si dist adonc mesire Yvains a Gyrflet:
>
> « Gyrflet, volés vous oïr une des plus beles aventures qui piecha mais avenist en cest païs ?»[18]
>
> [The companion asks Griflet where he comes from and where he is going, and he says that he comes from a mission that King Arthur himself had sent him on a few days ago; now he is on his way back to the court.
>
> "So let's go to the court," the other says. "Let's go there together." "That's a good idea," Griflet says.
>
> When they have talked a great deal about the court, they turn their talk to other things. So Sir Yvain says to Griflet:
>
> "Griflet, do you want to hear one of the finest adventures that ever happened in this country?"]
>
> (12)   Tant proie li chevaliers a monsigneur Tristran qu'il li otroie k'il herbergera avoeuc lui. Et lors se metent en autres paroles et li cevaliers dist a monsigneur Tristran:

---

[17] *Tristan* 4, p. 184.
[18] *Tristan* 4, p. 124.

«Sire, oïstes vous onques parler du tournoiement ki doit estre devant le Castel as Puceles?»[19]

[The knight begs Sir Tristan so earnestly that he agrees to stay with him for the night. And then they start talking about other things and the knight says to Sir Tristan:

"Sire, have you ever heard of the tournament that is to take place in front of the Castle of the Maidens?"]

The *Prose Lancelot* contains far fewer such changes of subject. The conversations it contains are not as playful as in the *Tristan* and that they have more of a dramatic purpose. It should be borne in mind, however, that (at least in manuscript BnF 768, which serves as the basis for Elspeth Kennedy's edition, reprinted in the Livre de Poche's *Lettres Gothiques* series) the scrivener uses attributive discourse to signal new thematic sequences. In this extract, Gawain meets a young girl who has gone in search of Lancelot and they converse while traveling together.

(13)   Il la salue et ele lui, et il li demande s'ele a besoig.

«Oïl, fait ele, mout dolereus. Et vos, o alez issi?

– *Damoisele, fait il*, ge vois en un mien affaire ou ge n'ai pas encor tant esploitié com ge vousisse. *Bele douce amie, fait il*, savriez me vos dire novelles del chevalier qui fist antrer lo roi en la Dolereuse Garde?

– De ce, fait ele, vos dirai ge bien novelles, se vous m'enseigniez de ce que ge quier. [...]

– Damoisele, fait il, conoissiez lo vos, lo chevalier?

– Oïl, sire, fait ele.

– Or me redites de celui dont ge demant.

– C'est il, *fait ele*, ce sachiez. Et comment avez vos non? *fait ele*.

– J'ai non, fait il, Gauvains.

– Ha ! sire, fait ele, vos soiez li bienvenuz. Et por Deu, volez vos que ge aille avoc vos ?

– De ce sui ge mout liez, fait il.»

Antr'aus deus chevauchent, et il li dist:

« Damoiselle, amez vos lo chevalier?

– *Sire*, oïl, fait ele, plus que nul home et non mie d'itele amor com vos cuidez. Ge ne voldroie mie qu'il m'eüst esposee. [...] *Sire*, fait ele, mambre vos il d'une damoisele que vos encontrastes l'autre jor?»[20]

[He greets her and she greets him back, and he asks her if she needs help.

"Yes, sire", she says, "I am in great distress. And you, where are you going?"

---

[19] *Tristan* 2, p. 219.

[20] *Lancelot* 1, p. 628. Voir aussi *Lancelot* 1, p. 804, Lancelot avec la dame de Malehaut.

> – *Damesel*, he says, I am on an errand which I have not yet accomplished as fully as I would wish. *Beautiful sweet lady*, he says, can you give me news of the knight who led the king into the Dolorous Guard?
>
> – I can give you news of him, sir, if you will do me a favor first. [...]
>
> – Damsel, he says, do you know him?
>
> – Yes, sire, she says.
>
> – So tell me of he whom I am asking about.
>
> – It is he indeed, she says. Believe it. And what is your name? she says.
>
> – My name, he says, is Gawain.
>
> – Ah, sire! she says. You are most welcome. And for God's sake, will you let me go with you?
>
> – I would be very glad to have you with me," he says.
> The two of them ride off, and he says to her:
> "Damsel, do you love the knight?"
>
> > – *Sire*, yes, *she says,* more than any man, and not in the way you might think. I would not want him to marry me. [...] *Sire, she says,* do you remember a damsel you met the other day?"

This lengthy conversation takes place in two times: first of all, the two characters meet, exchange news and decide to travel together; then they do so. The second part could be seen as a new conversation as it takes place in another space–time, but it clearly marks the continuation of the previous exchange and a deepening of the two characters' mutual knowledge, in a slightly more intimate tone. The beginning of the conversation is relatively phatic: the knight and the lady meet, greet each other and ask each other about their immediate situations: "Et vos, o alez issi ?" [And you, where are you going?], but Gawain does not prolong these questions on their circumstances and asks the lady for news of Lancelot (whose name he does not know at this point). This change in conversation is marked by a new, warmer term of address, "bele douce amie", and by a new parenthesis, "fait il". We find the same repetition of the parenthesis when the young woman asks her companion's name after revealing to him that they are both looking for the same man: "C'est il, fait ele, ce sachiez. Et comment avez vos non ? fait ele." [It is he indeed, she says, believe it. And what is your name? she says.] as well as when, after explaining the nature of her relationship with Lancelot to him, she suddenly asks him if he remembers the second damsel that the Lady of the Lake has sent in the wake of her young protégé: "Sire, fait ele, mambre vos il d'une damoisele que vos encontrastes l'autre jor ?" [Sire, she says, do you remember a damsel you met the other day?] At each change of subject, the term of address and attributive speech are repeated as if a new line were beginning on a new subject. The procedure does not occur often in the manuscript, but its use here shows the scrivener's evident awareness of conversational sequences. Such functioning of certain prose passages was previously observed by Bernard Cerquiglini, who saw in it a sign of the close link between speech and units of content in the prose system:

> Le discours que représentent les textes du Moyen Âge est conforme à la définition de *l'oratio* donnée par Priscien et reprise par Abélard: "la démonstration complète d'un sens" clôturant une unité syntaxique. Défini par l'unité de son contenu, le discours s'isole, se scinde en autant de parties tenues dès lors pour des discours autonomes et signalés comme tels. Une incise (pléonastique) peut ainsi apparaître au sein d'un discours, désignant ce qui précède comme un premier discours. (Cerquiglini 1981, p.87)
>
> [The speech represented in texts from the Middle Ages complies with Priscien's definition of oratio taken up by Abelard: "demonstration of a complete sense" closing a syntactic unit. Defined by the unity of its content, the discourse isolates itself, splits into so many autonomous pieces of discourse and is signaled as such. Hence, a (pleonastic) parenthesis can appear within a piece of discourse, designating what precedes it as an initial piece of discourse.]

I do not think that such a remark can be generalized, as is made clear by the very existence of topic changers, but in this extract, it is evident that each semantic unit corresponds to an enunciative unit, emphasized by the use of clearly pleonastic attributive speech.

Characters can also ask for the conversation to change subject themselves. This is an act of discursive authority, generally attributed to characters in high positions within the conversation. Such authority is expressed through use of more or less explicit topic changers, usually in the form of verbs in the imperative. These verbs may be in the first-person plural in order to initiate a change of topic jointly:

(14) Et Lanselos demande a Keu pour coi sa dame li avoit vee sa parole.

« Comment ? fait il, le vous a elle donc vee? –

– Oïl, fet Lanselos, voiant le roi et tous les autres.

– Ciertes, fet Kex, l'ocoison ne sai je mie, mais teus est guerredons de femme.

– Or laissons, fait Lanselos, et si com li plaira. Et comment l'avés vous puis fait?» Et Kex li conte le grant amour ke li rois lor avoit moustree.[21]

[And Lancelot asks Kay why his lady had forbidden him to speak.

"How?" he says. "Did she refuse to talk to you?

Yes, Lancelot says, in front of the king and everyone else.

Certainly, Kay says, I don't know why, but that's how women are.

– Now let's drop it, Lancelot says, and let her do as she pleases. And how are you now?" And Kay tells him of the great love that the king had shown them.

---

[21] *Lancelot* 5, p. 196.

Here, no doubt embarrassed by a conversation that likens Queen Guinevere to the fickle women of the world, Lancelot would rather ask his interlocutor about his health. Similarly, in the example below, when King Baudemagus shows excessive humility towards him, the hero changes the subject to something rather less delicate:

> (15) Et li rois s'umelie mout et li dist qu'il est ses sergenz et ses amis.
>
> « Ha, sire, fet Lanceloz, por Dieu merci, ne me dites jamés tex paroles, que vos ne me porriez plus couroucier, car uns rois ne doit estre sergenz a nul si povre chevalier comme je sui, mais sires et commanderres.
>
> – Ha, sire, fait il, vos n'estes mie si povres que je ne chanjasse la moitie de ma richesce a la vostre de tel povreté com vos avez, se vos m'an voliez faire compaingnon.
>
> – Sire, fait il, or laissons cels paroles, car ce n'est mie comparoison de mestre.i. povre chevalier contre.i. riche roi puissant, mais dites moi comment vos l'avez puis fet que je ne vos vi.
>
> – Certes, sire, fait li rois, je vos ai puis molt desirré a veoir. »[22]
>
> [And the king humbles himself greatly and says to him that he is his servant and his friend.
>
> "Oh, my lord", says Lancelot, "for God's sake, never speak such words to me again, for you could not make me angrier, as a king should not be a servant to any man as poor as I am, but his lord and commander."
>
> "Oh, sire", he answers, "you are not so poor that I would not change half my wealth for your poverty, if you would make me your companion."
>
> "Sire", he says, "let us leave such talk now, for there is no comparison between a poor knight and a rich and powerful king but tell me how you have been since I last saw you."
>
> "Certainly, sire", the king says, "I have wished to see you very much."

In this example, Lancelot has no trouble describing himself as a poor knight to King Baudemagus; his prestige is such that he compensates for his social status with his moral authority. Hence, he can express his disagreement with the previous topic and start a new one. These two examples from *Lancelot* show topic changers built around the verb *laissier*. Other formulas are possible, as below with the verb *parler*.

> (16) "Sire cevaliers, fait Helyes, bien saciés que, quand vous m'asaurés, je me desfendrai se je onques puis en nule maniere qui soit en trestout le monde. Mais quant je n'ai hui garde de vous, or parlons d'autre cose.
>
> – Vous dites bien, fait mesire Tristrans. Or parlons d'autres coses et d'autres affaires."
>
> En tel guise cevaucierent tant, parlant toutes voies d'aventures et de mervelles, qu'il viennent en une valee u il avoit une jonciere auques grant.[23]

---

[22] *Lancelot* 4, Micha, p. 188.

[23] *Tristan* 6, p. 342.

["Sire knight," says Helyas, "Know that, when you attack me, I will defend myself if there is nothing else in the world I can do. But as I have no fear of you today, let us speak of something else.

"You are right, says Sire Tristan. So let's talk about other things and other matters." And so they ride on, speaking of adventures and wonders along the way, until they come to a valley containing a large swamp].

The change of subject is proposed by Helyas and ratified by Tristan, who repeats it. It is normal for the hero to be in a position of authority. The dialogue is in direct speech and limited here to the confrontation between the two errant knights as long as it has a dramatic dimension. The lighter part of their conversation is left to narrative speech, but the topic changer puts an end to Helyas' challenge to Tristan. In all such examples in the first-person plural, the desire to change the topic is immediately presented as common to both participants. This may seem like a conversation coup, but I have not found any examples of protests against such changes of topic.

In *Tristan,* the expression most often used to introduce a new topic of conversation is "*Or me dites*", an imperative in the second-person which directly commits the interlocutor to the new topic provided, without the change being enunciated. The questioner simply indicates a new direction in the questions he is asking, without expressing his wish beforehand as we have seen previously. Although the change of conversation is noticeable, it is nevertheless in the continuity of an interrogation, as in the examples below:

(17)   Et quant il ont mengié et il se sont parti des tables, Persidés demande a monsigneur Tristran:

"Sire cevaliers, quel part vaurés vous cevauchier?

– Sire, ne sai, si m'aït Diex, fait mesire Tristrans. Et vous meïsmes savés bien que des cevaliers errans est tele la maniere que chil ki droitement voeulent aventures cerquier, k'il ne quierent onques droit cemin, ains vont tout adés ensi com aventure les mainne. Pour ce ne vous sai je pas a dire quel part je cevaucerai demain, car je nel sai mie, ce sace Diex!

– *Or me dites*, fait Persidés, savés vous nules nouveles orendroit de la maison le roi Artu?"[24]

[And when they have eaten and left the table, Persides asks Sir Tristan:

"Sire knight, which way will you ride tomorrow?"

– Sire, I do not know, if it please God, says Sire Tristan. And you know well that such is the way of knights errant. Those who rightly seek adventures never take the direct path, but always go where adventure leads them. So I cannot tell you which way I will ride tomorrow, for I do not know myself, as God knows!

– *Now tell me*, says Persides, do you have any news from the court of King Arthur?]

---

[24] *Tristan* 2, p. 225.

> (18) Et lors li devise la fontene et le jor.
>
>> « Et je vos di, fait Lanceloz, que je serai la a cele hore, se trop grant essoine ne me tient. Mes, por Dieu, *itant me dites*, est il si biax com l'en vet disant?
>>
>> – De sa biauté, fait Lamoraz, ne fait a parler, que je vos di qu'il est toz li plus biax chevaliers que vos onques veïssiez, ne en tote la Table Reonde qui gaires soit greignor de li.
>>
>> – Hé ! Diex, fait Lanceloz, tant desir que je le voie!
>>
>> – *Or me dites*, fait Lamoraz, dou Chevalier a la Beste Glatissant me savriez vos a dire noveles?
>>
>> – Nenil, certes, fait Lanceloz. Plus a d'un mois que je nel vi. *Mes or me dites* se del roi me savez a dire nule certeneté?
>>
>> – Oïl» fait il. Et puis li conte ce que il en cuide et ce que li dui chevalier l'en firent entendant, et li devise coment il l'avoit abatu.
>>
>> « En non Dieu! fait Lanceloz, encor apert a vostre hyaume qui est toz terreus. Mes quel part volez vos aler?
>>
>> – Je iroie, fait il, volentiers la ou je cuideroie trover le Chevalier a la Beste Glatissant. Je le vois querant, et ausi fait mesire Tristanz.»[25]
>
> [And then he names the fountain and the day.
>
>> "And I tell you", says Lancelot, "that I will be there at that hour if too great a hindrance does
>
> not prevent me. But, by God, *tell me*, is he as handsome as they say he is?"
>
>> – Of his beauty, says Lamorak, there is no need to speak, for I tell you that he is the most handsome knight you have ever seen, nor is there anyone in all the Round Table who is greater than he.
>>
>> – Hey! God, says Lancelot, how much I desire to see him!
>>
>> – *Now tell me*, says Lamorak, if you can, tell me news of the Knight of the Questing Beast?"
>
> I have not heard anything, certainly, says Lancelot. It is more than a month since I saw him. But *now tell me* if you have any certain news of the king?
> Yes, he says. And then he tells him what he thinks and what the two knights told him, and he relates how he killed them.
> In the name of God! says Lancelot, your helmet is still covered in soil. But where do you want to go?
>
>> I would willingly go, says he, where I think I might find the Knight of the Questing Beast. I'm looking for him, and so is Sir Tristan.]

In the first example, the conversation's illocutionary framework does not change even though the subject changes, because the speaker asking the questions is still Persides, Tristan's host. In the second example, however, alternation of speakers is accompanied by alternation of topics: Lancelot, informed of where he can find Tristan, asks Lamorak about his beauty; then Lamorak asks for news of the knight

---

[25] *Tristan* 3, Curtis, p. 109.

of the Questing Beast; and finally, Lancelot asks what has become of King Arthur. The speed of the switches from one individual to another is particularly striking (it is true that Lamorak's adventures with these characters have been related a few pages earlier). But the diversity of the topics is only apparent: the entire conversation is about the two knights' adventures.

Although these topics changers may make the conversation seem disconnected and fanciful, so turning it into a light-hearted interlude rather than a commitment to action, the open-ended succession of questions and answers is only apparent: the narrative rigor and requirements of the action conflict with this tendency and a visible effort to maintain dramatic coherence is often noticeable. If there is an actual thematic shift in the conversation, it remains limited insofar as the themes addressed are all related. It is quite natural to switch from the adventures of one to those of the others, and to inform each other of the latest news from the small world of knight-errantry. The change of topic serves less to diversify the dialogue's content than to depict the open-endedness of a friendly conversation. It structures the dialogue while giving the illusion of a random conversation.

2.2 Construction of the dialogue in the event of a change of topic

Topic changers make it possible to organize a dialogue's various sequences and make it seem credible. At literary level, their function is to emphasize changes of subject in order to make the conversation's fault lines clearer and so highlight the issues at play.

2.2.1 Topic change as dialogue closure

Such transition formulas can simply be used to close a dialogue. They indicate that a conversation continues without being recorded, so contributing to the impression of a coherent and exhaustive diegetic universe, as in example 16. The rest of the conversation then takes place in the narrative discourse:

(19)   « Vous avés trestout le bien du monde, et je tout le mal, et sour che avés encore esperanche de miex avoir et je tous jours encore pis !

– Palamidés, fait Dynadans, *or laissom mais hui ches paroles et entendom a autre cose*. Pensom de nous reconforter et de passer chestui jour au plus joiousement que nous poom.

– Vous dites bien, fait mesire Tristrans.»

En tel guise com je vous cont connut Palamidés monsigneur Tristran en chele prison.[26]

["You have all the good in the world, and I all the bad, and yet you still have hope of better things and I always of worse!"

---

[26] *Tristan* 3, p. 194.

> – Palamedes, says Dynadan, *let us leave such talk for now and see about something else*. Let us think of ways to comfort ourselves and spend this day as joyfully as we can.
>
> – A good idea, says Sire Tristan."
>
> So, as I tell you, that's how Palamedes met Tristan in that jail.]

While they are locked up in prison with young Dynadan, Tristan and Palamedes are forced to talk to each other and establish a friendlier relationship. Even though he is not supposed to have discursive authority, Dynadan not only intrudes upon their exchange, which is none of his business, but also offers to end it. The young knight certainly has enough conversational audacity to challenge his elders. However, by ending so arbitrarily, the conversation does not resolve the thorny issue of the relationship between Tristan and Palamedes, which is constantly put back on the agenda. It fails to settle the dispute between them. The arguments that Palamedes advances in order to show the injustice that Tristan's success has done him remain in abeyance. The author uses this technique to end a scene that is already long while leaving the continuation of their rivalry open.

2.2.2 Changing the topic as a way of highlighting what is essential

Examples 10 and 11 show the topic changer as a way of emphasizing the transition from information to action, and, in example 16, the transition from a conversation oriented towards action to a more light-hearted exchange after a decision has been made.

In the example below, the change in conversation has a psychological purpose: it enables the exchange's various levels to be organized in such a way as to highlight the relationship between the characters. Narrative discourse is of secondary importance here, but even so its very existence has major psychological value, illustrating the delicacy of Lancelot and Galehaut's relationship:

(20) Et quant li chevaliers oï parler de la roine, si s'anbruncha et comance a penser si durement que toz s'an oblie. Et Galahoz lo regarda, si voit que les lermes li sont venues as iauz et a grant poine se tient qu'il ne plore. Et *cil se mervoille mout et commança a parler d'autre cose.* Et quant il ot parlé longuement, si li dist li chevaliers:

> « Alez, sire, si faites a monseignor Gauvain et lo roi conpaignie et si escotez se vos orroiz de moi nules novelles ne nules paroles. Et demain si me diroiz ce que l'an vos an avra conté de moi.
>
> – Volentiers, sire» dist Galehoz.[27]

---

[27] *Lancelot* 1, p. 854.

[And when the knight hears about the queen, his brow darkens and he begins to think so deeply that he forgets everything else. And Galahaut looks at him and sees that tears have come to his eyes and he is barely able to keep from weeping. *And he marvels greatly and begins speaking of other things.* And when he has spoken for a long time, the knight says to him:

"Go, sire, and keep company with Sir Gawain and the King and listen to them if you hear news or words about me. And tomorrow, you can tell me what they said about me."

"Gladly, sire," says Galehaut].

Not only does Galehaut tactfully change the subject so as to steer the conversation away from the suffering he sees in his young friend, but Lancelot, who certainly seems somewhat consoled by the respite granted him, then sends him to the king to pay his respects. Expressing the friendship that has been established between the two men with much finesse, the change in subject also highlights it with considerable economy of means.

2.2.3 Changing the subject in a nested construction

In other cases, however, the change of subject is only apparent and the conversation returns to its initial subject. The divergent sequence is only a parenthesis nested in a larger theme which is returned to later:

(21) La dame de Malohaut se trait pres de li, la ou ele la voit plus seule, et dit au plus celeement que ele puet:

« Ha ! dame, dame, com est bone conpaignie de quatre!»

[…] Et la reine l'apela: « Dites moi por coi vos avez ce dit? […]

– Dame, fait ele, don lo dirai ge. Ge dis qu'il est mout bone compaignie de quatre, car j'ai veü un novel acointement que vos avez fait au chevalier qui parla a vos laïs ou vergier. Si sai bien que vos iestes la rien o monde que il plus aimme. […]

– Coment ? fait la reine, conoissiez lo vos?

– Dame, fait ele, oie. Tex jorz a esté oan qe ge vos an poïsse autresi bien faire dongier comme vos fariez ja a moi, car ge l'ai tenu an et demi an ma prison. […]»

Lors li commance a conter comment ele l'avoit tenu an et demi et por coi ele l'avoit pris et por coi ele estoit alee a la cort lo roi. Trestot li dit jusque a l'isue de sa prison.

« *Or me dites,* fait la reine, *por coi dites vos que compaignie de quatre valoit miauz que de trois.* Miauz est une chose celee par trois que par quatre.

– […] Mais s'il vos plaist que ge fusse qarte an la compaignie, si nos solacerions antre nos dames autresi com antr'aus deus feroient, si an fussiez plus a aise.

– *Or me dites,* fait la reine, *savez vos qui li chevaliers est?*

– Si m'aïst Dex, fait ele, naie, car vos avez bien oï commant il se crient vers moi.

– Certes, dame, fait la reine, trop iestes aparcevanz. […] Et puis qu'il est ansi, que vos l'avez aparceü et que vos me requerez la conpaignie, vos l'avroiz.

– Dame, nos serons ansanble totes les foiz que vos plaira.

– Or m'an laissiez covenir, fait la reine, car nos afermerons demain la compaignie de nos quatre.»

Et lors li conte de Lancelot comment il avoit ploré quant il esgarda vers eles.

« Et ge sai bien, fait la reine, qu'il vos conut. Et sachiez que ce est Lanceloz do Lac, li miaudres chevaliers dou monde.»

Ensi parolent mout longuement antr'eles deus, si font mout grant joie de lor novel acointement.[28]

[The lady of Malohaut approaches her when she sees her left alone, and says to her as quickly as she can:

"Oh! my lady, my lady, what good company four makes!" […] And the queen says to her:

"Tell me why you say this." […]

"My lady," she says, "I will tell you why. I said four makes very good company because I saw you make the acquaintance of the knight who spoke to you in the orchard. I know that you are the one person in the world that he loves the most. […]"

"How so?" the queen says. "You knew him, didn't you?"

"My lady," she says, "yes I did. There was a time this very year when I could have blocked your wishes, because I held him prisoner for a year and a half. […]"

Then she begins to tell of how she had held him for a year and a half, why she had captured him and why she had gone to the King's court. She tells her everything right up to the end of his imprisonment.

"Now tell me, the queen says, why you say that a company of four is worth more than a company of three. A secret is better kept by three than by four."

"[…] But if it please you that I might be in your company for a year, we could solace each other as two men would do, and you would be more at ease."

"Now tell me, the queen said, do you know who the knight is?"

"God bless me, my lady, no, for you have heard how he fears me."

"Certainly, lady," the queen said, "you are clear-sighted. […] And since you have seen him and ask for my company, you shall have it."

"My lady, we shall be together whenever it pleases you."

– Now leave it to me," says the queen, "and tomorrow we will organize our company of four." And then she tells her about Lancelot, how he wept when he looked at them. "And I knew well," said the queen, "that he recognized you. And know that this is Lancelot du Lac, the best knight in the world."

---

[28] *Lancelot* 1, p. 902.

And so, they speak to each other at length, and are delighted with their new acquaintanceship.]

This conversation, of remarkable psychological subtlety, highlights both ladies' finesse. Although it contains several pragmatic sequences in which illocutionary roles and types of discourse vary (interrogation, negotiation, and narrative), the thematic coherence focuses on the queen's adulterous love. But topics are raised upstream of their resolution, acting as cornerstones that structure the conversation and create expectation. The Lady of Malehaut does not have quite enough authority to open the conversation, above all on such a scandalous topic as the queen's illicit love. She chooses the right place and time and starts with an enigmatic sentence that does not spell things out and can certainly be sidestepped if the risk is too great. The queen, who pretends not to hear at first, presses her to open up a bit more and admit to what she saw and understood of her encounter with Lancelot among the meadow. So the enigmatic statement with which the Lady opens the conversation, "com est bone conpaignie de quatre!" [What good company four makes!] does not receive an answer until she has told her what she knows about Lancelot, after which the queen reintroduces her question: "Or me dites, fait la reine, por coi dites vos que compaignie de quatre valoit miauz que de trois." [Now tell me, the queen says, why you say that a company of four is worth more than a company of three.] Consequently, Lancelot's misadventures with the Lady of Malehaut are referred to between the opening statement and the later answer to which she is entitled, i.e. the pact of friendship between the two women, "car nos afermerons demain la compaignie de nos quatre." [and tomorrow we will organize our company of four.] Likewise, still using the formula "or me dites", the queen introduces the question of Lancelot's identity, but it is only after she tells of what she has seen of the young man that she answers the question she has asked herself: "Et sachiez que ce est Lanceloz do Lac." [And know that this is Lancelot du Lac, the best knight in the world."] Hence, the question of the pact of friendship is closely linked with that of the identity of the queen's young lover. Such interweaving prepares for the second topic within the first before it is resolved. As a result, each is highlighted by the resulting effect of expectation. The dialogue plays with this delay, which increases its dramatic weight. The stakes at play in the conversation are high: as the queen has discovered that the Lady of Malehaut knows about her secret love for Lancelot, she must bring herself to befriend her so as to keep her secret.

In the following example, although the change of topic seems more pronounced, coherence is maintained at a deeper level. Lancelot meets a damsel and asks her what has happened to Gawain without them recognizing each other. When she realizes who her interlocutor is, she tells him of the message that the Lady of the Lake has entrusted to her for his protégé, seemingly putting the question of Arthur's nephew's fate to one side. The two successive conversation themes are nevertheless linked at the level of the values they uphold:

(22) Et il s'an part et chevauche aprés la damoisele qui por monseignor Gauvain ploroit, tant que il l'ataint a l'antree de la forest. Si li demande que por Deu li die de monseignor Gauvain novelles.

« Ges vos dirai, fait ele, que gaires peiors ne pueent estre, car il est soi disoimes de compaignons en la prison a celui qui a esté sires de la Dolereuse Garde.

– Ha ! damoisele, fait il, puis que tant m'en avez dit, dites moi o cele prisons est.»

Et cele lo regarde, si li dit:

« Ostez vostre hiaume, si vos verrai. »

Et il l'oste. Et ele li cort les braz tanduz. Et il la conoist, si voit que ce est une damoisele qui est a sa Dame del Lac, si li fait mout grant joie. Et ele li conte que sa dame l'avoit a lui envoiee por une chose qu'ele avoit obliee a dire a l'autre pucele qui avant vint.

« Mais l'an me dist, fait ele, la ou messires Gauvains est pris, que vos gissiez morz en la Garde Dolereuse et por ce n'i vos ge onques antrer, car ge ne la pooie neïs veoir.

– *Quele, fait il, fu la chose que ma dame m'oblia a mander?*

– Ce fu, fait ele, que vos ne metoiz ja vostre cuer en amor qui vos face aparecir mais amander, car cuers qui por amor devient pareceus ne puet a haute chose ataindre, car il n'osse. Mais cil qui tozjorz bee a amender peut ataindre a hautes choses, autresin com il les ose anprandre.»

Et il li redist:

« Messire Gauvains, bele douce amie, o est il em prison?

– Ge vos i manrai », fait ele.[29]

[And he rides off after the damsel, who is weeping for Sir Gawain's sake, until he catches up with her at the entrance to the forest. He asks her for news of Sir Gawain.

---

[29] *Lancelot* 1, p. 556.

"I can tell you", she says, "that things could hardly be worse. He is shut up with his companions in a prison belonging to the Lord of the Dolorous Guard."

"Ah, damsel," he says, "since you have told me this much, tell me where that prison is."

She looks at him and says, "Take off your helmet, and I will recognize you."

He takes it off, and she runs to him with her arms outstretched. He recognizes her and sees that she is the damsel who serves his Lady of the Lake.

He is very glad to see her.

She tells him that her lady has sent her to him because she had forgotten to tell something to the other damsel who had come earlier.

"But I was told," she says, "where Sir Gawain was taken prisoner, that you had died in the Dolorous Guard, that's why I didn't want to go there, for I could not bear to see such a thing."

"What Was It," He Asks, "that My Lady Forgot to Tell Me?"

"It was," she says, "that that you must not choose a love that makes you lazy but rather one that improves you, as the heart that becomes lazy due to love can no longer accomplish great things because it no longer dares. But he who always seeks to improve himself can accomplish all great things because he dares to undertake them."

And he says to her, "Sire Gawain, my dearest friend, where is he imprisoned?"

"I will take you there," she says.]

Although it opens the conversation, Gawain's fate is only apparently the topic and his rescue is only a detail in the story. At a time when Lancelot is wondering whether he should let his life be dominated by an adulterous love, his adoptive mother's advice decides him: she makes his knightly prowess conditional on his having higher ambitions regarding love. The return to this first subject of conversation is not, as it may seem, a change of theme, but rather the implementation of her advice. Far from being disconnected, the conversation has real coherence: it marks further development in young Lancelot's knightly and amorous destiny.

Changing the topic therefore makes it possible to structure the conversation and bring out narratively important points, either by hierarchizing them by use of the various types of reported speech or by reinforcing a topic through its proximity to another, so creating effects of meaning. The transition from one topic to another always meets a narrative need, highlighting a psychological effect or preparing for a forthcoming event under cover of the conversation's naturalness.

Applying the tools of pragmatics to literary analysis enables us to identify many smaller, discreet phenomena along with those that may seem self-evident but whose presence is actually unusual in medieval literature and shows that the impression of naturalness and liveliness we get from the dialogues of these two romances has been skillfully created by authors who are sure of their effects.

At a second level of analysis, these stylistic devices also contribute to characterization of the protagonists and their dramatic relationships, constituting landmarks in the work's semantic and ideological development.

Such formulas for transition from one topic to another remain very rare. However, they testify to a conception of dialogue that says more than what is actually spoken. Dialogues are no longer exclusively at the service of action: the interaction phenomena that take place in them take on their own value and finally have as much importance as the jousts and tournaments that follow.

The consideration of pragmatic conditions for topic management to which these two romances testify is remarkable. Not only does it evidence their authors' sensitivity and talent, but it also creates dialogue stylistics that use such pragmatic conditions with all the means at their disposal in order to provide the dialogues with an impression of liveliness. By doing their utmost to imitate the content of real conversations, the authors show the confidence they have in the ability of a budding novelistic literary genre to provide an account of the world.

References

Lancelot du Lac, d'après l'édition d'Elspeth Kennedy : tome 1, Mosès François (éd. et trad.). Paris : Le Livre de Poche 1991. tome 2, Chènerie, Marie-Luce (éd. et trad.). Paris : Le Livre de Poche 1993. tome 5, Ollier, Marie-Louise (éd. et trad.). Paris: Le Livre de Poche 1999.
Lancelot : roman en prose du XIIIe siècle, tome 4, Alexandre Micha (éd.). Geneva: Droz 1979.
Le Roman de Tristan en prose, Renée L. Curtis (éd.), tomes 2 et 3. Leyden: Brill 1976.
Le Roman de Tristan en prose, edited by Philippe Ménard, Tome 1, Ménard, Philippe (ed.). Geneva: Droz 1987. Tome 2, Chênerie, Marie-Luce and Delcourt, Thierry (eds.). Geneva: Droz 1990. Tome 3, Roussineau Gilles (ed.). Geneva: Droz 2
Tome 4, Faucon, Jean-Claude (éd.). Geneva: Droz 1991. Tome 5, Lalande, Denis and Delcourt, Thierry (eds.). Geneva: Droz 1992. Tome 6, Szkilnik, Michelle and Baumgartner, Emmanuèle (eds.). Geneva: Droz 1993.
Berthoud, Anne-Claude and Mondada, Lorenza : "Traitement du topic, processus énonciatifs et séquences conversationnelles", in *Cahiers de linguistique française: Les différents plans d'organisation du dialogue et leurs interrelations*, 17/1995, 1995, pp.205–228.
Cerquiglini Bernard: *La Parole médiévale*. Paris: Éditions de Minuit, 1981.
Coltier, Danielle: "Introduction aux paroles de personnages: fonction et fonctionnement", in *Pratiques* 64, Dec. 1989, pp.69–109.
Denoyelle, Corinne : *Poétique du dialogue médiéval*. Rennes: Presses Universitaires de Rennes, 2010.
Durrer, Sylvie: *Le Dialogue romanesque*. Geneva: Droz 1994.
Kerbrat-Orecchioni, Catherine: *Les Interactions verbales*. Paris: A. Colin 1998.

Larmat Jean: "Le *Roman de Tristan* en prose, manuel de courtoisie", in Ruhe Ernst and Schwaderer Richard (eds.): *Der alt enfranzösische Prosaroman (Kolloquium Würzburg, 1977)*. Munich: Wilhem Fink Verlag 1979, pp.46–67.

Mondada, Lorenza: "Gestion du topic et organisation de la conversation", in *Cadernos de Estudos Linguisticos*, Campinas 41: 2002, pp.7–38.

Printed in the United States
by Baker & Taylor Publisher Services